SACRED
PRACTiCES
OF
unity,
POWER
&
EARTh
HEALiПG

ABOUT THE AUTHOR

James Endredy is a teacher, mentor, and guide to thousands of people through his books and workshops. After a series of life tragedies and mystical experiences as a teenager, he changed direction from his Catholic upbringing and embarked on a life-long spiritual journey to encounter the mysteries of life and death and why we are all here. For over twenty-five years he has learned shamanic practices from all over the globe, while also studying with kawiteros, lamas, siddhas, roadmen, and leaders in the modern fields of ecopsychology, bioregionalism, and sustainable living. James also worked for ten years with Mexican shamanic researcher Victor Sanchez learning to share shamanic practices with modern people.

On a daily level, his experiences have inspired him to live a sustainable lifestyle as much as possible while still working within mainstream society. He writes, leads workshops, mentors private clients, visits schools and community centers, speaks at bookstores, and volunteers in his community. His books have thus far been published in four languages. *Ecoshamanism* is his third book. Visit him at www.JamesEndredy.com.

ECOSHAMANISM

Sacred Practices of Unity, Power & Earth Healing

JAMES ENDREDY

Llewellyn Publications
Woodbury, Minnesota

FIRST EDITION
Third Printing, 2007

Book design and editing by Rebecca Zins
Cover art © PhotoDisc
Cover design by Lisa Novak
Interior illustrations by Llewellyn art department
Llewellyn is a registered trademark of Llewellyn Worldwide, Ltd.

The publisher and the author assume no liability for any injuries caused to the reader that may result from the reader's use of content contained in this publication, and recommend common sense when contemplating the practices described in the work.

Library of Congress Cataloging-in-Publication Data
Endredy, James.
    Ecoshamanism: sacred practices of unity, power & earth healing / James Endredy.—1st ed.
        p.   cm.
    Includes bibliographical references and index.
    ISBN-13: 978-0-7387-0742-6
    ISBN-10: 0-7387-0742-2
    1. Shamanism. 2. Ecology—Religious aspects—Shamanism. 3. Traditional medicine. I. Title.

GN475.8.E63 2005
201'.44—dc22

2005044241

Llewellyn Publications
A Division of Llewellyn Worldwide, Ltd.
2143 Wooddale Drive, Dept. 0-7387-0742-2
Woodbury, MN 55125-2989
www.llewellyn.com

Printed in the United States of America
on recycled paper

Dedicated to the memory of my father, Jeno Endredy;
my mother, Irma Endredy;
and to the nourishing spirits of
Grandmother Growth, Takutsi Nakawe,
and Grandfather Fire, Tatewari.

contents

contents

viii

contents

x

ACKNOWLEDGMENTS

I am fortunate beyond words to acknowledge first my principal teachers of shamanism, who ironically have no use for the written word: the spirits of nature, and the indigenous elders and shamans of Ixachilan and Cuexcomatitlan.

All my love and gratitude to the special companions that have encouraged and nurtured me during the writing of this book, and to all those who shared their personal experiences surrounding the Embrace of the Earth rite of passage, including Barbara Gross, Ed Calvitti, Joyce Calvitti, Jody Winters, Peter Stephenson, Lori Lichtman, Grace Clearsen, Renea Fuschino, Michael Stone, Benjamin Robin Mercer, Anna Digate, Jim Tolkien, Howard Koch, Angela Price, Deborah Derr, Christina Hagins, and Barbara Ligeti.

Very special thanks to Amy Gerber for providing me with such an inspirational and magical place in northern Arizona to finish and edit this book. May the butterfly spirit fly always with you!

Much appreciation to Natalie Harter, Rebecca Zins, and Llewellyn Worldwide for supporting this project. Visionary publishers such as Carl Llewellyn Weschcke, along with the many skilled people that produced this book, deserve a lot of credit for doing their part to help make the world a better place. Thanks also to Jaime Meyer and José Stevens for reviewing the initial manuscript and providing critical insights.

The reciprocal relationship of unconditional love with many canines has enriched my life in countless ways. During the writing of this book, Arwen, Byron, and especially my beloved sidekick Sophie have graced me with much laughter and many lessons.

ABOUT THE SOURCES OF THIS WORK

The animating spirits of nature and the informative qualities of the sacred landscape are the main sources of guidance and information for both my life and this book. The knowledge provided by these sources is direct and pure. It is not dependent on human concerns or concepts.

My fellow human beings have also significantly influenced my work. I have been fortunate to experience an extremely wide range of life circumstances, to be exposed to the writings of insightful authors, and to know a variety of human cultures throughout the world. But learning is far different than sharing or teaching. Translating experiences of altered states of consciousness, and also techniques of classical shamanism, to be shared in a context that is practical for the times we live in is a formidable task. The spirits that guide me were very wise when they led me into an intense ten-year relationship with Victor Sanchez, who not only helped me to learn how to teach shamanic techniques to modern people, but also introduced me to the Huichol culture, whom he refers to as the surviving Toltecs.

The ancient cultures and spirits of the Toltec, Maya, Zapotec, Mexika, Teotihuacan, Olmec, and Anasazi, as well as the lands that hold their sacred sites, have been significant sources of knowledge and inspiration to me. The descendants of the ancient cultures, the Wirrarika, Maya, and Nahua, have become my primary human companions on the shamanic path, although throughout the years I have also received considerable lessons from relationships with the elders of the Hopi, Navaho, Lenape, and Native American Church. Experiences with ancient cultures in Australia and throughout Europe and Asia have also affected my life significantly. In recent years I have been developing stronger ties to the many other indigenous people of the Unites States, Canada, and South America, and I look forward to deepening these relationships in the future.

It is an incredibly sad fact that most of the shamanic cultures of the world, primarily due to their mostly peaceful nature, have not survived into the twenty-first century. Within the few surviving cultures there exists various levels of shamanic knowledge. The tribal shamans that I have learned the most from, especially the elder shamans of the Wirrarika that live hidden in the mountains, are not interested in teaching people shamanism, taking money from tourists, or being in books or magazines. The only thing they have ever wanted from the outside world is for their people and their land to be left alone. I am not ashamed to say that the only reason they taught me anything was because they were not given a choice. For whatever reasons the spirits ordered them to help me to be a bridge between the primal world of the shaman and the modern world of humanity. Due to my respect, care, and commitment, I am happy to say that they have grown to become my companions, brothers, and sisters. But while no one can claim ownership of the spirit world, indigenous tribal cultures have rules and taboos that I must consider. This is why it is not possible for me to publish the names of the shamans and the indigenous communities that have shared their knowledge with me. Instead, when referring to an indigenous shaman or elder in this book, I will use the name *kawitero*, which is a term borrowed from my Wirrarika mentors that refers to a person who holds the knowledge of the spirits. Also, since there are, of course, both male and female shamans, I have tried to keep the gender of my pronouns neutral; however, simply for ease of reading, sometimes I use the masculine where the feminine equally applies.

The spirits of psychedelic plants have been allies of mine for most of my life. Although mentioned in a few places here, I have exempted the sharing of practices related to the use of these entheogens for several reasons. The ingestion of power plants is not only potentially dangerous but is simply one of many doors that can lead to shamanic perception, and in my opinion the use of that door can be a supreme waste of time and energy until one develops both a psychic and physical relationship of reciprocity with the land and the beings that provide us with life. Ecoshamanic practices can lead us into these relationships. The sources of love, light, and laughter are found in all the beings that we share this lifetime with. We all emerge and return to the same sacred source, and to learn to live in harmony with this source is the most worthwhile pursuit on the shamanic path.

A PERSONAL INTRODUCTION TO THE PROJECT

As I climbed higher and higher up the sheer rock face of the mountain, I knew that I was in big trouble. The route I was trying to climb was above my skill level of technical rock-climbing experience, and in this remote area of wilderness I was about to pay the ultimate price for my foolishness. I hadn't placed my safety gear properly and the safety rope was dragging me down. But even worse, for fear of more rope drag I stopped placing safety gear in the rock as I climbed, so now the rope was useless and if I fell I would surely drop to my death. My arms were burning from fatigue and my feet were continuously slipping off of the tiny crevices that were holding me upright. I couldn't climb any higher, I couldn't go back, and I couldn't stay where I was. I had come to the end of the road and I knew it. I was completely exhausted and it was physically impossible for me to hang on any longer. Death was on its way for me and I saw my life flash before my eyes.

That's when the spirit took me. I felt myself flying like Ebenezer Scrooge with the spirit of Christmas past, but the spirit speaking to me was the ancient spirit of the mountain that was about to end my life. My perception was dual. On one hand, I could clearly feel myself about to slip off the cliff and I could "see" my life flashing before my eyes. On the other hand, I also felt myself hovering next to the cliff, watching the whole incident with a feeling of detached awe while I had a silent conversation with the invisible spirit of the mountain. Everything was happening so quickly that I didn't have time to think or analyze. I somehow knew that this was the same spirit that had spoken to me during a vision quest I made a few months earlier on the same mountain. During that ceremony of three days and nights, the spirit had received my offerings and granted my vision. The mountain spirit knew my task in life even better than I did. And the spirit was about to make me a deal.

The deal was simple. My life would be spared, for now, if I would commit to stop goofing around with childish games and get busy accomplishing my task in life. It was a good deal, and I silently agreed. I found myself "whole" again and sitting safely on a wide ledge high above where I thought I would fall. On that ledge I learned many things. The spirit told me that I had been seconds away from my death, but because of my years of dedication in finding my true task in life, and because I knew that this important task was given to me by the spirits of nature, in my time of greatest need my own spirit was able to take the control of my body away from my mind and deliver me safely to the ledge.

But, more importantly, the spirit told me that it wasn't necessary to be knocking on death's door for my spirit to take control. This was a capacity that I could learn to use even during the course of my everyday life. If I would simply walk the path of my true calling I would learn how to do it. Fortunately I had already learned about my path with spirit years before. However, knowing it and walking it were two different things.

The mountain spirit also reminded me that I had allowed my own spirit to guide my actions countless times before, during other moments when I had almost died and while connecting with the spirits of nature, during ceremonies with indigenous shamans, and while learning about the medicinal properties of certain plants. But I hadn't yet learned to "will" my spirit out of my own volition, and the way to do that was to make my everyday life just as magical, mysterious, and urgent as those other special moments when my spirit was coaxed to emerge.

I took the advice of the mountain spirit and for years I tried to use my spirit to guide my daily actions. There were many moments of success, but much more often I succumbed to my same old habits. My spirit simply didn't have the strength to overcome a dominating ego that had been highly trained by an anthropocentric culture.

Until one day the spirits got tired of my ineptitude and stalling and sent the powerful spirit of the *hikuri* (peyote) cactus to kill me. I was in the sacred desert of Wirikuta in northern Mexico and the trickster spirit of the blue deer Kahullumari encouraged me to eat five huge hikuri buttons all at once. The spirit promised that if I ate the big pile of magical hikuri that was chosen especially for me, then I would learn the answers to all my questions and one day become a powerful shaman.

I was familiar with the hikuri. I had met the spirit many times with the help of my expert guides the Wirrarika, and I had also met the spirit alone. I always came to the spirit with respect and honesty and it had always been kind and gracious with me. But not this time. For almost twelve hours I vomited and had uncontrollable diarrhea while wandering and crawling around lost in the scorching heat of the high altitude desert. It was the worst hell I've ever been through. After the first four or five hours I would have given anything for it to stop, and each time I thought it was over it would start up again. I continuously spewed my insides out for so long that I couldn't even fathom where it was all coming from. But the purging continued nonetheless, and by the time of about the eighth hour I felt like there was no way I could endure it any longer and I was begging for the spirit to simply end my life.

After about ten hours I finally passed out, faceup, on the desert floor. I perceived that I was standing outside of my body and that the powerful spirit of the hikuri was all around me, as far as the eye could see in every direction, engulfing me. When the spirit spoke, vibrations shook the world and caused giant ripples in the atmosphere. It asked me if I knew why the Wirrarika came to this desert, and I answered that they came here to find their lives. Then the spirit told me something I didn't expect; it told me that I had come there to find my death. The spirits had already shown me my life path but I was too lazy to fully embrace it. But they knew that I was still the right man for the job they had given me, so the only thing to do was kill me and try again.

As soon as the spirit communicated that to me, I felt my whole being quickly disintegrate into millions of tiny multicolored specks. Some of the specks dropped to the ground, some mixed with the air, and some rose into the sky. Then everything went black and my consciousness was gone. I'm not sure how long I laid there, but for all intents and purposes I was dead. The spirits of the hikuri and the blue deer had finally killed me.

I am forever grateful that they did so. When I felt my awareness return to my body, the first thing I noticed was that even though my eyes were closed, I could "see" that there were five vultures flying in circles above my body. And I could somehow hear the air rushing through their wings. One of them swooped directly over my head, circled around, and then landed beside me. In that moment I realized that the vultures thought I was still dead, and they were anxious to feed. And then the smell hit me. I could suddenly smell the foul odor that my bodily fluids had left on and around me and that the hot sun was now percolating into the nauseating fumes that attracted the vultures. I smelled like death.

And then the worst thing of all happened. I tried to open my eyes, but I couldn't. I tried to sit up, and I couldn't do that either. I realized that I was either paralyzed or dead; I wasn't sure which. But a few things were certain: the effects of the plant medicine had subsided; I felt completely empty, both physically and mentally; and I was terrified.

After a while, I began to notice that my senses were incredibly acute and even though I couldn't open my eyes I could still see, in a strange kind of way, what was going on around me. I could also hear and feel, and the more I focused on each of my senses, the more I was able to perceive, until after a while I realized that the only limits to my perception were those that I imposed on myself. And, with that realization, everything changed again. Once I let go of what I thought were my perceptual limits, the doors of the spirit world opened, and as I lay there, helpless, I received a spiritual-energetic infusion from all the beings of the desert.

I could feel the individual energies of the plants, the butterflies, the rabbits, the birds, the mice, and even the soil, rocks, air, and sun each being poured into my body, as if my body were an empty pitcher being filled with many different colors of magical liquid. Even though my eyes were still closed, the sensations were also very visual, and I could clearly see how each being had its own unique quality and color of light or luminous glow that they were pouring into me. As the glowing spirits filled my being, they also spoke to me about my life and my place in the world. I was given specific instructions as to what to do. I wasn't told how I was to accomplish everything, but I knew clearly what the goals were.

From that moment on, my spirit took control and guided me through the changes in my life that I couldn't make before the hikuri killed me and the spirits of nature refilled my being. I was finally let up from the ground and, as I watched the vultures fly away without their meal, I regained control of my body. But I wasn't the same person. My rational mind wasn't in control any longer. It was still there in the background, but in a similar way to how my spirit used to take a backseat to my ego.

The most important part of this story is how my spirit was totally repulsed by the way of life that my ego had led when it was in charge. Now that I was literally looking at the world with new eyes, as I flew home from that trip and landed in New York City I was completely overcome by the sheer magnitude of the human enterprise: the noise, the grime, the foul air, the crowds, and especially the lack of psychic connection to the natural world. I could barely hear any input from any other living beings. I became painfully aware that the humans had killed or scared away all the natural spirits. They had created a spiritual vacuum—an island of purely human concerns.

Surrounded by over seven million people, I never felt so alone in my life. My spirit searched frantically for something to hook on to. It went from face to face, but no one's spirit would greet it. Everyone's spirit seemed to be locked away behind closed doors. I didn't know what to do, but I was sure that I didn't want to live that way. And then I felt a ray of light. Something beautiful and pure had touched my spirit. I turned around and it was a little girl. She was about three years old and holding her mother's hand while they waited to cross to the street. She was staring right at me and I knew instantly that she could see the glow of my spirit shining out from me. Her spirit still guided her; it hadn't yet succumbed to the ego-driven world. Unlike all the adults around her, I could see her spirit glowing as clearly as if she were a wild deer running across the plain or an owl silently watching over a stand of oaks. She smiled at me and then she was gone. But within that smile I found hope and the realization that just as I had done growing up, all these adults around me had also learned to lock away their spirit, but just like me they could all learn how to set it free again.

This has been my task all along, to help bring the spirits back to the island of humanity.

During the course of the last ten years, that is what I have been trying to do. The book you now hold is another step toward the humble completion of the tasks that the spirits have handed to me. And with guidance from the spirits of nature, I truly believe that the material contained in this book can help to save the world.

I say this because, more than anything else, this book has to do with the transformation of lifestyles and worldviews. Our modern lifestyles of consumption and unsustainable uses of technology have taken us so far off the path of harmonious living that we are now being required to radically reinvent the entire human enterprise. The spirits of nature that rule the world will not wait much longer for us to change our ways.

When the spirits told me about the capacity we all have to will our own spirit to guide our actions, they were referring to our daily life and not just the special moments that we are accustomed to calling "spiritual." There most certainly is a need for the special moments of enlightenment and peak experiences of our lives, but even more important is how deeply we listen to the guidance of our inner spirit as to how to live our life on a daily basis. It is only when the primal knowing of our inner spirit is shut out that we are capable of suicidal lifestyles that destroy the world even while we are fully immersed in it. And this is why a significant amount of this book relates to the lifestyle changes that I have had to make while listening to the guidance of my own renewed spirit.

Shamans are experts at listening to the guidance of the spirits at large, as well as the spirit of their own being. What I have learned through countless trials, successes, and failures in the shamanic world is that it is the lifestyles, ceremonies, and rituals steeped in reciprocity with the natural world that provide a shaman with his or her ability to see and feel the imbalances within both individual organisms and ecological systems. It is through this relationship of giving and receiving that the shaman discovers ways to restore the delicate balance necessary for health and happiness when discrepancies arise.

Many years ago, when I returned home after the spirits had killed me and my spirit began guiding my actions, the big questions in my life became "How does someone from our modern society reciprocate with the natural world? How do we heal our injured relationship with the land? How can we create a lifestyle in harmony with the ecological systems that provide us with life?"

Those of you familiar with my first book, *Earthwalks for Body and Spirit,* already know that part of my task as an ecoshaman has been to share with people how to restore our sacred bond with the earth through awareness-raising exercises and techniques for reconnecting with nature. The writing and sharing of that book, along with my second book, *The Journey of Tunuri and the Blue Deer,* which was produced for children, have given me a tangible outlet for transforming what I do for "work" into something that gives back to the spirits of the natural world. But in order to get into the deeper regions of reciprocity and truly answer those big questions that were pressing me, I needed to do a lot more.

What this means on a day-to-day level is that I try to live a sustainable lifestyle as much as I can within the realities of the twenty-first century, and without escaping into the wilderness to live as a hermit. I write, lead workshops and present seminars, mentor private clients, visit schools and community centers, talk at bookstores, and help preserve the traditions of my indigenous mentors. I volunteer for my local watershed conservancy and gently guide people into the wondrous areas of their local environments that they never knew were there. And I volunteer with a local organization that rescues animals, by bringing them into my home and fostering them until a caring family can be found for them. My diet consists of between 60 to 80 percent of food that I, or someone who I know and respect, has personally grown, gathered, or hunted. I am not against technology, but I am for the wise use of it. Even though for the past ten years I have lived primarily in the northeast United States, where the temperature fluctuates dramatically throughout the year, I do nicely without a fossil-fuel-burning heater or the nuclear-powered electrical demands of a central air-conditioning system.

On the other hand, I respect and appreciate certain other modern advances and I make wise use of the technology of my computer and telephone. For me, a healthy and sane life is a delicate balance between what is wise and what makes you comfortable; what sustains and gratifies you in this moment and what ensures a healthy and happy life for future generations. It has been this gradual and, at times, extremely difficult shift to a lifestyle that places much less demand on the environment that has provided me with the vision that there is light at the end of the tunnel and that I will not fail in the task that the spirits have given me.

With this in mind, I humbly offer my third book to the spirits, and to you. This book lays out what I consider to be a practical and holistic form of modern shamanic technology—an ecological shamanism, or *ecoshamanism* for short. Congruent with authentic shamanic practices, this book is not often subtle. The time for mincing words or remaining politically correct has long passed. The material comes directly from interactions with the spirits of nature and her human emissaries in the form of indigenous shamans. And let's face it, the lessons from Mother Nature can be far from subtle. She will just as soon kill you with indifference as allow you to live. If you are paying close attention to your surroundings and balancing your actions with what is happening around you, you stand a fair chance of survival. But if you attempt to go against the flow, or continually disrupt the natural cycles and systems, you will suffer and eventually perish. This is the situation we all now face. Our task is clear.

TOWARD A NEW WORLDVIEW:
A NEW WORD FOR A NEW AGE

The word *ecoshamanism* would seem like a very strange and redundant word to the tribal shamans that I work with, many of whom are Wirrarika Indians that live a traditional subsistence lifestyle without roads or electricity in the western Sierra Madre Mountains of Mexico. If the prefix *eco* refers to ecologic or environmental concerns, as it is most often employed nowadays, then placing *eco* in front of *shaman* would be useless to them, or at best unnecessary, simply because what these shamans do is "shamanize" with the more-than-human world of nature and her spirits. The function of these tribal shamans is much different to the way many New Age spiritualists now use the word *shaman*. In this modern age we now have people called urban shamans, corporate shamans, and a whole host of various kinds of shamans who have little or no experience in reciprocating with nature or, even more significantly, who lead urban and suburban lifestyles that are completely detrimental to the natural world.

Until very recently, the word *shaman* referred to a person that was a conduit to the more-than-human world in which a tightly knit tribal community lived. The shaman, through countless generations of acquired tribal knowledge coupled with a lifetime of personal experiences and quests with the more-than-human world, took on the immense charge of maintaining the balanced and reciprocal relationship between the human community and its environment. In contrast, most of the new urban shamans not only don't have shamanic training gleaned from the local natural environment where they live, but they also aren't part of a culture or community sustained in their day-to-day activities by a shamanic worldview. Without a life deeply embedded in the ebb and flow of the natural world, and without a community dependent upon the reciprocating relationship with that local environment, most contemporary shamans bear little or no resemblance to the indigenous shaman, both historic and current. Through the eyes of a tribal shaman that lives separately from the industrialized world, our contemporary version of the urban shaman lacks even the principal prerequisites to shamanize.

That is why, in this age of unprecedented ecological destruction, it has become necessary to distinguish shamanic practices that reciprocate with the natural world from practices that don't. Thus, the term *ecoshamanism*.

ECOSHAMANISM: HEALING THE TRAUMA

The very magnitude and complexity of humanmade environmental disasters and the ethical, psychological, and spiritual illnesses that allow them to continue necessitate a multifaceted approach at seeking to correct the dangerous imbalance in humanity's relationship to nature. Many current movements, such as ecofeminism, deep ecology, bioregionalism, ecopsychology, living systems theory, creation spirituality, and the revival of neopaganism and earth-centered religions, among others, are all trying to play a significant role in this task.

Ecoshamanism joins these movements by infusing into the modern mind, body, and spirit the psychic and physical reality of our interdependence with the life-sustaining forces of the earth. In its tribal form, shamanism is not a subtle practice; therefore, neither is ecoshamanism. It is practiced not on the couch of a climate-controlled office but rather in direct communion with the living intelligences of the natural world.

The world of nature as well as the nature of the modern human psyche has been severely damaged, in some cases irreversibly, and the healing of both will require deep revelatory experiences of similar or greater intensity to that which caused the trauma. The only powers stronger than man's technologies of mass destruction are the forces of nature and the underlying spirit that animates all life on Earth. Connecting and communing with the ancient wisdom of Earth's natural systems and sacred spiritual elements are at the core of ecoshamanism, and as such offer us a way to heal our separation from our environment, our physical bodies, others of our own kind, and our psychic connection with Earth.

Ecoshamanism must be the foil of mechanistic-materialistic existence: consumer antimatter, the breath of fresh air at the bottom of a landfill, the light of nature in the eye of the steer on its way to Burger King, the crystal in the radio of spirit. To break the spell of this modern world gone mad, we must turn it upside down, bring the innermost out, speak without talking. Then, as we heal ourselves, we can genuinely reflect the sacred elements of nature and artistically re-create our lives with the spirits of nature flowing freely through us.

Even though during many years of my life I have learned directly from tribal shamans that live separately from the modern world, the more I learn about shamanic practices the more I realize that human teachers are not nearly as important as learning to hear what the natural world is telling us in any given moment. Many of us have and will receive the call to learn from indigenous shamans, and we should certainly honor and respond to that calling. But even more important is to learn and apply our shamanic techniques just like the ancient shamanic tribes did—by immersing ourselves in our land, learning from the spirits of our place, and learning how to navigate on our terrain.

This implies that what is needed first is not the elaborate and complicated shamanic techniques of some faraway tribe, but rather a simple and down-to-earth encounter with the natural world in which we live. Developing a physical and psychic connection to the natural world that then leads to a spiritual connection, and a shamanic connection, will be the first order of business in developing our own conscientious and authentic shamanic practice. What we are really talking about here is the development of a worldview whereby shamanic activities can be born and employed in a healthy and constructive way.

This certainly cannot happen overnight. One's worldview is something developed over long periods of time, just as legitimate shamanic practices are. I realize full well that this prospect of working to develop a worldview and lifestyle congruent with shamanism here on our own turf is not half as appealing as flying to some exotic location and having exciting experiences with an indigenous shaman. But even if you succeed in finding an authentic tribal shaman willing to teach you, of which there are now too few, we still can't escape the real work that needs to be done. The real work starts here on our own soil, with the sky that's above our head, with the water we drink and the food we eat. To know the profound connection of the tribal shaman to the world and universe, we first must reacquaint ourselves with the most basic yet profound grounds of our own daily experience. Eco-shamanic practices can serve as our bridge to make the crossing to a holistic worldview where the path of the shaman begins.

THE SHAMANIC WORLDVIEW

Shamans were the earliest initiators of spiritual knowledge and were widely dispersed throughout the globe. Ancient shamans are generally associated with northern and central Asia, but they were also found in Africa, Australia, Europe, and the Americas, which is basically where they can still be found today among the few existing societies that have been able to preserve this ancient, sacred tradition. These shamans functioned in an extraordinarily wide range of activities. They were healers, visionaries, singers, dancers, psychologists, rain-makers, food-finders, and, most importantly, intermediaries between the human and nonhuman world. They were the spiritual leaders, whose expertise was both in the cosmic and physical worlds and whose knowledge covered the ways of plants and animals as well as spirits and deities. In modern times they also commonly function as intermediaries between their ancient culture and the modern world, as a kind of diplomat or politician.

As both a cultural platform and a discipline of consciousness, shamanism is ancient, perhaps the oldest system known to humankind. Therefore, it can be said that there were shamans even before there were gods. The masked, dancing shamans depicted in the earliest Stone Age caves were the ancestors of the world's earliest religions. Ancient and classic shamanism was not characterized by the worship of a single god or through codified scriptures; rather, it comprised specific techniques and ideology through which spiritual issues as well as ecological realities could be addressed. Shamans, realizing the integrity of the natural systems to which they and their communities were a part, were charged with maintaining the balance between society and nature as well as dealing with the community as a social unit and applying their talents to individual cases of healing. Consequently, the shaman personified the healer, mystic, and intellectual all at once. This, of course, is in marked contrast to our contemporary, fragmented view of the world in which "civilized" Western consciousness splits mind, body, and spirit, and therefore creates the rigid and separate roles of therapist, physician, and priest.

As a modality of healing, shamanism emphasizes the path of personal harmony as a way to health, instead of the idea of healing strictly coming from an outside source. In other words, while modern healing therapies focus on helping and healing the patient or client by diagnosing the malady and then prescribing treatment, shamanism promotes living in balance with the world so that the illness doesn't occur in the first place. If someone becomes ill, the first order of business is to locate and correct the imbalance in the patient's life, which will then lead to how to alleviate the symptoms of the illness. The values that this type of method encourages are those that promote the maintenance of balanced systems between humans and the more-than-human world of nature and her spirits.

What we are being asked for now, more than any other time in human history, is that we create a spiritual context for ecology; that we recover a reverence for the very sources that nourish us, that we rise above our childish rage against our earthly existence and abandon the industrial assault upon our natural spiritual home. Shamanism as a worldview promotes the reciprocal relationship between the human and nonhuman world, and this fact is, in my mind, the most important aspect of shamanism at the beginning of this new millennium. But in recent times, both from the standpoint of anthropology and New Age–type spiritualists, the main focus of shamanism has been concentrated on the esoteric trance states of shamans and the shaman's mystical abilities without close enough inspection as to how these functions of the shaman serve to uphold the worldview of the tribal community. Ancient shamanic practices originated and evolved from the life circumstances and experiences of human beings submerged in the reality of living in the natural world. The "place" where shamanic cultures lived was not seen as merely a location that they occupied, but rather the place—including animals, plants, sky, and especially the land—was inextricably tied to the basic identity of the people.

But nowadays we don't identify ourselves in such an organic way, and therefore if we are to engage in shamanic practices it is necessary to look at where these practices will fit into our lives. Ecoshamanic practices that attempt to reintegrate our mind/body/spirit organism with the natural world will be rendered ineffective if we simply try to introduce them into an ecologically impaired identity and lifestyle.

What this means is that our first order of business will be to work at constructing a platform on a rational level from where we can readily access the ecoshamanic experience. This is important because we have to remember that even the strongest types of shamanic and revelatory experiences must have foundation and grounding in the lived experiences of our daily world or else they will have no practical usefulness. This rational platform is our psychological and philosophical point of view, which is what I refer to here as our worldview.

This worldview platform must be solid and stable, but most of all it must be expandable in order to accommodate the weight of revelatory ecoshamanic experiences. Little by little, additions will need to be constructed onto the platform as we grow and mature and our worldview expands to include experiences we can't even imagine right now.

To help illustrate this, I'd like to share with you the current life situation of a Wirrarika friend of mine who received her call to be a *marakame* (singing shaman) about three years ago. This friend, whom I will refer to as Maria, was on pilgrimage to the sacred desert of Wirikuta. During one of the nights in the sacred place, she had many visions provided to her by the interaction of the hikuri (peyote) and Grandfather Fire. The most important vision was of two magical eagle feathers that were hovering over the fire. She was instructed to grab the feathers and take them with her, because she was to become a singing shaman and those feathers would help to guide her while singing with the fire and the sacred places.

Receiving this type of vision is one way in which the Wirrarika receive the call to become a shaman, but the really important point here is that from that moment on, she had the responsibility to learn how to sing with the feathers and with the fire. Maria had to begin learning the many songs that each of the sacred places had to teach her and, little by little, she had to begin modifying her daily activities and view of the world to include this new calling.

Maria's culture and local community completely accept this type of vision, so at a purely rational level her daily activities are now actually expected to include her obligation to learn about being a singing shaman. Each and every time she travels to a sacred place to petition for a song to progress in her shamanic abilities, her identity and activities must expand to include the new experiences she has. At the same time she is constantly being supported and encouraged by her community as her shamanic activities are viewed as supporting and nurturing the worldview, lifestyle, and cosmology of her community and culture.

I use this example because from it we can see that Maria's vision with the fire and her activities related to becoming a singing shaman are not at all compatible with the worldview, lifestyle, or cosmology of our modern culture. Maria's experience of going on the pilgrimage to the sacred place, which she had been preparing for since she was a child, along with the circumstances surrounding her vision with the fire, as well as her subsequent duties in learning the shamanic craft of singing the voice of the fire, all require such a radically different worldview from that of our modern society that we can easily say she is inhabiting a separate reality of human existence.

This is something that I personally discovered in a profound way while engaging in ecoshamanic experiences with the kawiteros of Maria's tribe. The staggering impact of discovering that, without major changes in my worldview, it would be impossible for me to integrate my experiences of this "separate reality" into the framework of my everyday life when I returned home from my visits with the Wirrarika, caused me to almost forsake the ancient ways that they were trying to show me. It was only through the patient reworking of my view of reality and my daily activities that I could integrate these experiences and work to construct a bridge between ecoshamanic practices and my modern identity and worldview.

It has become very clear to me that if we are to be successful in ecoshamanic practices, it is essential that we find areas of our daily lives that allow us to slowly and gradually construct such bridges to a new worldview. We need to be able to cross back and forth so we can, little by little, adapt our worldview to accept ecologically sound lifestyles and more profound levels of ecoshamanic practice.

As a basis for identifying areas where we can begin to build these bridges, I'd like to begin by mapping the contrast between the modern worldview and the ecoshamanic worldview, and then offer some clear and concise options that can be introduced into our daily lives at a purely rational level to build and support the ecoshamanic platform that allows us to jump into the ecoshamanic experience.

• **Modern Worldview**	Except for human beings, Earth, the solar system, the galaxy, and the universe are comprised of nonsentient and/or unconscious matter, and therefore they are open for us to exploit as we see fit.
Ecoshamanic Worldview	*Our sun—which birthed Earth, along with the rest of our solar system, galaxy, and universe—is imbued with a sacred life-force that is to be respected and honored.*
•	An individual is identified by the skin boundary—what is inside my skin is "me," what is outside is not.
	An individual is both unique and indistinguishable from his environment. The entire world shares one body, one flesh.
•	Identity is defined by occupation, social status, and material possessions.
	Identity is formed through intimate relationship with the natural world, especially the home territory and the sacred places.
•	Goals in life are based predominantly on self-fulfillment and compassion for a small group of family and friends.
	Service to the human community, as well as to the community of nature, is inseparable from the goals of the individual.

- Daily activities revolve around acquiring as much as possible while giving back no more than what is required or that you can get away with.

  Daily activities emphasize giving as much as possible while asking for no more than what is necessary.

- Success in life is based on material possessions and money to buy the "good life" of pleasure without discomfort.

  Life is not based on success or failure but comes to fruition through living in delicate balance and cooperation with the world.

- The value of the natural world is based upon what "natural resources" are worth monetarily and how much they can be sold for profit.

  All life has intrinsic value that is not dependent on human economic valuation.

- The rights of humans come before all else; with few exceptions, other life forms have no "legal" rights.

  Every living being has equal rights to live and fulfill its niche in nature's complex systems.

- Lusting for new things just because they are new, and for faster and more powerful technologies.

  Cherishing things that are old but still serve well, using and owning only what is needed.

- A tiny percentage of the population that is extravagantly "rich" dominates power of control over all the rest.

  Material "richness" and corporate power is irrelevant. Those who are seen as leaders are most often intentionally without material processions, but spiritually wealthy and grounded.

- The population is brainwashed into ever-increasing rates of consumption by mass media and advertising that is controlled by purely commercial interests.

  Forms of media are valued by their ability to provide accurate information and also advancement in the arts. Therefore commercial interests and advertising are irrelevant and have no power.

- Since goods and foodstuffs are shipped in, the local home environment has little to do with the sustenance of the community and therefore is open for exploitation.

  The community is completely dependent on the local environment for material sustenance and therefore is treated with utmost respect and reciprocity.

The more we integrate and live inside the worldview that is depicted as the eco-shamanic worldview of this chart, the deeper we will be able to jump into the experiences in this book and also integrate them into our daily lives. At a purely rational level, this worldview is accessible to us only when we begin to act in accordance with it through our daily activities and routines. Here are a few concrete ways that this worldview can be expressed by people currently living inside the modern worldview:

- Engage in anti-consumerism: purchase only products that fulfill vital needs and avoid shopping as a simple escape to life.

- Have a minimum of personal property and reduce the number of possessions.

- Maintain a material standard of living that is not significantly higher or lower than that of the so-called third or fourth world.

- Cherish old, well-kept things that still serve well, rather than admiring and purchasing new things just because they are new.

- Develop a career that makes a meaningful contribution to life, rather than just "making a living."

- Engage in actions that have intrinsic value, instead of doing things merely to "keep busy."

- Participate in and appreciate activities and lifestyles that do not blatantly disrespect or take advantage of fellow human beings or the natural world.

- Live in nature as opposed to merely visiting beautiful, overcrowded tourist destinations, such as national parks.

- Develop a feeling of responsibility toward local ecosystems.

- Try to leave no trace when visiting fragile environments.

- Purchase locally grown or raised food, or grow/raise your own.

These examples are basic prerequisites for making the transition from a consumer lifestyle to an ecologically healthy lifestyle, and can be used as a bridge to actual eco-shamanic experiences. Working experientially in this way is absolutely necessary as it affords one the possibility to explore from one's uniquely personal perspective and to formulate alternative possibilities from one's own lived and felt experiences. This allows us to take personal responsibility for, and practical guidance from, our own lived experience, which ultimately is what keeps us grounded and authentic.

This experiential process of ecoshamanism aims at cutting through the beliefs, concepts, rules, and limited worldview that we have either agreed to or have been forced to abide by as a consequence of having to adjust to environments and lifestyles that are both at odds with nature and also with our most deeply felt organismic needs and wants. We pay a high price for the alienation of our innermost psychic, physical, and spiritual connections lost through our consumer-based lifestyles. Vitality, creativity, spontaneity, sense of community, self-worth, and finding a fulfilling life path all suffer when we disconnect from our most primary organic needs. The very nature of an efficient factory, assembly line, or mechanized workplace suppresses the spontaneous, emotional, and casual aspects of human nature to the ever-expanding power of money and the corresponding decline of the sacred. Personally experiencing the profound connectedness of our sensory, psychic, and spiritual selves to the living body of Earth is our only true protection against the industrialization and corresponding dehumanization of our profound capabilities as human beings.

THE SSC AND THE ESC

The shamanic state of consciousness (SSC) is a blanket term that attempts to signify the states of consciousness intentionally induced to tap into the vast knowledge and power of the universe not reliant on human thought or concepts. In this state, the world is experienced without human theories, without written words, and without preconceived opinions or biases. In this state, there is no inner and no outer, and reality is perceived beyond the normal constructs of time and space. It is not some sort of obscure esoteric or supernatural state but rather a heightening of our experience of reality.

To simplify this discussion on how human consciousness relates to the world, I will place human consciousness on separate levels to illustrate the marked differences between the various levels:

1. This first level I refer to as ordinary for our modern culture, and for other cultures that have lost a sense of unity with nature and the cosmos. At this level, the ego is almost completely self-centered and isolated from the occurrences of the more-than-human world.

2. In the second level, there is a slight awareness of fusion between the self and the surrounding environment of nature and other beings. Because of this, the capacity for empathy manifests, but not at a level that would prevent the person from doing harm or damage to something or someone outside their narrow sphere of compassion if they deemed it was called for.

3. At the third level, we see the first signs of the ego temporarily melding with the environment or other beings.

4. The fourth level is significant for shamanism because here we identify our organism with a much larger unified body—with plants, animals, and other phenomena and forms of communication not accessible to the lower levels. We can experience consciousness free of human evaluations and judgments.

5. At the fifth level, the feeling of unity between self and environment leads to experiences of "silent knowledge" or knowledge without words, telepathy, the ability to transfer energy and/or heal, to compress or lengthen the perception of time, and other circumstances commonly thought to be supernatural or extrasensory. At this level many experiences simply cannot be explained by words.

6. The sixth level is the level free from all human attachments, as if your personal organism and consciousness were completely nondiscernable from the unified consciousness of the cosmos.

In terms of these levels, we could say that shamanic experience typically happens within levels three, four, and five. Now, with reference to an ecoshamanic state(s) of consciousness (ESC), I would add that the experience be stimulated by participation of the natural world, whether intentional or not. In other words, at each level an experience of unity to the natural world stimulates the shift to a deeper or more profound connection to the environment and the corresponding loss of attachment to purely human concerns. Through intentionally practicing and purposefully struggling through various actions, ceremonies, and rituals with the more-than-human world, a person realizes increasing states of unity, first with others of their own kind and their immediate environment, then with other beings and the wider world, and eventually with powers and forces inconceivable to our ordinary linear-rational mode of perception.

Also, it is imperative to make the distinction that the techniques I am presenting in this book are purely on the level of what I would consider to be positive experiences. In other words, there are no practices designed to empower a person in a way that would increase the ability or knowledge to do harm, or to put the person in a position that could be personally harmful. All shamanic cultures have practices of bewitching, and most now have an entheogenic or stimulant component that could potentially cause serious harm. However, while the practices in this book don't include either of these aspects of shamanism, the ecoshamanic experience does contain similarities to the documented positive experiences of the use of plant entheogens within the shamanic complex, and it is significant to identify them as a way to further define the ecoshamanic state of consciousness.

First is the importance of set and setting. This implies that the intent of the experience, and the place where the experience happens, are both relevant to the quality of the experience and the state of consciousness achieved. This is extremely significant because there are many anthropologists and New Agers that are too quick to place all shamanic experiences into the same category, and also because many modern people interested in shamanism don't even equate the local land into their experience. In terms of the ESC, the set and setting may be the most important phenomena of the experience.

Second, there is an experience of learning from a source of knowledge much larger than the confines of strictly human affairs. Visions, intuition, perception of sentience in plants, and communication with animals are common experiences.

Third is the experience of death and rebirth. Dismemberment, dissolving, exploding, and other experiences of being killed and then being reborn into a stronger and healthier state, although seemingly traumatizing, can be truly enlightening and empowering experiences.

Fourth, the experience can be heightened by external music, singing, chanting, dancing, drumming, and other activities that enhance the flow of the experience.

Fifth is the perception of spirit. This may come in many forms, but throughout this book there are many practices of feeling and working specifically with the spirits of nature.

It is important to note that these similarities between common experiences with plant entheogens and ecoshamanic states of consciousness are, for the most part, absent from the shamanic practices of modern people, which are often referred to as neoshamanism. In this respect, the practices and worldview of ecoshamanism are much closer to what could be defined as classical shamanism than neoshamanism. These two terms, along with the term core shamanism, can be somewhat confusing, so let's look closer at them before we move on.

Neoshamanism most commonly refers to the practices surrounding the revival of interest in shamanism by modern people, spurred on primarily through the hugely popular work of authors such as Mircea Eliade, Carlos Castaneda, and Michael Harner. Core shamanism is at the center of the latest neoshamanic revival; it was created by Michael Harner and is distributed by his Foundation for Shamanic Studies. Classical shamanism most often refers to the practices employed by indigenous tribal shamans, both historic and current.

Much of modern-day neoshamanism has gotten so far off the path from classical shamanism, and has become so commercialized, that the easiest way to begin understanding the differences between neoshamanism and classical shamanism is to simply note some of the differences between the two. The biggest distinction is that much of what is labeled as shamanic in our consumer-driven culture—listening to cd's of drumming, watching videos of bizarre body postures, reading shamanic fantasy stories conjured by city dwellers, replacing soul journey with guided imagery techniques, among many others—are not to be found in the practices of any shamanic tribe. Now, I firmly believe and give credit to the work of popular neoshamanic authors and workshop leaders for significantly raising the consciousness of the Western world toward shamanism. But I also know that many people are ready now for a deeper and more authentic encounter with the shamanic world.

Another obvious distinction between neoshamanism and classical shamanism can be seen with regards to service. While neoshamanism has at its core the personal and spiritual development of its practitioners, classical shamans endure extreme hardships and dangers in order to fulfill their obligations to the communities that they serve. Unlike the personal growth atmosphere of neoshamanism, where a modern person feels a longing to become a better person and explores shamanic techniques to "find themselves" and so more fully realize their true human potential, classical shamans have a completely different goal: to serve the community. Here is a basic overview of some of the other contrasts between classical shamanism, modern neoshamanism, and the goals of ecoshamanism:

• **Classical Shamanism**	All of the duties and practices of the shaman work within and around the specific culture of the tribe he is part of.
Neoshamanism	The practices are a blend of material drawn from different cultures or are even created independently without a specific cultural framework.
Ecoshamanism	*Our shamanic practices and duties come from a deep connection and devotion to the land where we live and address specifically the needs and wants of our modern culture.*

· Classical Shamanism	Although the duty is sometimes passed from one generation to the next in the same family, more commonly a shaman is "chosen" by the spirits through receiving a strong "calling" and therefore has no choice but to fulfill his vocation. If he refuses the spirits, or fails to fulfill his duty, it is common that he and/or someone in his family will become seriously ill or die.
Neoshamanism	Normally a person becomes interested in shamanism for any number of personal reasons, and of their own volition decide to learn more. Although they may feel a "calling" toward the shamanic arts, they are generally free to quit at any time without risk to their health or safety.
Ecoshamanism	*As people reconnect with the land, more and more are being called to service directly by the spirits of nature and are given tasks. When this happens, the choice to enter the ecoshamanic worldview has already been made. A person might be able to avoid their calling for periods of time, but eventually the calling will bring them back to service and completion of their tasks.*

- Once the spirits select a person to become a shaman, the next step is almost always the passing through of an intense and life-threatening initiation or near-death experience that radically and permanently shifts the perception of the potential shaman.

  Intense, life-threatening initiation ceremonies or activities are generally nonexistent. Shifts in perception come slowly and are more at the level of personal growth and/or small changes in lifestyle.

  Initiations and rites of passage are intentionally formulated to place shamanic practitioners into a direct encounter with the powers of nature. These encounters push the limits of the practitioner to such an extent that visions, guidance, and tasks are received at a level that dramatically alters a person's life.

- If the potential shaman survives the initiation period, being a shaman becomes his full-time vocation for the rest of his life.

  The time spent practicing shamanism is decided solely by the individual. It can be a full-time job or a weekend hobby.

  The time spent learning and applying ecoshamanic techniques is directly proportional to the time spent in nature. As a person receives messages and tasks from the natural world they spontaneously begin to incorporate them into their life. The challenge to remain faithful to their calling is a life-long task.

- Although a novice shaman is usually guided by either an elder shaman and/or the community he will serve, the actual lessons, skills, and power of the shaman is acquired through direct encounters with the spirit world after he has passed through the near-death experience or initiation period.

  The learning of shamanic techniques happens through workshops, seminars, and books. Although interaction with the spirit world may take place, this is usually at a very superficial level, as most practitioners have not "opened" the doors of perception through the near-death experience and/or have not received the direct call from the spirits to become a shaman.

The initial stages of ecoshamanic practice are learned through completion of specific tasks relating to connection with the powers of nature and the subsequent alteration of lifestyle toward a holistic worldview. Completion of these tasks is purely personal, but may be encouraged by participating in ecoshamanic work groups to safely accomplish specific rites of passage, as well as mentoring with an experienced ecoshamanic practitioner or indigenous shaman.

- A relationship with the spirits is maintained through the continuous making of personal offerings, and in certain moments blood sacrifices, to the spirits. Offerings vary in intensity, depending on the situation and desired outcome. It is not uncommon for an important offering to represent a full year's wages or equivalent amount of work. This high level of commitment is what gives power to the offering and the shaman.

  Offerings and sacrifices are basically nonexistent. Much is usually asked for from the spirits, but little or nothing is offered in return.

  Same as classical shamanism.

- The shaman radically and often alters his perception through a variety of means, some of which may include ingestion of hallucinogenic plants, multiple day and night ceremonies, fasting, many hours of continuous dancing, prolonged exposure to the elements, sleep deprivation, ritualized animal sacrifice, and body mortification, among others.

  The most common technique for altering perception is the use of repetitious drumming, or listening to recordings of drumming. This is often accompanied by techniques of guided imagery and is most often performed in a climate-controlled room.

  Perception and consciousness is radically altered as one receives visions, messages, and tasks from the natural world. Seasoned ecoshamans depend on prolonged exposure to the powers of nature to guide their life, help and heal others, and guide their communities toward balance with nature.

- Agreements and bargains are commonly made with the local spirits of nature and wild animals through the shaman. If the agreements are not carried out, the shaman will become seriously ill or is the recipient of some sort of physical tragedy or "accident," such as slipping off a cliff or falling off a horse.

  Practitioners are usually city dwellers and have little or no contact with the spiritual energies of nature and wild animals.

  As the ecoshaman gains experience, the offerings and agreements with the powers of nature become more and more powerful, as do the consequences of not living up to them.

• **Classical Shamanism**	Since tribes are usually completely or partially dependent on crops and/or domesticated animals for survival, the shaman is in constant contact with the spirits that ensure their life, growth, and health. Ceremonies, rituals, and offerings are made at the appropriate times during the year, according to the cyclical realities of nature and the cosmos, to ensure adequate sustenance for the tribe.
Neoshamanism	Shamanic practitioners deal with money in order to live within modern society. Rituals, ceremonies, and offerings related to the sowing or harvesting of plants, or the raising and slaughtering of animals that provide a significant portion of yearly sustenance, are nonexistent or very rare.
Ecoshamanism	*Ceremonies, rituals, and offerings are made at the appropriate times of year relating to the sustenance of the community and/or the restoration of balance between the community and nature.*

It's my belief that the time has come for us to acknowledge the people in our modern society that have received the call to shamanic service and to provide legitimate opportunities for them to learn and grow, while at the same time realizing that there is a radical distinction between becoming a shaman and using shamanic techniques for personal growth. In both cases, but especially for those called to become practicing shamans, the material in this book serves simply as a springboard into developing your own personal relationship with the spirits that will actually train you. Once that relationship is established, the spirits will prescribe for you the next steps in your transformation; your specific lessons, initiations, and your specific shamanic specialty will be revealed.

Perhaps the greatest service that surviving classical shamans provide for their communities is the continual re-creation of the shamanic worldview. With each new generation of shaman, each healing of a sickness, blessing of a child, and ceremony of reciprocity with the more-than-human world, they continue to uphold their culture's holistic view of reality. This is what modern culture has tragically lost but what our new shamans can help restore when they reconnect to the spirits, develop reciprocity, and guide people to a holistic worldview.

SHAMANIC INITIATION AND ALTERED STATES

Shamanic initiation is serious business. It includes many processes, both metaphorical and tangible, that include death and resurrection, ritual dismemberment and disembowelment, administration of power plant medicines including entheogens, isolation in wilderness, various types of fasting practices, ecstatic journeying into trance states, special relationships including sexual relationships with spirit beings, and many others.

Although a shaman might well receive their initial calling for shamanic work through a revelatory event of illness or tragic circumstance, the primary forms of initiation always include activities of purification and instruction that last many years. The shamanic path is a long and arduous road, full of hardships and the trials that come with having your walls broken down and your human masks pulled off. People of ancient shamanic cultures realize this, and most people don't voluntarily pursue the shamanic vocation precisely for this reason. But it is my point of view that this path needs to be taken by people in our culture, because without it we will continue to be lost in a techno-consumer wasteland that is completely detached from the numinous and most meaningful qualities of Earth and the cosmos.

The hardships and suffering encountered in shamanic initiations are absolutely necessary and should not be considered some sort of masochistic activity. On the contrary, they are tools of transcendence that allow you to soar. They break you free from complacent, repetitive, and unfulfilling lifestyles, and they prevent the mysteries of the world from leaving you behind, only to catch up with you in the end when it is too late. We are not talking here about the usual kind of suffering experienced by victims of life's sometimes-tragic circumstances. Suffering in the context of shamanic initiation is an intentional and specific form of experience aimed at pushing you into greater awareness, which is really not suffering after all. It is learning—learning through the pain (and joy) of breaking yourself open to what you are not. At first this may seem like suffering, but then it reveals itself to be an ecstatic journey. This is one of the paradoxes of shamanism—knowledge through distress, health through sickness, wholeness through fragmentation, dying of this life in order to joyfully live another.

Shamanic initiations and practices involve entering an altered state of consciousness. In this respect, we may generally say that a shamanic technique that produces an altered state is one that disrupts the normal stream of thoughts by producing a new rhythm or quality of psychic awareness. Shamanic states of altered consciousness may serve in the following ways:

- They play an important role in shamanic initiation.

- They promote enhanced states of physical and psychic functioning.

- They serve to significantly enhance and give life to the ceremonies and rituals of shamanic cultures.

- They are employed by both teacher and student during shamanic training.

- They are employed by tribal elders in order to develop fluid responses to cultural crises, including the influx of the modern world.

- They are used in reciprocal communication between the tribe and its environment, including flora and fauna, crops and animals, and the elemental and cosmic forces.

- They are employed during healing practices, as well as in bewitching.

- They are used in communication with spirits, including those of deceased ancestors.

In general, the main characteristic of the altered states of consciousness employed in the ecoshamanic project is unity. We are aiming to induce altered states that will illuminate and ultimately connect us with the numinous aspects of our world that we have been isolated from. In this way, we can transcend the way we are now and move in the direction of transformation, or transmutation, as it can also be called in this context. The table below identifies many of the contrasts between our ordinary, everyday awareness and consciousness and the altered states of awareness and consciousness experienced during ecoshamanic initiations and practices.

• **Aspect of Altered State During or After Ecoshamanic Practice**	Perception of the world and universe as a unified whole, and that we not only belong to this whole but that we have a specific place and niche within it.
Aspect of Ordinary State During Modern, Daily Life	*Feeling at various levels the existential void and loneliness of being an autonomous and independent entity.*
•	A melding of personal consciousness between the practitioner and other entities such as plants, animals, trees, and elements.
	Personal consciousness is limited to the boundary of the physical body, head, or brain.
•	Attention and concentration are intentionally focused in ways that foster a connection with other life forms and energies at a level that doesn't judge, evaluate, or compare. Everything that we perceive is accepted as equally important and awesome.
	We automatically evaluate, compare, and judge the people, places, and things around us.
•	A transcendental feeling of unity allows a person to be proud and humble at the same time.
	Pride is often a self-inflating emotion or response to a chaotic world, a kind of machismo that is not often associated with humility or humbleness.

- The world is perceived in a much larger context than strictly human concerns. Human beings are but one voice in a grand chorus.

  We perceive the world relative to human beings. The world is here for us to use, and the majority of our time is spent on our purely self-centered and human concerns.

- The experience is felt as having intrinsic value and many times the experience touches the soul so deeply that it provides real meaning and value to our life.

  We are in a continuous search to find meaning and value in our actions and for our life.

- Significant alterations in the perception of time occur. It is common for a moment to feel like a lifetime or a day to feel like an hour.

  Most often we are consciously in touch with the passage of time by very frequently checking our watch or clock to see what time it is.

- It is more common than not to experience the world as beautiful, magnificent, and meaningful. Positive and negative, moral and immoral are equally accepted as part of the greater whole. This most often leads to focusing attention and action on that which makes life valuable and worthwhile.

  Because of all the perceived crises of modern times, we often get stuck dwelling on the problems of the world and of our personal lives.

- The capacity to receive, as in sensing, feeling, and listening, is enhanced through a more passive and humble state of being.

  Our actions are often aggressive in order to "succeed." We tend to miss a lot by rushing around to accomplish tasks.

- Emotions and feelings such as awe, humbleness, wonder, mystery, reverence, and sacredness are experienced.

  Much of the everyday feelings associated with the sacred or divine have been lost through our hectic and fast-paced lives.

- A peaceful acceptance of death is commonly felt, which fosters a deep feeling of harmony with the world during life.

  We tend to view death as tragic. We do everything we can to avoid it, and we often go to our graves with feelings of resentment for our life being taken away. This cultural view of death tends to make us more aggressive and belligerent during life.

- We awaken to the fact that there is so much more that we don't know than we do know. Mystery is embraced as we humbly acknowledge that some things may be forever unknowable.

We feel like we know more than we don't know. Mechanistic-materialistic views attempt to reduce everything to the knowable.

- Experiences of awe and unity give a person increased ability to transcend their perceived limitations. A renewed confidence is felt so that daily life is more self-directed toward an authentic calling in life.

  We are often trapped by feelings of inadequacy, anxiety, and confusion. Our life path is commonly guided by society and authority figures rather than the unfolding of our life occurring naturally and spontaneously.

- It is common to feel that "heaven" is what you make of it during life here on Earth.

  Our earthly existence is normally felt as being subordinate to what might be described as "heaven."

- People are often described by others as more loving, accepting, kind, compassionate, and less selfish after deep ecoshamanic experiences.

  The modern world often creates very callous and malicious individuals.

- People tend to feel more "in the flow," blessed, lucky, and fortunate.

  People tend to dwell on the negative. "If it weren't for bad luck, I'd have no luck at all."

- It's common to receive messages and visions pertinent to our life situations from beings and entities that we normally don't communicate with.

  We are accustomed to solving life problems chiefly through personal thoughts and human knowledge.

Obviously, this table is designed to list the positive aspects of the ecoshamanic experience and not the positive aspects of the modern world, of which of course there are many. But please keep in mind that at the deepest or highest levels, the ecoshamanic states of consciousness defy explanations with words, or at least the words of our current English language, so many aspects of altered states cannot be included in this table.

In summary, while exploring and experiencing altered states of consciousness during shamanic initiations and practices, we are bringing to light the other side of things, turning them upside down and inside out toward a positive goal, which at first is the transformation of our worldview. Once our view has expanded, our inherent communicative faculties are free to touch and be touched by various other dimensions of consciousness. The awareness and practical utilization of these dimensions offer us the hope, healing, and power to call back to the island of humanity the spirits that we have so tragically estranged.

2 | THE PROJECT OF ECOSHAMANISM

Shamanism and ecoshamanism, as living traditions, cannot be easily reduced or defined. Therefore, I propose that ecoshamanism be thought of as a project, a multifaceted undertaking that evolves and expands as it is learned and practiced.

In a similar way to how shamanism has evolved differently amongst tribal groups throughout the world, the project of ecoshamanism must develop in a fluid way that takes into account not only circumstances and conditions at a global level but also the needs and wants of the local area where it is being practiced. This will likely mean that specific eco-shamanic practices will develop in different ways in different environments. And this will invite ecoshamanic practitioners to grow and develop knowledge pertinent to their local flora, fauna, history, and current situation, including threats to their local environment. Ide-ally, a network of locally based groups will spread throughout the world and develop and share practices, techniques, and visions with each other.

For those even a slight bit open to the necessity for change, the project of ecoshamanism can easily come into view when looked at through the initial tasks that I will now lay out. In wrestling for many years with how to explain and define what an ecoshamanic model might look like, in the end it was Earth herself that provided the very simple and appropri-ate answer to me while I was participating in the Embrace of the Earth ceremony (see page 181). Planet Earth as a magnificent entity, nature as our spiritual home, and our natural envi-ronment as the source of our sustenance all must be infused and embedded into the deepest regions of our mind, body, and spirit. Following this lead, I will describe the project of ecoshamanism from four levels of consciousness: mental, physical, environmental, and spiri-tual. This mind/body/environment/spirit approach will affect the total human organism in a way that aims to bring together and unify all four levels. Any enlightenments in one of the areas will help to advance the others, and the connections and interrelation between the four areas will develop strength, balance, and cohesion within our total human organism and between the human and nonhuman worlds.

Throughout the text of this book I will use the abbreviation MBES to shorten the reference to mind/body/environment/spirit consciousness. I will also add A (MBESA) for "awareness" to this abbreviation, in order to refer distinctly to being conscious of MBES instead of simply referring to MBES as a phenomena. During the experiential sections that comprise the majority of this book, the practices that I lay out necessarily affect the MBES levels of awareness, but be aware that sometimes one level or two levels can be much more dominant, or all can be equal, or each could occupy various levels of your awareness, depending on what you are doing. For example, if you are sitting in a quiet place reading, the workings of your mind will probably be the dominant awareness, as you are being affected by the written text. The awareness of your body may be next, and then your environment, and then spirit. But if someone suddenly knocks on the door your awareness may radically change from MBESA to EBMSA or MEBSA. Likewise, if you are outdoors performing a ritual to connect with the spiritual properties of a lake and you are submerged in the water, you may be experiencing BEMSA or SEBMA or any other combination, depending on what is happening to you in a given moment. I bring this up so that you can be aware of where your attention is flowing and at what levels you are aware of what is going on around and inside of you.

Also, I will be using the phrase "total MBESA" to describe the moments that signify or attempt to invoke a state of consciousness where your total organism is aware of being placed into a situation of unity. This implies a state of awareness not commonly used in the course of everyday life that helps to invoke the ecoshamanic states of consciousness that will be experienced throughout the practices in this book.

TASKS AT THE LEVEL OF MIND

> *Dispel the illusion that the human psyche is somehow separate from the natural world by acknowledging and granting psychological status to our relationship with the natural world.*

Little public recognition is given to the fact that many of the crises of our times, including the ecological crisis, have at their bases a psychological crisis. The critical situation we all face right now is obvious enough. Our society is in an advanced state of disconnection from the organic reality of life, as witnessed on a daily basis by the expanding ecological crises and daily ecological catastrophes. The lack of recognition that these crises are psychological extends to the field of psychology itself, as has been discussed in recent years through the emerging field of ecopsychology. The challenge now faced by psychologists, as well as the general public, is to recognize the psychological impact of the relationship between humans and the natural world—to acknowledge that human behavior is rooted deeply in nature's rhythms and systems, and that when we lose our psychic connection to the natural world, our religious, political, and cultural systems become sick; people and society become sick; nature is exploited; species become extinct; and the whole biosphere is threatened.

To place "psyche" and "consciousness" exclusively inside the human mind limits the psyche of the universe to personal human ownership and denies the experience of psychic relationships with the larger world that we need in order to be healthy and whole. Ecoshamanism, as a tool of psychological intervention, works from the assumption that at its deepest level the human psyche is bonded to Earth and the cosmos that birthed us into existence and that nurtures and sustains a countless number of other living beings and organisms. Some will see this view of placing psychological awareness into the natural world as a way of romanticizing nature, or simply as being overly sentimental or even corny. But it is a matter of pure common sense, as well as a basic wisdom that guides shamanic tribal societies, that health for human beings depends on harmony with the natural world with respect to the land, water, sky, and living entities that share our psychic space.

There is nothing romantic, mystical, or esoteric about this view. From the standpoint of ecoshamanism, neither is there anything subconscious about it. Many noted psychologists and philosophers, including some that acknowledge the trauma caused by our disconnection to the natural world, have been quick to place our psychic link to the natural world into the realm of the subconscious by hypothesizing that, in a similar way to Jung's ideas of the "collective unconscious," we all have an even deeper unconscious that could be referred to as the "ecological unconscious." According to Theodore Roszak, "repression of the ecological unconscious is the deepest root of collective madness in industrial society; open access to the ecological unconscious is the path to sanity."

While this "open access to the ecological unconscious" seems like a great idea, it doesn't provide any practical usefulness for a society so deeply alienated from its natural environment, and therefore tends to sound like just more psychological mumbo-jumbo. Our knowledge of the environmental crisis is not deeply buried in some part of our unconscious that we don't have ready access to. We know about our impact on the environment, we can see, read, hear, and feel the effects of our actions on a daily basis. It's just that, for myriad reasons, we don't attend to this knowledge; we disassociate from it or repress it, just like our mainstream economic, political, and educational systems do. This isn't some sort of unconscious problem to be solved on the soft couch of a therapy session. This is a tangible and real situation of the concrete, material world that is right in front of our noses every single day.

Our psychic connection to the natural world is available to us in every moment, and this is precisely why many of us now feel as sick psychologically as our environments are physically. It is time we acknowledge that our psychological health is directly tied to the health of our environment and the relationship we have with it. Under the impact and severity of current psychological conditions, the prudent course of action is to focus on mending our conscious psychic connection to the natural world, for the healing of humanity as well as for the planet that provides us with life.

🍃 *Overcome our deficient childhood psychological development stemming from insufficient reciprocal and harmonious relationships with the natural world.*

When I first started visiting shamanic tribal communities living at a distance from the modern world, my initial feeling was of being a child among adults—not in the way of age, but in the quality of what I can only describe as a sort of calm wisdom. It was as if when they spoke to me they were speaking with the voice of the mountains where they live, the corn that sustains them, and the sun that is their father. The maturity of their thoughts and actions, even among the children, was astounding, and gave me my first glimpse of what humanity can be like without the constant competitive atmospheres of our schools and marketplace, the sterile and lifeless environments of our urban and suburban communities, and the technological hyper-reality of media, computers, and video games.

Did these tribal people have problems? Of course. They are as human as you and I, but the difference that I felt from them was the security that comes from knowing their place in the world. Their way of life depended on cooperation between the human and nonhuman world—the study of the mysterious, dangerous, and breathtaking natural world where everyday life was immersed in a sense of spiritual significance and encounter, and where individuals of all ages and both sexes celebrated life's stages and passages through group ceremony and ritual with the spiritual entities of their natural home.

I soon came to understand that what I was observing and feeling was not only a matter of cultural differences between them and me. At a much deeper level, somewhere deep in their bodies and souls lived an inner knowing that began at infancy and continued to grow until death. They displayed an inner strength born from generations of connection to the rhythms and cycles of the natural world.

It should come as no surprise how these tribal people come to be so grounded and at home in their natural environment. From the time of infancy, a child is immersed in the rich texture, smell, and motion of the natural world. Sunshine and rain, the sounds of wind and water, earth between the toes, the touch of tree bark, and the warmth and glow of the fire are constantly being infused into the mind, body, and spirit of the child. Along with this, the stories, rituals, and even regular, everyday language and activities of the tribe all revolve around the natural environment in which they live.

What is perhaps most generally missing in the childhood of modern people is this sense of place, the grounded relationship of community with the human and nonhuman world.

Bring to light our current valuation and affiliation for the natural world to critically assess both our lifestyles and philosophical views.

The way we understand the natural world depends on the quality of our relationship to it, our point of view mentally, physically, and spiritually, and our historic perspective, both culturally and personally.

Stephen Kellert, while writing about the biophilia hypothesis (that humans have an innate affiliation to other living organisms), very nicely delineates nine possible categories in which humans place value on to the natural world (from *The Biophilia Hypothesis* by Stephen R. Kellert and Edward O. Wilson, eds. Copyright © 1993 by Island Press. Reproduced by permission of Island Press, Washington, D.C.):

Utilitarian	Practical and material exploitation of nature
Naturalistic	Satisfaction from direct experience/contact with nature
Ecologistic-scientific	Systemic study of structure, function, and relationship in nature
Aesthetic	Physical appeal and beauty of nature

Symbolic	Use of nature for metaphorical expression, language, expressive thought
Humanistic	Strong affection, emotional attachment, "love" for nature
Moralistic	Strong affinity, spiritual reverence, ethical concern for nature
Dominionistic	Master, physical control, dominance of nature
Negativistic	Fear, aversion, alienation from nature

From these basic values, we can see a huge spectrum of perspectives that we modern humans have in relation to nature. When addressing the values of shamanic or animistic cultures, these categories must also be added.

While examining these nine categories of valuation, there are two main points I'd like to note. The first is that while these categories explore the values that we give *to* the natural world, they also clearly demonstrate our deeply embedded human dependence *on* the natural world. Our innate need for nature ranges from material sustenance to emotional and cognitive development. And even while we are destroying and dominating the natural world, we are still experiencing an undeniable interaction.

Second, while thoroughly describing the valuations of the modern man, many of the seemingly "positive" values delineated here are barely even discernable within modern culture, and within these nine categories it is only in the moralistic that we see any hint of the extremely high spiritual values that shamanic/animistic cultures place on the natural world. But lumping the shamanic/animistic into the moral category does not do justice to the profound differences between spiritual values and moral values. Moral/ethical concerns surely can arise from one's spiritual beliefs, but they are not dependent upon them. Moral and ethical values can be held toward the natural world without placing nature or the earth into a spiritual context; this is much different than the worldview known as animism, which most shamanic cultures ascribe to, "which sees all life-forms, including animals, plants, rocks, forests, rivers, mountains, fields, oceans, winds, as well as sun, moon, fire, and the total cosmos, as pervaded by, and interconnected with, spiritual energy and intelligence" (Ralph Metzner, *Green Psychology* [Rochester, VT: Park Street Press, 1999]).

Ecoshamanic practices that place not only value but also spirit into the natural world open us to the animated world in a way that deflates our necessity for purely human values, archetypes, and icons. The heroes and heroines of the ecoshamanic universe—the rising sun, the nourishing rain, the selfless salmon, Grandfather Fire, Grandmother Growth—

all of these place value and affiliation with life outside of the purely human sphere. Valuating the natural world from the purely human standpoint is one of deepest underlying sources of disconnection between humans and nature.

🍂 *Identify specific psychological imbalances in our relationship to the natural world.*

The values we have toward the natural world are a consequence of upbringing, cultural worldview, and spiritual orientation. I've already discussed the notion of the drastic differences in childhood between shamanic and Western culture as a root cause of the rift in the human-nature relationship. Now let's briefly explore other diagnostic metaphors in an attempt to broaden our understanding so as to offer in upcoming chapters specific ecoshamanic practices that could help in healing these ailments.

Through the writings of such great thinkers as Henry Thoreau and Ralph Waldo Emerson, we get the very clear notion that the great civilizations of man may be maladjusted to the realities of nature. Those that followed, including Rachel Carson, Aldo Leopold, Paul Shepard, and Gary Snyder, among many others, offered that this maladjustment was a consequence of an anthropocentric (human-centered) worldview and that from there we easily made the jump to assuming human superiority in our relation to the nonhuman world. The rise of agriculture and animal husbandry, mechanistic science and technology, the conquering of the pagan worlds by religions holding aloft a righteous monotheistic version of god, and many other historic occurrences have been put forth as the historical roots of the split between humans and nature.

From these historical perspectives come a variety of diagnoses to our current situation. Theologian Thomas Berry has put forth the idea that, as a result of the mechanistic-technological worldview, the human species has become autistic in relation to the natural world. Like an autistic child that does not seem to feel or even see or hear the presence, voice, and gestures of its mother, we have become autistic to the voices and psychic presence of the living being that birthed us. Dolores LaChapelle and Chellis Glendinning, among other authors, offer the diagnosis of addiction. According to this theory, the phenomenal growth of the capital-accumulating industrial society, the rampant spread of consumerism, and the obsession for faster and more powerful machines all point to signs of an addicted society. Other diagnoses, such as traumatic amnesia (that we have actually forgotten our interdependent relationship with nature as a consequence of major disasters, both natural and manmade) and narcissism (our relentless pursuit of more expensive and high-tech goods feeds our inflated and grandiose self-image, which masks deep-seated feelings of emptiness) have also been postulated.

Although clearly these diagnoses shed light onto possible treatments that could lead to healing the split between humans and nature, with regards to the psyche of the Western mind I believe a diagnosis that includes dissociation must be included. Dissociation, a normal cognitive function that allows us to concentrate or focus our attention by screening out what we are not immediately focusing on, becomes unhealthy when taken to extremes. Modern society has extremely dissociated itself from the physical, spiritual, and psychic realities of nature, while at the same time also dissociating the mental and spiritual from physical sensations, impulses, and instincts.

The healing of our dissociative splits is not so much a matter of simply forsaking our science and technology to return to some pre-industrial way of life, but rather to re-infuse the human mind, body, and spirit with practices and activities that enable us to examine the value systems with which we develop and apply our technology, and also foster the desire to maintain a respectful and spiritually sound, balanced relationship with both the human and nonhuman worlds.

TASKS AT THE LEVEL OF BODY

> *Reclaim the awareness that our physical body is the most obvious and intimate component of the natural world that we could ever know, and that alienating ourselves from our body also alienates us from nature.*

The current crises that planet Earth faces could be caused by capitalism or industrialism, or loss of spiritual vision, or psychological disease, or patriarchy, or all of the above plus many other circumstances all wrapped into one. But one thing is very clear, and that is that we are all a part of it, each and every one of us, simply because we all share in the body of this magnificent planet. We are not born into the world, but out from it. We are part of this enormous life form; we are an expression of its creative being. Each of us is a small fragment of a greater whole, an extension of the ancient, unfolding experience of planet Earth.

Our mortal body is an extension of Earth's body, which makes it our most precious connection to this sacred, life-giving planet spinning within a vast galaxy and universe. The organic reality of the earth is thus found not only in the ranges of mountains and in the depths of oceans but inside the human body as well. Alienation from our bodies by over-intellectualizing and technologizing causes us to feel like disembodied minds with disenchanted bodies that are separated from the earth. Our true identity becomes weak and vulnerable when divorced from our bodily feelings and from the earth. To reconnect the sense of self with one's earth-grounded body is also to reclaim a connection with the body of Earth and the dynamic interaction between body, mind, and environment.

Reconnecting with our physical body can also affect us spiritually. Nonincarnated spirituality that is disconnected from our bodies and from nature contributes directly to alienating us from the sacredness of Earth and the profoundly spiritual reality of the natural world that our body surely is a part of. When we discover that our body is not the dwelling place of spirit, but is the physical manifestation of spirit, we move to a place of honoring and cherishing our own flesh, and also the flesh of the whole world and universe.

> *Realize that our physical health is continually affected by the health or sickness of our environment, and also by what our body is receiving as sustenance.*

Before the advent of polluting technologies, our ancient ancestors lived and died within the context of a healthy environment of pure air, water, and foods harvested from fertile soil. Even within just the prior few centuries, humans living within a city environment could still depend on the purifying qualities of the natural elements. But this is no longer true. Our home planet no longer rules itself, but is now subject to the domination of one single species that is overwhelming the natural systems of the planet with toxic and non-biodegradable materials. The devastating effects of human technology threaten the survival of every living species, but since humans flourish only within the healthy complex of the planet's ecosystems, any damage done to other species, or ecosystems, or the planet itself, ultimately damages the human organism as well.

From a shamanic perspective, as well as spiritual and utterly practical, the topic of food is key to individual and ecological education as well as for the inherent rights and well-being of an enormous number of living species on Earth. Unless humans across the globe can open themselves to developing a sacred relationship with the food they eat, they will continue to decimate the planet, and our existence here will continue to seem insignificant.

In a similar way to re-owning the body, the alienation of our consciousness with food can seem like an extremely trivial topic, except when viewed from the perspective that this aspect of alienation contributes significantly to the alienation of both our personal body and the earthbody. In this light, our food becomes a highly important ecological, as well as spiritual, issue.

Viewed through the eyes of the tribal shaman, our current cultural experience with food is one of complete spiritual disconnection, to the point that our relationship has degenerated into food being simply the fuel that supplies the energy for our seemingly insatiable appetite to consume the world around us, which then still leaves us searching for what will fill the hungers of our soul. To understand that food is not simply a metaphor for spiritual nourishment, but rather that it is spiritual nourishment of the most tangible kind, is to place oneself in a most intimate relationship with the divine energies that keep us alive. When we engage in the sacred gathering, preparing, and presenting of food, we enter a spiritual communion that places us inside the circle of life and the seasons. In contrast, eating takeout food, microwaving a packaged dinner, or purchasing chemically grown or raised food at the supermarket to prepare at home does not illicit inside of us the sacred feelings of our membership within the community of all earthly beings.

Even organic food purchased in the large, "healthy" markets that are becoming quite popular, although certainly a major step in the right direction, is still grown by people and places we don't know, and packaged, shipped, sold, and profited from in a way completely separate from us. We can certainly be thankful for these more wholesome organically grown and raised food products, but the sacred acts of raising, gathering, and hunting are still completely lost, not to mention the ecologically unsound shipping and retailing energy used to get them on our table.

The sacrament of food, then, becomes central to the project of ecoshamanism. So important is this that it is included at many different levels throughout this book. While transforming our attitudes and actions revolving around what we put into our bodies, we will also be transforming our relationship to everything around us. By relating to our relationship with food as sacred, we then begin to see the soil of gardens as holy ground, and one who farms the soil in a sacred way as acting in the service of spirit. The roles of farmer/gatherer/hunter are then transformed into most honorable and sacred professions. In the same way as surviving shamanic cultures, sacred farmers and hunters will be shamans who work through the mysterious forces of creation to bless and help nourish their community. When this happens, then engineered food will be replaced with sacred agriculture nurtured by pure air, water, and love. The *milpa* (garden, field) becomes the spiritual center of the community, the rhythms of the seasons are restored to our bodies, and our flesh becomes the same as the sacred flesh of the world.

🌿 *Reconnect with the inherited ancient wisdom held within our human body.*

Our physical experiences and intentions are the threads that connect us to this world. The body gives us the grounds for our experience. The unfolding of our lives is not just the realizing of our inner potential but also a process of interaction with our environment. It is through this interaction with others and the corporeal world that we discover and invent meanings that allow us to blossom and flower into mature beings. We encounter, adjust, exchange, engage, transmit, and interact with the world through our contact with life. Without this contact we wouldn't be perceiving the emotional, imaginative, instinctual, impulsive, or desiring relationship with all we encounter.

Being in contact with the world is therefore a fundamental aspect of life, and one that, whether we realize it or not, can happen at significantly different levels or depths. For example, in the current Euro-American worldview, we have become largely alienated from the deep bodily knowledge so familiar to nature-based and shamanic cultures because we live chiefly in the mind. This causes us to live and interact with the physical world on a very superficial level. Upon close inspection of our lifestyles through the looking glass of nature, it becomes apparent that our life experiences, in many ways, resemble those of a disembodied mind in a bubble. This is a disturbing realization but one that has to be made if we are to reclaim our body and our relationship to the body of the living Earth.

By educating ourselves predominantly in indoor classrooms with books and media, feeding ourselves with genetically manipulated food that someone else raised or slaughtered, and dedicating most of our life to a workplace that is founded on the abstract reality of growth economics, we divorce ourselves from the web of life experiences shared by the rest of the species of the planet, including the human cultures that still live a nature-based existence. We actually have placed ourselves in an artificial and sterilized bubble of reality where it is not only possible, but also very common, for us to experience life with a minimum of meaningful physical contact with the world, and to utilize a mere fraction of our sensory and bodily awareness. Our modern technological lifestyles also repress the need for authentic bodily experiences that connect us in a meaningful way with our natural environment.

One of the primary ways we become alienated from the body is through our endless pursuit of control. In our world, success is largely seen as the attainment of financial security and independence. A "well-adjusted" individual with a loving family that he or she can provide for, and owning a nice car and home, is a common dream that millions of people truly work hard toward every day. But with this dream comes the need to control as many circumstances as possible. The more that we can control and manipulate, the more successful our illusion of success becomes.

Our ego attempts to control as many of our life circumstances as it can and as such becomes the controller of all of our voluntary activities. But the body, on the other hand, functions as a highly complex system of mostly involuntary actions (blood circulation, digestion, metabolism, etc.) that we have little or no possibility of consciously controlling. It is precisely due to the inability to completely control our body that we develop the feeling of being trapped by it—by the pain it makes us feel when we are injured or sick, and by the perceived chain of flesh that promises only one final outcome. In response to this we become alienated from the body, and many times we long and search for means of escape, even if just temporarily.

Our temporary escapes often lead to serious addictions where our body is abused and degraded and from where not only our body but also our larger mind-body organism suffers extremely, or even dies. In many shamanic cultures, alienation and abuse of the body (not to be confused with intentional deprivation and mortification in certain rituals) is one of the strongest taboos, since it is well known that all life contains spirit and if one doesn't care well for the body, its spirit or soul will lose interest and leave. A retrieval of the spirit and rebirth of the person into a new life is then required if the individual is to be healed and live healthily again.

Since our bodies are inextricably connected to the earth, the issue of control relates not only to our personal physical body but to the earthbody as well. In both cases it is necessary to let what is ultimately beyond our control simply live on its own behalf. The natural world surely doesn't need human beings to make order of and control it. Quite the contrary; Earth has evolved quite nicely without us, and the last few moments of Earth's history reveal that the destructive force of humans strikes considerable resemblance to parasites that attack and consume their hosts—in this case, the earth and all its living species. The wilderness areas and wild animals of the world do not need to be controlled and exploited by us. They are self-regulating systems; that is what makes them wild. The same goes for the human body. It is a highly complex self-regulating system that more properly belongs to the wilderness than to a sterile building, whether it be home or office. In terms of control, we will be much better off when we allow our body to be wild instead of continuing to drive it around like a car or control it like a lab rat. We need to learn to let our body drive us. Our body is perfectly capable of telling us where it likes to be, what it prefers to eat, what level of activity it needs, and what relationships are healthy for it.

But the sad fact is that in order to continue living in our lifeless environments and persisting in our abstract lifestyles, we have most brilliantly developed to a super high degree the ability to intercept and then repress our body's needs and wishes. We are born from (not into) an organic reality that perfectly coincides to our physical needs, yet day after day we almost completely ignore this most primal connection. Our body needs and wants the more-than-human world. Denying this and repressing it has caused a frustrated and unconsummated relationship between our bodies and our natural environment. A lifetime of these unlived, blocked experiences becomes jammed up inside our bodies, to the point that it is not to be wondered why there are so many of us suffering from anxiety, depression, rage, hatred, sexual dysfunction, and chronic illness.

Our bodies carry the inherited wisdom of countless generations and bear the historic past of our species right up to this very moment. The communication that our bodies employ with the world is older than words, older than intellectual thought. Through our bodies we have an inborn sense of the interrelation we are to have with the world, and we are "made" in accordance with what our bodies are expecting to receive from their environment. In this sense we are born *from* the world, confident and adapted to the historic organismic patterns of our ancient ancestors, but if these patterns are changed or deprived, then psychic and physical distress is inevitable. This distress—the deprivation of our bodily felt interactions and psychic connection with the natural world—is being evidenced in countless ways by the actions and lifestyles of our modern society. We have deviated so drastically from the lifeways that have nurtured us over countless generations that we are now being born from and into a kind of ecological and cultural vacuum that prevents the complete unfolding of our life process. Without this natural unfolding and maturation, we are left with feelings of frustration, incompleteness, agitation, dissatisfaction, and a general nonrealizing of both our innate bodily and psychic needs.

The end to this suffering will require us to make contact with our deeply felt bodily longings and connect with a wider view of reality than just the human hyperworld we now live in, and also to work with our psychic intuition and silent knowledge to create the conditions that will allow us to unfold and fulfill our sacred niche as part of the earth community.

> 🍃 *Learn that our bodies are capable of an awareness that is distinguishable from and complementary to the awareness of our minds.*

Being fully aware of the myriad processes of perception that our human organism is capable of can truly open us to a new understanding and experiencing of the world. Traditionally, human perception is thought of as a one-way process whereby data is collected from the surrounding environment and organized by the human organism. Our interior human mind is kept apprised of what is happening around us through the use of our sense organs that register and transfer sensory information into our nervous system. We perceive the objects and facts of the outside world through the passive one-way operation of our senses. In this traditional view of perception, there is a real and tangible perceptual boundary between what is inside of me and what is outside of me. In this case, I perceive the world but I don't perceive the world perceiving me. Perception is a passive and one-directional experience.

The shamanic worldview, on the other hand, does not limit the senses to simply being passive collectors of information; rather, they are viewed and felt as exploratory organs in constant interaction and exchange with their living environment. Direct and nonverbal communication with other organisms and persons is not viewed as some sort of "extrasensory perception" but is simply a normal function of our human organism. This communication is far deeper and more primordial than the verbal communication we carry on among ourselves and describes a bodily felt exchange, a reciprocal interaction between the body and its environment. This communication is corporeal rather than intellectual—a communication without words. When our perception is felt as a bodily exchange of intelligence between our human organism and the living environment, we experience birds, trees, rivers, mountains, and even stones as living and communicative presences.

> 🍃 *Develop and engage in ecoshamanic practices to acknowledge that our human flesh is the same as the flesh of the world.*

For most of us, the skin of our body simply represents the boundary in which we delineate what is me and what is not. However, what is usually not kept in mind, or is easily forgotten, is the fact that our skin is actually a highly sensitive organ that is in constant interaction with the world in every moment we are alive. Our skin is the largest organ we have, weighing 8–11 pounds for most adults. This remarkable multilayered organ allows us to touch our environment in the most sensual way possible. It constantly renews itself, heals with astonishing speed when injured, and is such an important element of our human organism that approximately one-fourth of our blood flows through our skin at any given time.

For our discussion here, I would like to make note of the fact that our remarkably sensitive and complex skin organ is not only that part of us that binds together the flesh of our body but also that joins us to our environment. That we have such an important organ on the outermost portion of our body is a significant feature of the human anatomy that goes largely unnoticed by a culture that spends most of its physical and psychic time inside.

The fact that we don't have a hard shell, scales, or fur is one reason why we build structures to live in, but without these protective coverings we also have the inherent potential to feel the physical world in a super-keen manner. Our super-sensitive skin organ puts the very flesh of our soul in direct contact with every element of the world we touch, and helps make us the highly sensitive beings we are.

An important viewpoint held by both shamans and certain forward-thinking contemporary philosophers—and one that I would like to introduce here in our search for bodily consciousness—is the psychic correspondence of flesh. In this context flesh is viewed as a primary element of the world. Just as water, air, earth, and fire, flesh too is primary and elemental. Our bodies are born from the flesh of our mother, from the flesh of the world. The flesh of our body, the flesh of fruit, the flesh of the deer and whale—all are one flesh, one elemental fabric of a living world.

In this sense, when flesh touches flesh, it is touching itself. When my fingers touch my body, I am touching myself; as I breathe in and out, my lungs touch the air—we exchange, part of it becomes me and part of me becomes it—and so when the air flows into my body, the atmosphere is actually touching itself. When I breathe in the air, I am touching myself. In this same way I touch the trees and plants and animals in my environment.

This is utterly personal and primary; it is experienced at a level deeper than thoughts or words. When I eat the flesh of an apple or the flesh of an animal, the flesh becomes me, and as I live and grow I become the flesh of the earth. The shaman knows this. Through the reality of living experiences with the unity of body-mind, the shaman perceives the world as a single living tissue encompassing all phenomena in a mutually informative and reciprocating body comprised of the identical primary elements. There are no lines drawn; each form of life, each level of reality, is a reflection of the other. The plant, animal, human, and spirit realms flow into each other in one grand continuum of mutual multidimensional kinship.

Therefore, imperative to the project of ecoshamanism is the transcending of the traditional mind/body schism for which so many healing modalities where born. But the shaman does not enter clinical therapy or learn intricate body movements in order to know or reclaim their body, for the shaman is an experientialist (or more properly a phenomenologist) in the purest sense—all they need in order to know is phenomena, the reality of lived experience that comes before thought or reflection.

The shaman's phenomenology is really the study of relationships. The shaman sees human relations in the context of a large web or network where our existence is continually unfolding throughout this web of interactions and not simply inside the human skull containing the human psyche or ego. He knows that if he were to literally cut up the flesh of our bodies and slice open the brain, he wouldn't find there any thoughts, perceptions, emotions, or behavior, because these phenomena occur in relation to our experiences with the world. To reclaim the body, then, is simply to increase and optimize our direct and primal contact with the flesh of the world.

It is at this level of awareness that the shamanic abilities to somehow know or see things happening in the natural world that escapes general awareness, which to the Western eye are viewed as clairvoyant, extrasensory, or supernatural experiences, are revealed as simply highly developed forms of body-mind-environment awareness that places the shaman in communion with the ever-unfolding intelligence of the natural world in which he resides.

Acknowledging the psychic correspondence of flesh also helps us to deal in positive ways with our relationships to death and dying. Our repressed, blocked, and unlived experiences with the natural world results in a less than healthy body-mind-environment state that has not fully lived, and so therefore is also not prepared for, or even fears, death. Nothing could be of greater evidence for this than the colossal structures that we build to represent our immortality—or rather our fear of mortality.

This is one of the most striking and noticeable differences between nature-based cultures and ours. While we are obsessed with constructing permanent buildings and homes from ecologically devastating materials, nature cultures create beautifully crafted impermanent structures from all-natural sources. Our nature-dominating structures that first destroy and then completely shut out the natural world clearly represent our self-inflated egoistic lifestyles filled with unfulfilled hopes and dreams, while the ecologically sound homes of our nature-oriented relatives that return to the earth every few years represent the cyclical reality of birth-death-rebirth on which life on Earth is founded. While we feel our technologically superior buildings somehow represent a more evolved or mature culture than our so-called primitive cousins, in many ways this couldn't be further from the truth. Our massive and sterile edifices clearly symbolize our immature and myopic worldview that attempts to deny the natural life cycle of all living things.

The human life cycle, under the best conditions, ends with the last desire, after all others are fulfilled, to rest, to know no more, to be content. A satisfied life comes full circle as one's life projects are fulfilled; the desire to do becomes the desire to see one's offspring do, in a way that the cycle of life continues. As this happens, the struggle to hang on to life loses its immediacy and is replaced by the wish to simply rest and conclude. For shamanic cultures, this manner of leaving the world is common and normal, but for us the opposite is usually the case, as we try at all costs to prolong our lives with drugs and machines in the hope that one more day will allow us to feel complete. This war we fight at the end is another example of the war against our body. In the final analysis, our feeble body is blamed for not giving us enough time to realize our dreams, for never being able to see our loved ones again; and so the body becomes avoided during life because it is seen as merely the abode of death, rather than the gift of life.

From the perspective of shamanic and nature-based cultures, we avoid death so vehemently because a major part of our lives has never been fulfilled. Born from the natural world but then immediately taken from it, and then later taught precisely how to exploit it, we have missed a whole life's worth of experiences that the incomprehensible amount of living species and places of the world had for us. It is no wonder we go to our death in tragic ways or psychically kicking and screaming.

One of my indigenous shaman mentors once commented to me, after being invited to travel for a few weeks to the United States and Japan, that "The lives of you modern people mirror the lives of the animals in your factory-raised meat farms—born inside, kept in the dark, fed artificial food, exploited for profit, and then finally, when a little light seeps into the cage, it is merely the door being opened by the great huntress that ends your life."

This strong comment, said through tears of bewilderment over all the destruction he witnessed, has served as a strong reminder to me while on this path of trying to realize an ecoshamanic worldview and developing practices to share with others.

TASKS AT THE LEVEL OF ENVIRONMENT

🍃 *Recover the moment-to-moment awareness that every one of our thoughts and actions are tied to the web of life that encompasses the entire planet.*

Thanks to the technology of mass media, we are all aware of the major environmental problems such as ozone depletion, acid rain, toxic waste, and deforestation, to name a few. But the sad fact is that most modern people still don't attend to the connection between these global catastrophes and the lifestyles we lead as individuals. People just don't seem to make the connections between fast-food burgers and deforestation, between electrically powered households and nuclear waste, between hour-long commutes to work and toxic drinking water.

Environmental problems are not the result of someone or something "out there," they are directly related to the way we live our lives, from the big decisions like what house to live in or what car to drive all the way down to the smallest actions like what brand of coffee to drink or what magazine to read. Every single one of our actions, and all of the thinking (or thoughtlessness) that surrounds those actions, is part of an intricate process that affects our environment.

The concept of saving the environment has been externalized and trivialized to such an extent that people now view "the environment" as something "out there" to be saved, while really paying little attention to what is happening to the earth under their feet and the sky above their heads in this moment. Major automobile manufacturers sponsor TV programs about endangered species and try to sell to us that they are defending the environment even as they continue to develop, market, and sell the most powerful and gas-guzzling SUVs to date—and we continue to buy them. Seemingly caring families donate money to environmental groups while continuing to feed their kids agro-business packaged food and sending them off to schools that have the primary goal of teaching them how to become "successful" in the economic growth marketplace.

A new level of environmental awareness is needed. Most people in our society are ecological illiterates. It is much too difficult, if not impossible, to ask someone not to drive their car so much if they have absolutely no understanding of the hydrologic cycle of water that provides for their very life, or to suggest they buy organically grown foodstuffs when they have not a clue about soil depletion and its effects on the immune system. I'm not talking here about purely scientific matters, but rather about the most simple and basic functioning principles of life that we have all but completely forgotten. Healthy soil complete with earthworms cycling upward and downward, clean rain formed by water cycling through healthy rivers and seas, magically invisible air cycled through vigorous forests and jungles—these healthy ecological cycles and the interrelationships between them and between humans are the most basic realities of living on Earth.

Ecoshamanic practices must get people back in tune with the underlying energies and cyclical realities of healthy living, not through guilt or shame but through direct sensory experiences with the interconnectedness of all life. When we engage in practices that honor and connect us to the cycles and systems of the living planet, our eyes are opened to how we interact within those systems.

🍃 *Promote environmental education with a holistic systems approach.*

The way we have all been educated is a big part of the environmental problem, and although the ecoshamanic practices I'm outlining in this book certainly don't propose specific curriculum to be used in schools, what they do provide is the opportunity to begin understanding how our narrow and negligent educational systems have created a society of ecological illiterates, and how to begin learning in a more proactive, healthy manner.

The biology, ecology, and even environmental awareness programs in our schools tend to be classroom-based memorization exercises where bits of knowledge are learned outside of the natural context that would give them meaning, and therefore are quickly forgotten. We receive explanations, charts, and diagrams, and we do experiments and outdoor activities designed to supplement the overall curriculum, which ultimately leads to issues of resource management. But what is really needed is an integral program designed into the entire educational system that is based in the natural world, is not activity oriented but outcome based, is not management oriented but lifestyle based, and that demonstrates for us the interconnectedness of all life in a way that teaches us where we as human beings fit into the living systems of the planet. Most people simply don't have a systems view or approach to the natural world because they weren't taught that way. Neither were the leaders of our governmental, social, and religious institutions.

Educating ourselves about the earth's systems is also a proactive way to move past the environmental activist stereotype that portrays those who care deeply about the environment as messengers of doom or moralist preachers. Too often we are reminded, or we remind others, about ozone holes, toxic waste, species extinction, global warming, etc., but what would be much more productive is learning instead of blaming. Instead of preaching about the morals of environmental awareness, immerse yourself in the natural systems and energies of the natural world, learn about your place within those systems, make your lifestyle changes accordingly, and then teach other people in a humble and experiential manner.

Environmentalism and ecoshamanism can work together when environmentalists are land-healers and earth-teachers that solve problems not through quick technical fixes but by connecting with and therefore understanding the ecosystems they are part of, and by demonstrating and living the lifestyle changes necessary to restore the physical, psychological, and spiritual wellness of the beings living within those ecosystems.

🍃 *Develop a deep, genuine connection and affiliation for the land where we live.*

If there was one task that stands out as singly important for the project of ecoshamanism, as well as for many other earth-honoring projects and environmental programs and reforms, this would be the task, because this is where it all begins and ends.

We are an uprooted culture and society. Most of our families have only a few generations living on this continent, and many of us have only one or two generations. Most affluent people don't live where they grew up, and many people move dozens of times during their life. With consumer-based lifestyles, equipped with massive transportation systems that relieve us of any connection to our local land for sustenance, the actual place where one lives has become a trivial circumstance to life. But this illusion couldn't be further from the truth.

Our immediate environment directly influences, at the most primal depths, the way we think, the way we eat, the way we dress, the way we earn a living, the things we own, the way we relate to each other, and the way we relate to the world. Our sense of place is what roots us and grounds our experience of life. Without a deeply grounded sense of place, we magnify the feelings of the existential void that accompanies our modern lifestyles that provide no significant meaning to our lives. Recovering this sense of place, this rooting that is the basis for a stable psychological, physical, and spiritual well-being, is a vital task in healing many of the crises of our modern times.

This recovering has been called "re-inhabiting place" or "becoming native," among other terms, and forms the basis for bioregional thought and action as well as forming an ecological aspect to personal identity and arousing notions of sustainable lifestyles and community. But it also connects us in a tangible way to the bigger systems that "our" piece of land is dependent on. For example, we may discover how our watershed is affected by the health of surrounding rivers, lakes, and seas, or how our air quality is affected by weather coming from the Gulf of Mexico or the Canadian Arctic. We may begin to notice the migration of birds and butterflies in and out of our land, and the impact that other regions have on local wildlife and fauna.

It is just this sense of place that at once connects us to a piece of land in such a way as to love and nurture and preserve it while at the same time providing the realization that we are also dependent upon the health of the surrounding regions and also of the entire globe. This sense of place transcends borders of nationality, social class, religion, or color, for it places all human beings and human activities into the context of being just one part of the greater community of life on Earth.

Learn to see a deeper reality by removing the façades and disguises that obscure the true identity of objects, situations, and circumstances.

Our society has been all but completely blinded by the promises of technology, the black magic of corporate advertising and marketing, and the general "unburdening" of life encouraged by modern conveniences. We have been taught to look at the surface of things and to ignore what lies beneath and behind. It has become so easy for us to just consume things without question that the obvious questions rarely even get asked anymore.

In this age of ecological and social decline, we are being asked to take a much closer look into the things we purchase and why we purchase them, why we engage in the activities that form our day-to-day lives, and how our actions are tied to the ecological systems that sustain us. It's time that we asked where the food that we put on our table comes from, how it got here, how it was made, what exactly it was made from, how it is being preserved, and what will happen to the packaging it comes wrapped in. Where do the clothes we are wearing come from, who made them, from what, and who profited from our purchase? Where does the paper that our books, magazines, and newspapers we read come from, at what cost to those environments; who profits? What materials are our homes, cars, and office buildings made from? Where were the materials extracted from and at what cost to the environment? Where does our trash go? And so on . . .

TASKS AT THE LEVEL OF SPIRIT

> ❦ *Identify and heal the spiritual-ethical illnesses that allow for the continued degradation of our natural spiritual home.*

The current environmental crisis is also a crisis of spiritual beliefs. Without a physical experience of the sacred, both for people and the natural world, there exists a gaping chasm between spirituality that enhances and heals the well-being of individuals, other groups, and the environment, and those religious expressions that hurt and even destroy other persons, other groups, and the environment. All across the globe there exists fanatical, authoritarian systems of faith that fuel violence, including violence against the natural world. When religious cosmologies are detached from the earth and lose their sacred connection to the corporeal world, a plethora of spiritual, psycho-spiritual, and ethical illnesses manifest. With regard to the earth, the notion of human superiority and the resulting "God-given right" to exploit the natural world is just as ethically unhealthy as a monotheistic religion's attempt to extinguish the earth-rooted spirituality of "pagan" animistic and shamanic cultures.

Idolatries of a psycho-spiritual nature are deeply rooted in the contemporary spiritual crises. Idolatry of oneself, idolatry of the human species, one's ethnic group, religion, nation, economic system, or even the now-commonplace idolatry of materialism constricts one's values to a small sphere of self-interest that blocks caring for the world on a global spiritual level.

As a result of psycho-spiritual and ethical illness, many people suffer from a kind of spiritual deadness that prevents them from fully experiencing the incredible gift of being alive. For these people, spirituality has become like a vacuum of empty space where nothing is sacred.

There are also individuals and groups that maintain the fantasy that we will somehow be saved from the brink of ecological destruction by God—that simply praying or going to church is all that is required, even while continuing to engage in and ignore the effects of ecologically destructive lifestyles. This is also a form of spiritual deadness because it kills the appropriate ethical responsibility to do all that we possibly can to respect and protect our natural spiritual home planet.

Confronting the spiritual dimension to the ecological crises and expanding our spiritual-ethical horizons to create a more viable human identity is an essential task. Spirituality has no possibility of being whole or nurturing if it doesn't promote both healthy human relations and a healthy relationship with the natural world.

🌿 *Engage in spiritual practices that allow the controlling aspects of our ego to dissolve and our consciousness to flow outward in connection with the sacred elements and entities of the natural world: air, water, sun, fire, earth, moon, and also with the animating spirits of trees, birds, animals, insects, and flowers.*

The self-reflective consciousness that we humans possess has enabled us to glean incredible insights about ourselves and our universe. However, the capacity for self-reflection also allows us to see ourselves as separate from the natural world even while we are fully immersed in it. With regards to the contemporary ecological crisis, this feeling of separateness is not the cause, but rather it is this feeling of separateness taken to an almost incomprehensible extreme that allows us to continue degrading the planet. We have placed ourselves at such an isolated distance from nature that we have lost our kinship and deep feelings for the other beings and entities that we share the planet with. To feel as though we are each unique and special human beings is completely normal and isn't the problem; it's just that we have submerged ourselves so deeply into our own egoistic concerns that we have lost the deep affinity for anything else.

Throughout human history, spiritual awareness of nature supported the complex task of maintaining balance between our self-reflective human ego and the environment of living beings and entities with which we share the earth. Through skillful interaction with the environment, rituals, myths, and altered states of consciousness, tribal communities forged agreements with animals to avoid overexploitation, developed relationships with plants to learn of their nurturing and healing properties, and generally made spiritual exchanges with the natural world based on reciprocity, courtesy, and respect. The shamanic worldview, pervaded by kinship toward the nonhuman worlds, acknowledges the uniqueness of human nature but does not participate in the self-conscious struggle between our nature as human beings and the rest of the world, like modern people do today.

By overseparating ourselves from the natural world, through losing our kinship, the modern human has become ungrounded to reality and has separated the ego into isolation. The isolated ego, terrified of being alone in the universe, while also fearful of the eventual prospect of its own annihilation at the body's inescapable death, searches for security by controlling and dominating the natural world (among other things, including people) around it. In this light, the antagonistic and dominating aspects of ego must be overcome through integration of the only thing that can make it whole—a healthy spiritual practice.

The paradox of this situation is that the only way for the ego to become healthy and whole is to merge with what it is most fearful of and dissociated from—the dissolving of the rigidly controlling ego into the expansive matrix of the more-than-human world. To experience, even temporarily, the expansive freedom from the confinement of a purely egoistic mode of existence is to identify with the greater rhythms and cycles of both this world and the cosmos. By intentionally releasing the confined ego outwards into the world, our consciousness is allowed to flow with the sacred elements and powers of the earth and galaxy as well as with the community of beings with which we share the planet. This type of spiritual experience, and the practical aspects of personal transformation that it can bring about, can help in healing the deep-seated feelings of isolation that are so apparently a part of contemporary human nature.

> *Develop a spiritual connection to the natural world that allows us to listen to and understand what Earth and her living entities are telling us.*

Through ecoshamanic practices and experiences, we allow for the intentional identification of mental, bodily, and spiritual associations and relationships with the more-than-human world of nature and spirit. These practices develop our mind-body-spirit connection to the sacred elements and powers of earth, sun, water, air, and fire. These five main fundamentals of life not only comprise and give life to the major structural components of our human organism, but they are also living spiritual forces that have many modes of expression and ways of communicating with us. From an ecoshamanic perspective, the body or physical form of each of these five fundamental energies is associated with a particular expression of spiritual being. In a similar but grander way to the expression of spirit that lives inside the beings that we call eagle, or snake, or whale, or even human, the physical form of the earth, sun, water, wind, and fire is the bodily manifestation of each of these divine entities.

The possibility of spiritually communicating or, more appropriately, communing with the divine beings that are at once part of us and all around us is our sacred inheritance that we have largely squandered through living inside of our heads, but it is one that we can reclaim and use for the healing of both humanity and the earth. What is needed now is not a human solution to healing the sacred earth, but a sacred earth solution to the healing of humanity.

In this respect, the ecoshamanic task comes into view: to open the doors of communication through ceremonies, rituals, and ecopsychological practices of reconciliation and rebalancing with the spirits and forces of nature. Intentional effort must be made at making peace with the spiritual manifestations of our biosphere, as well as with the animal and plant communities within our local bioregion and throughout the world.

🍂 *Find our individual reconciliation with nature's cycles of life, death, and rebirth.*

For the isolated and impoverished ego of modern man, the idea of death is marked by fear and denial. This fear is often so strong that it causes us to oppress others and even kill them by making war. The denial of death can also be seen every day through the lifestyles of those constantly putting off their hopes and dreams of today for a possibly nonexistent tomorrow, by the monolithic shrines called banking towers, and by the abstract financial concepts of "life insurance."

Overcoming the destructive and numbing effects of the fear and denial of death calls for us to transform our relationship with this inevitable consequence of life, to acknowledge this fact and turn it into our friend and ally. If the acceptance and recognition of our death is viewed as the anticipated and happy ending of a great journey, then there is no need to fear and deny it. Death, when viewed as the transcendent continuity of life, actually can give rise to profound feelings of connection and joy, both during life and at the end of the life process.

There are countless ways to experience a transformation in our view of death through observation, immersion, and connection with the natural world. The natural cycles of life, death, and rebirth are ongoing and will not stop after we are gone from this body. That we have a place at the banquet table now simply means that we will be part of the feast later. This is not a morbid concept but rather a completely inevitable event, and as such there is no good reason to fear or deny it. The shamanic/animistic worldview supports that there is no possibility of attachment to our individual life form, that we are all part of a much larger body. Even through modern science we see that two to three million of our cells die each second, while equal numbers are being born, so that every seven years or so all of the cells in our body have died and been replaced.

Ecoshamanic practices and ceremonies that put us in direct contact with the life and death processes surrounding us in every moment can help us achieve a more healthy view of life, a heightened sense of being part of a wider community of life, and give strength and immediacy to our actions.

🍃 *Create and utilize spiritual ecoshamanic rites of passage and initiation in order to grow into wise, mature members of the earth community.*

Many of the psycho-spiritual maladies that have been identified here, such as the alienated and isolated ego, fear and denial of death, lack of ethical/moral concerns toward nature, and deficient childhood development, among others, point to the general lack of maturity displayed by the modern human being. I believe this is due, at least in part, to the guiding of the younger generations by adults who have never become much wiser than that of an adolescent who has not yet been initiated into a sacred adult cosmos.

Important ecoshamanic/spiritual rites of passage for the modern adult living inside an adolescent worldview will necessarily include transformational experiences that convey the reality that to be alive is to share the sacredness of the world and the cosmos. Only when an individual can clearly see into this spiritual reality will he attain the maturity of an adult human being. The finding and/or inventing of ritual forms that genuinely meet our needs within the context of our own time and place will be an important task for the modern world.

3 | THE ART OF COUNTERPRACTICE

To open the experiential portion of this book, I'm going to start with a short story told to me by an indigenous friend that lives in a traditional tribal community in Mexico.

In this community there is a man who has discovered that beneath the communal cornfields is a great deposit of stone that is precious to the surrounding modern world. Little by little, he secretly begins to dig out the stone and sell it in the nearest towns. One day the members of the community realize that areas of their priceless fields are being dug up, so they investigate and find out what is happening. They immediately tell their brother to stop, but he can't. He's been touched by the lust for profit and, despite the disapproval of the community, he keeps digging. It gets to the point where the man won't listen to reason and his excavations will soon threaten the community's food supply.

The elders decide there is only one thing to do—they take the man and hang him by the feet, upside down, from the branch of a large tree. Outraged and yelling obscenities, he hangs there for a few days until he starts begging for food and water. They give him water, but instead of corn tortillas, which is the food he is accustomed to eating, they give him some of his precious stones to eat, which of course he can't. This goes on for a few more days, until the elders decide to have a ceremony to help the man. They say to him, "We don't like what you're doing, but you are our brother and we want to help you, so we will have a ceremony here under this tree and we will bring you your sacred objects so that you can give cornmeal to the fire and deer blood to the earth, as is our tradition, just as you always have done." But the man refuses, yelling, "No! Why don't you do this? Let me down and we can all share the precious stones and be rich together." So the elders, realizing that being "rich" would just mean paying someone and depending on them to grow their corn, decide to have the ceremony anyway. They make it away from him but near enough for him to see and hear as they asked the spirits to help him.

The following days after the ceremony, the elders did not try to speak with the man again, but instead they let the forces of nature do their work. The sun shined on the man, the rain washed him, the wind spoke to him, and the living beings around him continued their ways with little interest, except that once in a while a bird would land on him and sing. In this way and through time, the spirits of nature emptied the man, and his illusions of profit fell away. After the second week of being left alone, hanging in the elements, had passed, he lost all thought of the precious stones. On that night, he saw a small fire where the elders had had the ceremony for him, but instead of people there by the fire, he saw a blue deer standing. The magic deer walked over to him, let him down from the tree, and next to the fire gave him some tortillas to eat. The next morning, the people found him sitting next to the fire, and he told them, "The sacred deer set me free and gave me his flesh of corn to eat. I no longer wish for stones or money. I hope that you can forgive me; I've been a fool and want to come back to the community." The elders laughed and said, "Of course! There is no need to come back, you have never left. It was just your turn for a strong lesson, and so you don't forget too soon, your new name will be 'Stoney.'" At that all the people laughed, including Stoney, and they welcomed him with hugs and food and water.

This story told to me by the kawitero may seem harsh, but the figure of the man digging up the cornfield is not unlike the modern entrepreneur that continues exploiting the common ground solely for individual profit. In my opinion, these destructive entrepreneurs should all get hung upside down from a tree and given oil, plutonium, lumber, or whatever their consumptive fixation is for dinner for a few weeks until they're ready to come down and act as responsible members of the earth community.

The story, although a little crude by modern standards, contains some significant insights that are important to begin this chapter with. First is the transformation of the man as he starts to identify with the precious stones and away from the corn that has always sustained his life. Second is the fact that our physical bodies are sustained by what they eat, and without proper care our body will suffer and therefore so will our entire being, including our mind and spirit. Third, the elements of the natural world that give us life also have the ability to either kill or heal us, whether we want them to or not. Fourth, the underlying spirit that animates life on this world can speak to us in many different ways when we are fully open to listening.

The fifth insight of the story is the one I would like to continue with here—the wisdom of turning the world upside down—because this will be one of the central aspects of shamanism included in this chapter. As the kawitero once said to me when I asked him what modern people should do to heal their relationship with Earth, "If I understand clearly all that you have told me, I would have to say that your people would do well to just stop doing everything they do and begin doing exactly the opposite."

When the elders hung that poor man upside down, they acted with beautiful simplicity. What an outrageously pure action! In shamanic culture, inverting the world, inverting perception and consciousness, is a means to fuller understanding. That man became sick but in the end he was healthier than when he started, and because of his sickness he became healed and also, I am told, became a great shaman many years later.

This kind of story is one of hope for modern people who suffer the same kind of illness. Granted, our lives are infinitely more complicated due to the many financial, social, and political webs we are all tied into. Oh, how refreshing it would be to simply choose between precious gems or sacred corn! But the underlying truth remains the same. Our sicknesses can be the beginning of our true healing. The illnesses, when inverted, can be the source of the remedies.

This concept will be central to the shamanic journey laid out in this section. By inverting the harmful process, we find that the contraries are dissolved—narcissism and selflessness, intolerance and compassion, materialism and voluntary simplicity. Dissolving the boundaries removes the negativity, and from there the seeds of an expanded and improved worldview can be planted and grown. Thus, our contemporary inner personal crises are in actuality no less than a major rite of passage on the way to freedom. Our successful transition through this crisis heals the fragmentation of consciousness caused by modern lifestyles and elevates an individual beyond an egocentric perspective and into an expansion of perception.

In classical shamanism, one of the significant rites of passage for the shaman initiate is symbolic death and rebirth, which sometimes includes dismemberment of the initiate's body, the eating of his flesh, and the scattering of his bones, so that he can be reborn into a higher state of being. In a metaphorical sense, the fragmented psyche of the modern consumer could be seen as the cut-up body parts of consciousness that are ready and waiting to be reborn. From this perspective, the fragmentation of consciousness exhibited by modern humans can be viewed as not only a significant occurrence but also a necessary step in the evolution of human consciousness. This, of course, only becomes true if we are able to realize that we have been dismembered, and if we can then be enlightened through the process of raking up our scattered fragments.

This is the journey I would like to invite you on. It is not a quick-fix guide to self-improvement, of which there are already too many. On the contrary, it is an invitation to discover the simplistic complexity that is the paradox of humanity's current condition. Here we will dissolve the boundaries, give up the notions of gratification and mere comfort as goals for life, and boldly unify our consciousness to be healed at many different levels. But all of this will only lead us to another beginning, for once we can clearly see the emergence of a new worldview, we then have much work to do to develop and sustain it. But this should not daunt us. The shaman dares to tread forward where others have stopped. The beginning of his journey starts at the end of the known road. This attitude is one that we can internalize as we start walking the razor's edge of paradoxes that will be the way of modern ecoshamanism.

INVERTING THE WORLD: INTRODUCTION TO COUNTERPRACTICE

In these complicated times, it's helpful to have simple ideas and solutions. Simply put, the initial task in the project of ecoshamanism is to counteract the patterns we are currently stuck in with regards to our mind/body/environment/spirit disconnection with the natural world. At the most basic level, the counteracting of these patterns can be accomplished through what I will here refer to as counterpractice.

As the name implies, counterpractice involves actions that move counter, or in a contrary direction, to a habitual pattern or practice. It turns our habitual way of doing things upside down and inside out so that we can see and feel from a place other than our habitual point of view. In terms of shamanism and shamanic training, counterpractice is employed specifically to enlarge and expand one's consciousness by experiencing shifts in one's perceptual point of view. Shamans accomplish this in many ways, such as exploring the consciousness of a specific animal or converting their perception to experience the energy of the wind, sun, or rain. Shamans use counterpractice when they engage in isolated excursions into the wilderness to obtain vision and guidance. By completely removing themselves from their normal environment, people, and food, they open the door to perceive the mystery of the world from a fresh perspective. Many times I have also witnessed elders of shamanic tribes use counterpractice when assigning tasks and roles for people in ceremonies.

For example, a person that is known to be shy or introverted is given the task to be one of the supportive singers to the shaman during a ceremony, while at the same time a normally gregarious person is given a task that requires sitting still and quiet during the ceremony, such as the continuous stirring of the sacred corn beverage that is cooked next to the fire. In both of these cases, we see the elder using counterpractice to help each person experience the ceremony from a perspective that they wouldn't if left to their normal habits. Although the assigning of these tasks initially caused each of these people to feel anguish and apprehension, and actually doing the tasks was extremely challenging, in both cases there was much laughter and feelings of accomplishment afterwards, as each person recounted their experience to friends and family. This form of counterpractice employed by the elders is often used to help create well-rounded individuals in the community.

As we can see by way of these two simple examples, the assigning of specific forms of counterpractice depends highly on the personal characteristics of the individual. In this respect, tribal shamans have a somewhat different job than we do because within their community they have a very deep understanding of the cultural worldview shared by the tribe, in that they share a similar upbringing, environment, diet, and general way of life. The shaman very probably knows each individual extremely well from a lifetime spent in the same community. With all of this accessible information, the choosing of specific counterpractices for shamanic initiations or ceremonial matters comes quite naturally and spontaneously.

Our case, however, will be somewhat different. In our great melting pot society, there is no possible way to generalize with regards to a person's upbringing, family structure, religious affiliation, economic status, etc. This means that our individual forms of counterpractice will have to be just that—very individualized.

There is, however, one common theme of counterpractice that will be somewhat similar for the majority of people in our society, and that is with regards to our disconnection to the natural world. In this respect, ecoshamanic counterpractice will involve concrete experiences designed to help develop an ecologically healthy worldview.

It is important to note that it is not easy to let go of our habitual ways of doing things, or to convince ourselves that something like counterpractice is even necessary. This becomes especially true when introducing counterpractice to those already involved with psychology or those already on a shamanic path. It has been my experience working with folks in both of these groups that they are often the most resistant, because counterpractice at some level challenges the significant amount of time and effort they have put into learning about their respective fields of inquiry. But at the same time, once members of both these groups move past a steadfast clinging to what they already know and can open to fluidly experiencing the heart of shamanic counterpractice, they are often the most deeply affected by it and the first to endorse it.

To get to that point, the first thing that needs to be stressed is that counterpractice cannot be overanalyzed if it is going to be useful. Counterpractice is not an exercise of thinking; it is an exercise of simply doing. There are, of course, guidelines to follow and moments when our rational mind must be engaged not only for safety's sake but also in choosing and then processing the specific experiences of counterpractice. So to continue our discussion, let's take a look at the criteria for counterpractice and how to choose productively.

Luminous Acts

Specific acts of counterpractice must be life-affirming, respectful, and enlightening actions that continue our evolution and imply growth and heightened awareness, or else they would make no sense to practice. This is why I call them luminous acts. An authentic and powerful counterpractice will be one that "illuminates" a side of ourselves that has been obscure, or situations that we normally see only one side of, or qualities of existence that we haven't even dreamed were possible.

This is what makes counterpractice at once joyful and challenging, tender and terrifying. In terms of growth, it is an adventure to accept the unacceptable and discover the hidden. This process of counterpractice—of engaging in luminous acts of enlightenment, of bringing light in—is the perennial journey of shamans.

But enlightenment can come at many different levels. On one hand, we can be enlightened by the keen words of a person, a television program, or a book in a way that sheds light for us onto previously unrealized facts or concepts. This is the rational acquisition of knowledge that brings to light for us things on the mental plane. In this manner we are using light as a metaphor and as an abstract symbol to represent a process of gaining knowledge. This, however, is not the same as enlightenment when received through the total human organism. Experiences of light for shamans are not abstract concepts, but rather they are lived and felt directly in the heart and spirit; they illuminate the body and its environment at once, so as to be joined and felt together as one single being. This is not merely a metaphor but rather an experience of sublime illumination, where one sees and feels their essence as a being of light, both internally and externally. While in this state, there is a lucid awareness and the ability to see with clarity and depth.

This is the quality of ecoshamanic counterpractice that we are striving for. Therefore, we can continue by saying that counterpractice is not at all the simple "opposite" of something we currently do. For example, the counterpractice of working at a job just to "make a living" is not simply refusing to work, but rather working at something that fills an authentic calling from deep inside of you. Counterpractice for a nonsmoker will not include starting to smoke, just like a counterpractice for a vegetarian would not necessarily be to start eating meat. Counterpractice and developing luminous acts are very delicate art forms that require sensible and sober judgment, but in a way that allows for creative and innovative practices to be employed.

NECESSARY AND UNNECESSARY SUFFERING

Ecoshamanic counterpractice will, by design, challenge you at the deepest levels because it will go against everything you've been taught about comfort, suffering, burden, satisfaction, gratification, and mystery. A major part of the promise that our technologically advanced culture makes to us is that of being relieved of the burdens, toils, and suffering that our ancestors had to endure. But while I don't mean to seem ungrateful for the many technological advances that legitimately have raised the quality of human life, there is another side to the coin that is not often considered.

By the consequence of our own human nature—that is, by our historical and hereditary physiological and psychological makeup—we require certain experiences, stimulation, and interaction with the world in order to be healthy and whole human beings. Unfortunately, many of our technological advances have isolated us from a wide range of these life experiences.

To illustrate, if you were to place a lion cub inside of a cage in a climate-controlled warehouse and raise her there, if she didn't die, she would still be a lion, but she wouldn't be a psychologically healthy and whole lion. The lion is built for running and hunting, for holding down its live prey with its massive paws, for roaming the savanna by the cover of night, and playing and resting in the shade by day. Without the unfolding of those life experiences, the lion is not fully a lion, and it will suffer from not being allowed to be who it truly was meant to be. By simply handing the lion her food instead of having her endure the run of long distances to catch and kill her prey at physical risk to herself, you are not just relieving her burden of performing the work for her meal, you are actually making her suffer by not letting her be a lion. And the same goes for human beings.

When human beings are deprived of the natural and hereditary unfolding of their lives, they suffer and are not allowed to develop into being fully human. When our technology unburdens us from the most basic experiences of life, we are not fully living. Long before man ever dreamt about planting crops, and for hundreds of thousands of years (a time period so long as to hardly be imagined), men were long-distance runners involved in the chase for deer, antelope, horses, and a wide variety of small game. At the same time, they were continuously running for their lives when pursued by other predators. That is how our physical body evolved. Our legs are made for running and walking and our arms for climbing and swinging. To sit a man in a chair or bind him to a machine for most of his life is a madness that results in physical ailments of the heart and vascular systems, and the suffering of chronic illnesses from a deprived physical existence. Am I suggesting that we all start chasing around wild animals? No. But we need to be much more aware that we went from running to planting to sitting in such a short time period that our total human organism is suffering in a similar way as the caged lion, only maybe worse because our psychological makeup is so much more complex, and the way we lash out is so much more destructive.

The psyche of our species was shaped by living within a diverse environment of plants and trees; a vast playground of scents, colors, and sounds; rock structures; animals; wind; clean running water; fish; birds; and countless other ecological and psychological constants that formed individual experience and behavior. Without immersion in these things human beings still survive, but they do so in poor mental health, in constant crisis, and without the full development and true unfolding of life and what it means to be a healthy and whole human being.

In our culture we are constantly being sold secondhand versions of life where the push of a button, the turning of a handle, the purchase of this new thing or that latest technology will relieve us of our burdens and make us happy—all the while destroying the beautiful and mysterious natural world, our sacred inheritance, and the one historical constant that can truly make us healthy and whole human beings.

To be awakened from this spell is to realize that many of the things we are told are burdens are not really burdens at all—that many things considered suffering are not suffering at all, but rather necessary and healthy experiences of being human. Below I have created a small chart that might help to shed light on this from an ecoshamanic perspective.

• Current practice (unnecessary suffering)	Seeing the natural world from the outside looking in. Nature (including parks and preserves) is a controlled resource for human beings to use.
Counterpractice (necessary suffering)	*Seeing the world through the eyes of nature. Feeling the pain of seeing the misuse of plastic, metal, and noxious fumes as heresy against our organic existence.*
•	Eating processed and genetically altered food that is raised, processed, packaged, and transported in a way that causes both human health problems as well catastrophic damage to the environment and needless suffering by billions of animals.
	Raising, gathering, killing, and eating of organic, sacred food that is either wild or raised/grown on a free range by you or someone you love or implicitly trust.
•	Working a job that degrades you into a "human resource" to support a marketplace based on the insane assumption of never-ending economic growth.
	Making the difficult transition to exploring ways of sustainable and sane livelihood.
•	Allowing your self-worth to be judged by your appearance, the clothes you wear, the car you drive, or the neighborhood you live in.
	Taking off the masks and breaking free of the need for approval, and simply doing and living in a way that feels authentic to you.
•	Spending your whole life in the overcrowded urban environment of a techno-consumer wasteland.
	Periodically going alone into the wilderness to rediscover the miracle of life.
•	Depriving your body of its hereditary physical needs by spending the majority of the day seated or engaged in docile or repetitive activities.
	Engaging periodically in highly stressful but rewarding physical activity such as running, swimming, and climbing.

- Sleeping in a lifeless and artificial environment where even the smallest ant or spider is killed immediately upon discovery.

  Sleeping out in the open, under the stars, taking the chance to be exposed to the elements in order to feel communion with all the living creatures around you.

- Limiting your life experiences to the purely human realm; knowledge of nature and wild animals gleaned superficially through television and other media.

  Exploring, gathering, and hunting in the wilderness community and making intentional quests into the wilderness to mark significant rites of passage.

The methods of "counterpractice" will not be easy to employ or seamlessly assimilate into a consumer lifestyle—and that's the point. The lifestyle of the "current practice," and therefore the worldview accompanying it, must be altered and the patterns counteracted. But that is just the beginning. For these simple forms of counterpractice to become truly ecoshamanic, they will have to be explored at the deepest levels, where the altered states of awareness and consciousness they produce will touch the very core of your being and carry light into those areas of your being that have so far been left obscure.

Sleeping out in the open and under the stars is one thing, but having the living beings surrounding you—the trees, plants, animals, and insects—form a psychic imprint deep enough to allow you to dream with them is quite another. The intricacies of the sacred hunt, when time, place, and living flesh come together at the level of spiritual offering and renewal, demands nothing less than full organismic surrender to the greater powers surrounding you. Even just learning how to leave your many years of social training behind you in order to truly see the world through the eyes of one of nature's children is a major breakthrough and profound experience.

The activities and circumstances described in the above list happen at varying degrees of intensity and at many different levels. A person who has a physical job—for example, a carpenter—and who goes rock climbing for fun on the weekends will obviously approach the physical aspects of counterpractice differently than someone who sits in front of a computer most of the day and watches movies or goes to the mall for fun. It's impossible for me to design specific and personal ecoshamanic activities of counterpractice for an individual without spending time and getting to know the person, so that job will be left for you. The forms of counterpractice I introduce in this book are designed for the general public of modern society to work with while exploring ecoshamanism. If you have a close companion to work with, great; if you have a group, especially a group that has already weathered the trials of working effectively in a group dynamic, even better. But if you are going at this solo, it's okay, too, because you aren't really alone, and the sooner you realize that, the better off you will be.

COUNTERPRACTICE I: Seeing in Systems

Ecoshamanic seeing starts with perceiving the world around us at a deeper level than our normal habits of perception and language allow. Instead of labeling complex objects, entities, and circumstances with simple one-word names, this practice requires you to identify the connections and the systems that tie everything together.

Light Switch

You can start this practice anywhere, but a good place to begin is inside your own home. Begin by gathering some note cards or pieces of paper and a pen, and stand in front of an item in your house. For example, let's begin with a simple item like a light switch. The idea is to take a perceptual journey with your light switch in order to become aware of what it really is and what it really does. A light switch is really an object that transfers energy from the place where the energy is generated. When your finger touches that switch, it is touching miles of electric cable that directly connect you to a number of different energy-generating systems. Currently these generating systems in the United States include fossil fuel-burning power plants (64 percent), nuclear power plants (17 percent), hydroelectric plants (17 percent), and renewable energy (wind, solar, biomass) producers (2 percent) (source: *State of the World 2003,* Worldwatch Institute, page 87).

Since only 2 percent of the energy coming through that light switch comes from ecologically healthy sources, 98 percent of your finger on the light switch is touching all of the other ecologically disastrous systems. If you were to write down on your note card what that light switch really is and what it really touches, the list would look something like this:

Plastic and metal switch	Nuclear waste
Plastic manufacturing and molding factories	Metal manufacturing plants
Thin-gauge copper electrical wire	Resource extraction consequences; air, soil, and water pollution; acid rain; biodiversity loss

Heavy-gauge electrical wire	Refineries
Copper mines	Coal mines
Electrical poles	Tankers—truck and ship
Underground cable	Nuclear accidents
Transformers	Carbon dioxide emissions
Local distribution centers	Hydroelectric power plants
Fossil fuel-burning plants	Nuclear plants
Dams	Stockholders of thousands of corporations

This, of course, is the short list, which you will now tape onto the switch to remind you to see that switch for what it really is whenever you use it. Now move on to another item, such as the refrigerator, dishwasher, toilet, TV, computer, stereo, carpeting, heating system, air-conditioning system, etc. Each time you use one of these items, take a moment to view the whole system you are touching and what the consequences are. The more clearly you can see the systems that the common items you use are all connected to, the deeper will be your experience of reality.

Another way to see in systems is by tracing even normal, everyday items to the places and people involved in creating them. This may require researching on the Internet or through books and periodicals, but the insights gleaned can be well worth the effort. Everything that we purchase, use, and discard originally came from somewhere, a real place on Earth, and will eventually go to some other real place when we are done with it. Everything we buy has a history, a past that leaves a trail of causes and effects. And everything has a future, another set of causes and effects. To illustrate this, let's look at the manufacturing and supplies needed to make a common pair of tennis shoes that you would typically find in an American or European store.

Tennis Shoes

Most sneakers are composed of three main parts: the leather upper, the foam midsole, and the rubber outer sole.

Upper: The upper has about twenty different parts comprised mostly of leather from a cow raised in Texas. After the cow is raised, slaughtered, and skinned, the hide is covered with salt and shipped to South Korea for tanning. The chrome tanning process involves twenty steps where the hide is dehaired, delimed, pickled, tanned, retanned, dyed, and lubricated, using solutions of chrome, calcium hydroxide, and other strong chemicals. The hair from the hide, the epidermis, hide scraps, and processing chemicals are typically dumped into the river next to the tanning plant. This is why most of the hides from the United States are tanned overseas, because environmental regulations are minimal and labor costs are much cheaper. Much of South Korea's tap water is contaminated with metals and other pollution from industrial plants. From South Korea, the tanned leather is sent to Indonesia.

Midsole: The leather upper is the only part of the sneaker not made from petroleum-based chemicals. The midsole is made of EVA (ethylene vinyl acetate) foam that is made from synthetic chemicals distilled from Saudi petroleum refined in Korea. The ethylene and vinyl acetate are mixed with pigments and various other chemicals and then poured into a mold and baked.

Outer Sole: The outer sole is also made from Saudi oil and benzene that is synthesized into styrene-butadiene in a Taiwan factory. The synthetic rubber is transported to Indonesia in large sheets, where machines in the shoe factory cut and mold the tread.

In the shoe factory, machines cut the component parts of the shoes, but even today the actual assembling of the shoes is done through hand labor. The workers, who typically make the minimum Indonesian wage (about twenty-five cents an hour), assemble the shoes with glue, then trim, polish, and insert the laces.

Seeing the interconnected systems of light switches and sneakers is the tip of the iceberg when it comes to the items we are all used to buying. This is one of the biggest things that hits you when you contrast the lifestyle of cultures that live subsistence lifestyles with the lifestyles of modern consumers. Everything in the indigenous world can be traced back in just a few easy steps to the item of the natural local environment where it came from. And there is relatively no waste or byproducts from the things they grow and make to live healthy and satisfied lives.

This practice of seeing in systems is not to try and convince you to live a subsistence lifestyle, but rather to open your mind to see the whole picture and to question everything. Start asking where things come from, and why. Who profits and who loses? Where does the material come from and where does the waste go? How does this or that system work?

Seeing in systems is the first step to altering your consciousness to perceive the difference in the linear mechanical systems of industry and the larger reality of the interconnected web of consciousness that make up our multidimensional universe.

THE SPIRALING REALITY

Everything in our galaxy is rotating around some central point. Electrons revolve around the nucleus of an atom, Earth's moon revolves around the planet, while Earth itself rotates around the sun. Our entire Milky Way galaxy has a three-dimensional spinning vortex shape, as does the swirling "double helix" of the DNA containing our genetic code.

The curious thing about the rotating quality of the universe and the corresponding shape and symbolism of the spiral pattern and concentric circles is that once you become aware of this phenomena and how it manifests in the reality of the natural world, you begin to see it everywhere, which has a profoundly counteractive effect to purely self-centered thought.

The flushing of a toilet, a spinning hurricane, the whirlpools of water in streams and rivers, the spirals of seashells, the circular outward growth of a tree trunk, and the concentric shape of a spider's web, among countless other examples of both the centripetal (moving toward a center) and centrifugal (moving away from a center) forces of this physical reality, are around and inside of us in every moment.

Due to the profound significance of the spiraling reality of our universe, it is not to be wondered that even the most ancient civilizations, such as on the island of Malta or those that inhabited Newgrange in Ireland (dated to be somewhere in the second millennium BC) carved the spiral shape into stone, as did the ancient Anasazi people of Chaco Canyon. In ancient Crete and Babylon, the spiral shape was associated with the internal organs of the human anatomy as well as the underworld, one being a microcosm of the other.

My first meaningful encounter with the spiral happened when I first starting exploring the Southwest desert. I had spoken to some locals near to Moab, Utah (long before the town became a mountain-biking Mecca), who told me about a little-known canyon where petroglyphs and ancient paintings could be seen. I hiked into this beautiful canyon that had high and sheer cliff faces on both sides and a clear running stream that formed an oasis of lush green plant life down the meandering and curving center of the canyon. It was like no place I had ever seen, and there wasn't a soul around.

I walked and explored the canyon, which in itself was a remarkable experience. I came upon a fairly deep pool of water in the corner of a tight bend in the stream, and in that isolated place, as I swam and submerged myself in the clear, cool water, I literally felt a purification of my body and a cleansing of my mind. But I still hadn't seen any petroglyphs or paintings, so I climbed the canyon wall above the place I was swimming and onto a wide, flat area where I could survey the canyon. Feeling super-relaxed and not in any hurry, I sat down on a surprisingly comfortable rock and gazed across the stream and into the deep canyon, and I remember thinking to myself what a great place this would be to spend the night; however, I hadn't brought anything with me, so I made an internal agreement to come back and stay overnight in the future.

But in the meantime, I felt so unusually comfortable just sitting there that I stayed still and quiet for a very long time, gazing into the canyon and down into the streambed. And that's when it happened; without any effort, I slowly began to see a circular-shaped whirling spiral of multicolored energy. I closed my eyes and it was still there. In that moment I was amazed by what I saw; it was much more than a visual experience. I'm not sure how long I gazed at it, but not having experienced this before, I remember trying to see if I could go into it or control it or understand it in some way. At one point I remember acknowledging the fact that I was thinking about going into it in the wrong way. Instead of thinking of it as a typical physical sensation, I switched to feeling the spiraling energy field with my entire being, and as soon as I did that I experienced the sensation of being pulled into and through a door into a new level of awareness and perception, where the physical aspects of the canyon where still "there" but I was perceiving them as differentiated energetic areas. For example, the stream running through the canyon was an amazingly alive feature that seemed to have its own spirit and volition. The pockets formed by the curves of the canyon had a different quality than the sheer walls on the top of the canyon; the plants and trees all had a unique and sort of vibrating glow; and so on.

One of the most noticeable features of this vision was that some parts of the canyon felt infinitely more attractive to me than others, and after I felt like I got all I could out of the experience, I eventually moved on to continue my exploration of the canyon. I began by heading toward an area of great attraction for me during my vision. After seeing the spiraling vortex I somehow felt different, calmer, and very at home with the canyon. After a short while, I arrived to the place I saw in the vision and there I found my first petroglyph. Again, I was completely astounded—it was a perfectly shaped spiral carved into the rock face directly across from where I had been sitting above the water hole!

What a remarkable feeling of connection I had just then, a feeling that the ancient people who used to live in this area where not so different from myself, that we had seen the same thing, and a shiver of excitement ran up my spine. Just then I saw something equally amazing. Looking back to where I had been sitting, I could clearly see the outline of where ancient footholds had been carved into the rock to make it easier to climb out of the waterhole and up onto the flat place above it where I had just been sitting. I had unknowingly made the climb following in the footsteps of the ancients!

Needless to say, over the years I explored and camped in that canyon many times, and I actually discovered over a hundred petroglyphs and cave paintings in just a short two-mile stretch of canyon where I would thereafter come to see, feel, and learn from the vortex. But it wasn't until many years later that I would come full circle with the spiraling vortex, or *nierika*, as the Wirrarika call it. Those experiences are too numerous to recount here, but the important thing to mention is that the people of this ancient shamanic culture hold the nierika as a sacred portal of vision. They actually paint the spiral onto their faces when on the sacred visionary pilgrimage to Wirikuta, and through their help I began to see the original and basic truth of the whirling energy vortex as the source of all life in the universe.

COUNTERPRACTICE 2: Seeing the Spirals of the World

The modern world of boxlike houses and cars, rectangular TV and computer screens, and square, flat books and magazines homogenize our perception of the world into straight lines and corners that almost completely cause us to disregard the innate spherical reality of our universe and home planet. What is perhaps most enlightening about the naturally spiraling shape of vortex energy, as well as the configuration of concentric circles, is that it is not a reality or intellectual concept made by human beings but rather a tangible and readily available phenomenon of the universe that we can connect to in a way that enlarges our perception of who we are. Seeking out, seeing, feeling, and experiencing the circular and spiraling manifestations of life in the natural world are simple yet profound luminous acts of counterpractice. This begins by simply looking around you and acknowledging the spiraling gesture made by the pinecone, sunflower, and rose. Watch the spiraling vortex shape of the universe as you pull the drain plug out of the sink or find a beautiful spiral-shaped shell on the beach.

Once you find the spiraling gesture of the universe all around you, you will begin to see things in a completely new way. For example, my whole view of the ocean changed radically when I realized that the flesh of the beautiful yellowfin tuna that I caught for dinner was one of the most perfect examples of outwardly spiraling energy I had ever seen or tasted. From that moment on, whenever I am on the ocean I see the water as filled with countless spiraling life forms of energy, all manifesting in their own unique way . . . what a miraculous and life-affirming experience!

Another example is seeing the spiraling energy of trees and plants. Every tree has the outwardly spiraling growth that at its center holds the heart of the tree from when it was born, while its outermost layer places it in immediate contact with the airborne elements. Seeing in this way transforms a forest of simple trees into a countless sea of outwardly spiraling energies that are both alive and present to this moment and to an ancient remembering of the past.

One of my most enlightening experiences of relating to the spiraling energy of trees came once when I was visiting the Wirrarika sierra and helping a group of the community's spiritual leaders clear and bless an area for a new corn field. I was using my machete to cut the small limbs off a tree that they had felled and I was having a hard time. As I was hacking at the limb one of the elder shamans came to me and gently grabbed my arm. He proceeded to tell me that what they were doing there was not simply the mechanical clearing of the land with their tools, but also an energetic connection with the land that included many offerings to the plants and trees and other beings that lived in the area. He explained to me that when working in this way it was important to join our energy with the land.

I didn't quite understand and he must have seen it in my face because then he told me to walk through the portal, the nierika, and I would learn how to do it. I must have then looked even more puzzled because he took my machete and swiped a limb off with one clean stroke, then he took my hand, palm-side up, and placed it next to the end of the severed limb. He told me to look closely at the tips of my fingers and then to the flesh of the tree. At that moment I finally understood. The concentric circles on my fingertips were the same shape as the concentric circles of the flesh of the tree. Both myself and the tree carried the same mark of the nierika. From that moment on, I felt a profound connection to everything in that field, and to this day all I need to do to remind myself of my sacred connection to the natural world and the spiraling universe is look at the tips of my fingers.

DEPTH

People like to look as far and deep as the eye can see over the land. We like to look out at the world from the top floor of a tall building or out the window of a plane, we pull the car to the side of the road to enjoy a scenic view, and we climb the highest mountains in part because we are enamored by catching a view of the world that few others have witnessed. We are attracted to seeing the depth of the world in a similar way to how we stare into a campfire or listen to the endless chant of the ocean. Something primordial connects us to these things in a way that no explanation is needed. But our primordial perception of depth is severely impaired when we continuously submerge ourselves in the reading of two-dimensional text, driving on roads that have bulldozed away the natural contours of the land, and by reducing our view of the world to the flat surfaces of billboards, fast-food signs, and strip malls.

One of the saddest changes I have witnessed over the last decade is the almost complete transformation of our small towns and suburbs from interesting and unique localities into exact replicas of franchised reality. The charm of the old town and neighborhood now sits in the shadow of the towering signposts of the various fast-food chains and super-mega department stores. Now you know you are leaving one town and entering the next merely by the passing by and emergence of a new set of chain stores. In short, the depth of our experience has been taken over by the abstract reality of consumerism and the narrowing of our perception to the world of strictly man-made objects and circumstances.

One of the ways we can counteract the effects of our flattened perceptual field is to engage in practices that intentionally expand our view of the world both visually and perceptually. In a similar way to the story I previously mentioned of the Wirrarika Indian that was hung upside down from a tree limb, the first part of my prescription (although not quite as harsh) is to climb up into a tree and view the many degrees of depth in the natural world for long periods of time. This is the counterpractice for the continuous experiencing of the grid of urban housing developments and storefronts; the commute back and forth to work via car, bus, or train; and visually flat media such as TV, newspapers, magazines, etc., all of which limit our view and promote a flattened-out visual and physical reality.

COUNTERPRACTICE TOOL: The Tree Stand

The idea here is to get yourself out of the straight-lined urban grid and into a natural environment such as a forest, and then up off of the ground and into a tree so as to be able to look out and over a natural area in a way that you feel safe and comfortable enough to remain there for a number of hours. Although this can be accomplished in a number of ways, I'm going to outline my preferred way, not only because it is a safe practice but also because it allows you to be very still and comfortable, which is really important in order to inspire you to keep practicing.

The ideal conditions I like to have for this practice are to locate myself approximately eight feet up a medium-size, straight-trunked tree located on a gently sloping hill in a forest lying at a distance from the hustle and bustle of the modern world. I look for a tree in a nice location that is approximately twelve to eighteen inches in diameter and is relatively free of branches from six to eight feet above the ground. I don't really want or need lower branches because I'm going to sit in the tree by anchoring a tree stand to the tree. A tree stand is a piece of equipment that you can find at any good sports shop that caters to hunters, and of course you can buy them online.

The tree stand is a small lightweight platform that folds up for carrying and unfolds for placing onto a tree trunk by way of a heavy-duty strap and locking mechanism. When properly installed, this type of platform is completely harmless to the tree. Never buy a tree stand that uses chain or bolts to attach to the tree, always use the strap-on type; I recommend a lightweight model unless you are a very heavy person. In any case, follow the manufacturer's recommendation as to which tree stand is best for you.

The tree stand platform straps to the tree and then locks into place when you unfold it to create a platform for your feet and a seat for you to sit on. Once you have the tree stand in place and you are up in it, you can secure yourself with a safety strap to the tree so you now have a very comfortable, safe, and unique way to submerge yourself in the magic of the forest. In order to get to the proper height, I usually use either a lightweight ladder or strap-on steps that can be purchased with the tree stand. Strap-on steps are great, especially if you have a private wooded area that you can return to frequently, so you can leave the steps attached to the tree for periods of time.

Please make sure to prepare properly before using the tree stand. You must familiarize yourself completely with how to anchor your steps and tree stand to the tree before you go up. I suggest practicing the anchoring of the tree stand at waist level, and sitting and standing on it, and climbing on and off of it numerous times before going up any higher. Also, familiarize yourself with and *always* use the safety strap. Commercially available tree stands are well built and very safe once you get the feel for them, and once you are comfortable with your tree stand it will become a good friend. A word of caution—they make possible such a wide range of enlightening experiences that they can become quiet addicting.

COUNTERPRACTICE 3: Depth of Vision

Once you are up in your tree, the first thing to do is take some deep breaths and relax. Try to become as still as the tree trunk. In the first moments it's not important to do anything special except for simply getting yourself comfortable and quiet. This will be happening both internally, as you become relaxed, and also externally, as your local environment relaxes to your being there. After you practice with the tree stand a few times, you'll get to recognizing the brief transition time between your entrance to the forest, with the corresponding intrusion felt by the beings that live there (which feels like everything is holding its breath), and when after you have become quiet, the forest returns to its normal activity.

When the transition time has passed, you now have open to you myriad opportunities for discovery in the realm of perception and experience. For this exercise of depth perception, the first thing to do is gaze as far as you can into the forest and focus your vision way out in front of you. After a few minutes, turn your gaze 360 degrees around you and continue looking as far as you can into the forest, but move your head from front to back in one direction and then the other. In this way, get a feel for where you are sitting in relation to the forest that is in your farthest field of vision on all sides. Take your time.

Now shift your focus to a tree that is very close to you. Examine the tree very closely; the bark, branches, leaves, insect or bird holes, nests, etc. When you have done that, shift your focus out again to the limits of your view and then back to the close tree, and then back and forth a few times. Now explore the areas between your farthest view and immediate surroundings. Gaze at everything around you and at all the varying depths. Try doing this in a causal way; in other words, don't start a methodical search of the area but rather just let your focus rest on whatever draws you. But for now keep your focus slowly but continuously shifting from tree to tree at various depths. Forests are perfect for this exercise precisely because they contain natural spiraling entities at varying distances and of various proportions, and in moving your focus between them you can saturate your perception in the natural depths of this visual experience. The most important aspect of this exercise is simply to experience the actual reality of depth formed by the relationship of all the living and previously living entities within your field of vision and to actually allow your focus of vision to dance between objects, thus counteracting the perceptual flatness of ordinary modern-world experiences.

The next step of this practice is to "catch" the movements of the forest within your visual circle. Everything in the forest is moving: leaves swaying in the breeze, birds flying to and fro, twigs dropping, shadows shifting and changing, all these movements and countless others add enormously to the depth of the forest and convert what may ordinarily be viewed as stagnant scenery into the constant unfolding process of life. To get the most out of both these steps, I recommended spending from two to four hours in the tree at least five times during one month.

COUNTERPRACTICE 4: Sensory Depth

From the moment you stepped into the woods, through the time spent getting into the tree and the transition period, right up to the present moment, you have also been submerged in the sounds made both by yourself and those of the environment around you. Now is the time to focus on the individual sounds within your auditory field. Distinguishing them, and also the distance each source is from you, adds to your perception of the depth formed by the natural environment you are sitting within. Close your eyes for a few minutes (or an hour) and submerge yourself in the auditory reality and depth of the place.

The next phase is adding to your experience of depth by consciously placing attention on to the smells, colors, textures, shadows, and other qualities of the area and the moment, such as wind, rain, sunshine, or animal movements. By intentionally engaging all of your senses into the various depths of the forest, you encounter a depth and quality of experience that far surpasses the flat and mundane one-dimensional perception of urban life.

COUNTERPRACTICE 5: Concentric Circles

By the time you have had a few months of experiencing the forest from the depth of perception that the tree stand allows, you will naturally become very sensitive to everything happening within your perceptual field. You probably have started to enjoy the ability to distinguish the sounds of many animals and birds, and your body is becoming accustomed to feeling the different qualities and directions of wind and sun and rain. When you have reached this point, it is time to go completely undercover in order to view the forest without being seen or heard.

Begin doing this by setting up your tree stand in a tree that has branches to help camouflage you, and/or make or purchase a camouflage suit that blends into the forest. Hunting outfitters carry a wide range of camouflage patterns for all types of terrain, and if you are going to buy one I recommend getting the reversible-type suit that has two patterns—

one for spring and summer foliage and one for fall and winter. It is also important to camouflage your hands and face if you really want to go to the next level.

This next level begins by staying silent and hidden in your tree stand for long enough periods of time to view the depth of wildlife in the forest. What I mean by depth of wildlife is that there are some animals and birds of the forest that are "surface" dwellers: easy to be seen, not easily scared, if scared they will return soon, etc., but there are whole other classes of animals that won't come anywhere near you if they see you move, smell you, or receive messages that you are there (we will be discussing these "messages" shortly).

The first part of this is simply learning to be absolutely still. This is a skill that requires you to be calm and patient with yourself, to not fidget, to not scratch every itch, to not move your head all around every time you hear or see something. This is not easy, but the benefits are so rewarding that for many years they took control of my life. When you have a great horned owl or a wild turkey land on a branch just a few feet from you, or watch baby deer chasing each other around the base of the tree you are in, you will understand what I mean. And when you have experiences like that you will also understand that seeing those beautiful creatures is just the bonus. The real lesson and prize is the internal calmness and confidence that comes along with those experiences as you begin to identify with a wider range of species and habitats and away from the grimy urban jungle of human beings.

The second part of this practice is to become aware of the circles within circles of experience and perception that are happening all around you. Every animal and entity in the forest is at once giving off concentric circles of sound, smell, and volumetric information at the same time it is receiving the same sort of information. All of this happens at different levels of intensity and depth. For example, let's start with humans.

When you have spent enough time in your tree stand that you are invisible enough to have an owl or hawk land in your tree and stay awhile, the other side of the coin is that you also become painfully aware of how blundering, noisy, and destructive people are. When the average person steps a few feet into the forest, every living thing that is able runs or flies away. This causes a chain reaction. The animals that are the sentinels of the forest sound the alarm, birds fly away, chipmunks dive into their holes, deer leap into thickets, and squirrels climb up trees. Waves of noise and scent are carried off in every direction in widening circles to all the beings in the area. No other animal causes this kind of panicked reaction, but it is important to experience this in order to feel the full effects of how the simple action of a person walking in the woods is carried off in concentric waves out into the forest.

Once you've experienced the concentric waves given off by modern humans and domesticated animals, you'll realize how they don't harmonize with life in a wild setting. But given time, patience, and practice, you can begin to feel the different levels of expression and information being given off and received by the various animals and forces that are at home in the woods. For example, the intensity and type of call made by a blue jay or crow will send a message in a circular pattern out into the forest that other birds and animals recognize and react to. If the sound made by the birds and their pattern of flight indicate the presence of a predator such as a hawk, the other animals wary of hawks will respond, but other animals who don't feel the threat of the hawk (like deer or bear) are not much affected. When you have experienced this particular sounding of the birds, the resultant reaction of the various animals, and then the actual sighting of the hawk, after a few times you get familiar enough with the scenario that you can perceive the concentric circles of information coming to you in a way that you'll know when a hawk is coming long before you actually see it.

Perceiving the concentric circles of information that a person is entering the woods is pretty easy, that a hawk is coming is more difficult, and that a male deer is on the scent of a female is a little harder, but the point here is that all of this information is out there and it takes not some form of extrasensory perception to experience it. Rather, all you need to do is tread lightly, be silent, and develop awareness of concentric waves of information, and the doors of perception will open to you in remarkable and healthy ways.

COUNTERPRACTICE 6: Engaging the Flow

When you have gleaned the ability to identify concentric circles of information and communication, you are ready to embark on the challenge of engaging the flow.

What this involves is entering into a perceptual experience of joining the natural entities and forces around you in both the depth and flow of the living moment. You do this by first throwing away the calendar and forgetting all about what "time" it is in the modern world and instead focusing on what is happening right now in that area of nature. In a general sense, this means feeling the energy of the season. Are the trees budding or the leaves falling? Are the squirrels building nests or collecting nuts? Is it warm or cold, is a storm approaching, or maybe one has just passed through? Is the land dry or wet? What birds are around? What are they doing? There are countless processes going on in the forest at any given time, and connecting to them can place you into temporal sync with the natural world and away from the abstract "rat race" where there is never enough "time."

When you successfully meld your perception and the rhythm of your human organism to the natural flow of the place where you are sitting, and add that dimension to your full sensory awareness of the place, you discover a whole new complete dimension of existence. It may take months or even years to get to this place, but it is well worth the trip. The human body and mind have been formed through hundreds of thousands of years of being immersed in the rhythms and cycles of the natural world. We are born to relate to the world in this way and to be a part of the natural flow of life that is continually unfolding around us. When we engage in an awareness of this flow, we regain a healthy sense of temporal reality by leaving behind the one-dimensional feeling of time imposed by human clocks and calendars, and we are able to see and feel the many dimensions of time that are simultaneously being experienced by the other living beings of the natural world.

CONSTRUCTION IS A EUPHEMISM FOR DESTRUCTION

For someone who truly loves the land, one of cruelest circumstances of our modern world is the never-ending bulldozing of forests and natural areas, and the cutting, digging, hammering, welding, and pouring of construction. It is not the concepts or skills involved with construction that makes the skin crawl, it's the bad dream behind it all.

Over the last twenty years I've had to endure watching almost every single natural place where I learned and played as a child be completely destroyed and replaced by housing developments and strip malls. Practically every pond, meadow, and forest that was etched into my psyche as a child is now gone forever—not to mention the poor creatures that called those places home. And the destruction by construction continues throughout my life. Just yesterday the big news in economic circles was that new housing starts in the United States had risen to a twenty-year high of 2.07 million new houses a year.

Although I no longer live where I did as a child, just this past year the natural area near to the house where I live now, my sanctuary and the local place of the biosphere that gives me my sense of identity, was systematically destroyed to make way for giant, obnoxious homes that stare back at me like the menacing characters of a bad dream. But they are no dream. They have permanent concrete and metal foundations submerged deep into the ground, and every morning when I wake up they are still there, and the beautiful forest that once stood there is gone forever.

This obsession to continuously construct buildings and manufacture "durable" and "long-lasting" cars, appliances, tools, and other products from raw materials mined from the earth and transformed into cement, metal, and plastic must somehow be counteracted. The concentric circles of pollution and death emanating from these products and businesses must be recognized and felt in the hearts of both the consumers and the manufacturers. Ecoshamanic counterpractice must therefore include practices that put us in touch with another way of being so that we can see what we are doing from a fresh point of view and make changes accordingly. The only living beings found at modern construction sites are humans; every other sensible creature runs away from them as fast as they can. Doesn't that tell us something about ourselves?

Human beings have always found it necessary to shelter themselves from the infinity of space. The differences in how this is accomplished become apparent in how the shelter structures are built. For shamanic people, the architecture in their lives has always been significantly associated with the sacred. For example, the tipi, hogan, longhouse, or tukupi defines and shelters the people but also serves as a model of the world and universe. These structures establish the sacred center from where the family and community revolve both microcosmically and macrocosmically. The relationship between nature and man can clearly be seen in the homes and buildings of each culture, and the quality of that relationship is a major indication of the character of a culture. What do our structures and urban sprawl say about us?

COUNTERPRACTICE 7: Impermanent Structure

Just as learning to see with depth and perceiving the concentric circles of the world can help counteract a flat and narrow view of your daily activities in the modern world, spending time in an impermanent structure can help counteract the effect of ecologically traumatizing technology and lifeless, artificial, permanent structures. This implies living for a period of time in a debris hut, tent, yurt, teepee, or other kind of structure that is impermanent or portable and that contains little or no modern technology. Engaging in this type of counterpractice is not merely some form of romanticizing what life used to be like before technology or an attempt to re-create such lifestyles. It is more of a process of discovering what we have lost and gained by our technology so that we can claim knowledge of more appropriate uses for what we know and have.

It is easy to list the ways that technology has made our lives more comfortable but sometimes this perceived comfort masks many of the benefits that have been lost by the "old ways" of doing things, especially when viewed from the perspective of how we relate to the natural world at the most basic levels. Take, for example, the technological introduction of the central heating system.

Prior to the use of automatic heating with fossil fuels, most families relied on the heat from an old-fashioned wood fire, whether in a wood stove, hearth, or simply on the ground. The fire was not just a source of heat, but was also the center of a plethora of social, physical, and psychological activities. Firewood needed to be collected, cut, and stacked, typically with each household member contributing to the work. The kindling of the morning fire marked the start of a new day, and in the evening the fire was the center for the evening meal and a place of gathering for not only warmth but discussion, stories, music, and sharing.

This example is cited not to simply arouse the romantic feelings of the old days or suggest that we all use wood for heat. I mention it to shed light on the fact that the technology, which in this case is a heating system, has replaced not just the source of our heat but also a whole set of relationships and circumstances that for many millennia was a central focus of human life. The simple wood fire connected us to the local landscape as well as to each other. The furnace, the pipelines, the tankers, and the entire enormous fuel industry has replaced whole worlds of relationships and reduced them to the flipping of a switch and the paying of a bill.

In general, this same situation applies to many of our technologies where once we related to the world in a visible give-and-take manner but now we simply push a button, turn a handle, or look at a flat screen. All this happens, many times, with the technology that we use hidden from us "behind the scenes." We know how to turn the knobs and push the buttons, but most of us really have no idea how the specific technology we are using actually works. This is part of the great promise of technology—to alleviate us from the burdens of life. But so many of the so-called burdens aren't burdens at all, they are actually necessary experiences that ground and connect us to life. When we disconnect from these life-affirming experiences, we reduce some of the most important aspects of life to simply commodities and products that we depend on someone else to sell us. There is probably no better example of this than the supermarket, but we will dive more into that topic shortly.

The counterpractice I want to introduce here is that of living out of an impermanent structure that will place you squarely into the natural world with a minimum layer of padding between you. The exercise is quite simple. First make the arrangements necessary to spend at least a week living out of your impermanent structure. The more time you spend in and around your impermanent structure, the more you will get from the practice. In other words, try to avoid going into your house or other permanent buildings as much as possible. Figure out alternatives to meet your basic needs. The level that you do this will depend entirely on your personal situation, but the idea is to fully embody the exercise and push your limits of creativity, patience, and discipline.

This type of experience forces you into reevaluating everything in your life, starting from the simplest things, like where am I going to go to the bathroom? How will I stay warm and dry? What will I eat? And so on. Facing these realities opens your eyes to all of the circumstances and experiences of the natural world that we insulate ourselves from by always being inside, and also brings to light many of the activities and skills that have been lost through our dependence on technology and machines.

COUNTERPRACTICE 8: Fasting

As a form of counterpractice, fasting is an extremely potent and obvious luminous act of cleansing and awareness. Fasting from food empties the body so that both the body and the spirit can be cleansed of toxins while at the same time an awareness separate from the time schedules of meals can be invoked. The psychological schedule of feeding is left behind and so, then, is part of the rigid structure of everyday modern life. In this way the natural rhythms of your body are given the chance to meld more deeply with the natural rhythms of the world.

Although fasting is part of practically every spiritual tradition known to man, its roots go back much further and are not so much part of spiritual tradition as simply a consequence of ancient life. The physical structure of our bodies shaped by the 99 percent of our history spent as hunter-gatherers prepares us both physiologically and psychologically for the times when the belly is empty for extended periods. We humans can go only a few days without water, but we can live quite easily for a week or more without food.

Intentional fasting is a very healthy practice often overlooked by modern people. This is not just the skipping of a single meal but the prolonged abstinence from food that carries with it the sharp edge of awareness capable of bursting the "quick fix" bubble and the instant gratification mentality of consumerism. Through conscious and intentional fasting, you create an extremely personal ritual time that at once draws your attention inward and outward.

Your journey inward is a journey of discovering how you organize your day around mealtimes and how the absence of those moments has you searching elsewhere for nourishment. You hear your empty belly talking and turning inward upon itself for food while it eats up the stores of glycogen and other bodily sources of nourishment and energy. Without the meal to occupy your time, you are given precious moments of inner reflection that deepen your awareness to the sacredness of the earth's sustenance and the gift of life it provides.

Your outward awareness focuses on the condition of your physical body—your stomach, your genital area, your hands. You study the backs of your hands, the palm side, and your fingers. They may clench with the empty shiver that clenches your jaw but that also delivers the resolute strength and clarity that comes with an empty stomach.

Periodic fasting can be combined with any of the other activities included in this book, or can be an exercise on its own. Start by intentionally skipping a few meals at a time. As you begin to learn how your body reacts during the fast, as well as the best things to eat when breaking your fast, gradually increase your fasting period. When you are confident in fasting for a day or two at a time, to go further it is advisable to intentionally place yourself in an environment where your physical activity level is reduced and you do not need to operate a car, machinery, or engage in any other activity where momentary lapses in concentration could be dangerous. Fasting for long periods alters your perception, as well as your physiology, significantly enough that it is best to remove yourself from normal modern activities and instead replace them with activities in the natural world. The activities laid out in this book are perfect for use while fasting, as are the activities in my first book, *Earthwalks for Body and Spirit*.

COUNTERPRACTICE 9: Letting Your Body Drive

Another potent form of counterpractice relating to the physical body is to periodically set aside time for intentionally listening to your body in a way that your body, not your mind, guides your actions. So many times our body is giving us clear signals but we don't listen to or attend to those signals and messages because they interfere with what our rational mind and our responsibilities are asking of us, for example, when you awake in the morning still tired and your body pleads with you to stay in bed, but you have to go to work, so you get up anyway. Or, after being indoors working in an office for extended periods of time, your body is silently begging for fresh air, natural light, and physical activity, but you tune it out and suppress your body's natural urges in order to keep being "productive."

While we certainly need to fulfill responsibilities in our lives, which often means temporarily suppressing our physical, emotional, and mental urges until our tasks are complete, this type of suppression becomes unhealthy when it becomes a habitual way of relating to life. The spontaneity and the creative forces that come and go with the seasons of nature and the phases of moon and sun are completely disregarded as we train ourselves, year after year, to endure excessive periods of time cocooned in our indoor environments and to neglect and suppress our natural urges and the needs of our organic being.

Our bodies have a unique way of communicating to our mind what we need to be healthy, and by renewing that flow of information and then developing and deepening the dialog between body and mind, we place our entire human organism in a more healthy and happy position. Setting aside specific times when you let your body "drive" your actions is the first step to developing this awareness. This can be easily done when you have time to "yourself" after work or on weekends or at any time when the demands of life are not totally consuming your attention. Once you have experienced the positive effects of taking a nap when you need it, prying yourself away from the computer to take a walk outside, or eating a certain food that was not on the day's menu, and you consciously feel and acknowledge the positive effects of listening to your body, you quickly learn that your human organism has its own rhythm and pattern of needs that may be much different than the schedule you are imposing on it. From these initial experiences, the simple exercise of letting your body drive can transform into an integral part of your life whereby your daily actions, as well as the habits, patterns, and cycles of yearly, monthly, and weekly activities, become more in tune to what your human organism is asking of you.

At its highest level, this form of counterpractice does not conform to the rigid accounting of wristwatches or calendars and becomes much more a way of living life rather than simply another activity within our lives. Nowhere is this more apparent than in the shamanic communities in which the whole cycle of activities of the year are determined exclusively by the interaction between the environment and its human inhabitants, between the bodily felt connection and intuition of the people themselves.

For example, more often than not when I arrive at a Wirrarika ceremonial center on the date that I was told a certain ceremony or pilgrimage would happen, it's common to either have to wait for a week for all the people to be "ready," or to find out that I already missed the whole thing by a week or more. Many times it is the shamans themselves that "disappear" around the time of a special event because they know that the proper time has not yet come or maybe has even passed. This completely unpredictable way of relating to the world is something that has driven Western researchers of indigenous people crazy for hundreds of years, but it is the very thing that makes these people so aware and thus so precious.

The shaman that is leading the ceremony for blessing the arrival of the baby corn in the fields will not give a hoot about what day the calendar says it is, and neither will he care that the documentary film crew that is there to record the ceremony is waiting with their expensive equipment, time schedules, and monetary budgets. When the time is right, both for the baby corn and for the shaman and the community, the ceremony will happen. The ceremony will not start precisely at 8 AM and it will not end at precisely 5 PM simply because the shaman is not driving, the corn is driving the shaman's body and the shaman is letting his body drive.

COGNITIVE MAPS

A glimpse of Earth from space tells the whole story. It shows the planet whole, without the arbitrary political boundaries of man. What a beautiful, colorful, and miraculous place, this ball of circulating water, continents of land, and swirling clouds. Few people have ever actually seen Earth from outer space, but even just seeing photos of this view of Earth immediately alters our perspective, our sense of place, and enlarges our perception to identify with the planet as a whole. As human beings we all have something precious in common: we all call this amazing blue-green spinning and rotating planet home. A more primary identity we will never know.

Identifying our self as an individual inhabitant of planet Earth is such a primary awareness, and the planet is so incredibly large in comparison to our view from the ground, that our planetary awareness goes largely unnoticed during the course of our normal day and so we tend to identify ourselves more readily with the imaginary lines placed on globes and maps that give the areas where we live borders and names. It is important to realize that these abstract concepts of place that portion off the planet according to the politics of the human species have absolutely zero basis in the organic reality of the planet. As can readily be seen from viewing the planet from space, our home biosphere is one interconnected whole.

But here in the United States we attempt to carve up the land with imaginary boundary lines of states, counties, and city limits, which are divided into even more abstract governing lines of congressional districts, legislative districts, judicial districts, fire and police department districts, school districts, postal zip-code districts, telephone area-code districts, and so on.

Where most of these lines are even located is unclear to us, and so we end up identifying with a whole set of imaginary lines and abstract places that impede our sense of the organic reality of the soil we are actually standing on. The geological terrain that forms the place where we are actually becomes trivial when identifying and communicating where we are to another person! But what is worse is that it also becomes trivial to our sense of personal identity. This preposterous situation is one of the underlying causes of the ecological crises of our times.

The key to reclaiming an organic, primal sense of place, an awareness of place that has literally formed the cognitive evolution of human beings and that is embedded at the deepest levels of our psyche, is to experience the soil, landscape, and ecosystems of the places where we live and work at a level of reality much deeper than that imposed on us by political boundaries, zip codes, and school districts.

One process of reclaiming a sense of organic identity begins with understanding and altering the maps inside of our mind that provide us with a sense of where we are. All of us have images of places and spaces in our memory that we associate with our lives presently and in the past. These "cognitive maps" are used, for example, when we leave home to go to work or the grocery store, on the trip back home after we have gone out, when thinking about past places we've been, or when we give someone directions. At the most basic level, the cognitive maps inside our mind provide us with the landmarks of the areas we know and enable us to navigate to and from them easily.

Cognitive maps are very complex because they are not like a static map that is drawn on a piece of paper. Cognitive maps also take into account time, patterns, observations, and the perceptions of the human mind.

Our ancient ancestors, as well as contemporary people living a nature-based existence, employed a mental mapping system that could process the complex ecological realities of the world around them. They needed to remember how to find trails that led to water and successful places of hunting animals and gathering different types of plants and fruits and roots, where dangerous animals had been seen, places to cross rivers, lookout posts, and so on. All of this was, of course, influenced by the time of year and changing of the seasons. Hunting patterns, plant growth, river levels, and hundreds of other considerations were constantly changing throughout the year and so, in turn, were the cognitive maps that enabled people to adapt quickly and efficiently to changing circumstances.

In modern times we have traded in most of the natural geographical "landmarks" that our ancestors used for street signs, gas stations, and convenience stores. Instead of animal migration patterns we now register weekend traffic patterns, rush hour, sporting events and holidays, when we decide a particular way to navigate from one place to the next. Similarly, when we describe the places where we live, we automatically tend to use a cognitive map that exclusively employs human-imposed features of the land. For example, a person living within the imaginary borders of Colorado might describe where they live by saying "I live in Colorado, just outside of Frazer, off of Route 40" instead of saying "I live next to a small lake in a wide valley on the eastern side of the Rocky Mountains, north of the Continental Divide." A New Yorker might say "Fifth Avenue, Manhattan" rather than "In the Hudson River Valley, very close to where the Hudson flows into the Atlantic Ocean."

Both of these perspectives are useful in different ways, but it is important to realize how different they are. One way identifies with the organic world and the other with the human-created world. One way utilizes manmade districts and boundaries that have been created for the purely human purposes of property rights, political control, supervision and exploitation of nature as well as other humans. In short this way of thinking is in competition with organic reality. The second way describes a cooperation with nature, a thought process that takes into account the organic qualities of the land formed by rivers and mountains and valleys. By adding a layer of organic cognitive maps on top of, or underneath, the maps of our mind that identify with the purely human world, we can begin to reclaim our organic sense of place and identity.

COUNTERPRACTICE 10: Organic Mind Map

This technique begins by going outdoors and entering an ESC by taking the "view from the moon" perspective of Earth—from where all the imaginary human lines that indiscriminately carve up the world are wiped away—and then slowly zooming in on the planet to identify the connected parts of the whole; natural parts of the whole that share various organic realities such as altitude, climate, vegetation, fauna, and so on. Using the cognitive maps you already have inside your mind relating to the geology of the planet, zoom in on your continent, then your region, then your neighborhood, until you arrive to your home and the exact place you are standing.

Now walk around and begin to create a new cognitive map based on the organic reality of where you are. Notice and register all of the natural features of the landscape, such as hills, valleys, individual trees, shrubs, flowers, birds, puddles, insects, rocks, and so on. Now look up and realize that you are standing in the center of your local "home" circle, a circle inside many other larger ecological circles. What you find inside your immediate home circle will tell you a lot about yourself.

The next step is to expand your awareness to include the next larger circle, which could be called your neighborhood. This might be a very small area, or a mile in diameter. It might include just 5 people in a rural area or 500 or more in a heavily urbanized area. Walk around your neighborhood and identify the geological and biological realities of the place. Notice where your smaller home circle fits within this larger neighborhood circle.

Now walk or even drive around inside the next larger circle, which could be called your community. Again, depending on where you live, this could include a few hundred or many thousands of people. Remember, you are working to produce a cognitive map of organic reality, so "community" does not simply refer to people, buildings, and streets. Inside of this circle will be countless members and features of the natural community that include those in your home circle and neighborhood circle, but now at the community level you will find much more diversity of plant and animal life, bodies of water, geologic formations, and so on. Try to maintain or deepen your ESC as your circle of awareness grows larger and larger. Don't be depressed if your community circle is detrimentally over-populated; notice what it says about your life.

The next larger circle is the bioregion in which you live. At the most basic level, this could be described as a large area of similar topography, or the rough boundaries of a watershed whose climate and geography supports similar types of vegetation and fauna. Even among seasoned veterans of the bioregional movement, there is still debate as to what defines a bioregion. Don't get hung up on this; we are not involved with a scientific experiment but an exercise in altering consciousness. One helpful way to determine bioregions is by investigating native tribal groups that once inhabited the area. A bioregion (absent of nonsustainable human construction) should be large enough to be relatively self-sustaining to its human occupants; native people often formed tribal boundaries inside of these realities.

When discerning your bioregion, keep in mind that the edges of bioregions emerge out of the land itself, rather than being drawn as an arbitrary line on a map. Edges are formed by watershed divides, mountains, climate zones, fault lines, and so on. Careful and patient observation coupled with a shift in consciousness toward relating to the organic reality of a place is needed when discerning the edges of your bioregion.

There are, of course, even larger natural regions that we can identify. Often called biomes and sub-biomes, these large land areas include many bioregions that eventually comprise a whole continent. But for this exercise it is enough to simply acknowledge the place of your home bioregion inside the larger biome and continent without getting lost and confused. Realize and understand that continents, biomes, sub-biomes, and bioregions all exist without the help from any line drawn on a political map. They are the true borders of the natural world, and we can enter into cooperation with the natural world when we learn how to live and plan our human communities while paying close attention to the organic reality of the place where we live.

COUNTERPRACTICE 11: Sense of Place Map

An extremely enlightening counterpractice exercise is to throw away all concepts of modern map making and create your own map of your local area and the sacred places in nature that are most important to you. In *Ecological Identity* (Cambridge, MA: MIT Press, 1995), Mitchell Thomashow describes the sense of place map as the following:

> [A] rite of passage that links ecological identity to life-cycle development . . . [The making of the map is] a process of self-reflection through which we perceive the places in which we live: the people, community, land, and species that form our networks of domesticity and exploration, the sources of sustenance and struggle. Sense of place is the domestic basis of environmentalism; it's the foundation of our deepest connection to the natural world. At the same time, we may observe how hard it is to establish a meaningful community—how places are so easily eroded, how we dwell in so many mental spaces . . . It's about our habits of familiarity, the places we visit every day . . . It also reflects how we earn a living, the things we do to survive, the material basis of our life. In what ways are we bonded to the landscape? What are our emotional attachments to the place we live in? How do we coexist with other people, with the flora and fauna? How do we understand the local ecosystem? How do we define our bioregion?

There are many mediums that can be employed for mapping your local area while entering an ESC. Maps can be drawn on paper, tree bark, or on any other medium. They can be made three-dimensional through use of fabric or other natural materials, or can be expressed through mobiles, mandalas, poetry, or any other creative medium that moves you. Ancient people have historically employed sticks, stones, and seashells, drawings made from deer blood on bark and hides, and even carved sacred maps into living rock that can still be seen today.

When making your map, the most important thing is to not feel constrained by impersonal scientific mapping techniques and to simply place your organic consciousness into the map in a creative way that encourages greater awareness and connection to your natural surroundings. Making the map is much more than simply symbolizing the physical properties of the area; it is more like transferring the feelings of the living essences of the entities that inhabit the area into your map so that the map becomes alive to you.

COUNTERPRACTICE 12: Then and Now Map

The processes of altered consciousness employed in the previous two exercises encourage the start of greater awareness and involvement with one's homeland at a deeply organic level. And when we become more conscious and connected to a place, it becomes easier to protect and serve it. When one develops an identity with the home soil, then honoring the land becomes honoring the self, and vice versa. This "local identity" is an extremely important transformation in consciousness, even for those people that are already inspired to contribute to environmental and wildlife protection groups. While many people now feel the impact of the global environmental crises, it has become more common to contribute money or other resources for the protection of rare and threatened animals and rainforests in faraway lands. We would do well to continue with these efforts, though not while we are doing nothing to conserve and protect our own local home environments.

Our local environments are changing so rapidly and are being managed so poorly that they deserve our immediate attention. It seems so natural that we would feel responsible for our local area, but that simply is not the case for so many people. Since groceries come in trucks from far-off places and people habitually commute to work outside of their local neighborhood, the home area is not seen as a source of life and so becomes just a "place to live." In the next section of this book, I'm going to go deeper into this last point. But right now I'm going to approach this theme from the perspective of counterpractice map-making. In this counterpractice, you employ an ESC while recapitulating a place from your past: the sense of place and the lessons from the natural world that that place gave you.

The first thing to do is pick a place from your past where you had direct experiences with the natural world. It could be a large tract of land, a backyard, park, garden, orchard, or any other place that is significant to your experiential awareness of nature. Now you're going to draw a map of the place while reliving the events that took place there.

As in the previous exercises, don't limit yourself to adhering to traditional mapping techniques. Although scaling your map to resemble the size of the component areas may help you in piecing together your map, the scale of different areas may have more to do with the intensity of experience that happened in a certain place than the literal size of the place. For example, a tiny section of woods behind a house can seem like a huge wonder-world for a small child or even to an adult in a deep ESC. In terms of conventional map-making, this place would scarcely exist, but for this exercise it could be your entire map.

To illustrate this technique I've included a map I made of a place where my family lived when I was ten years old (see page 84). Since I lived in a semirural area and kids were always encouraged to play outside, I had the opportunity to deeply know this wonderful area of nature, and although it has now been almost completely covered with roads and houses, it still lives inside of me to this day. During that part of my life I spent so much time outdoors and loved to explore all the different areas around where we lived that my identity of what was "home" included a large natural area. The map I've drawn here depicts the core region of my home area and the places I spent time on a daily basis.

When making your own map, take your time and start over as many times as you need in order to feel comfortable with it to the point that it comes alive. What you are doing is transferring a cognitive map of your mind on to a tangible medium. Try to do this without losing the feeling of the place or, even better, as you draw the place let the act of drawing carry you deeper into the essence of the place.

Reliving the essence and spirit of the places on your map is key to this practice. The combination of essence and spirit in an area, together with your MBESA, is what accounts for your actual experiences and lessons. To understand this better, let's first look closer at the phenomena of essence and spirit.

The essence is the quality of feeling exuded by the entity or place that is being perceived by you. For example, the Thorny Thicket on my map has a particular feeling that the essence of the thorny bushes exude. This essence is far different from that of the Quiet

Pines. Sitting in the Thorny Thicket is something that would rarely happen, unless one wants to brave the cuts, scrapes, and torn clothing that come with trying to get through or under the thorny bushes. The cottontail rabbit feels completely comfortable and secure here, as you won't find an owl or hawk perched on a thorn bush. The Quiet Pines, on the other hand, provides a quite comfortable place for one to sit. The soft bed of pine needles, the shade, and the relative shelter from wind and rain make this a nice place to visit. But the rabbit will be very wary there, as the owl and hawk are waiting. These are two areas with distinctly different essences.

Now, the thorn bush, the pine tree, the rabbit, and the owl all have their own essence and spirit. The essence is the form and the feeling; the spirit is what animates it. Everything in nature has both. One simple way to look at this is at the species versus the individual level. For example, a particular species of rabbit or pine tree will have a similar essence, but each individual will have a unique spirit that animates it. The same can be said for places, which means that spirits of nature come in many different sizes and forms.

At an individual level, a rabbit, a hawk, or a tree has a spirit that animates it, but also the collective essences and spirits of an area have a larger essence and spirit. Walking into a cedar forest puts you into contact with the collective essence and spirit of that particular forest. The way the forest feels and grows and dies, the animals and birds that live there, and the function of the forest within the larger geographic area is unique and different from a stand of oak trees over the next hill.

When trying to speak of spirit, it is best not to fall into the trap of intellectualizing. The only way you can really know the spirit of a place, and therefore even prove to yourself that it exists, is to interact with it personally with your entire MBESA.

Experiences are only as real as your ability to have them. For example, there is no way you could explain or speak about the color red to a person that was born blind, in a way that they would actually experience "red." You could talk about wavelengths and color spectrums until you were blue in the face and that person would still not actually experience what we who can see call the color of a rose or sunset. In the same way, talking, thinking, or trying to describe "spirit" will not lead you to know it. The only way to know it is to experience it.

I would say that the place I have drawn on this map contains the essence and spirit of many component areas that form a larger spirit that extends much farther than this map shows. The spirit of this place in the northeast United States is not the same as the spirit,

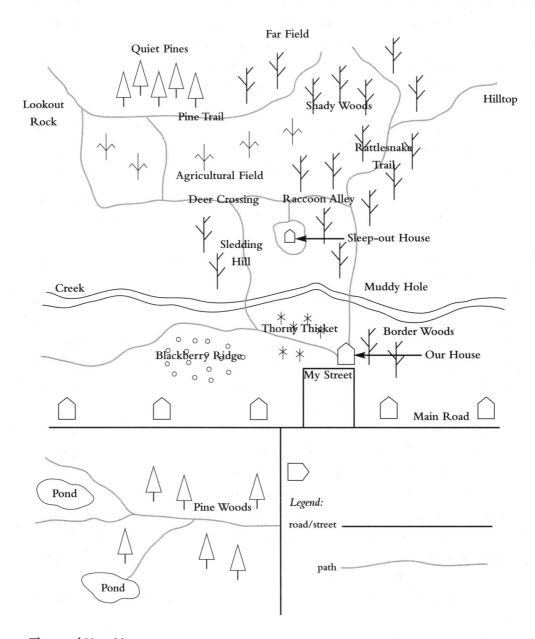

Then and Now Map.

for example, in another extremely special place for me that is located in a region of canyons in the Southwest. Intimately knowing them both for many years has allowed me to learn their unique personalities, traits, and wisdom, and the friendship with both has provided different experiences and lessons.

The essence and spirit of the place that lives in this map is made up of countless components in a somewhat similar way that individual human spirits comprise the collective spirit of a culture. Each individual has unique and important lessons to share, as does the collective spirit of the larger culture. With this in mind, and keeping in mind that this was just one tiny place on Earth, let's look at what this place had to offer and teach.

Thorny Thicket was located on the hill right in back of my house, between the house and the stream. During three seasons of the year, this area was basically impenetrable, due to the thickness of the bushes and quantity of the razor-sharp and extremely strong thorns. It made a perfect place to hide if you were willing to crawl on your belly into it. Although compared to other places in my home range, I didn't spend much time inside the thicket, but it had plenty to teach. I was humbled by the little animals that frequented the thicket because they moved effortlessly in places where I struggled to even get to. Rabbits could literally disappear before your eyes in there. Little birds flew so fast in and out of the thorny branches that they were like a blur before my eyes and were easier to hear than they were to see. It was amazing to discover how many beings called this place home and were completely comfortable in a place so difficult for me to penetrate. Even many bigger animals like deer would go in and out with little difficulty. I learned patience and perseverance trying to navigate my body through the thorns, and also what clothes functioned best when going in. The Thorny Thicket also taught me to cooperate with the landscape. The more I tried to bull my way into the thicket without paying attention to its nuances, the more difficult and frustrating the place became. But when I moved calmly and carefully I could navigate the thorns much easier, and the experience of the place was far more enjoyable. Also, it was a great place to hide things because people (especially adults) never went into the Thorny Thicket.

Blackberry Ridge: Not all of the thorny bushes in my area produced the delicious blackberries found on the left side of the hill, and that's why this area is called Blackberry Ridge. The sense of accomplishment felt coming out of the thorns with a full tub of succulent blackberries is indescribable. This place provided me with a sense of the gathering of wild food and the feeling of kinship with the diverse communities of birds that visited the patch. Because of the short berry season the bird activity was pretty intense, and I think that it was in this place that I first started noticing the interactions of the different bird types, the different vocalizations, and even the different sounds of flight between the species as they fluttered to and fro. Perseverance in working around the thorns and amidst the flying insects was needed, as was a lot of patience in waiting for the berries to ripen and not getting too mad when the birds picked the berries clean if I didn't time the days for picking correctly. This place was also one site of continued confusion and mild anger for me because a main part of the blackberry patch was directly over an underground natural gas pipeline that every couple of years would be mowed down for easier access by the gas company. No matter how many times my parents would try to explain it, I couldn't fathom why they needed to cut down my beloved blackberry bushes for something that I couldn't even see. On a positive note, I was always astounded at how quickly the bushes grew back again.

Muddy Hole: Along the right side of the Thorny Thicket and the left side of the Border Woods was one of the main trails in my life. It was a well-worn path that was part of my highway system. But during many times of the year this path ran smack into a muddy bog formed by a low spot in the terrain where the creek ran through the valley. There was really no escape from it. On the one side was the bottom of the Thorny Thicket and on the other was the border of the land where the wild farm dogs of the spooky farm lived. So when the muddy hole got really deep I would carry down a couple of long boards to help with the crossing, but normally I would just plow through it and accept the mud as just part of my world. Muddy Hole was the best place in the world to see animal tracks. The consistency and odor of muddy soil, and the insects, frogs, and garter snakes all provided a unique essence to this place. Muddy Hole taught me a lot about animals' tracks and also tuned me in on a daily basis to what was happening with the stream, the amount of rainfall, whether the dogs had been in my area recently, etc.

Raccoon Alley was the most mysterious place in my world, not because of the essence being exuded by the place as much as what went on there in the night. A couple of years before we built my little sleep-out house, which was right in Raccoon

Alley, I would lie in bed at night during certain times of year and hear the most mysterious and spine-chilling animal noises coming from the woods just below the farmer's field. It didn't happen often, but when it did it filled my head with images of fangs and glowing eyes in the night. My father and I thoroughly investigated the sounds and the area with a respected outdoorsman and we all concluded that the mysterious noises were territorial raccoons. Well, knowing this didn't quench my curiosity, it merely fueled it. So when I received permission to build my small sleep-out house, I immediately decided to put it smack in the middle of the mysterious Raccoon Alley and thus began my spotting and stalking of raccoons, foxes, deer, possum, owls, and a host of other creatures large and small during the night. The whole experience of discovering the mystery, fear, and curiosity of the nighttime wilderness was like opening the door to a whole new secret world for me. One of the most tragic circumstances of modern life is that it completely disconnects us to the nocturnal reality being lived by millions of beings every night, and these precious beings are almost never considered when an area such as Raccoon Alley is eventually destroyed by development, which is exactly what happened about ten years after my first full-night experience there.

Deer Crossing: The most profound lesson of this small area between Raccoon Alley and the Agricultural Field where the deer would often cut through was humility. Because although I saw deer quite often and I somewhat knew their patterns of movement and where they liked to be during the different seasons of the year, the numerous signs of activity like the big deer paths, antler rubs, scrapes, and scat provided me with the realization that even as well as I knew my little area of wilderness, the animals knew it infinitely better. This realization, even at a subconscious level, always kept me humble in the face of all the mysteries of the wild, and kept me hungry to always keep learning and experiencing what the woods and fields and animal messengers had to teach me.

Sledding Hill: On the steep, wooded hillside next to Deer Crossing was a large path cut into the woods and maintained by the gas company for their underground pipeline. As a kid, this long, steep hill appeared to be specially designed for us to go sledding in the winter. If I was mad at the gas company for ruining my precious blackberry bushes on the other side of the valley, I was almost equally happy to have part of the big hill cleared for our wintertime entertainment.

Agricultural Field: This field had annual rotations of corn, soybeans, and alfalfa, and as such provided one of the reasons for my intense relationship with the white-tailed deer that often visited the crops to feed during the night. But it also struck a deep chord inside of me as I would sit quietly during the day and watch the dust rise in columns through the air as the powerful tractors would tear up the ground like butter. I would cover my ears as the mechanized monsters came screaming back and forth across the land, and when they were gone after the plowing, the silence they left behind was so sweet that I would just sit there for a long time listening to the wind and birds and the creaking of branches, which eventually soothed my ears enough that the rumble of the tractors seemed to only be a bad dream.

Rattlesnake Trail: The trail above the Agricultural Field was always greeted with special appreciation because I would always have to cross the field in order to get into the Shady Woods and up the mountain, and the field always felt so unnatural to me, especially when the corn was full grown, that I couldn't wait to get through it and come out the other side. Once I made it through the field I was back in my comfortable environment of woods, and at the beginning of this particular trail the woods were very thin and full of large boulders for the first 100 yards or so before the trail dove into the big and shady oak forest. In this open area is where many of the local snakes, especially the rattlers, would come to sunbathe, and so even in the times of year when I knew the snakes weren't out I always kept very alert and especially watchful while walking through this area. Even though I met rattlesnakes and copperheads (both poisonous) countless times, only once (when I was being careless) did I ever feel truly threatened or in danger by one of these incredible beings. Mostly I just felt reverence and respect for them, and we seemed to have an unspoken agreement that when we met we would just leave each other to our own business and go our separate ways. Although once in a while, if I came upon a really large rattler, I couldn't resist sitting down on a large boulder and just watching it lie motionless in the warm sun. Curled up completely still yet vigilantly aware in the sun on a large boulder, these snakes were my first teachers of meditation, and they also taught me how to pay attention to the vibrations of the earth and atmosphere while lying perfectly still on the ground. It's unexplainable, and my connection to snakes has faded as my connection to other animals has grown, but lying with those snakes for long periods of time as a boy I know that I felt what they felt, and they knew I was there and that I was learning from them and they approved and accepted me and what I was doing. This type of connection is at the heart of my dream to share with people the ecoshamanic project. I dream of people having this type of connection with birds and whales and wind and trees and snakes in a way that places us humans in the service of nature, and not the other way around.

Shady Woods: This large area of mostly oak trees was constantly teeming with wildlife and was on the outskirts of my home area. Past the Shady Woods was a field and then a great expanse of woods that ran for miles, which I knew fairly well but no way near as well as I knew my immediate areas like the Shady Woods. This large area of woods started my love affair with wooded areas and mountains in general. It is so deeply etched into my human organism that thirty years later I can still see in my mind and feel in my bones many of the individual trees, both the live ones as well as those that had fallen; the unique quality of light in that place; the smell; the individual rocks alongside and on the trail; and the countless experiences with the wildlife. It is this kind of remarkably deep imprint of a place on the total MBESA that fosters my profound respect for my Wirrarika shaman mentors that have walked the same trails in their homeland, and to and from their sacred sites, for not only a lifetime but many generations. They know the places and the places know them, at such a profound level that they are the land and the land is them. There is no way to possibly separate the two.

Quiet Pines: More than any place in my home area, this felt the most secret and private to me. I can't recall ever seeing any traces of human activity, other than mine, in these woods, and I would go here at those times when I was feeling sad or upset about something, or when I just wanted to sit and think or rest. The lack of undergrowth in the pine forest and the thick cover above gave these woods a kind of cathedral-like quality that always invoked a feeling of reverence and stillness within me.

Two Ponds: Across the main road that ran through my home range were two small ponds that I loved to go visit because they were truly an endless source for discoveries and adventures. Between Two Ponds was a pine forest that was perfectly situated for hiding in while watching the animals come to drink or to watch certain birds come to catch small fish. It was like the two ponds were a magnet for all the wildlife in the area, not to mention that just past the ponds was an enormous apple orchard that helped support a wide variety of birds and animals. There was never any doubt to me that the water of Two Ponds was a sacred and magical substance that held within it the power of life. Although the house my family lived in was supplied by a well and not city water, the magical fluid of the two ponds seemed so different and special to me that I have to admit that I never even made a connection in my youth between the sacred water of the ponds and the water coming from the tap. But even though I somehow missed this connection, the two ponds certainly instilled into my being the sacredness of water that later in life opened doors to magical experiences of connection and reverence to the sacred fluid of life.

The main part of this practice is the creating and re-creating of your representation of the place, and the reliving of experiences and feelings associated with the place while you are mapping. Once you have your map and it has been sufficiently refined to portray your lived recollection with the place, try to focus on each place within the map and relive the feelings of some of the experiences you had there.

The last part of the practice is to go back there and visit with the spirits of the place. Depending on the condition of the place, the same spirits may or may not be there. In the case of the map I gave as an example, the only spirit of those lands that was still living when I last visited was in the upper forest, but it was shaky and felt very distraught, nervous, and afraid. All of the other places on the map have been completely destroyed by housing developments and their roads and drainage systems. I hope your experience with this practice will be as enlightening as mine, and I encourage you to do it with as many places as you can. But keep in mind, especially if your experiences are similar to mine and most of the places you've known are now destroyed, you still have the chance to know and bond with sacred places that are new to you, and you can use all your experience to try and preserve the new lands that fill your heart, mind, and spirit.

SUSTENANCE

Every one of the authentic shamans that I have worked with have known exactly where the food they put into their mouth comes from, and every one of them was (is) intimately involved in the planting, raising, growing, hunting, harvesting, butchering, and blessing of the life-giving nourishment they receive. This is simply a consequence of living an organically based lifestyle, and is one of the primary differences between indigenous shamans and the neoshamanic practices of American and European cities.

One of the main circumstances that originally gave birth to shamanism was the necessity for food. Those that possessed superior perceptual abilities, even when compared to the best hunters of a group, were acknowledged for their gift of somehow knowing and seeing things that others could not. This aspect of shamanism has been part of human history for tens of thousands of years, right up to the advent of agriculture. And this still remains true today, even if in modified form. As many indigenous peoples also began raising crops, the shaman's duties expanded to include service to the plants, the rain, and the soil. Even in this more modern capacity, the shaman still has significant duties related to the sustenance of the community, and is intimately involved in the reciprocal relationships between the people and the spirits of nature. The shaman is responsible for maintaining the balance between the seen and unseen forces. At the most basic level, this implies the balance between people and the life-giving energies and forces that provide them with life.

Food is a sacrament. But the tragic fact is that modern people, including many of our modern spiritual leaders, have all but lost the sacred connection to what truly sustains them. We don't know who grows our food, or where it comes from. We can't even pronounce half the ingredients of the food we eat; much of it has been genetically altered, contains chemical preservatives, and comes wrapped in a plastic package. Furthermore, by depending exclusively on others in faraway places for our sustenance, we place ourselves in a dangerously vulnerable position as we give up the knowledge and the ability to provide for ourselves. When this happens we also miss out on the psychological, physiological, environmental, and spiritual benefits, connections, lessons, and strengths that come with directly providing for our most basic needs. Humans can't eat dollar bills, stock certificates, or insurance policies. When we are completely disconnected from producing what we put into our mouths and we reduce the whole sacred complex of sustenance and nourishment to a monetary transaction with a multinational corporation, we simply deepen our role as human resources in the great industrial machine.

If you think the above statement is too strong, ask yourself these questions: What would happen to you and your family if the tractor-trailers stopped delivering food from far-off lands to the local supermarkets, restaurants, and quickie-marts? How would you provide for yourself and your family? How would your neighbors? How would you survive?

LONG–DISTANCE NOURISHMENT, MANUFACTURING NOURISHMENT

Incredible as it may seem, several recent studies show that fruits and vegetables now typically travel between 2,500 and 4,000 kilometers (an average of 1,300 miles) from farm to market in the United States. In the United Kingdom, trucks moving food now account for about 40 percent of all road freight, and in the last two decades the imports of fruits and vegetables arriving there by plane has more than tripled. Throughout the world, part of the reason food is being moved around so much is that there are more people living bunched up in cities that are far from the centers of food production. Also, scientific advances that control the ripening of fruits and vegetables, and the preservatives added to other perishable foods, extend shelf life and make them available for long voyages and long-term storage. But the most significant circumstance promoting food travel has been the subsidizing of the transportation and agricultural industries by governments throughout the world, with the United States as the leader and model.

In the United States, the federally subsidized interstate highway system spreads coast to coast. Cheap fossil fuels, which the government is willing to go to war for at the horrific loss of human life and the cost of billions of dollars, encourage long-distance shipping. With the global agricultural trade valued at around 500 billion dollars, the immense agro-industrial system in the United States easily controls governmental policymaking in favor of factory farming, mega-supermarkets, and long-distance trade while at the same time all but squashing local farms, farmers' markets, and food cooperatives.

The systems of growing and distributing of food are so absurd in the United States, and the monopolizing of the food market is so complete, that even locally grown produce typically travels thousands of miles before it reaches the table of a family that might live just a few miles from where the produce was grown. Food monopolies such as Safeway and Wal-Mart have massive distribution and refrigeration centers where all the produce must be shipped in order to be inventoried and inspected. On the East Coast, one of the largest centers is in Maryland, which means that, for instance, produce grown in Georgia must get shipped all the way to Maryland to be inventoried and inspected, and then shipped all the way back to the local supermarket in Georgia before it is sold. To agro-business and retail executives this massive distribution system represents cost-effective control and efficiency. But that is only because of governmental fuel and highway subsidies that we all pay for.

In the short term, and for those who can afford it, this wasteful system provides the ultimate in convenience. If you have access to a mega-supermarket, any food is available virtually anytime. But the hidden costs of this system are enormous and unsustainable. And by industrializing our sustenance we take away the practical, as well as the sacred, beneficial aspects of locally grown food. Below is a listing of some of the main malicious components of the current long-distance food system run by the agro-industrial complex (primary sounces are *The Fatal Harvest Reader*, edited by Andrew Kimbrell, and Bernard Jensen and Mark Anderson's *Empty Harvest*):

- The system is totally dependent on staggering amounts of fossil fuel for transportation, which contributes greatly to smog, global warming, and oil wars.

- Food products in this long-term storage system are more susceptible to contamination and require preservatives, additives, and refrigeration.

- Consumers are subject to the intentional or unintentional hazards of E. coli bacteria, pesticide residue, genetically modified foods, and biological warfare agents. Under this system there is virtually no security in knowing what you are eating or where it came from.

- Advances in food processing, long-term storage, and transportation have promoted the formation of huge industrial conglomerates that have decimated the family farm and local farming communities.

- The deserted family farms have been replaced by housing developments, strip malls, and asphalt.

- Farms that once grew a diverse range of crops for local consumption are now forced by the system to specialize in one or two crops for distant markets. This lack of diversity causes even the farmers to also be dependent on outside food sources.

- Modern farms that limit growth to only one or two specialized crops threaten the biodiversity of the planet.

- Small grocers, farm markets, butchers, canneries, and bakeries are replaced by a handful of national chain stores.

- Money spent on food is no longer circulated locally but given to distant corporations.

- The long-distance food system does not return organic matter back to where the produce was grown, and so promotes the use of polluting chemical fertilizers.

- Packaging of processed foods results in staggering amounts of trash that, along with food scraps that would be better composted, account for a third of all land-filled waste.

- The profit-oriented supermarkets have left the inner cities in order to capitalize on more lucrative suburban areas. This results in inner cities that are crammed full of fast-food joints but often have no grocery store where produce is even available, so inner city people are often left only to purchase nutritionally deficient food from behind the bulletproof glass of fast-food joints and quickie-marts.

- Giant food companies influence people's eating habits through extensive market-ing and advertising of profit-rich but nutritionally deficient products such as candy, breakfast cereals, and fast food, which directly contributes to half of all Americans being overweight and one in five being obese. Food is the most heav-ily advertised commodity in the United States.

- In North America and Europe, sugar and fat now comprise more than half of caloric intake.

- Lack of dietary variety in the high sugar and fat diets of developed countries such as the United States accounts for a significant portion of the population to be micronutrient deficient, even in those who are overweight and obese.

- Packaged food and fast food promote meals being taken outside the home, on the run, and especially in the car, which is the second most popular place for Ameri-cans to have breakfast.

- Current reports indicate that by 2005 many people of consumer societies will have never cooked a meal from "scratch" (using basic ingredients).

The most ironic (and tragic) consequence of the long-distance food system is that it ultimately destroys what it is supposed to nourish. The climate change and pollution induced by the fossil-fuel-burning transportation system, the packaging trash, the deficient diets, the soil depletion, the smog, and the inability for consumers to know what they are eating all together create an almost criminal abuse inflicted on such a basic and sacred human need.

What to do?

From the perspective of ecoshamanism, the solution to this awful situation is simple. If you (or someone you love or respect) didn't grow it, raise it, hunt it, or harvest it—**_don't put it in your mouth._**

Big statement, I know. The first problem is that people just don't equate their land, or their local farmer, with their food. The long-distance food system is now so deeply seated that most people think it is the only option. This is why a total mind-body-environment-spirit approach to the problem is necessary. The greatest realizations come when we feel our body responding and changing to the physically and spiritually nourishing food provided by our local, sacred land. We need to reclaim the land and stop the urban sprawl by raising our own diverse foods (or supporting someone locally to do it; many large towns and cities now have local farmers' markets and co-ops that are perfect for rediscovering a sacred connection to both the food we eat and the people that grow and raise it) instead of raising more housing developments and mega-malls. The fear of the collapse of our long-distance food system when cheap oil runs dry, and the knowledge of the system's devastation to the environment, are perfect reasons to change, but the positive experiences revolving around being a part of a locally based and nourishing food chain are the most powerful agents of change.

Now, being a realist, I understand full well that even those who truly want to gain independence from the industrial food system and reclaim a sacred connection to the spiritual energies of the plants and animals that they put into their mouths will find this an incredibly daunting task that might take years to accomplish (as I can attest to myself, in my own life). What we are talking about here is a change not only in certain actions related to food, but major lifestyle changes that affect every aspect of life. And that is exactly why this is so important.

COUNTERPRACTICE 13: Food Journeying

Ecoshamanic counterpractice relating to the food we eat can be something we engage in multiple times a day, every day, and so what begins as a novel exercise expands gradually into a new state of being and way of life. One of the simplest yet profound forms of counterpractice is to "journey" with the food you put into your mouth before you eat it. This implies learning all you can about the journey your food made to arrive at your mouth by reading the packaging that your food comes wrapped in to find out where it came from, researching about the companies that have manufactured it, and asking at the point of purchase where the produce or meat you are buying actually came from. This is a similar exercise to Counterpractice 1: Seeing in Systems, except that this is far more personal. When you put something in your mouth and swallow it, you have now allowed it to become part of you and to penetrate the barrier between what is "me" and what is "not me."

The difference in awareness and perception between knowing at an intimate level what you are making you by putting in your mouth, or not having a clue what it really is or where it came from, is astounding at both an immediate level of consciousness as well as in the context of how one's life unfolds through intentional actions or mindless following. Discovering this level of reality was very frustrating for me in the beginning, and at some level continues to be even to this day because it changes everything; it is an extremely difficult situation to resolve while trying to live in and relate to modern society, especially while traveling away from your known sources of nourishment.

COUNTERPRACTICE 14: Eating Spirit

Whether you are a meat eater, a vegetarian, a vegan, or whatever, the simple truth is that everything you swallow as nourishment for your body is either still alive or is the dead carcass of something that was once alive. With this sometimes overlooked fact in mind, it becomes easier to understand why nourishment is such a sacred and central aspect to so many shamanic cultures. And in this context, nourishment is far different than simple nutrition.

Ecoshamanic counterpractice relating to food therefore must view nutrition and nourishment in a much wider and more organic sense, where the food that one puts into the mouth has spirit and a meaningful and tangible connection to the life and lifestyle of the person eating it. Simply by making the attempt to put locally grown or raised food into your body, you raise your level of awareness at the most primal and basic level. And growing your own food connects you to a level of organic awareness that those trapped in the world of packaged food can't even imagine.

A simple form of counterpractice is to gather together and compare locally grown organic heirloom produce with the factory-farmed and genetically manipulated produce from a normal supermarket. The heirloom tomato or corn won't look as perfect, but what about the spirit? Which was naturally grown with pride and harvested with sweat, and which was chemically grown to satisfy stockholders and harvested with machines bigger than a house? Which promotes the organic reality of life in the place where you live, and which promotes the abstract reality of dollar bills and national debt?

When engaged in this counterpractice, one of the first noticeable shifts in conscious awareness relating to food will be the difference in uniformity between organic heirloom produce from small farms and gardens and the biotechnology-created produce available at the supermarkets. To be sure, genetically modified crops may have some outwardly impressive characteristics, such as uniformity, increased yield (in some cases), and inherent resistance to certain diseases and pests. But this comes at a heavy price in the long run because it is only in the wild that the mixing of genes continually replenishes the vitality of a food crop. Naturally proliferating plants develop into countless varieties, with each having unique shape, color, flavor, yield, and natural abilities to ward off predators. When we interfere with this grand process and the dance between species and predator by selectively manipulating the genetics of the crops, we interrupt or even cancel out the ongoing evolution of the species and end up with nothing more than a genetically stagnant and spiritually devoid food product.

When you look over the sea of uniform vegetables available at the super-mega mart, you witness a profound loss of individuality—similar in many ways to the monotony of continuous commercial advertising that promotes everyone to do and buy and think in the same way. But when you see the uniquely imperfect qualities of hand-grown organic heirloom produce, you see a mirror reflecting the individual personality of both the local land where it was grown and the diverse personalities and spirits of those who grew it.

COUNTERPRACTICE 15: Psychic Food

Ecoshamanic counterpractice relating to food, if approached in a way that openly pervades our consciousness at many levels of MBES awareness, can transform into a deep form of relating to the world at a psychic level. In most cases the way that modern humans, especially city dwellers, approach their sustenance is devoid of any kind of intentional psychic connection, primarily for two reasons. First, much of the overly processed foodstuffs that we eat have been bleached, dyed, synthesized, formed, and packaged to such a degree that the ingredients of such products are barely recognizable, and normally we wouldn't have a clue what was in them unless we read the package they come in. In terms of "spirit," these food products are pretty much dead and don't elicit any type of psychic response in us. Also, when it comes to meat, especially poultry and red meat, people that are open to a psychic connection many times feel an immediate revulsion to factory-raised meat products because at some level they feel a psychic connection to the horrible lives that these animals led and the way they died in the factory slaughterhouses. Tragically, many people that feel this sickening psychic energy become turned off forever to intentionally fostering a psychic connection to animals that live a natural, healthy life and that die in a sacred and appointed way that provides sustenance for other creatures, including humans.

Second, most of us have never experienced a positive psychic connection to our food, and so we don't even know how to do it or even that it's possible. If you have never learned and experienced the sacred arts of gathering wild foods, hunting game in a respectful and sacred way, or growing your own vegetables and herbs, there is no way that you could be expected to even know that the reality of a psychic connection to your food is even possible.

As a first approach to entering into a psychic connection with food, a powerful form of ecoshamanic counterpractice is to intentionally go to where the food you will eventually eat is being grown or raised. Seek out an organic farm and ask to be present at the time of planting, and then go and sit with the plants periodically, sharing with them the sunlight, rain, wind, and sense of place they are growing into. If you are a meat eater, go to a free-range farm and spend time with the animal you will later eat, and then pay to be there when the animal is killed and butchered. Or engage in a sacred hunt, as described on page 225 of this book. Learn about what it takes to get that meat onto your plate. In most suburban areas it's possible to find a small-sized meat farm that will take special requests, and in many places where there is diverse ethnicity among the community there will be meat farms that cater to the special butchering requirements of religions that have not forgotten some of the sacred aspects and respectful actions that should be taken to honor the animal whose flesh you make your own.

When you sit down to a meal that includes plants that you knew and that you gave thanks to when they were being harvested, or an animal that you bonded with in a psychic or spiritual way that feeds more than just your physical body when you eat it, then the act of making the flesh of plants and animals your own flesh becomes something infinitely more nourishing and powerful than simply fulfilling your appetite.

COUNTERPRACTICE 16: Relating to the Elements

Initiations with, and knowledge received from, the five fundamental elements of life—earth (soil), water, air, fire, and spirit/space—is at the heart of ecoshamanism. The names that we give to these elements are purely symbolic; they simply describe the fundamental forces and energies of the world, both internal and external to the human organism. There is nothing in our world that is not formed and sustained by the interactions of these five elements of life.

Although working with the five elements is such an important aspect to ecoshamanism that we will be dealing with this topic in many upcoming sections of the book, I am including a first approach to the elements here in this section on counterpractice because it is imperative that we engage the elements with a form of awareness that begins not in the typical way of the ego looking out, but rather from the perspective of what is seemingly outside of us looking in.

This perspective is the reverse to what we are accustomed. The world of the shaman doesn't start with his own mind and extend out, but rather the shaman learns to make what is "out there" a seamless part of his own perception. The world, and the reality of all life and spirit, was here far before us; it is we that are born from it. We are not unlike a flower that has sprung from the earth and receives its nourishment by taking in the sun and the rain, by circulating the sacred air through its body and turning the nutrients of the soil into a creative expression of its true being. When we work with the elements at a shamanic level, we need to proceed with this kind of feeling in mind or else all we are doing is projecting ourselves into the environment. The way to relate to the elements on an eco-shamanic level is to become initiated by them, to encounter and learn from them on their own terms and truly experience that what is without is within.

The waters of the earth are fundamentally no different from the water of our bodies. The heat of the fire is the same as our metabolic fire within. Our flesh is the flesh of the world from which it is destined to return. The air in our lungs is communal to all aerobic life. The space that holds the world and all the elements is the universal continuum of matter and consciousness that we are at one with.

It is easy during the course of everyday life to forget our primal connection to the elements, and so many times the innate sacredness of the elements is most readily appreciated by their temporary absence. When we are deprived of any one of the elements, we at first yearn for it, then we crave it, and if we are deprived further from any one of them, we die. It's that simple. In the freezing cold we yearn for fire. In the desert we rejoice at the sight and nourishment of water. When at sea for many days we often kiss the ground upon returning to land. It is often forgotten that far beyond our physical and psychological reliance on the elements, which becomes readily apparent in extreme conditions, is the simple fact that the elements are sacred because they provide and sustain our very lives. What could be more sacred than that? If you need to be reminded of the sacred aspect of the elements, just try not to breathe for a few minutes!

Working at an ecoshamanic level with the elements doesn't necessarily mean we need to give up our modern understanding of physics, chemistry, ecology, or psychology. Working with the elements provides us with the most fundamental and underlying aspects of these disciplines. The optimal functioning of any species is in a healthy environment, and as human beings our quality of life is directly related to clean air, pure and plentiful water, fertile earth, and moderate temperatures.

In the same way, the condition of our internal elements also affects the quality of our lives. When we are in balance, our blood pressure, insulin, hormones, and so on are within a certain optimal range, but when there is an imbalance, we suffer or even die. Our emotional state naturally fluctuates in a healthy way, but severe imbalances are debilitating. When our internal elements are balanced we can more easily face environmental extremes, such as cold temperatures or intense physical work, and internal pressures, such as stressful relationships or frustrating tasks. But when we are out of balance not only is it more difficult to handle challenging situations, but even moments and situations that should be happy and rewarding lose their flavor. Through working with the elements, we can deepen our understanding of what it means to live in a healthy environment, both inside and out.

As we learn to associate the elemental essences and energies underlying them with the qualities of our life experiences, emotional states, personal decisions, cognitive modes, and physical tendencies, we gain insight into our balance, within and without. The first step is greater understanding of the dynamics and interplay of the elements. From that basis of understanding we can then apply our knowledge of the elements to any situation, any circumstance, in any context and in any dimension. The descriptions of the elements that follow in this section are intended to make a first approach to this immense field of study and practice.

The context I am using for these descriptions is that of an ecoshamanic practitioner, not a medical doctor, traditional psychologist, or ecologist. These descriptions aim toward arousing in you a sense of how your life corresponds to elemental essences and energies, to recognize imbalances and tendencies, and make creative and practical adjustments based on honest observation, intuition, and critical assessment. The descriptions are general and simplified, and one needs to always remember that the elements are constantly interacting with each other, they are always part of one another, so dividing them up into five is merely an exercise to emphasize the core qualities of each element.

This last point should also be remembered when applying elemental knowledge to your personal organism. The elements inside you are never wholly separate; they are always dynamically interacting, and the balance between the elements is always fluctuating. With this in mind, there are two main ways that we can specifically relate our physiological and psychological makeup to the elements.

The first is more like an overall assessment of our personal elemental makeup. It is very enlightening to raise awareness of particular elemental essences that are naturally strong or weak within us. For example, some of us are naturally more creative than others (strong fire). Some of us are naturally more steady and grounded (strong earth). The important thing to notice when corresponding the elements to these traits is whether or not they apply to you because they are naturally strong or weak within your personal makeup, or if certain traits that you associate with yourself are merely a consequence of your past life experiences, some of which may no longer apply.

The second way the elements relate to us is on a more immediate level of experience. For example, situations that arouse strong emotions correspond to elevated levels of the elements associated with those emotions. Also, habitual behaviors and reactions are associated with certain elements being dominant of the others. The most important thing to remember is that within the microcosm that is your human organism, and the larger macrocosm of the natural world around you, the balance of the elements is always dynamically shifting, changing, reacting, counteracting, and so on. Because of this, all of us have the inherited and innate ability for transformation.

In the descriptions that follow, I have listed as "luminous" the human qualities that we readily identify with because they are usually seen as positive traits for a person to have. On the other hand, those qualities that we tend to not associate with who we are, even though they may be perfectly visible in us to someone else that knows us, are listed as "shadow" qualities, as they are often seen as being less than positive traits to have, but are equally tangible and valid.

Earth

Luminous qualities: grounded, steady, focused, strong, stable, earthy, practical, dependable, conservative, sensual.

Shadow qualities: dull, slow, possessive, overly materialistic, stubborn, bull-headed, self-centered.

If we are lacking earth qualities we feel like a ship lost at sea, constantly looking for a place to land. We move from this to that without completing what we have started. We move in and out of relationships or jobs, never quite feeling secure with other people or with ourselves. We tend to change living spaces a lot and never seem quite satisfied with our home. We lack a sense of place and we are constantly searching for things that will make us feel secure, whether it is material items, people, or situations of authority or control. Lack of earth energy tends to cause us to neglect our physical needs or abuse our body. It also contributes to dissociation toward environmental concerns as we become lost in the world of imagination. This can lead to a lifeless view of the natural world (Earth as a chunk of rock) and identification with purely human concerns.

When the earth element is too dominant within us we are inflexible, rigid, dull, sluggish, and narrow-minded. We are closed to new ideas and experiences and stifle our creativity and passion with rigid routines and predictable actions. Oftentimes we can spend years or even an entire lifetime stuck in the same rut, unable to shift or change. This can lead to depression, melancholy, and despair. Too much earth energy dulls our senses, makes us insensitive to the problems of others, and allows us to turn our heads and shun responsibility. We may become overly practical, cynical, and skeptical. Too much earth energy can make us antisocial, reclusive, or obsessed with triviality. It can lead us to feel a compelling desire to acquire an escalating quantity of material possessions and/or money. We may become reliant on only the physical aspects of touch, taste, sight, smell, and hearing, while neglecting our creative and intuitive potentials.

When the earth element is balanced within us we feel stable, confident, and grounded. We are keenly aware and not easily swayed, deceived, or knocked off balance. Comfortable and secure in our actions and intentions, we are neither too rigid nor too flighty. We have determination to succeed in our goals, without being obsessed by them. We have resiliency to accomplish tasks that can lead us to opportunities for success. We embody the stability to be aware of greed and manipulations in others and ourselves. We have a reverence for all life and the ability to see the true web of connections and circumstances of our actions. The cycles and seasons of the natural world are alive within us, and we renew ourselves and honor our relations. Connected to the unconditional love of the earth, we are able to love unconditionally. We honor and learn the knowledge of growth, sustenance, and the use of plants and minerals to heal diseases.

Activities steeped in earth energy include gardening and land reclamation projects, and developing relationships with and reclaiming forests and populations of other rooted beings. Intentional burial (which will be discussed in depth in chapter 6), and deep connection to caves and caverns are also appropriate for earth energy.

Air

Luminous qualities: communicative, spontaneous, flexible, refreshing, intellectual, open-minded, idealistic, and objective.

Shadow qualities: impractical, insensitive, tactless, and inconsiderate.

When the air element is deficient within us we have difficulty expressing ourselves to others, as well as not honestly listening to our own inner guidance. We can become stuck in the middle of things, and we can't shake off worries and concerns and lack the ability to move on. We may lose common sense and not think things through before acting. We lack the motivation to reflect on issues, and our curiosity is stunted. Without the air element it is more difficult to engage in spiritual practices and transformational activities. An imbalance in air restricts the channels of breath and visualization.

If the air element is too dominant we lack inner gravity and fly from this to that, or we can be easily pulled along or dragged into things. Our emotional state can change and switch with lightning speed. Our mind becomes overactive and must be guided and brought back to center or else our thoughts become scattered and fragmented. We can become interested in hundreds of things all at once and we delve into concepts and activities but we never master any of them. Tending to overanalyze everything, we seldom are able to make a firm decision. The flightiness of too much air separates us from the physical, grounded, and mundane but necessary activities of life. Overintellectualizing can cause us to not deeply relate emotionally, physically, and sexually to other people, and we may have a general lack of sensuality.

Balanced qualities of the air element within us promote open and clear communication with other people, with ourselves, and with our environment. Air energy promotes the power of speech, the written word, poetry, and music. When air is balanced we acknowledge the interconnectedness of all life and the relationships between all things. We are inspired toward mental balance, freedom, and curiosity. We are open conduits for creativity, inventiveness, and intellectual discourse. Air also opens us to the magic of spiritual and mystical phenomena.

Air energy is stimulated by direct exposure to the wind at the top of mountains, and in wide valleys, canyons, deserts, and plains. Breathing techniques that promote the opening of creative and meditative channels, as well as social activities that engage in spontaneous expression and creative writing in any form, all help in the movement and deployment of air energy.

Water

Luminous qualities: fluid, sensuous, calm, relaxed, receptive, emotional, sensitive, compassionate, and complex.

Shadow qualities: moody, raging, easily influenced, self-pitying, and wavering.

If the water element is deficient within us we live a rather dry emotional life; we lack joy and feel uncomfortable with other people and with ourselves. We don't appreciate things and find little pleasure in life. We may appear cold to others and lack sympathy, empathy, and compassion. We have little passion for life. As a result of diminished emotional expression, we may develop acute psychological and physical problems. We retreat from any form of challenge or confrontation. The lack of dynamic fluidity may leave us feeling cold, as in a lack of blood flow, or it may cause a buildup of emotional or physical toxins.

When the water element dominates us we may feel like a pebble being constantly tossed and turned in the great sea of our emotions. Oversensitive to our emotions, we bounce between laughing joy and weeping sadness, self-confidence and self-pity. Common to holding too much water energy are mood swings and extreme emotional behavior. Or we may feel as though we are drowning in our emotions, and feelings of vulnerability may arise. If we retain too much of the water element we may feel overwhelmed or even paranoid and so turn to secretiveness. The sensual qualities of water may cause us to become compulsively amorous and overly sexual.

With a balance of water energy we experience contentment and joy in being alive in a way that is not reliant on joyous external circumstances. As we embody joy, it tends to flow from us to the people we meet and the situations we encounter. We are able to fluidly move in and out of situations, knowing that sometimes we are required to be calm and gentle, and on other occasions forceful and dynamic. We are flexible and cooperative. Compassion is embodied as a calm, mirrorlike wisdom. When water is in balance, it makes the soil of earth fertile to the creativity and passion of air and fire.

The water element is stimulated inside of us when we simply let things flow, when we don't hold back our emotions, and when we intentionally place our body into the flowing water. The acts of giving and sharing also encourage this energy, as does the sharing of sweat and tears with others.

Fire

> *Luminous qualities:* passion, energy, inspiration, creativity, will, eagerness, spontaneity, independence, and enthusiasm.
>
> *Shadow qualities:* forceful, consuming, domineering, and overbearing.

Without enough fire within us we lack vitality, vigor, and inspiration. Lacking proper levels of energy, drive, and spirit, we may become pessimistic, distrustful, and aloof. Deficient in enthusiasm, it is hard to find joy in our work or in our relationships. Life becomes a plodding cycle of boredom. A lack of fire energy can also cause one to lose faith and connection to their spiritual path. If spiritual practice perseveres with a lack of fire, it is often an uninspired and repetitious practice that doesn't lead to greater understanding or fulfillment.

Too much fire energy can cause one to be easily agitated, insensitive, and even hostile. Anger and irritability are ignited easily, resulting in impulsive actions and lashing out at others. Too much fire makes us intolerant of other people's views, philosophies, religions, and race. We can fly off the handle over any little thing and quickly shout blame at others. A dominance of fire energy can make it hard to sleep, meditate, relax, or even just sit still. When fire dominates us there is a general lack of peace and quiet in our lives.

When fire energy is balanced within us we have a high degree of passion for life, but we don't let our fire rage uncontrollably. We have the drive to create, initiate, and complete the important undertakings in our life. Guiding our impetus are the intuition and insight that are the essence of the fire element. Balanced fire allows us access to our most primal awareness of the interconnectedness of all life. Fire connects us to our star, the sun, and the sun connects us the universe. When we attend to this interconnective awareness, we may become more mindful not to waste our life force on self-centeredness and self-indulgence. Fire teaches us the true meaning of power and how every one of our actions reverberates through the universe. Mindful of our actions, we begin to understand and develop ways of using our energy in proactive ways that may facilitate healing and purification. In this way, the fire element inside of us becomes an agent of transformation, transcendence, and regeneration.

Fire energy is stimulated by bursts of physical and creative action. Activities that speed up the rhythm of our organism, metabolism, and cognitive functions raise the level of fire energy. Think of it this way: when you connect to a tree, your rhythm slows and you could touch or hug the tree indefinitely, but if you put your hand in a flame, you will draw it back as quickly as possible. This applies to fire activities as well. Strong physical activities, such as chopping wood for the fire, will only last a short while, but during that time the fire level inside of you could be very high. This also goes for creativity. Those moments when your creative expression just seems to pour out of you normally don't last continuously for days on end. But when you are inside those moments, your organism is filled with fire energy.

Spirit

Luminous qualities: being, clarity, animation, expansiveness, and spaciousness.
Shadow qualities: lack of presence, spaced out, lost, and wandering.

Spirit is the animating force imbuing all life. Although what we call spirit has no mass, volume, or any other physical or chemical qualities that allow us to measure or quantify it scientifically, the mysterious animation of life itself has traditionally placed spirit as one of the five primary elements. In the context of the elements, spirit can be seen as analogous with life force, imbuing inanimate matter with life and giving it purpose and meaning within the vast reaches of space and the cosmos. Therefore, a lack of spirit or life force would leave a person weak and feeble, not exactly as with a deficiency of the other four elements but more in the sense of "being." Without strong spirit within us we lack a sense of purpose, and although we may have lots of fire, air, water, or earth energy, we lack a sense of a higher purpose for our actions and life. Without the binding force of spirit we can be more easily dominated by the other elements. Spirit can also be correlated to space since everything emerges, exists, and disperses in space. When we lack a sense of space we feel the world is closing in on us; we don't have enough time for everything; we rush, forget what is truly important, and lose sight of the bigger picture.

Having too much spirit may sound absurd when thought about rationally, but spirit, and a sense of spirit, is a mysterious thing, and when it dominates our life too much it can throw other aspects of our existence off balance. For example, when a sense of spirit is absent we lack direction, and everything is a bother. But when spirit is overly present, things aren't perceived as bothersome, but neither are they important. Our job isn't important; our relationships are superficial; if things get done, okay; if they don't get done, that's okay, too. In terms of space, too much spirit correlates to being somewhat "spaced out." There is undoubtedly a certain wisdom to be found in emptiness, but when the sense of expansiveness and space dominates us, it becomes difficult to take care of ourselves and we lose touch of what it means to be a healthy, functioning human being.

When spirit is balanced, we feel fully seated in our sense of being. We have time and space for everything. The other four elements of our being are brought into harmony and balance. We have clarity and focus and purpose, but our actions are tempered with an awareness of expansive humility. A sense of our vast, spinning universe is combined with the immediate presence of the moment.

Spiritual energy is stimulated when you touch the spirit of other beings and places of the world so that you feel the universe as a continuum of spirit-consciousness. The best ways to find the spirit inside of you is to become aware of the spirits surrounding you. Explore the world at the numinous level and see into the deeper meanings of the activities and circumstances around you, and look deeply into the hearts of animals, plants, and trees, and then stand back and feel the collective spirits that form the sacred places on Earth. When you feel at one with those spirits, you also have found new strength and meaning to your own spirit.

Elemental Energy Flow

Along with relating the essences of the fundamental elements to ourselves and our lives, we can also focus on working with how these elements energize the actual physical functions of our human organism. The five main functions of energy within us can be correlated to the five elements in this way: the life-force energy animates spirit, the upward-spiraling energy is related to earth, the downward-spiraling energy relates to water, the centrifugal-spiraling energy refers to air, and the centripetal-spiraling energy relates to fire.

These five energies have often been also referred to in shamanic terms as the five "winds" or "lights" that animate and flow through our body. At the most fundamental level, the energy, wind, light, or spirit that animates the universe pervades everything and is, as such, indistinguishable. However, we are able to discern a multitude of unique physical and conscious phenomena that are given life by this pervading force. And we can also discern how this force manifests and flows through our body in different ways and at different levels.

Life-force energy: Life-force energy is the fundamental animating force of our human organism and corresponds to the heart. Highly trained shamans, yogis, martial artists, and other disciplined practitioners of balanced life-ways often display seemingly supernatural abilities that arise from strong life-force energy. When this energy is potent within us we are vital, when it is absent we are dead. Life-force energy is contained by everything that is alive. The ultimate shamanic expression of this energy is manifest when one can transfer it from one center to another. This traditionally is a technique that enables a person in a deep ESC to embody the life force of a particular element, plant, or animal, or also in the imbuing of energy from the shaman into an object, a person, or any other entity.

Upward-spiraling energy: Upward-spiraling energy manifests in the human body as cognitive awareness and also gives life to the main five physical senses of sight, hearing, smell, taste, and touch. This energy is that of the earth itself; the complexity of the functioning and balanced systems of the earth correlates to the complex systems of the human body, particularly the brain. This upward-spiraling energy gives rise to thought, perception, and intellect, as well as awareness of the spirit essence. It is associated with the flight of consciousness; the ability to jump, rise above, fly, and enter the upper regions of consciousness and spirit.

Downward-spiraling energy: Downward-spiraling energy is the movement of physical connection to the world through such phenomena as urination, defecation, orgasm, and child delivery, among others. It is the water energy, the most prevalent of the tangible elements, and its energy connects our fluid internal cycles to both the great flowing hydrologic cycle and the mystical forces revolving around sexual union.

Centrifugal-spiraling energy: The outwardly moving, centrifugal-spiraling energy totally pervades our human organism and is responsible for the complex interconnected systems of communication throughout our body. Nervous-system function, blood flow, oxygen and nutritional distribution all occur as expressions of this outwardly spiraling energy related to the all-encompassing and continually moving element of air. This energy of movement expresses our connection to the world through our body movements, facial expressions, vocalizations, and attitude. The centrifugal-spiraling energy is widely used by shamans in an enormous variety of ways. It is related specifically to shamanic forms of seeing, clairvoyance, and communicating with the numinous realms.

Centripetal-spiraling energy: The centripetal-spiraling energy is our inner fire and is responsible for our body heat and metabolism. Our bodies are like small furnaces, and the inwardly spiraling energy accountable for this can be subtly affected though our normal day-to-day activities, states of mind, and physical activities. This inward energy is often related to meditation, contemplation, and dreaming. Inner-fire energy is not easy to significantly manipulate, but through conscious long-term practice of techniques related to this internal energy it becomes possible to affect the rise or fall at remarkable levels. Shamans who learn to become aware during dreaming, or exhibit an imperviousness to the influence of the other elements, are said to be highly connected with the centripetal-spiraling energy of inner fire.

Developing counterpractice relating to the elemental energies involves critical awareness between healthy levels and deficiencies or imbalances of these energies in the function of your human organism. Sometimes it is difficult for us to recognize these imbalances for ourselves, and if that is the case for you it is a good idea to work with someone you trust and simply ask them to review the material I have just provided and give you their assessment about what they see in you. From there, you can take the suggestions of how to stimulate a specific energy from the text above and develop a strategy of practices to balance your energies. In any case, whether you have the ability to recognize the current balance in the energies of your human organism or not, if you try a variety of practices with each of the elements and energies, and you find some that are much more uncomfortable or unappealing to you, those are the practices that, more than likely, are the ones you need.

That is the secret challenge of counterpractice: identifying those areas of yourself that you don't identify with, and then forming a strategy to incorporate them. Sometimes the realization of what areas to work with come spontaneously, but other times, especially when dealing with the fundamental elements, which is a subject we are not normally accustomed to dealing with, we can become confused or unsure and we need something or someone to jar us or free us up so that we can look at ourselves from a different perspective.

When relating counterpractice to the fundamental energies, and to get a feel for what this type of counterpractice implies, I sometimes have clients go through a list of common expressions that include the elemental energies, because through finding the obvious and also the hidden meanings behind these verbal expressions, you can view each of them as they relate to your life and your current personality. For example, if you are in a long, heated discussion or involved in an emotional situation that just has you flabbergasted, you may decide the best thing to do is go out and "get some air" to clear your head, so that you might then "clear the air" with the other person. It is interesting to note that when taken literally, these expressions are somewhat strange, but in a deeper context they are perfectly natural, and at a shamanic level they hold the power to awaken us to our multilevel relationship with the energies that sustain us. Here is a short list of phrases that can be used to stimulate the sometimes-hidden aspects of our relationship to the fundamental energies:

Air	Up in the air (unsure)
	Get some air
	Walking on air (to be happy)
	An air of . . . (characteristic look, appearance)
	Clear the air
	On the air (like radio or TV)
	Air thick with anticipation
	Out of the blue
	Kiss the sky
	Winds of change
Earth	Down to earth
	Move heaven and earth
	Unearthed
Water	Above water
	Hard water

	Holy water
	Hold water
	Pass water
	Tread water
	Troubled waters
	Mouthwatering
Fire	On fire
	Go through fire and water
	Misfire
	Open fire
	Play with fire
	Set on fire
	Set the world on fire
	Under fire
	Fire an employee
	Fire up
Spirit	Brave spirit
	High spirits
	Show spirit
	School spirit
	Be there in spirit
	Aromatic spirit
	Holy spirit
	Out of spirits

COUNTERPRACTICE 17: The Way of the Clown

The way of the clown is a shamanic counterpractice with the power to explode the limiting confines of identity and behavior imposed on us by others that would judge us. As the policeman and the banker represent authority in the "civilized" Western world, the clown represents authority and counterbalance in the shamanic world. These are not the clowns of our children's parties, whose role is limited to blowing up balloons and performing parlor tricks. The clown of the shamanic world ritualizes and satirizes human behavior on a ceremonial stage and possesses extraordinary power, privilege, and license to express outrageously antisocial behavior that to an outsider would seem utterly disrespectful, perverse, or even psychotic. This type of clown exists in almost every indigenous culture in North America and in most shamanic traditions throughout the world, and the role of the clown is always embodied by a person that has been given great powers of vision and insight.

The shamanic clown speaks to the contrary, rides his horse backwards, and not only converses openly about those things usually not spoken about, but acts them out in public displays. The complete freedom of expression granted the clown is not limited, and so shamans, chiefs, and other high-ranking authorities are often the subjects of the clown's metaphysical comedy. By fooling around and poking fun at everyone and everything, even the most sacred of things, the clown is in reality performing his own type of spiritual ceremony.

The way of the shamanic clown need not be limited to these insightfully perverse indigenous people who live on the border of counter reality. In my experiences with the Wirrarika, as well as other surviving shamanic cultures, the way of the clown becomes in certain moments a state of mind that everyone in the community openly participates in. Before I realized what was happening, and so could enter that level of reality with them, I have stood absolutely mortified on more than one occasion as I witnessed what appeared to me as totally inappropriate behavior by some indigenous people during extremely important rituals and ceremonies.

On one occasion during a three-night-long ceremony inside one of the principal ceremonial centers of the Wirrarika sierra, I was seated around the fire with four shamans and a host of assistants and kawiteros when one of the younger men began speaking intimately with the fire, an act which in itself is absolutely normal for Wirrarika. As he continued to speak, his voice became louder and his gestures more animated, until at last he started sobbing and tears swelled up in his eyes and ran down his face—which, again, is completely normal for Wirrarika when they speak with the fire. But as soon as the young man began to cry, all the others around the fire began to laugh! And the louder the young man sobbed and spoke pitiful words to the fire, the harder the other Wirrarika laughed, until some of them were actually rolling on the ground, holding their stomachs and covering their faces in unquenchable laughter.

Finally, when things started to settle down a bit, I managed to ask one of the shamans why everyone was laughing so hard at the poor guy. The answer caught me completely off guard. Everyone was laughing because the young man was doing a hysterical impression of the oldest kawitero, who later that night, with the whole community gathered by the fire, would recount a very long and ancient Wirrarika story in which he always cried and sobbed for hours on end while reliving it for the people. Apparently, while there was a short "break in the action" of the ceremony, and anticipating what was to come, the young man spontaneously began comically imitating the old kawitero to the absolute joy and humor of everyone there, including the elder kawitero, who was laughing at the comical impression just as hard as everyone else.

It is important to note that this type of behavior is not uncommon in their world; in fact, it is completely normal and it is one of the features of their culture that to me is so fascinating and ultimately empowering for those who live it. In one moment these people will be engaged in the most sacred and solemn activity, and in the very next moment they will be joking and laughing uproariously. They live inside this amazing reality where every part of life and every action is serious and sacred while at the same time nothing, absolutely nothing, is above ridicule, absurdity, and humor—especially between family, friends, and spiritual companions. That is the way of the clown, and in terms of shamanic counterpractice it can be a powerful tool for altering consciousness and raising awareness.

COUNTERPRACTICE 18: Moment-to-Moment Counterpractice

As I said in the beginning of this section, since ecoshamanism is the antithesis of the materialistic worldview, one of the ways that the shamanic world can start to appear in front of us is when we engage in activities completely foreign to the habitual modes of being imposed on us by modern society. The techniques of counterpractice that I have laid out so far have been some of the big ones that are aimed at deep levels of awareness. But there are also thousands of smaller forms of ecological counterpractice that, when combined, can create significant momentum and radical shifts in consciousness. Therefore, to end this section on counterpractice, I'm going to list some smaller conscious-raising forms of counterpractice that can be performed during daily life. Keep in mind that I'm not considering all of these simple things to be shamanic practices, but when taken all together these types of actions, when done on a daily basis, can affect considerable changes in the way you perceive the world, and that is one of the main goals of the ecoshamanic project.

- Reclaim your mind and revolt against the brainwashing of commercial advertising. If you see a product being advertised, don't buy it. Seek out local products and those from small businesses that aren't mass marketed.

- Every time you see or hear an advertisement, state out loud what button it is trying to push inside of you.

- Try to never buy another disposable battery.

- Don't kill insects. Adopt a spider.

- In the summertime when people are watering the biotic desert they call a lawn, turn off their sprinklers that are running during the heat of the day, and adjust the ones that are watering more driveway and sidewalk than they are lawn.

- A sheet of paper has two sides. Use them both.

- Create something beautiful and then give it away to someone you don't know and will probably never see again. While you are giving it you may feel regret, but you will learn that you need not possess something to own it.

- Read *The Man Who Planted Trees* by Jean Giono, and then see how it feels to be like him.

- With the help of a friend for safety, blindfold yourself for twenty-four hours while still performing many functions of your everyday life.

- Spend a whole day exploring various tasks in a wheelchair.

- Walk backwards for a half an hour each day for a week.

- Take a tape recorder with you and record yourself during various conversations and situations. Is that really you?

- Tell a total stranger a secret that you've never told anyone before.

- Tell yourself lies in front of a mirror. Tell yourself how great you are, how good looking, how intelligent, smart, funny, successful . . . after a while, the lies and the truths are all the same. Do it now.

- Read out loud all the ingredients of the packaged food you eat each time before you eat it.

- Put the specialness back into simple items—only use one plate, glass, fork, pair of shoes, socks, or underwear.

- Color your world without petroleum-based paint products.

- Never buy or eat anything that comes in Styrofoam. Tell businesses you currently frequent that you will go elsewhere unless they provide alternatives.

- Use a cloth rag, not a paper towel.

- Each time you flush 3–5 gallons of water down the toilet, become aware of how wasteful it is to defecate into water that is made pure for drinking.

- Say "thank you" to everything. If you stub your toe, say "thank you" to the kid's toy that caused you pain. Before you start to eat, say "thank you" to your fork.

- We've all seen the "adopt a highway" signs. What about adopting something really important, like a stream or an old-growth forest?

- Revolt against helium party balloons. They always seem to end up where they don't belong.

- Make peaceful rebellion your church. Revolt against your own self-imposed limitations, and those put on you by society. If your rebellion feels uncomfortable, then you're doing it right.

- Adopt an endangered species.

- Don't put your groceries into anything but a reusable cloth bag.

- Don't speak for at least two days. Spend your time listening instead. Write it out if it's really that important.

- Just like a child who knows the world is still a mystery, ask the question "Why?" to everything and to everyone.

4 | ECOSHAMANIC CEREMONY AND RITUAL

The first thing to do when thinking about ecoshamanic ceremony and ritual is to throw out all preconceived notions about ceremony and ritual as fixed, repetitive physical and verbal formulas. Ceremonies and rituals that don't adapt and change through time and along with current circumstances leave us lost as the moving and changing world passes by. If there is one thing that we can be sure of, it is that the world, both at micro- and macrocosmic levels, is always changing and evolving. The desperate clinging to rigid and outdated religious ceremony and ritual leaves one standing in a stagnant pool of ideas and expression. There are, of course, some truths that may be viewed as universal and in that context seem to be timeless, but the inner balance of one's personal self and the outer balance between self and world necessarily must include what is happening in the current moment at personal, societal, ecological, and cosmological levels—and so must be the ceremony and ritual employed to create and maintain that balance.

That is not to say that the old ways must be completely thrown away. It is more of a building upon and co-creating of an evolving stream of growth that I am trying to promote here. Earth still revolves around the sun, and the seasons still come and go in sacred cycles, but the way we live has evolved and will continue to evolve, and so must the ceremonies and rituals we use.

This is one of the core beauties of shamanic cultures, the regeneration and rebuilding of the sacred life through each succeeding generation. In this way the spiritual traditions continue to grow, adapt, and expand with the identity of the people. In place of dogmatic and repetitive procedures, the rituals of shamanic cultures spring from primary human need, and so form a medium of expression unique to the time and place of the particular tribe. Although custom and tradition do provide a framework to the rituals, once inside and engaged in the process spontaneous activity emerges. It is from this spontaneous response inside of the ritual framework that the creative psychic powers of human potential arise and fuse with the creative force of the cosmos.

In the modern world where the process of registering events with the written word creates the illusion of certitude and authenticity to the actions being written about, it is often difficult for us to accept that which arises spontaneously and continues to reflect immediate reality while at the same time avoiding capture by the rational mind or written word. But these spontaneously creative moments are what shamanism is all about, and the more we do to promote the occurrence of rituals that advance authentic and profound moments of sacred unity the more effectively we will be able to apply our spiritual convictions to the problems and challenges of day-to-day life. When this happens the secular and the spiritual cease to oppose one another and instead mingle and combine to form meaning in the midst of mystery.

PRACTICE 19: The Ecoshamanic Temple—Joining the Vortex Circle

The ecoshamanic experience of "place" is not linear; it doesn't conform to the straight lines and grids of orientation that modern mapmakers impose on the land. It doesn't reduce a place to a simple set of coordinates or an address that provides no sense of the experience of the place. The ESC comprehends place and space as an experiential relationship. That is why, when manipulating earthly space, the ecoshamanic mind mirrors not only the local flora and fauna and the historical significance of the place, but also the workings of cosmic space. In this way a union of relationships is created between the interwoven realities of nature, humans, Earth, and the cosmic rhythms, so that the conception of place and the creation of sacred places reflect the interconnected systems of life we all share in.

The creation and continued usage of sacred places can promote deep forms of ESC when deliberately forming cooperation between the builder and the place/space. Such places create reciprocity and express a deep desire to delve into and learn from the natural world, which is much different from a church or temple that is inherently designed to keep nature out. When creating earth-honoring and reality-based sacred places, the defined space serves as a model of the world and cosmos. It gives one a center, a place from which to relate to the world, the universe, and life itself. Without such places, the complexities of life have little grounding and more easily soar out of control.

Although there may well be a structure built, or other form of demarcation to the temple, such as a stone ring, this merely serves to ritually define the center from where the actions inside the sacred place revolve and evolve. In this way the actual process of making such a sacred place is as important as the use of the place when it is complete. The creation of such a place is really a co-creation with forces much larger than yourself. It is at once a partnership and an internship, and it is a conscious expression of the desire to be one with a greater power.

Working with Stone and Other Natural Materials

Historically, many of the world's great monuments and sacred places have been constructed with stone. The mere physical presence and durability of the earth's bone, along with internal qualities representing cohesion, strength, and wholeness, among others, make stone an obvious choice for many types of shamanic sacred places. Included among these are stone circles, medicine wheels, cairns, dolmens, and various types of pyramids. Oftentimes within these places stone is used to form lines and avenues, or stone monuments can take the form of standing or recumbent stones placed in meaningful and creative ways.

An interesting aspect to stone-made sacred places, and other sacred structures of indigenous shamanic cultures, is that in many cases the builders and users are in a continuous state of constructing and renewing the site. For example, the ancient site of Stonehenge shows almost continuous change in construction during a period of around 2,000 years. Many of the pre-Columbian pyramids of Mesoamerica, which have personally touched my life while I've explored their shamanic past, are actually pyramids built on top of pyramids, sometimes many times over. And the sacred building that has had perhaps the greatest impact on my life, the round ceremonial temple of the Wirrarika, is renewed ceremonially every five years by the painstaking replacement of the entire thatched roof and all the main supporting wood beams, all of which directly correspond to the structure and various components of the earth and cosmos.

Anyone who creates a sacred place is in communion with something larger than the self. Although ecoshamanic practice surely includes communion with existing earth-honoring sacred places, there is no substitute for creating your "own" place. When this small place on Earth is constructed as an embodiment of your spiritual evolution, it can have even more power to you than the biggest pyramids ever created by someone else. With this in mind, I'm going to lay out suggestions for constructing a small open-air ecoshamanic temple that can be used for the following:

- Communing with the earth energies in the area of the sacred place, such as wildlife, flora, and the various expressions of the five elements.

- Connecting with the earthbody as a whole and developing a reciprocal healing relationship.

- Consciously joining in the spinning reality of the vortex circle of our galaxy by honoring the solar and/or lunar movements through placing them at the center of the temple's design.

Choosing the Place

This ecoshamanic temple will take at least one year to construct. For this type of temple, one of the main supporting elements will be the sighting and marking of the rising and setting points of the sun in relation to the temple on the four major solar/earth days: spring equinox (approximately March 21, equal night and day); summer solstice (June 21, longest day); fall equinox (approximately September 23, equal night and day); and winter solstice (December 22, longest night). In order to facilitate this your temple will have to be located on a relatively flat area of ground, and this in itself will help dictate where you will place the temple and also its size. Since the sunset point on the summer and winter solstice mark the turning point of the light of the sun, it is best to be able to clearly see either or both of these events on the horizon in relation to your temple, and locate and design it with this in mind.

Beside the solar considerations, there are a huge number of other circumstances that you could employ while planning where to locate your temple. Some people suggest using ley lines to locate sacred sites, or building them over underground blind springs or deposits of certain types of stone. In the final analysis, my best suggestion is to simply construct your temple in a place that is convenient for you to get to so that you will actually use it. That should be the first criteria. From there, use your intuition and inner guidance to choose a place that feels right to you. All the ley lines, underground water, or quartz rock in the world won't help you if you don't feel comfortable in the place. Spend time in the proposed place, explore the environment and how it feels to you, and then make your decision. Of course, if you already have a special place or area that you are intimately familiar with, that is the best place of all.

Defining the Area

Once you have located a flat area with a good view toward at least one of the solstice sunsets, place a stake in the center of the proposed area, tie a string to the stake, and walk out from the center until you reach what will be the outer circle. Let's say, for example, that you walk out fifteen feet from the center. In this case, your circular-shaped temple will be thirty feet in diameter. To initially mark out your circle, attach a stake to the string at fifteen feet, pull it taut, and then mark the ground with stones or wood stakes while walking around the circumference. Be sure to treat with respect all of the beings that live in and around your circle. Talk to them, explain to them what you are doing, ask to share the space with them, and apologize for disturbing them.

Sighting the Solar Movements

It is best to have two people for this, so that one person can do the sighting for the other person to mark the location. Arrive at the location in plenty of time to be ready before the sunrise. Position one person at the center of the temple facing toward where the sun will rise. Locate the other person at the edge of the circle near to the point where the sun will rise over the horizon. At the moment of the first beam of light from the sunrise, the person at the center directs the other where to place a pre-sharpened stake into the ground, marking the place on the temple circle where the sun rises on that day. The procedure is the same for sunset. Since these special days only come once a year and there is a chance that rain or fog could inhibit your view of the sun on the special day, it is well worth the effort to do this same sighting a few days before and after the actual day so that, if needed, you could very reasonably "guess" where to place your stake until it can be verified the following year.

It could be that your particular site won't have views into the distance on all sides, or that trees, mountains, or even buildings might be blocking certain areas of your view. Don't fret, just remember that the sun's movements will still be obvious and the ritual journey of the sun will still be intimately connected to the solar aspects of your temple.

As this temple will incorporate the honoring of the sunrise and sunset of the four major solar/earth days, at the least you will have six points of your circle marked. Following the traditions of many cultures, you may also want to mark the days that "cross" these four and so divide the year into eight. These special days have historically been associated with the planting and harvesting of crops, as well as ceremonies and pilgrimages of fertility and

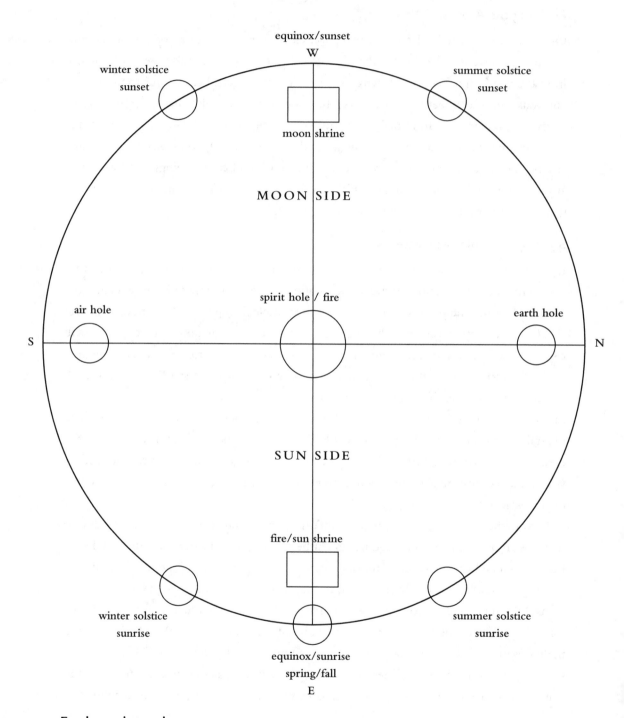

Ecoshamanic temple.

renewal. The cross days are roughly halfway between the solstices and equinoxes: November 1, February 1, May 1, and August 1. However, there is no expressly "correct" date for celebrating these days, for they are merely a window in time.

Regardless of exactly which day you celebrate them, the cross days mark the times of year when most everyone really becomes aware that the length of the daylight is changing. During the November cross, the days are getting noticeably shorter. By February 1, the darkness breaks and the daylight hours are getting noticeably longer. At the beginning of May, you first become aware of how much later the sun is setting in the evening, and by August for the first time you really begin to notice that those long summer evenings are beginning to get a bit shorter. In essence, the solstices and equinoxes mark the beginnings of the great seasonal changes, and the cross days mark the midpoints of the transitions.

Working with the Elements and Directions

Another important aspect of the temple will be honoring your relationship to the five fundamental elements of life, and having the presence of the essence and energy of the five elements will add significantly to your temple. Aside from building a *rirriki* (discussed later in this chapter) for each element, many other powerful items can be used; since this temple is a reflection of you or your group, use your intuition, inner guidance, and creativity as your guide.

For this type of open-air temple, the following are important considerations:

- The sacred fire is almost always placed in the center of the temple. In this case, the center fire represents the spirit/space element. A stone circle (seat of honor) is formed (as in chapter 6 or in a similar way) for the sacred fire. In the center of the fire circle, a small hole (approximately 6–8 inches in diameter, 24–36 inches deep) is dug for the placement of sacred offerings to spirit, and a special stone (preferably round) that is larger than the hole is placed on top of the hole to protect the offerings. In contrast to other locations of the temple, where offerings are routinely made, this hole is reserved for very powerful offerings that mark major life changes like birth, death, etc.

- Since in this case an actual fire will be the center, the fire element will be properly represented by the sun, which is already being honored by the inherent construction of the temple. However, a powerful practice is to place a special shrine or altar either at the equinox sunrise marker (east) or anywhere on a line from that marker to the center fire.

- A powerful way of honoring the earth element is the digging of another hole specifically for offerings (6–12 inches in diameter, 12–24 inches deep). Again, this hole will have a special stone covering the hole. It is good to adorn this stone with engravings or symbolic painting. The placement of this hole is on the planting and growth side of the temple, signified by the sun rising more toward the north in the time of year when flora and fauna are in accelerated growth.

- Ritual objects of the air element, such as ribbons, flags, feathers, etc., are typically placed on a pole or staff located on the winter solstice side of the temple, associated with harvest, hunting, and pilgrimage.

- A shrine for the water element is located on the western side of the equinox line so that the water shrine and the fire/sun shrine complement and balance each other. This shrine could be anything that holds water, such as a large rock with a natural depression, a cauldron, a wooden or stone planter, or even a special cup or vase.

The previous five suggestions related to the five elements can be employed with or without the construction of a rirriki for each; however, incorporating these suggestions into the construction of a rirriki for each element will provide the most flexibility, creativity, protection, and therefore intensity to your work. For example, the water rirriki could include a bowl for catching rainwater, the earth rirriki could sit over the sacred hole, the air rirriki could be adorned with air objects, and the sun rirriki could be designed to track the angled rise of the sun, if sunrise is visible at the equinox. As far as a center/spirit rirriki goes, one option is to not place the fire in exactly the center but place it slightly toward the east/sunrise equinox, and so place the center/spirit rirriki over the center hole instead. This is basically how the Wirrarika do it; I suggest placing the fire in the center just out of personal preference and also because many times space inside the circle is at a premium and simply having the fire over the spirit hole requires less space.

The Feminine and Masculine

Whether you are male or female, what we are trying to create with this temple is balance. From the forming of the foundation to the placement of the tiniest object, the ingredient of balance will be what ultimately sets this temple in place as a microcosm of the universe. This temple is inherently balanced with male and female energy. In fact, the whole temple itself, being constructed on the soil, can be regarded as a woman's womb that, when the sun rises, is impregnated with the ray (or arrow) of the sun to bring fertility throughout the daily, seasonal, and annual cycles. Extending this concept is the offering of masculine and feminine offerings at the equinoxes and solstices. These offerings (which can include prayer arrows for men and votive gourds for women) are placed at the equinox and solstice markers throughout the year.

Working with the Moon

Designing a functioning temple based on lunar movements is extremely complicated. The moon's movement through the sky is like a celestial dancer whose ever-changing phases and monthly swings can challenge even the most dedicated sky-watcher. Basically, the moon makes the same movements through the sky in a month that the sun makes in a year. However, the moon is also part of another cycle that takes place during a period of 18.6 years—whereas the sun has only four positions that mark the limit of its movements (sunrise and sunset on the solstices), the moon has eight. Accurately tracking and marking the course of the moon and its phases in relation to the temple is beyond the scope of this book.

However, honoring the moon and the significance of the moon's movements to all life on Earth is an integral part of ecoshamanic ritual and ceremony. The moon is Earth's natural satellite, and the many relationships between Earth, moon, and sun are truly remarkable. The moon spins on its axis in the same amount of time it takes to revolve once around Earth. From Earth, the sun and moon have an almost identical angular size, which accounts for nearly perfect solar and lunar eclipses. The moon radiates no light of its own. It is the partnership between sun and moon, like a ray of light that a shaman directs into a sacred mirror in order to see, that delivers "moonlight" to Earth's soil and to our eyes.

Placing ritual and ceremonial objects in the temple can be organized by the phases of the moon and the points of rising or setting, if visible or known. Many knowledgeable people, especially female practitioners of earth-honoring spirituality, have written about the significance, symbolism, and rituals that can be associated and employed throughout the various moon cycles. In my experience with indigenous shamanic cultures, it is usually the women who are tied closest to the moon's cycles and associate their corresponding cycles of fertility as a sacred connection.

In addition to these important correlations, many other circumstances make it clear that the moon is central to the sacred balance of our world. Working in concert with the sun, the moon controls the tides of all major bodies of water, and for this reason the moon is associated with water in shamanic lore. Bodies of water, plants comprised mostly of water, animal species both aquatic and terrestrial, and of course human beings (which are mostly water) are all significantly influenced by the complex cyclical force of Earth's companion.

The honoring of the moon inside of the temple can be accomplished through several different dynamics. Since the foundation of this temple is unity and balance, the sun and moon—the two most important cosmic entities to Earth—each symbolically occupy half of the temple. The sun occupies the eastern half, the half that says good morning to the night and greets the day. The moon rules the western half, the half that says good night to the day and greets the night. Following this, the placement of the moon shrine or rirriki will be at the western point or in the west near to the water shrine.

If you are a person that already works closely with ritual significance to moon cycles, another way to work with the moon in this temple would be to create a moveable shrine that could be easily moved with the moon cycles, or a new shrine could be created for each ritual symbolizing your current energetic correlation to that particular moon, as in some Native American traditions.

Other Considerations About Placement of Ritual Objects

There are countless other celestial bodies that can be honored with a special place within the temple. Venus or the Pleiades are two good examples. Also, shrines honoring loved ones who have passed, a new or upcoming birth, or shrines for sacred animals or plant spirit helpers can be created and used effectively inside the temple. Another consideration are sacred places. Sacred places can be re-created inside the rirriki or shrine that correspond to the direction that the actual place lies in relation to the temple, or, in the case of extremely important sacred places, they can have their own rirriki, hole, or shrine inside of the temple.

In any case, the placements of the ritual objects that I have recommended here for inside of the temple are simply suggestions, and you could certainly design your temple however you like. But keep in mind that the design of the temple that I am suggesting follows not only my experience with the ancient and time-tested traditions of indigenous shamans but also demonstrates many design factors that are more or less universal to shamanic cultures throughout the world. The fact that so many ancient and profound traditions, located so very far from each other, could share so many features attests to the validity of the basic founding principles, as well as the more subtle intricacies of this ecoshamanic temple's design.

Opening the Temple

Since the time that you sighted the first solstice or equinox that formally began the construction of the temple, you have gradually added the other main solar days and the many other elements that sing together inside the circle of your personal re-creation of the sacred cosmos. The opening of the temple will commence on the year anniversary of the first solstice or equinox. From this time forward, your temple can be the magical center of your universe and a place of renewal and power. Ask the spirits of the place to help you in knowing the appropriate way of opening the temple. I have laid out dozens of practices in this book that are perfectly suited for integration and use within the ecoshamanic temple and are perfect for use in opening the temple. As you explore these practices, the shifts in consciousness created by them will create a natural momentum for the heightened use and significance of the temple as a grounding source of energy and local point of power in the multidimensional universe. The keyword here is *momentum*—the more you use the temple and add ecoshamanic experiences to both the energy configuration of your human organism and the extension of that energy in the form of the temple, the greater the power of the temple will be as it also merges and becomes part of the conscious-energetic fabric of the larger geographic area.

ECOSHAMANIC DANCE

Our bodies come alive through movement. Beyond the body's basic functions of digestion, metabolism, and procreation is the facility and gift of expression that our body provides for our human organism. This capacity for bodily expression finds its ultimate expression in the art form referred to as "dance." It is through myriad forms of dance that our body gives expression and visible form to sacred aspects of life and being alive. In this respect, the use of bodily motion, of sacred dance, has been a significant aspect of spiritual life for *Homo sapiens* since the earliest of times.

That the body could be used to express relationships between beings and entities living on Earth, and also to connect with even larger spiritual forces, is an idea older than organized religion. The engravings of masked, dancing shamans found in Paleolithic caves provides clues to our earliest connection with this scared art of movement. By the time of the dawn of civilization, dance had become perhaps one of the most highly developed and skillful human activities. But throughout the greater part of Western civilization, and especially in Christian-dominated society, sacred forms of primal and shamanic dance were considered savage activities and were not only rejected but abhorred. Not until the founding of stylized and "proper" forms of dance, such as European ballet, was dance even considered a serious form of expression and art by the Western mind. But this was and is not the case for nature-based indigenous cultures throughout the world, where dance is perhaps the most pervasive and universally accepted mode of connection to the spiritual aspects of life.

For native peoples worship is dance. "Dancing and praying—it's the same thing," said the famous Sioux shaman Lame Deer, and this is precisely why sacred dancing doesn't belong to the rational sphere, and why it's so very difficult to talk about without reducing it to something that it is not. Ritual dancing embraces and fuses together MBESA in a way that expresses the complex relationships between our conscious and unconscious, between our body and mind, between the essence of human spirit and the essences of spirit pervading the plant and animal kin-doms *[sic]*, between the life-giving forces of nature and the total human organism, and between the complex notions of past, present, and future.

Among my shamanic experiences with the Wirrarika, I have found in the union of song, dance, and music the uniting of scattered fragments of my MBESA caused by my internal battle between my felt primal connections with the natural world and the thoughts and images of commercialism and consumerism constantly being implanted into my mind by corporate America. During ritual dancing experiences around the sacred fire, singing responses to the shaman singer, feet stamping rhythmically to the drum and ritual instruments of violin and guitar, beating the pulse of the earth while connecting the universal energy of the fire and stars in the sacred round, I found a unity that transcends any verbal explanation. All I can say is that everything becomes one. The other people dancing the circle, the pulsing vocalizations, the music, the movement, the whirling horizon, the earth, fire, and sky all unite into a timeless space where there is no front or back, beginning or end. There is no order but neither is there confusion; all is one mind, one complex body, undivided and undifferentiated, everything fused together in a spiraling, whirling circle of life.

This type of ecoshamanic activity has immense transformational value, especially in the sense of bringing the spiritual back into the body. This is a most natural form of expression that has a definitive physiological basis. Our body provides us with hearing, sight, touch, taste, and smell, but also other important sensory inputs, such as balance and rotation. From the semicircular canals of our inner ear emerge the impulses sent to our brain that contribute to the fusing of the sense of motion between our MBES and the cosmos when we are engaged in sacred dance. We also have a kinesthetic sense that operates through the feeling of pressure in our muscle tissue receptors that provides us with the sense that we are moving, the speed of our movements, and what kind of surface we may be moving on. Far beyond the purely practical function of these senses is the more primal awareness that we are provided with when we attend to them.

Although I never condone the direct copying of native traditions simply because they don't apply to the day-to-day lives of modern people, there are many models of indigenous dance that can be extremely helpful in developing modern ecoshamanic practices. While developing practices such as ritual dance we must be careful to accentuate rather than bypass the underlying expression and understanding of how the dance connects us to the sacred. For example, if we are to embrace the spirit of a dance such as the Hopi Kachina Dances, where tribal dancers embody the spirits depicted by the famous Kachina dolls through elaborate masks and costumes, we must attend to the fact that the dancers are not merely impersonating the natural or supernatural being the costume represents, but rather they are living those spirits through their human organism. This means that the outrageous, grotesque, and humorous actions sometimes exhibited by the dancers are not at all confined to, or overtly planned by, the mind, personality, or ego of the human being inside the costume. And the dance, the costume, and the whole public ritual is but one small component to a complex spiritual life that is intricately woven into the very fabric of everyday life. This, of course, is not at all witnessed by those spectators who are simply viewing the dance.

This type of dance, along with other native dances such as the Sioux Sun Dance or Pueblo Deer Dance, is for the dancer a way of unifying self-expression with self-surrender. It is a harmonious example of cooperation between humans and the greater forces of the cosmos. When we enter into this kind of activity, we transform ourselves into beings of an expanded world; thought and action become fused, and we become the embodiment of the mysterious forces of creation.

PRACTICE 20: The Five Directions Dance

The type of dance I will now introduce is characterized by what is called "homeopathic ritual," in that the intention of the dance aims to influence or unite the outside forces of the dance it is concentrating on. For example, in homeopathic hunting rituals, the depiction of the pursuit and slaying of the animal during the ritual that is held prior to the hunt is aimed at influencing the actual spirit of the animal on the day of the hunt in order for the animal to willingly sacrifice itself for the benefit of the tribe. The rites of the ritual before, during, and after the hunt are all necessary components in the respectful and reciprocal relationship between the humans and the entities that support their lives. This type of homeopathic ritual is commonly used in shamanic cultures for everything from the growth of crops to the birth of a child or the bringing of rain or peace.

In this dance, we are transforming our total MBESA into a replica of our universe, from the minuscule spiraling strands of our DNA to the whirling mass of energy/matter/spirit that is our Milky Way galaxy. This is accomplished through the rotating movement of our body around a central axis, while at the same time revolving around the circular area of a sacred fire. Inside of this celestial movement we add the honoring of the five main elements of life within our body and throughout the world, and the five sacred directions through the careful and rhythmic steps of the dance. By way of this simple yet profound act, we can deliberately:

- Connect to the revolving, circular, spiraling reality that pervades the life of our body, the earth, the solar system, and the galaxy.

- Acknowledge the spirit in Earth and flesh by bridging the earth and sky with the human body.

- Employ both physical movement and psychic interchange in active cooperation with the forces of nature.

- Alter our breath, circulation, groundedness, metabolism, and creativity, thereby achieving a new relationship with our internal chemistry of air, water, earth, fire, and spirit.

- Use rhythmic body movements, and the rhythmic sounds resulting from the movements, to "drive" us into altered states of consciousness.

- Honor and connect to the five directions, and the sacred places associated with them, through the steps of the dance.

- Join the single bodies of the group of people together into one spiraling microcosm of the universe.

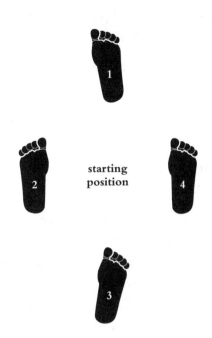

starting
position

Steps for the Five Directions Dance: At the end of the first four steps, your left foot will be at the fourth position and the right foot at the third. At that point, simply step with your right foot to the first position and start over again. Once you do it a few times it becomes very fluid. The fifth direction is the center (spirit, yourself).

These are just a few of the main circumstances promoted and nurtured by this eco-shamanic dance. With practice and through time you will no doubt discover many more of your own personal aspects and reasons for engaging in it.

To perform the five directions dance:

• Stand with feet shoulder-width apart, facing the fire.

• There are four main foot placements to the dance. At this moment, your left foot is in position 2 and your right foot is at position 4. Position 1 is one step directly in front of you and position 3 is one step directly in back of you.

• To start the movement, step forward with your right foot, placing it from 4 to 1.

1. At the moment your right foot hits position 1, lift your left foot from position 2 and return it to position 2; thus you have just stepped "in place" with your left foot.

2. At the moment your left foot lands back on position 2, step to the back with your right foot from position 1 to position 3.

3. At the moment your right foot hits position 3, step across with your left foot from position 2 to position 4.

4. At the moment your left foot lands on position 4, step with your right foot from position 3 to position 1.

5. Start the circular movement again by stepping with your left foot from position 4 to position 2.

During the movement, your left foot is going between 2 and 4 alternately, while your right foot is moving between 1 and 3. This will feel a little awkward while simply stepping slowly between the four positions. The next step in learning the dance is to simply speed up the movement slowly and create a rhythm to your four steps. The way to do this is to perform the steps while only having one foot on the ground at a time. This means that the other foot that has not landed in one of the four positions is off of the ground and moving to its next spot. This creates a sort of one-foot hop or jump from one position to the next. While learning the dance, it is perfectly fine to exaggerate this hopping movement in order to get the feel for the movement.

The principal idea while learning the dance is to alternately place, as fluidly as you can, your right foot, left foot, right foot, left foot, while following the circular pattern of the 1–2–3–4 positions of the circle. The fifth direction is the sacred center, in this case honored and symbolized by your human organism.

The Five Directions Dance is almost exclusively performed around a fire that was brought to life in a sacred and intentional way. The "seat" or "bed" for the fire is formed by a circular ring of stones. Once you have learned how to rhythmically "dance" the movement of the five directions dance, your momentum will naturally pull you to move from the place where you started. When this happens begin to "steer" yourself in a circular manner around the circle of stones containing the sacred fire. When a group of people is engaged in the dance this normally occurs spontaneously as each member of the group becomes a satellite for the fire.

Another element of the dance that usually arises spontaneously, or can be introduced intentionally, is to accentuate the placement of stepping toward the fire (position 1). There are many ways this can happen. One powerful way is to reach with your right arm toward the fire while you step in toward the fire with your right leg, and with your hand "grab" the energy of the fire and bring it back toward your body. You can bring the fire energy back to your chest, stomach, genitals, head, or wherever you spontaneously need it. Another way to accentuate the inward step is to vocalize something during the step. A word, a shout, a guttural noise, a soft whisper—any type of vocalization can be used. When sharing this dance with modern people in groups, I have seen many forms of spontaneous expression arise from the inward step, but normally the most powerful occur when the whole group is vocalizing the same sound or word.

Because of this, in the beginning it is sometimes helpful for groups just learning the Five Directions Dance to have an experienced person "lead" the dance in a way that pulls the group into the vortex and then keeps them there when some of the satellites might start thinking about it too much or begin to let their mind talk them into being tired, or hot, or whatever else could be thought up to prevent the dance from continuing. With groups of people unfamiliar to dancing around a sacred fire, an experienced ecoshamanic practitioner familiar with the dance will be invaluable for helping to ease the people into the vortex, and also to be there if any of the participants are overcome by emotion or fall too deeply into some kind of primal trance state.

When performed at a high level of intensity, the Five Directions Dance affects multiple levels of MBESA and an ESC is fostered to a degree unexplainable by words.

PRACTICE 21: The Spiral Dance

Another dance that creates heightened states of awareness and that can be performed with large groups is the Spiral Dance. This dance is also performed around a center fire and begins with the group holding hands and forming a complete circle around the fire. The performers follow the leader and at the dropping of hands the leader turns and begins a walking/skipping/dancing movement that draws one end of the circle around and inward toward the center in a gradual spiral (usually clockwise). Upon reaching the center, the leader turns and reverses course so that the spiral folds around itself. As the spiral grows outward again, the leader can bring it back to a circle or begin the spiraling process again.

This dance is aided by the use of drums, either one or many, played to the beat of the dance, and by songs, chants, or costumes. It can be used in a wide range of situations and for different intentions. The rotating effect of the Spiral Dance is perfectly suited for celestial observances such as solstices and equinoxes, or anytime a group has the intention of joining energy and honoring the spiraling reality of the cosmos. These occasions include ceremonies for healing, where all the dancers are uniting their energy toward a common feeling or goal, to mark a special occasion, or to honor a sacred site. The unique folding of the dancers within the various parts of the spiral provides a powerful space and pattern for the mingling and uniting of energy in a naturally occurring shape the pervades the universe.

Another way I sometimes use this dance is to connect the dancers to each other by having them move very slowly and look briefly into each other's eyes as the spiral folds back and forth on itself. When night, fire, shadows, reflections, and movement come together and meet with the profound wells of emotion and intelligence found in your companion's eyes as you dance the spiral, a connection beyond words is formed and doors of perception that are rarely seen become open and accessible.

PRACTICE 22: Dancing Our Relations

When "civilized" people view the primal behavior of shamanic tribes as they dance wildly around dressed as animals, stomping their feet, and drumming and rattling with their homemade instruments, they are usually inclined to feel themselves wholly separate, with nothing in common to these unsophisticated humans. But what I have learned through more than twenty years of exposure to shamanic rituals, together with a lifetime of experiences in the "civilized" world, is that the same impulses that drive shamanic tribal people are also embedded in modern people. It's just that the process of civilization has caused us to withdraw from the natural world and so our primal awareness is rarely or never given a chance to unfold and express. When civilized people are given the proper setting to unfurl their primal awareness and express it through movement and vocalization, a miraculous transformation occurs that expands the consciousness and breaks a person free from the one-dimensional, rational-linear perception they had been stuck in.

One of the effective practices of movement that can draw out primal awareness is the ecoshamanic ritual of dancing the spirits of animals. This type of dance is the ritualistic embodiment of the embedded relationship of humans in the more-than-human world of nature and spirit. The dancing of the animal spirit is not simply an imitation of the animal but rather a transformation of consciousness—so the dancer doesn't just perform an emulation of the animal, the dancer becomes transformed into what animates the animal. Although the overall experience of dancing an animal spirit may be enhanced by a costume made from the actual animal, it is the movement that is most primal to the dance.

Every animal, including the human, expresses itself with movements that are not purely utilitarian. These movements are made from the spontaneous relationship between the genetic makeup of the animal and the life that is unfolding in the environment surrounding it. Even more than the utilitarian movements of the animal, these spontaneous expressions are what give the animal what we would call its "personality." When these movements are embodied by a dancer, they provide access to the essence of the animal in a way that the dancer can become part of the movement in a primal and non-self-reflective state of consciousness.

Dancing an animal requires for you to have intimate, bodily felt experiences with the animal at a level that allows the animal's movements to appear spontaneously in the form of your dance. In the following section on animals and animal spirits, I have included specific practices that can lead to this level of connection to an animal.

At this level of connection, dancing our animal relations becomes a magical action of participation and celebration with the larger community of life. This ritual form of movement is perfect for celebrating with others during ceremonies or festivals, and especially when in the company of the fire, which assists in calling the primal awareness out from the depths of your soul while you dance.

CREATING CELESTIAL RITUALS WITH MEANING AND HEART

Rituals form an intricate part of our lives. From "putting on our face" in the morning before work or how we tie our shoes or stir our tea, to the annual family vacation or celebration of holidays, we all have countless rituals that we play out on a daily, monthly, annual, and continuous basis. But the kind of ritual involved with marking and celebrating celestial events is completely unique in that these events are so much larger than our merely human concerns that they go on happening whether we are aware of them or not. These events are so grand in scale that they are even beyond holy in the ordinary sense because they were happening long before the human concept of holy even existed. They provide the basis for everything we know about space, time, and the continuum we call the universe. Rituals that connect us to these events can be joyous occasions because they have the inherent power to join people together in a sense of unity that is rarely felt outside of ritual time.

Creating and performing ecoshamanic rituals to synchronize with celestial events can be given extra power when performed in a sacred placed designed for honoring these windows in time (such as the ecoshamanic temple described earlier). However, the most important criteria for creating or participating in these rituals is that you do it in a manner that has meaning to you. The depths of experience and the knowledge and understanding that follow them is a continuing process of unfolding that evolves along with your efforts, your desires, and your offerings. Right now, our moment in time is different from any other time period in history and our rituals must express that or else they are just repetitive exercises. My best suggestion for learning about, creating, and participating in celestial rituals is to glean all you can from reputable people, books, and media while always keeping an open heart and mind, but at the same time never losing touch with what feels right to you. Then test everything you learn from secondhand knowledge by doing it yourself firsthand. At that point, let your own unique energy and circumstances guide you in unfolding your creative response to what you feel in your heart and what you feel deserves sacred honoring and offering. Be true to your newly acquired knowledge by not turning your back on it just because it's difficult to continue or you feel pressure from others who may not fully understand. And most importantly, never, ever, fail in completing a shamanic offering, especially if it was made during a ritual where a significant connection was made with powers much greater than yourself.

An enormous quantity and variety of written material now exists on how our ancestors, other cultures from throughout the world, and current groups of people celebrate and ritualize celestial events, such as solstices and equinoxes. This information can be an important starting point when beginning to engage in these practices, and I will not go over them again here. However, I feel it is important when formulating our own personal rituals to have a clear understanding (even if we don't completely agree) of the more or less universal concepts and concerns that have historically been associated with what we are doing. Since it may take you a considerable amount of time to gather the relevant information as pertains to celestial ecoshamanic ritual, I'm going to briefly summarize some of the main points to provide a foundation from where your own creativity and circumstances can take control of the construction. Be aware, however, that since celestial rituals coincide with different life circumstances according to the location of each unique place in relation to the sun, moon, and other heavenly bodies, these suggestions may be more relevant to your location at a different time of year. My suggestions here are most relevant for those in the Northern Hemisphere, and they particularly incorporate my personal blend of experiences from northern Mexico and the southwest and northeast United States.

PRACTICE 23: Solstice and Equinox Rituals

Ritual celebration of solar and lunar events have, by and large, been deemed archaic, outdated, or "pagan" by modern societies and not included in what might be considered spiritual or religious activities by the mainstream Western religions. But these celestial events transcend religious ideology, as they are numinous astrophysical episodes that have been celebrated by intelligent and highly spiritual people for tens of thousands of years. They give order to chaos and provide the very foundation of our seasonal cycles and temporal being.

To a large extent, what defines a culture is the way it relates to temporal reality. The rhythm or pulse of society is defined by its activities, its rituals, and its calendar of special days and events. This is an intricate kind of synchronized dance that underlies the culture and provides order so that individuals, families, and groups are joined to a much larger functioning unit. But today, instead of our activities and cycles being determined naturally through the interaction between our pineal gland and the seasonal rhythms of the sun, we have all but ignored our body's natural rhythms and replaced them with "clock time," nanosecond "computer time," and economically staged holidays. The result of this is that we have become a kind of temporal anomaly because much of what would instinctually and naturally determine our temporal reality is now culturally orchestrated by our human-centered concerns rather than by human–nature/cosmic realities.

The acknowledgement, celebration, and ritualized significance of the cyclical celestial events such as solstices and equinoxes, along with many others, are the perfect and most obvious way for us to rejoin the temporal realities of organic life on Earth, as well as the spiritual mysteries of being alive. Although this type of cosmological awareness can be experienced quite unexpectedly during the course of our lives, we can intentionally set ourselves in a place of receiving (and offering to) the perceptual revelations of cosmological awareness by consciously synchronizing our total human organism with the cyclical foundation of our solar system, our galaxy, and ultimately the great mystery that moves all. Within these experiences of direct perception (or in shamanic terms, "silent knowledge") the perceptual boundaries that we are normally aware of fall away, inner and outer dissolve, and we are left with a primary awareness of the whole.

Winter Solstice

Ceremonial Dates: December 20–23

Modern Observation: December 22

Traditional Date: December 22

For nature-based cultures in the Northern Hemisphere, the season of winter is a very difficult time. The growing season has ended and the tribe has to live off of stored food or whatever animals they can find. The people feel the dormancy and death in the environment as the life-giving sun sinks lower in the sky each noon. In ancient times, they even feared that during these days of the year the waning sun would eventually disappear and leave them in permanent darkness and extreme cold.

But although the day of the winter solstice is the shortest day of sunlight in the year, after this shortest of days and longest of nights the sun slowly begins to rise again on the horizon each noon. This is why winter solstice is not only a time of awareness of death and darkness but also a day of celebration, because even though many hardships and some of the coldest days of winter still remain, the rebirth of the upward movement of the sun will begin with the dawn after the longest night, and so the return of the warm season is promised. The concept of death and rebirth is naturally associated with the winter solstice and is at the core of the rituals and celebration of this time.

Suggested themes for rituals: Death and rebirth, self-examination, resurrecting dormant projects, conservation.

Winter Quarter

Ceremonial Dates: First week of February

Modern Observation: February 1 or 2

Traditional Date: February 5

As the days lengthen while the sun has been gradually gaining in height and strength since the winter solstice, by the midpoint between winter solstice and spring equinox the land begins to slowly awake from the winter slumber, seeds begin to stir in the womb of the earth, and the living beings rejoice at the return of light and life.

This is a time for inspiration, initiation, and purification. Although there is no set date, among my Wirrarika companions this is the time of year when the annual pilgrimage to the sacred desert of Wirikuta is usually made. The waxing (increasing) light of the sun is both a tangible and symbolic reference from which to gain inspiration and manifest renewal and rebirth at personal, ecological, and spiritual planes. As the land has been purified by winter in preparation for renewal in spring, our synchronization with the cycles requests that we do the same. Many shamanic cultures include rites of passage and initiation in their ceremonies for this part of the year, especially concerning puberty rites and rites of fertility.

Suggested themes for rituals: Purification, transition, initiation, fertility.

Spring Equinox

Ceremonial Dates: March 21–23
Modern Observation: March 21
Traditional Date: March 23

With the light restored and the darkness driven off, the land fully awakens, and the life force smiles and sings throughout the land in the form of flowers, bees, and new life of every kind being born. Balance has been restored to the world as day and night are equal. The trees have begun to bud and put on their coats of green, and the fields are beginning to show signs of new life. Animals are bearing young, and for subsistence cultures fresh meat can be had for the first time since the culling in the fall, and the first fresh sprouts of greens are gladly received to nurture the body. Birds are laying eggs, an ancient symbol of fertility and of the circle of the seasons, and these will soon be hatching into new life.

This is the season to celebrate new life. Now is the time to begin new projects that you have thought about throughout the cold months. Now is the time for action.

Suggested themes for rituals: Birth and creation, balance, life force, creative inspiration.

Spring Quarter

Ceremonial Dates: First week in May
Modern Observation: May 1
Traditional Date: May 6

For shamanic cultures that live solely or in part by subsistence farming, this time of year is critical to the well-being of the community in that the success of the planting done at this time will help ensure life or guarantee death later in the year. This is a time of propagation and procreation at every level. In terms of mood it is one of the lightest and happiest times of the year, as the natural environment is full of life and love and light. Inspiration and motivation for song, dance, and creative pursuits abound.

Suggested themes for rituals: Planting of seeds (both literally and figuratively), song, dance, opportunity, good fortune, happiness.

Summer Solstice

Ceremonial Dates: June 20–23
Modern Observation: June 21
Traditional Date: June 22

Even though midsummer is a time of abundance, the longest day and shortest night marks the imminent decline of the sun's light. As the sun peaks in strength and power, in one magical instant it begins to wane, and so just as the switch in the sun's power brought hope and happiness to the difficult times during winter solstice, the waning of the sun during the time of summer solstice brings a tinge of sadness and sobriety to the abundant celebration of summer. But our awareness of the impending decline in the sun's power during summer solstice only serves to fuel our appreciation of the gifts of summer. One of the most powerful and precious of these gifts are the healing herbs and flowers available in summer that will later be used in winter to treat a wide range of maladies. These herbs hold a place of honor at the summer solstice rituals, as does the sacred fire that from summer solstice on will gain in importance as the nights grow longer and the days get colder.

Suggested themes for rituals: Abundance, strength, energy, fulfillment, fire, fruition, flowers.

Summer Quarter

Ceremonial Dates: End of the first week in August
Modern Observation: August 1
Traditional Date: August 7

The tiny seeds planted in spring have matured and the sacred relationship between earth and sun has produced the first fruits and grains. As we hold these miracles of sustenance in our hands, we are humbled by the mysteries of life and thankful for the gifts of food that have been created for us. As we take in the energy of the first grains and fruits, this is a time of robust health and erotic energy. But it is also the last chance for us to celebrate in the warmth of the sun, and our minds are beginning to concentrate on the safe completion of the harvest that will see us through the winter.

Suggested themes for rituals: First harvest, joy, celebration with fruits and vegetables, sexual vitality, planning, completion.

Fall Equinox

Ceremonial Dates: September 20–23
Modern Observation: September 23
Traditional Date: September 21

Everything seems in perfect balance. The day and night are equal, the crops that we planted are providing for us, all the work we put in has come to fruition. The September equinox is a beautiful and magical moment in time, and it deserves our recognition and honor. Of all the important celestial moments, this may be the most important for modern people to reconnect with because it is the one that has been the most tragically lost. While other important celestial days have been transformed into modern economic holidays, without a Santa Claus, Easter Bunny, or Great Pumpkin, this important moment in time goes by largely unnoticed. And so, for those of us that are in tune with the sacred cyclical reality of organic life, we cry and we laugh, we recognize and we rejoice, we try to make a difference and we celebrate, we prepare for the future and we reflect on how far we have come, we feast and we give thanks.

Suggested themes for rituals: Harvest, bounty, cooperation, balance, thankfulness, cautiousness, preparation.

Fall Quarter

Ceremonial Dates: End of the first week in November
Modern Observation: October 31
Traditional Date: November 7

This being the last festival before the sun begins its revival, it has historically been associated with completion, change, and death. Although some customs treat this with ghoulish morbidity, the organic response to this moment in time is more practical, and in shamanic terms can be viewed as a moment infused with positive energy and filled with hope for the healthy future of our planet. The fall quarter is a time to look into the future, and so it is a time for recognizing change and opportunity and what we hope to accomplish in the coming year. As we honor the passing of the crops that nourish us, we also honor the passing of loved ones. With full awareness of the coming winter, we remember the happiness of the harvest just as we remember the loving memories of our departed. A simple and practical activity that touches the spirit of this time and prepares us for winter is the ritual making of candles.

Suggested themes for rituals: Impermanence, change, honoring the dead (both humans and other beloved beings), final preparations for winter, firewood, candle making.

PRACTICE 24: Pilgrimage

For indigenous shamanic cultures the land is everything, and their land-based spiritual practices are rooted in the specific places that comprise the sacred landscape. The stories of creation and the oral history of the tribe are embedded in the land. These narratives educate the people about tribal history, ethics, and spiritual values. They contain oral maps of sacred places, information about kinship with plants and animals, and most importantly they continue the cultural identity of the tribe through the retelling and passing of the stories to the next generations. Since each tribe has developed, as part of its own sacred landscape, the oral stories that accompany them will, of course, be unique to each tribe. But although the stories and history may be different from one tribe to the next, one common component to shamanic cultures is the periodic visiting of the places sacred to the tribe in order to honor the spirits of the places and the bones of their ancestors, and to continue the sacred traditions of reciprocity with the land.

Since before written records, pilgrims have traveled great distances to venerate the sites most holy to them to receive visions, instructions, and guidance. In the bottom line, it is the interaction between the people, the land, and the spirits who reside there that sustain a nature-based shamanic culture. And that is why shamans, whose charge it is to ensure reciprocity, regularly endure great hardships to travel the sacred road of the pilgrim. Having spent many years engaging in pilgrimages to sacred mountains, deserts, canyons, and bodies of water, I can attest that this is a road that also can be taken by modern people in order to enlarge our view of reality and seek vision for our lives.

A pilgrimage is fundamentally a journey, but it is a sacred journey that is infinitely more than just a there-and-back-again trip. Although all pilgrimages have their own unique dynamics, to aid in the illustration of what this may imply I'm going to lay out eight basic steps or circumstances commonly found in the pilgrimage experience.

1. There is a reason, a calling, a longing, or some other type of hope, desire, goal, or obligation that produces the inspiration to depart on the journey to the sacred place.

2. There is preparation for the journey. This includes mental, physical, spiritual, and logistical preparations that often include ritual purification, the making or purchas-

ing of offerings to give to the sacred place, the saving and collecting of resources including food, clothing, and money to make the journey, and arrangements for taking care of your affairs at home while you are gone.

3. There is the moment of departure when the sacred time officially begins. This occasion is sometimes marked with great happiness or can be very solemn, depending on the circumstances. In any case, from this moment on there is no chance that the pilgrim will return unchanged.

4. There is the journey into the mystery. No one can say what will happen to the pilgrims once they leave home for the sacred place. The journey itself is full of messages and hidden meanings for the pilgrims as they deal with the internal and external circumstances of sacred travel. Sometimes there are other special points or places during the trip that mark significant thresholds to cross along the way.

5. There is almost always a major hardship or obstacle that creates doubt but fosters strength once it is overcome. Sometimes there are many of these, and if they become too great it may be a sign that the moment is not right and the pilgrims should turn back. I have seen obstacles as large as a baby being born prematurely to a pilgrim in the middle of the desert, which at the moment seemed like a tragedy, but in the end was a blessing of the largest kind imaginable.

6. There is the arrival to the sacred place and the joy of having made it. In many cases this is just another beginning, because there may be a lot of work to do once the pilgrims arrive. For example, although the trip may be exhausting and full of difficulties, when I travel on pilgrimage with my Wirrarika mentors to the sacred desert of Wirikuta, once we arrive we have two full days of hunting and gathering the peyote, at least two sleepless nights of visionary experiences with the fire, the spirits, and the shaman singing or the kawitero retelling the stories of creation, and then the demanding physical hike to the top of the sacred mountain for the making of offerings. Other times there may be work to do in order to help preserve the sacred site or special duties of reverence to perform, such as the building of a rirriki. In any case, during this step the reason for the journey is addressed and the spirits of the place are petitioned and honored.

7. There is the turning around and bringing home of the gifts and/or the pain. If one has found what they went for this could be a joyous time, or if one has been

disappointed or injured it could be very hard, but in all cases there are lessons to be learned and circumstances to be contemplated.

8. There is the welcome home when you return and the integration of your experience into your life. Sometimes you will tell your story to your loved ones and other times you will keep it to yourself. But no matter what, you will have to assimilate your journey into the context of your life and your future.

In a similar way to the Embrace of the Earth rite of passage described in chapter 6, you should be very clear about why you are going on the pilgrimage and what you hope to find. Fasting and any other types of purification are helpful prior to departure in order to help you gain clarity. When traveling to a sacred place in nature to ask for something important to your life, you should always make a reciprocal offering in return, and it is a good idea to leave a representation of that offering in the sacred place and/or make the offering out loud in front of your companions/witnesses in order to seal the deal.

Once in the sacred place, be sure to be open and attentive to absolutely everything around you because you cannot predict in what form a message or signal might come. There is a vision of some kind waiting for you and it is your responsibility to make yourself available and not to let it pass you by. Stay true to your reason for being there and do not let small obstacles grow into large distractions.

There are many reasons to make an ecoshamanic pilgrimage, but none better than to seek a vision to guide your life. For this reason I go on a special pilgrimage once a year, usually in December or January to the same place if possible, and this journey represents my New Year no matter what date I go on. In this type of pilgrimage you recount your year to the sacred place; I usually do it during most of the night in the company of the fire and some other pilgrims. Then I present a handmade physical representation of my perceived goals for the following year and petition the sacred place for any information relevant to what I aim to do. After that is done, either directly or after being witness for my companions, I go alone to the sacred place and ask the spirits of the place to communicate with me about what I have shared. Depending on what I learn from the place, I make one or more concrete offerings to carry out during the coming year.

For example, after a recent pilgrimage where I learned a great deal from the sacred place, I was guided to offer something back to the spirit of the indigenous people, specifically to the Wirrarika children. I made the offering to the sacred place but I did not know what it would specifically be until one day shortly afterward. I was talking to a Wirrarika friend and he mentioned that he thought it would be great if the Wirrarika children could see the children's book I had made with two other Wirrarika friends who created the illustrations. I immediately knew that was what the sacred place had in mind for me and I spent about six months arranging everything. In the end, with the generous help of the publisher, I acquired a large number of books to be donated to the Wirrarika children.

This is just a small example of how the procedure of commitments and offerings give strength to the whole process of learning from sacred places, and especially in those moments when you have journeyed a long, hard road during a pilgrimage. The pilgrimage process, when used as a catalyst for personal and spiritual growth, healing, honoring, and offering, is a powerful vehicle that can help steer us into the heart of the sacred place so that our heartbeats become one.

ECOSHAMANIC TOOLS AND SACRED OBJECTS

The tools that shamans use to assist their work are usually very sacred objects; however, sacred objects are not necessarily shamanic tools. This distinction is extremely important, especially for people learning about shamanism through secondhand sources and books. Many modern people interested in shamanism are under the erroneous assumption that finding a beautiful feather in the woods or a special pebble at the beach is a valid way of acquiring powerful shamanic tools. While these items may be sacred to the one who finds and treasures them, and they certainly may have the potential to be used in shamanic work, they lack the powerful force of intention characterized by shamanic tools that have been painstakingly earned, made, and imbued with the power of sweat and blood, which acts as a catalyst to join the shaman with the natural spiritual essence of the object.

A treasured object of a deceased loved one, a family heirloom, a special gift from a respected teacher or famous person, a magical eagle feather found in a special moment on a pilgrimage, all of these objects can be considered extremely sacred to the owner. Their unique significance holds a special power over the owner, maybe even to the point that they would defend the object with their very life. The implications of this, and the special meaning of the objects to the owner, cannot be overstated. However, a powerful and sacred shamanic tool such as a deerskin drum that is handmade by the shaman through successfully accomplishing a sacred ritual hunt, skinning, scraping, tanning, and seasoning the skin, fabricating the drum frame, assembling, and ritually consecrating the drum, among many other tasks in the making, is a far different type of sacred object that carries an exceptional form of intent.

Also, the sacredness or the apparent power of a sacred object or shamanic tool doesn't automatically mean that it is the best tool for a shamanic task. For example, a few years ago I was given an incredible gift from a powerful and famous Wirrarika shaman. This man, who is now in his late 80s, and is the father and grandfather of literally dozens of my Wirrarika companions, some of whom are now respected shamans in their own right, was once so well-known for his shamanic abilities that the famous Mexican artist Diego Rivera painted his portrait. During one of my stays in his remote mountain community he surprised me by walking unannounced into my hut (which he enjoyed doing quite frequently) and presented me with two of his feathered *muvieris* (the name of the staff or wand used by Wirrarika shamans). Needless to say, I was greatly honored, and to this day I keep those muvieris with my most sacred shamanic tools. But in my shamanic work (unless I want to invoke the presence of the old shaman) I almost always use my own muvieris that I painstakingly made myself from my own connection to the spirits. For working with the ESC, the muvieris that I made from material that I acquired, consecrated, and have ritually used hundreds of times are always my first choice.

One of the main points here is that shamanic tools work in the same way as any other tool except that here we are dealing with the sacred, spiritual, or healing aspects of the cosmos. Shamanic tools are made with very specific purposes in mind. The making of these tools is a fine and delicate form of art that combines the unique essence and energy of the materials used with the intuition, skill, knowledge, and internal force of the creator.

MUSIC AND SOUND

Some of the most potent shamanic tools are those used to produce sonic vibrations and melodic rhythms. The drum is by far the most widely used shamanic instrument of sound. But many other instruments are employed by shamanic cultures, and can be grouped into four broad categories:

Idiophones: instruments that are shaken, struck, or rubbed

>*Rattle:* The most common instrument of this type. Types include gourds with seeds, pebbles, or teeth inside, or multiple strung objects such as shells, bones, teeth, or hooves fastened to a frame of some kind or a simple object that is easy to grasp.

>*Bell, chime, gong:* Often made of stone, wood, or metal, and struck by hand.

>*Concussion drum:* Gourd or hollowed-out wood that produces sound by hitting the open end on the ground or other flat surface.

>*Rasp:* Typically made of wood, bone, or stone that has been serrated so that another object can be rubbed across it to create a unique sound.

>*Clapper:* Usually either a single cylindrical-shaped piece of wood or reed that has been split partway, or two such objects hit together.

Aerophones: breath or wind instruments

>*Whistle:* Usually thin bone or reed hollowed to create a single tone.

>*Oblique whistle:* An object that makes sound by blowing across the top (like a thin-necked bottle).

>*Bullroarer or buzzer:* An object that is attached to piece of cordage and swung in the air.

>*Flute:* Reed, bone, wood, or clay instrument designed to create multiple tones using one's breath.

>*Trumpet:* Usually a shell, horn, or gourd, but sometimes wood, as in the didgeridoo.

Membranaphones: taut skin drums

>*Frame drum:* One or two heads with skin stretched over the frame.

>*Talking drum:* Skin tension can be manipulated to change pitch.

>*Cylinder drum:* Usually shaped like a barrel, cone, or hourglass, sometimes with feet or a hole in the side.

Clay or ceramic drum: Sometimes these drums have water just underneath the skin of the drum head.

Chordophones: taut string instruments

Mouth bow: String held by mouth and either plucked by hand or tapped with a stick or bone.

Resonating bow: String is run between the sides of a gourd, basket, or other hollow object.

Harp: Multiple strings that are plucked or strummed.

Violin: Wood-carved instrument with single or multiple strings that is played by dragging other strings across it.

No matter what instrument or manner is used to produce shamanic music or sound, the most distinguishing feature that all shamanic forms have in common is that they are not composed or written on pages as notes to be followed. This unwritten form of making sound arises from the immediacy of the moment and is not so much dependent on the well-respected skill of the musician but on the sound itself as representative of one of the primeval forces of creation. In this sense, ecoshamanic music is the sound of the natural world made immediate and audible through the miracle of the interaction between instrument and ear—a resonance without, becoming within. This dynamic interplay recognizes sound as a spiritual space itself, rather than a particular space containing sound.

The impulse to create shamanic sound arises from natural inspiration, an inner longing to connect with a harmony much larger than oneself. It addresses the total MBESA toward the promotion of ecstatic experience *inside* the sound, rather than trying to understand the perceptual meaning of the sound or the music. Some sounds are created in festive atmospheres, while others are the product of lonely suffering or visionary experiences. Sounds and songs of healing arise from the mysteries of life and death, while diligently carved instruments provide the music of courtship and love. Some shamanic songs are utterly personal and never shared, while others, when shared, have the power to join entire nations.

The making of musical instruments as ecoshamanic tools at once connects us to our ancient ancestors while at the same time provides us with an immediate experience of a primal nature. One of the main reasons for this are the basic ingredients of ecoshamanic instruments: bone, stone, wood, skin, and cordage. Working with these materials gives the instruments an elementary form so basic that they inherently contrast with the modern tools and technology that we are accustomed to using. Within themselves, they create a primacy in the user and creator that is seldom, if ever, felt in the modern world.

By far the most popular shamanic instrument throughout the world is the drum, and there is no experience quite like the ritual making of a skin drum from start to finish. Even though most modern people interested in shamanism don't make their drums from scratch, the popularity of drumming and drum making have led to a proliferation of books, courses, and workshops where when one can learn about drum making, so I will not get into the specifics here. One point I would like to stress, however, is that no matter what instrument you are making, it is important to realize that the instrument will only sing through you as loud as your connection to the instrument. In shamanic drumming there is no replacement for the vibration of personal energy emanating from a skin that you personally removed from an animal. The act of skinning and fleshing, more so than the act of killing, which any fool can do, is a skillful and ultimately personal, primal way of connecting to and honoring the spirit of the animal whose skin you will be drumming on. In an upcoming section on working with deer I will talk more about this.

PRACTICE 25: Gourd Rattle

The gourd was such a singly important natural item to early man that it is often referred to as the womb from which the culture of mankind emerged. It lives in human consciousness as the mother of cultural life where nature meets human, where human meets the spherical universe and the seeds of life. The gourd is the universal womb incarnate on Earth. It floated in the world's oceans, crossed the Atlantic, and spread its seed throughout the globe long before humans existed on Earth. In every early human culture the gourd was used as water bottle, cup, bowl, plate, and spoon. Its buoyancy helped create floats for fishing and the construction of rafts. Gourds were used in medicine, masks, games, penis sheaths, and shamanic offerings and charms. And, of course, the gourd was one of the first musical instruments.

The gourd rattle is an extremely potent ecoshamanic tool that is relatively easy to make. Its potency derives from many sources and symbols, both on the physical and metaphysical planes. For ecoshamanic work, what you place inside the womb of the gourd is what provides the central power of the instrument. Dried corn kernels (especially if you grow the corn yourself) will sing inside the rattle of the interplay between earth and sky, rain and sun, fertility and life. Small pebbles from a riverbed sing the voice of the water spirit, while pebbles from an anthill re-create the unique energy of the place from where the evenly sized pebbles were collected. Another powerful choice is to use the teeth of animals or the beaks of birds so that they can walk, fly, and sing once again through the voice of the rattle.

The sound that the sacred items you place inside the rattle make will correspond to the energy of the objects. Soft as rain will be grains of rice or beans; hard as stone will be pebbles or crystals. Each different rattle will have not only its own unique sound but its own unique aura and life, for when you truly place items that mean something to you, that are alive to you, inside the rattle, the rattle becomes alive when played. The significance of this cannot be overstated. A rattle handed to you by someone else can surely create magic in the right circumstance, but a rattle that you make and that sings to you of the place of the rattling objects, or the life of the being whose essence is inside of the rattle, every time you pick it up, will be the type of powerful instrument you will want for deep ecoshamanic experiences and practices.

Gourd rattles are fairly simple to make and there are many informative books on gourd craft available to get you started in fashioning your own rattle. But no matter what style you choose to employ in the making of your rattle, in order to transform it into an ecoshamanic tool the most important aspect is your relationship to the spirit of the items that will sing through the rattle. The deeper your connection, the more powerful an ally your gourd rattle will be.

PRACTICE 26: Bone Whistle

The whistle is one of the most ancient shamanic tools. Throughout the world thousands of bone whistles have been found in Stone Age graves, and throughout Europe they have been found in archeological sites from every era. In many of the most sacred and important rituals and ceremonies, many ancient and contemporary shamanic tribes of the Americas also use whistles of bone, wood, and reed, and horns made of shell and the horns of animals to call the spirits.

In a setting of shamanic ritual, the blowing into a sacred whistle or horn breaks the surface of our consciousness to begin a streaming flow of what lies beneath. The unique sounds that vibrate out of the various types of whistles and horns call out to the natural world and cosmos of both the seen and unseen to mark the beginning and ending of ceremony and ritual, to announce the arrival of pilgrims to a sacred site, to awaken the energy

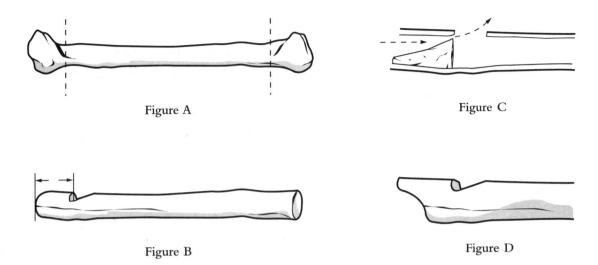

Figure A

Figure C

Figure B

Figure D

How to make a bone whistle.

and spirit within and without, and to honor the significant moments in time when communion, sacrifice, and ceremony create their own space instead of space merely containing them.

On the tops of sacred mountains, in the canyons and valleys of holy lands, and inside ceremonial circles and temples, the reverberating sound of breath blown through bone and horn ignites the fire of the mind in such a way as to be joined and integrated into the sacred landscape. Whether one is on a solitary quest outside of the range of human affairs or melding the sound of their personal wind with others of like mind, the energy of sound resonating from a sacred wind instrument raises the skin in a call of human flesh to join with the flesh of the world.

You will need a raw bone to make a whistle. The "drumstick" of a wild turkey or the tibia of a deer both work well. Remove all of the flesh by scraping with a knife and/or boiling it in water. Don't overcook the bone in water or roast it, because it may become too brittle. Use as straight of a bone as you can find and saw off the ends, as shown in figure A.

Then, with a very thin awl or other strong but thin tool, hollow out the bone. Measure approximately one inch from the blowing end and make an air hole. This is the most difficult step. Use a drill, awl, knife, and whatever else you need to cut the hole, but make sure that the side of the hole away from the mouthpiece is slanted toward the other end (figure B).

Now fashion a wood or cork plug so that it fits into the mouthpiece and ends at the beginning of the air hole. Make the plug so that air can pass through the mouthpiece to the top air hole (see figure C).

Blow gently through the air hole and adjust the plug to make the sound stronger or weaker and then glue it into place. If desired, you can bevel the mouthpiece, as shown in figure D.

Soak the bone in lemon juice or bleach to whiten.

WORKING WITH DEER

In terms of raw materials for the making of ecoshamanic ceremonial tools and sacred objects, in the United States the white-tailed deer presents us with a unique and extremely potent opportunity that should not be overlooked. Even if you don't believe in hunting and/or you are a strict vegetarian, the tragic mistreatment of this sacred animal demands the attention of all people interested in shamanism and especially ecoshamanism. Although the venison acquired through a sacred hunt is for me a staple of my diet, one of the qualities I respect most in my strict vegetarian friends is that for many of them the abstinence from meat is just one part of a larger lifeway that usually also includes high levels of dedication to recycling and voluntary simplicity. Of the millions of deer that are killed annually in the United States, only a tiny percentage of each of these animals is *not* tragically wasted. And for this reason it matters not if you eat meat or you don't. The tragic situation of the white-tailed deer provides all of us with a perfect opportunity for actions that can at once correct the wasteful abuse of a sacred animal while at the same time learning about and connecting to the amazing practical and spiritual gifts that are the deer's essence.

Modern hunting of deer is for sport and venison. In 2002, the state of Pennsylvania, only one of many states with large deer herds, reported 517,529 deer taken during the hunting season. Of course, this huge number doesn't take into account illegal hunting or deer killed in other ways, such as by collisions with automobiles. Some states with large deer herds report upwards of 40,000 deer-automobile accidents a year (something like one every eight minutes).

These numbers are staggering, but the saddest part is the waste. Even deer hunted legally are often used simply for the meat, with the rest of the deer going to waste. And many deer hunters only hunt for the "trophy" of the male deer's antlers and don't use any of the deer meat at all. Most deer involved in car accidents die in the brush on the side of the road and are completely wasted.

In the seemingly never-ending sprawl of suburban housing developments, the once-sacred deer has now been officially labeled a "pest" for eating ornamental plants, "causing" traffic accidents, and spreading ticks. Some communities, such as Princeton, New Jersey, hire private contractors to kill deer by sharpshooting and a technique called "net and bolt." This killing technique starts by luring the deer to bait such as cornmeal. Then the deer are captured in a net, and while they are struggling to get free they are killed, one at a time, by a device that punctures their skull.

The sane management of deer herds is a hot topic, mostly because it affects hundreds of millions of dollars annually and also because deer-automobile accidents claim thousands of human lives. Many circumstances contribute to this clash between deer and humans, and there are certainly no quick remedies. However, there are numerous factors contributing to the situation, and most of them are human made.

In most states, all of the natural predators of deer have been systematically eliminated by humans. Reintroducing the wolf and the mountain lion would help in restoring the natural balance. Clear-cut logging produces an abundance of browse vegetation that normally would not be available to the deer. Sustainable logging practices, which selectively take trees from different stands, is not only sane land management but would also promote smaller deer populations. Mechanized industrial agriculture contributes to the overabundance of food supplies available to the deer. This is just one of hundreds of factors supporting the transformation of our industrial food system into a system more viable for both humans and the natural world. As the number of automobiles and highways continue to increase, so will the number of deer-automobile accidents and deaths. Again, this is just one factor of hundreds supporting the reduction of automobiles and urban sprawl.

Whether we realize it or not, the management of deer is intricately tied to the management of our daily lives. There are no instant solutions in either case, but in the meantime, while our society either moves closer to balance and health or further down the road of destruction, all of us on a shamanic path can do our part in honoring the sacredness of the deer by treating them with respect, whether they are alive or dead. If you hunt, learn to use *all* of the deer and integrate your hunting practices into your spiritual life through rituals of honor and offering. Discourage friends from trophy hunting (the killing of male deer with the biggest antlers for sport) through educating them in ways that promote higher awareness and compassion for life. All of us interested in ecoshamanism have a sacred responsibility to honor the spirit of the deer and to help counteract the daily desecration of this graceful animal. One of the ways we can do this is by not allowing their life to be completely wasted when they suffer the consequences of our culture's casual indifference to their brutal slaughter. At the very least, the carcass of a dead deer can be utilized in countless ways.

Deer hides make wonderful drums, bags, pouches, sheaths, etc., and they are easy to come by, especially during hunting season. Most hunters don't want the hide, so it is either disposed of or the butcher that processes the deer meat has to try and sell it. Up until a few years ago, deer hunters were usually given one dollar for the hide, but now hunters usually have to pay an additional ten dollars if they bring the deer to the butcher with the hide still on. This situation is causing even more deer hides to be wasted, as many hunters are now skinning their deer in the field and leaving the hide in the woods to rot in order to avoid the ten-dollar charge by the butcher. A thoughtful and powerful gesture for those practicing ecoshamanism is to utilize these deer hides. Whether you obtain them from a hunter, professional deer processing business, or honor the memory of a road-kill deer by removing the hide, by intentionally placing yourself inside of this loop in a proactive way you open yourself to gifts of knowledge and a powerful energetic connection with the spirit of the deer.

Many other parts of the deer can also be utilized for a variety of things. For those interested in naturally tanning the hide, the brains of the deer are the best substance to use. Although brain tanning is a challenging skill to master, there are few activities that have a greater power to connect one with the essence of the animal. In terms of usefulness, the lower leg of a deer is probably the least-appreciated part of this beautiful creature. Once you learn the technique, the lower part of the deer's legs can be removed from the carcass easily with just a sharp knife. The skin can be made into a pouch or sheath, and the long bones (cannon) of the leg provide material for knife handles or for actual tools, such as bone knives, garden implements, needles, hair pins, and chisels. The foot bones can be ground, shaped, and decorated to make buttons, earrings, and pendants. The sinew can be used in many ways to bind things, such as feathers on a prayer arrow.

PRACTICE 27: Hoof Rattle

The hooves of a deer make powerful shamanic rattles. They sing the running motion of the deer and keep the spirit of the animal alive and moving even after physical death. Since the lower leg has little edible meat, this part of the deer is almost always discarded by hunters and can be readily obtained by simply searching around hunting areas after the hunting season is over, removing the lower legs of road-kill deer, or by going to a deer processor. Once you have the lower legs, the easiest way to remove the hooves is to boil them in water. It is advisable to find a place to do this outdoors, as there will be a unique odor during the process. Boil the lower leg for 5–15 minutes and, while still hot, use a twisting motion to pop off the hoof. If it doesn't want to come off, put it back in the hot water a little longer, but be sure not to overboil the leg because the tendons will cook and then separate, making the whole process more difficult.

Once the hooves have been removed, they are much easier to trim while they are still soft and flexible. Trim off the whitish tissue and the underside of the hoof that is softer and less shiny. From here you can trim the hoof into whatever shape you desire, and you can punch a hole into it in order to attach it to the rattle. If you make a really small hole, you may want to place a small stick or something else into the hole so that it doesn't close up as it dries. If you plan on drilling a hole instead, you might leave that for after the hoof dries.

Dry the hooves for 3–5 days, and then clean them up and polish them with a brush or steel wool and lightly oil them with tallow or mineral oil. Now you can string them on a piece of deer skin or whatever else you have. Use your creativity combined with the guidance from the deer spirit to create a unique and extremely personal rattle that will sing and honor the deer, and give voice to your newly found connection to this sacred animal. Suggestions for completing the rattle include simply stringing the hooves on to a single piece of cordage, stringing each hoof singly and then bundling all the strings together, or wrapping the bundle of strings on to a special bone or carved piece of wood.

OFFERING

Within the shamanic worldview, the fundamental reality of the universe is a fabric or unified field of energy and consciousness that constitutes the "web of life." This web is multidimensional in that it forms a spectrum of realities dependent on the perspective of the viewer, but it also forms an inherent symmetric polarity such as light and dark, male and female, and positive and negative charge. Within this reality our modern culture resides within the narrow confines of what psychologist and shamanic researcher Dr. Tomas Pinkson refers to as a "monophasic" worldview.

The monophasic culture is able to tune into only one channel of the multidimensional universe because it has elevated a single cognitive mode—the shared trance of a patriarchal, consumer-based, and technology-driven consciousness that emphasizes power and the control of others—to a position where all other states of consciousness are subordinate or nonexistent. But shamanic cultures live within a polyphasic model of reality that continually tunes into multiple states of consciousness within the unified web of life.

One of the ways that the shamanic, polyphasic culture tunes into the other channels of the multidimensional world is through the powerfully unifying act of making offerings to the beings and sacred places that comprise the unifying field of consciousness that human beings are just one small part of. These actions represent an honoring of the interdependent nature of our world and universe from which we can never truly be a detached observer because we are forever a participant. However, while offerings can be viewed as an act of unity, even in a scientific sense as we learn more about unified fields and systems, for shamanic cultures it is actually much more than that because their view of unity resides more in the feeling of kinship, which makes the whole relationship extremely personal, emotional, arousing, and even sensual.

This sensual relationship with the kinship of the world carries over into every part of life. For example, the language of shamanic tribes can sometimes be very confusing to us because it is based on the reality of the unified field. When a kawitero was holding his head in his hands and I asked what was wrong, he said, "This head aches" instead of "my" head aches. When he spoke to me of troubles in finding deer to hunt, he said, "The deer aren't offering themselves" instead of "I can't find the deer anymore."

In trying to understand this, I was constantly encouraged by the kawitero to look at things from beyond my linear Western training and to see the circumstances of my life from a multidimensional perception. The making of offerings to the sacred places, the cardinal directions, and the fundamental energies of the world became, for me, a large part of my initiation into perceiving the multidimensional universe of interdependency.

PRACTICE 28: The Female and Male—Gourds and Arrows

Shamanic offerings can be as simple as the offering of a sip of your drink to the five directions with five sprinkles in each direction before you drink, or as complex as rituals of sacrifice that take many days or weeks to complete. Maintaining balance, petitioning for healing or guidance, and requesting protection are some of the core circumstances for connecting with the kinship of the polyphasic web of life through offerings, and usually the spirit of the offering is symbolized through creating a physical representation of the offering.

Any type of creative expression in physical form can be used to represent the energy of an offering. But be clear that the physical representation is not the offering, it is the energy you are giving that is the actual offering. Your offering is like a mirror that you are reflecting to the spirit and that will represent you when you leave the physical offering in the sacred place. Two powerful mirrors representing the female and male energies are the gourd and the arrow. Women connect the creative power of their womb to the symbol of the gourd and place representations of their offering inside the gourd, while men make small arrows representing the phallic complement to the womb and represent their energetic offerings through the making and decorating of the arrows.

The people in my workshops and retreats usually attach right away to the notion that the physical offering is just a representation, and they often make extremely beautiful physical representations, but knowing what to actually offer can sometimes elicit great confusion for modern people. The only thing I can say is that you have to just open your total being to the kinship of the multidimensional world and listen. From there, your offering will take shape as a result of why you are making it. For example, if you are going on a pilgrimage to a sacred place to seek a vision for your life, you might make an offering to the sacred place, such as helping to protect it through legislation, giving money, or your time. Or your offering might come from your daily life and be an offering to the spirit to stop a wasteful activity or to improve yourself or your relationship with nature by learning a new trade that is more in line with the reciprocal nature of the universe.

Holding your gourd, arrows, or other offerings in your hands and raising them to the spirits to present them or invoking a blessing is a powerful gesture of kinship and respect. By raising the offering to any of the sacred multidimensional phenomena described in this book, such as the five fundamental energies, the five directions, or any of your sacred places, you are crossing over the threshold from the normally one-way relationship of always taking from nature and spirit and entering into the two-way, multidimensional way of giving and receiving, nurturing and being nurtured, listening and being listened to. This is what shamanic reciprocity is all about, and what sets shamanic practices apart from other spiritual systems that frequently ask but seldom offer.

PRACTICE 29: Rirriki—House of the Spirits

A rirriki is a small house that is built to hold offerings to the spirits. Depending on the configuration of the rirriki, it can also serve to physically represent a particular spirit or be a dwelling or visiting place for the spirit. Since the rirriki holds the energy of multidimensional offerings, and is created with the energy of the spirit it contains (in a similar way to the jicara described on page 271), the rirriki is much more than the physical materials made to construct it. When the rirriki is built with the spirit's energy and then infused with offerings it manifests and exists in multiple dimensions and becomes much greater than the sum of its individual parts, much like any living being.

There are different types of rirrikis, a word borrowed from the Wirrarika language meaning "spirit house" or "god house." Some rirrikis at major sacred sites are durably constructed and permanently maintained so that pilgrims coming from far away with offerings can be sure that their offerings are kept safe. A few years ago I helped to collect funds for the Wirrarika to build a brick rirriki at the top of one of their sacred mountains that lies near to a popular Mexican town because tourists were stealing the beautiful handmade offerings that the pilgrims would leave there. But the type of rirriki I want to focus on here is somewhat different in that the actual materials of the rirriki bring it to life in a special way.

For example, a rirriki built for one of our sacred places will be constructed from the materials found in the sacred place. A rirriki for the spirit of a lake or stream is constructed from materials of the lake or stream and from the area of life that it supports. The main structure of these types of rirrikis are typically built with stone, wood, mud, or sand, and then finished with leaves, branches, flowers, grass, or any other type of natural material in the area where the spirit lives. The way that you construct the rirriki is completely between you and the spirit. I usually build mine in a way that it has a roof and sides to make the offerings feel "at home" with the spirit.

The more attention you pay to the energy of the rirriki, the more power it will reflect. For example, if the rirriki is built for a body of water, it is appropriate to incorporate into the construction something that will hold water; if the rirriki is for the sun, it could face east and be positioned to catch the rays of the sun during significant celestial days; if the rirriki is for an animal, it could be built to physically represent the animal or hold specific items that connect you to your relationship with the animal, and so on.

It is important to note that this type of rirriki is built with the intention of developing a relationship and acknowledging kinship with the spirit in its numinous form and also with its physical body through the actual building process and through the offerings that the rirriki holds. It is not for performing some kind of supplication to appease a god that may become angry with you if you don't honor and obey it. And it is not for simply giving gifts to the spirit, although this can be done at times in a subtle way. The rirriki is really more for the development of a friendly and mutual relationship with the spirit that it holds and reflects. Using the rirriki as a spiritual source of fulfillment is a healthy and holistic alternative to the judgmental threats imposed by many of the popular mainstream religions. The rirriki, and the whole process of offering behind it, acknowledges our presence in a multidimensional universe in a peaceful and reciprocal way.

5 ECOSHAMANIC CHANTING

The power of the chant connects us to the ancient spiritual art of singing shamans, swamis, lamas, rabbis, ministers, and priests. However, just as many of the world's religions have neglected to adequately promote the sacredness of the land, so the modern versions of these faiths employ many forms of chanting devoid of any meaningful connection to the natural environment. The ecoshamanic chants described in this section, as well as earth-centered spiritual chanting in general (including, of course, the chanting of ancient and current indigenous peoples), work in a very special way that actually expands one's identity outward into the natural world instead of driving consciousness inward or toward a non-incarnated god, as in many traditional forms of spiritual chanting.

Chanting encompasses an enormous variety of musical and vibrational expressions of the human voice. While some forms of chanting employ a repetitive series of sounds or words, other forms allow for improvisational melodies and rhythms. Chanting includes recitations of sacred texts and stories as well as prolonged single tones; it can be performed *a cappella* or accompanied by drums, rattles, flutes, and countless other instruments of sound. Traditional chanting is done in temples, churches, ashrams, mosques, and kivas, as well as in forests, on mountaintops, and by the sea. It graces meals and weddings, the rise and fall of the sun, and the passing of a loved one.

Through the chant we engage sound and silence with the resonance of the world so that our perceived boundaries of self melt away as we perceive ourselves being part of something much larger. Chanting is moving meditation, it sings our prayers, and at the deepest levels we no longer sing the chant, the chant sings us.

When employing ecoshamanic chanting, we are not merely working with the mechanics of "singing" so much as we are experiencing a bodily connection with the world through the use of our voice, which then can lead to a psychic connection and spiritual dimension. For this reason it matters not whether you have a "good voice" or not. The only criteria for ecoshamanic chanting is that you come to it with an open heart and mind.

LEARNING TO CHANT

Before going into the specific practices of ecoshamanic chanting, it's important to "find your voice," which is really more about opening your heart than learning how to sing. Listed below are some important aspects to toward this goal.

Breath

One of the main physiological benefits to chanting is simply the deep and rhythmic cadence of breathing that chanting encourages. While learning to chant, you will also be learning a new form of breathing that will develop quite naturally as you progress. To begin, it is enough to simply notice and place attention on the difference between shallow breathing, which mainly comes from the upper part of the chest right below the throat, and deep breathing, which develops much lower, toward the abdomen. Both levels of breath, and all levels in between, will be used while practicing ecoshamanic chanting. However, it is good to practice the deep breath coming from the abdomen because this breath will provide for a wider and longer chant cadence, and also will help you develop a deeper and healthier breath, especially if you are a smoker or if you are not accustomed to physical activity.

Toning and Resonance

For those of us that lack previous affirmative life experiences with singing (including yours truly), one of the basic boundaries we need to cross is simply allowing ourselves to use our voice in a manner other than simply talking. This can be easily facilitated by exploring the basic vowel sounds that we already know. Thoroughly exploring these tones and the vibrating resonance they create in your body will also help you to explore your various levels of breathing. To start, simply breathe in and then vocalize the "A" sound (as in the word *play*) through one exhalation—"a a a a a a a a a." Then breathe deeply and vocalize "AH" (as in *father*)—"ah h h h h h h h."

Now do the same with the other vowel sounds. "E" as in *free*—"e e e e e e e e." Then "I" as in *fly*—"i i i i i i i i i i." Then "O" as in *boat*—"o o o o o o o o." Then "U" as in *cute*—"u u u u u u u u." Vocalize these individual tones through one fully extended breath a few times, and then vocalize all six in the same breath a few times. Now explore all the various sounds and tones that surround these vowel sounds. Our English language is very flat and choppy when compared to many other languages, and those of us who are currently limited to the use of only the English language have probably not even experienced many of the sounds and vibrations that we are capable of creating. Start with a familiar sound like "O" and then sing through all the variations of the sound—play with it, let it dance on your tongue, and feel it vibrate throughout your whole body. Take your time. Then explore different sounds, invent sounds, manipulate them, and sing them through long, sustained breaths and short, choppy breaths, at high volume or mere whispers. Let the sounds lead you.

Let It Flow

Truly engaging the chant takes disciplined practice, but also requires a certain amount of abandonment. This is another form of the shamanic paradox—to fly while keeping your feet on the ground. During the chant we surrender to the flow of the world and the merging of our voice to that flow, but we also ground that experience by attending, at varying degrees, to what is happening with our human organism. This is especially true when chanting while engaged in physical activities such as walking, climbing, attending the fire, immersing in water, etc.

Although we certainly don't want to injure ourselves by losing touch with the physical reality of the moment, the one trap we have to overcome is to not let attending to our human organism interfere unduly with the flow of the chant. For example, it is common for us to wonder if we are "doing it right" or to ask ourselves, "How long have I been chanting?" or "I wonder how much longer I should continue?" When these types of mental questions disturb the flow, it is usually best to try and simply meld these thoughts with your chanting experience. Treat the thoughts as just one more input that you are receiving. You can even sing these questions out and see where they lead. When you are engaged in the chant, normal timekeeping by clocks and watches loses its value and is replaced with unscheduled and spontaneous events.

PRACTICE 30: The Freeform Chant-Song

There are many advantages to introducing this first form of chanting to begin the process of learning ecoshamanic chanting. This chant:

- Is best practiced initially while you are alone in nature, which in itself will make you feel more comfortable if you feel awkward chanting in front of others.

- Initially is best practiced while moving (walking), which promotes the movement and flow of your chant-song.

- Encourages your creativity to join with the creative energy of the world, thereby placing you in the position of co-creator with the world.

- Connects you in a tangible way with the area in which you are chanting.

- Exposes your total human organism to receiving and joining with the flow of energy and the various perceptions of time being experienced by the entities around you.

- Opens you to receiving messages coming from the world and from specific entities.

- Disengages the purely rational side of your being while at the same time introducing healthy new dimensions for relating to the world.

- Is an inspiring, creative, and dynamic practice that is at once enlightening and enjoyable.

This form of chanting is not the simple repetition of known words or phrases but rather a spontaneous and dynamic journey accomplished by connecting with an element, or multiple elements, of the natural world. As you unite the consciousness of your mind/body/spirit with that element(s), you express that unity by spontaneous vocalization.

This type of journey is much different from the popular journeying practices employed by modern shamanic practitioners that use a drum or a recording of a drum to provide the auditory driving into a trance state. That type of journeying practice can be performed inside of a closed room because the trance state requires only the medium of sound in attempting to give your consciousness access to a journey into "another world" that is supposedly lower or higher than this world. The key difference between that kind of auditory driving journey and the journeying of the ecoshamanic chant-song is that the chant-song uses the medium of the natural world, which is incomprehensibly diverse and spectacularly beautiful, to connect and commune with tangible forces and energies of this world. With the ecoshamanic chant-song the goal is utterly tangible, and there is no degree of imagination or eyes-closed visualization required; instead, what is needed is just the opposite: full organismic immersion into the magic and mystery of the world of nature and nature's animating spirits. The deeper you can place your psyche, your bodily felt perception, and your spiritual being into the natural element(s) surrounding you, the more profound your chant-song journey will be, and the more tangible and practical the experience will be to your daily life.

This type of chanting can become highly specialized by focusing and connecting over long periods of time on joining with specific places, powers, and entities. For example, the Wirrarika shamans that first inspired my ecoshamanic chanting practice are experts at chanting with the fire, with the other main powers of the world, with the sacred places, and also with specific plants and animals. However, since this type of chanting is not normal to our culture, it will be more productive for us to begin learning this type of chanting without attempting to focus on one entity. Rather, let's try and connect with the overall flowing and mixing of the various fields of activity happening in the area where we are.

Chant-Song Journeys

There are numerous ways of beginning the freeform chant-song, but for this first example let's assume that you are in an area of nature and this is your first time practicing this type of technique. As this form of chanting is most easily learned while you are walking, begin to walk in a relaxed way and "loosen up" your voice by either vocalizing vowel sounds or any other sounds that spontaneously arise from out of you. After a few minutes of this, begin to make vocal contact with the world around you. The basic way to do this is to begin acknowledging the various living entities around you with your voice. Even though our English language is very reductionist in form, it is plenty useful for saturating our perception, and one way of doing this is to vocalize the names of the entities around you in a fluid stream of words that you "sing" to a rhythm that takes form as you proceed. What is many times helpful while learning how to vocalize with the natural world is to simply add a refrain to your chant-song. The refrain can come spontaneously or be one that you are familiar with. A potent refrain to begin with is "be my voice." For example, if you are in an area of deciduous forest, you might start by chant-singing—

Pebbles and trees and sky and wind, be my voice . . .
Leaves and spiders and willow and flower, be my voice . . .
Hill and valley and river and clouds, be my voice . . .
Grasshopper, blue jay, squirrel and snake, be my voice . . .

From this beginning you could chant-sing for a long time while celebrating the diversity of the place you are walking. This version of the chant-song imprints the specific elements of that place into your being and the deeper you go, the stronger the effect. There are so many natural entities that come into your field with each step that you can't possibly sing them all. The idea is to just let your attention flow deeply into what is surrounding you and to immerse yourself not just at the mental, physical, and spiritual levels, but also at a vibrational-vocal level. Your vocalizations are part of your presence in that place; they are an expression of your being, of who you are. Giving voice to the entities around you, even by just simply naming them in your chant-song, places you in a tangible relationship with all of those entities and allows your spontaneous creative abilities of forming the rhythm, tone, volume, and vibrations of your chant-song to join with the natural unfolding of life where you are walking.

The next natural step to the ecoshamanic chant-song is to give voice to the movement of that unfolding of life. This is where it begins to get more difficult to explain, so I will simply suggest what I think will help lead you into your own experience. What you do first is attend to the movement around you. The most obvious movements will probably be either wind blowing through leaves and branches, or the flow of water if nearby, or the movements of birds, animals, or insects. These are the obvious movements of the world that you start to chant-sing first. How you do this will be entirely up to you. At first you could chant-sing the words describing the actions that you see, for example—

Robin flying from ground to tree; grass moves from birds' wings.
The branch sways as robin lands; its head moves up and down,
its tail moves like a conductor's wand . . .
Robin jumps up a branch; maybe it feels me watching.
It hears something, hops to turn; the leaves move to its movement . . .

This simple example of singing the actions of the bird's body and flight, the movement of the grass, the tree branches, the leaves, and the perceived interaction between the bird and the world and the bird and the singer is merely one of the countless movements and actions that was happening in that same area at that moment. Once you begin to chant-sing at this level be aware that it is not important that the words rhyme or form some sort of catchy phrase or song. You are not singing to entertain, you are singing to shift consciousness in order to connect and therefore perceive in a unique manner. This journey you are on is the unfolding of life in the area you are chanting. The slow methodical growth of the oak tree, the busy activity of ants and birds, the washing of stones in the creek bed, the dropping of leaves by the breeze. This journey is incomprehensibly rich and filled with activity that eventually will require you to move beyond using simple names in order to sing them.

For example, let's continue with the chant-song of the robin from above. This chant-song developed at a certain level of complexity that is only one of myriad levels that depends on the singer's particular point of view and life experience. The singer of this song identified the bird as a robin, which means they must have had some experience with robins before. But how much experience? Do they know the difference between male and female? Do they know what color variations the robins have? How big is its territory? Where does it build its nests? Or, for that matter, what about the grass on the ground where the robin flew from? What kind of grass was it? What does the type of grass tell us about what the robin might have been doing there? What kind of tree did the robin fly into? Is that a favorite type of tree to robins in general? Is there a favorite tree for the robin?

As we can see, the first chant-song of the robin, even though it was about a very simple activity, was only touching the surface of what a more experienced person might have seen. The chant-song at a deeper level might be something like this:

Mr. Robin hunting worms in the wet soil.
Feels my footfalls, alights into ancient willow.
Marsh grass sways with flight; willow branch sways from landing.
Mr. Robin shifts his head tries to see me; back, forth, up, down, sideways—
Tail conducts movement; yellow-beaked robin keeps hunting . . .

A this point it is natural that you begin to express the movement of the world through vocalizations that are not merely words. This will have two primary effects. The first is that you will be able to leave your normal word-forming process behind and replace it with vocalizations that come spontaneously as a result of your interaction and experience. And secondly, by doing this you will start on the journey of discovering how vocalizing tones at certain vibrations helps you to connect in a different way with the world. In other words, at this level it is the tones of the voice and not the actual words that are the main tools.

The discovery of this possibility first came to me while listening to Wirrarika shamans chant-singing all night long in a language I didn't know, but somehow understood at a certain level. There are two main reasons for this. The actual words of that language sound very much like the elements and activities that the shaman is singing about, and interspersed throughout the chant-song are descriptive vocalizations (not words) that arise spontaneously during the journey. The first time I realized this was the morning after participating in an all-night ceremony with a singing Wirrarika shaman. I was singing softly to myself a line that I heard the shaman repeat many times during the all-night ceremony. When one of my Wirrarika friends asked me what I was singing, I sang it louder for him and then asked the meaning of the words. That's when he told me that they weren't really words. They came from the shaman's vocalizing the flight of the eagle that gave him the feathers for his shaman's wand (muvieri). In that moment I remembered seeing the bird flying while the shaman was singing, but at the time I thought it was just my imagination projecting the image, when all along I really was hearing what the shaman was communicating! From that moment I realized how the human voice is capable of communicating so much more than just words.

To continue with our simple example of the robin, the next level of chant-song might be something like this (words in parentheses are explanatory and not part of the chant):

> Red-breast (male robin) chick chick chick chwosh (hunting in the wet grass)
> from me fla, fla (robin flies from my footsteps) to wooweeyawoolalana
> (vocalized name for this particular ancient willow tree)—
> yellow beak red breast ba, ba, ba, ba (head bobbing up and down)
> no me floonana (flies away from me) chick chick chick (continues hunting) . . .

This type of descriptive chant-song is obviously not going to precisely detail the actions of the bird so much as it will convey the actual sounds and feelings of the event at a vocal level. From here the leaving behind of words altogether is a natural occurrence. It is common during your chant-song, especially while walking for long periods of time, that the literate part of the mind is not fully engaged and the vocalizations of the chant take form spontaneously and creatively in a way that "speaks" the environment you are walking in. This is an important step in discovering new ways to perceive and relate to the world, and it is especially important while initially learning and experiencing ecoshamanic chanting. When you are able to leave the words behind and feel the pure meaning of the vocalization through the sounds and vibrations rather than through the dictionary, you open yourself up to the possibility of engaging in the flow and the unfolding of life that is all around you in a way that is beyond our habitual rational-verbal perception.

Practice this ecoshamanic chant-song in many different environments and experiment with vocalizing your journeys while feeling the tangible forces of the sun, wind, water, earth, sky, mountains, deserts, hills, valleys, trees, birds, streams, deer, mice, flowers, carcasses, arroyos, rain, dust, corn, lizards, and all the other magical entities and beings that form the earth community. The connection between your voice and the unfolding life around you can truly be your vehicle. When this type of shamanic journey begins to work for you, other popular types of journeying and guided meditations that begin by "close your eyes and imagine" will seem trivial and superficial, as will merely seeing the images of wild landscapes and animals on television and in magazines instead of really seeing, feeling, and singing them. Imagination and media are certainly important tools, but they cannot replace the actual felt experience that stimulates you physically and spiritually, as well as mentally and emotionally.

PRACTICE 31: Receiving a Power Song

Messages from the multidimensional world can be received through the gift of a song that is given to you in a special way. These songs, sometimes called "power songs" or "songs of power," have special significance to the singer/receiver or to the community of the singer/receiver. These songs very often come to you during the various practices of vocalizing during ecoshamanic chanting and in some way they stand out due to the very specific message they carry. In this way they are usually fairly easy to remember, and often stay with a person for the rest of their life. One of my very first power songs was gifted to me while singing with the fire during a three-night fasting/vision quest. It was delivered to me in Spanish; here is the translation:

When you have nothing, you are free . . .
When your body is empty, you feel . . .
When your mind extends outwards, you see . . .

This simple chant-song was a message of power that I associate, even to this day, with the place where I received it—the Shawangunk Mountains in New York State. Whenever this little song comes back to me, so do the feelings, emotions, images, and the psychic/physical/spiritual connection that I felt with that place. This is one of the most remarkable and practical aspects of using your total human organism to communicate with the natural world: the experience stays with you and gives you strength. Over the years and with continued effort you accumulate dozens or even hundreds of these experiences and songs, and your life begins to shift as it starts to reflect the wisdom of the natural world that you have gathered. Songs about the fluidity of life gifted by a mountain stream, the cyclical reality of the world sung by the movement of a vulture or the patience of a large cat, the hidden treasures of life in a desert, the blossoming creativity of a forest in springtime—all are experiences that add real depth and flavor to life. But even more importantly, these experiences expand our view of the world.

Once you get accustomed to letting the land sing through you, songs can come to you spontaneously even when you are not already singing. Many times this happens to me while sitting in my tree stand, planting or harvesting, chopping firewood, hunting, or sometimes even while traveling by plane or riding my bike. At any moment the land and spirits can sing through you.

Most recently this happened while taking two Wirrarika friends to visit the ruins of the World Trade Center in New York City about a year after the tragedy. Casimiro and Maria were staying with me while working on the illustrations for my first children's book. Since I lived only a few hours from the city, I took them to Staten Island and we got on the ferry to Manhattan. Just as we approached the Statue of Liberty, it started to become obvious where the WTC used to be. I'll never forget the feeling in those moments. My two Wirrarika friends had never seen skyscrapers, nor been on a huge ferry, nor ever witnessed the devastation of man on this scale, and since I was so close to these two people, having them in my home for over a month and knowing Casimiro's whole family for many years, it was like I was living the experience through them as well as dealing with it on my own level. Well, there were no words that needed to be said; our eyes and our faces expressed to each other the complex emotions we were all feeling.

But what also did happen was that a chant-song was given to mark the crossing. It was a metaphorical crossing in the sense that by crossing over the river to Manhattan, they would never be the same—a part of their innocence as simple peasant farmers would be gone forever. Also, it was a tangible crossing, as they would see and feel in a most intimate manner the gaping hole, both deep and wide, of the physical loss of the buildings, and the mental and spiritual effects of the unimaginable horror and loss of life. This is a vital aspect of the chant-song—especially for oral cultures like the Wirrarika, who don't write their language—that it expresses experiences through tangible human emotions and through real vocal vibrations, real tears, and real bodily felt expressions of feeling. I'm sure that when Casimiro and Maria returned to their tiny village, hidden in the mountains, they would share the chant-song with their people and that the song would convey human sentiments and feelings far beyond what written words or photographs ever could.

PRACTICE 32: Chanting Your Place

Similar to the positive experiences gleaned from mapping the ecological region you are inhabiting, which I covered in chapter 3, using the ecoshamanic chant-song to allow the place where you live to sing through you can be a truly enlightening experience. Even though we may see and interact with a certain place on a day-to-day level that, after a while, embeds a certain familiarity into our being, the world is constantly changing and no two moments or places are ever the same. While standing outside of my front door, the wind being delivered to me might come from the Canadian Artic today, tomorrow from the Gulf of Mexico. During the seasons the migrations of birds are changing continuously, the flora endlessly transforming, the sunlight gradually waxing and waning. The tiny corner of the globe that we are inhabiting at any given moment is so deeply connected to the rest of the world that when we connect to it in the immediacy of the moment, and join with the dynamic flow that that moment represents in the passage of the seasons, we can actually join in the magical journey of unfolding life even while we are rooted to a single place. In this sense, the terms *local* and *global* can merely be seen as current states of mind.

Through periodically using the ecoshamanic chant-song technique to sing your place of residence, you open yourself to letting your place, including all of the living entities in and surrounding it, sing through you in a way that provides you with tangible information about the health of the place, patterns of growth and decay, what the flora and fauna are doing, what new ecological threats have appeared, and so on. Singing your place can introduce you at much more personal level with the living beings that you share space with. While you may only see a specific bird, butterfly, or insect once in a while, there will be other entities that have a more personal presence, such as trees, flowers, or permanent animal residents such as squirrels or deer. One of the most positive and life-affirming outcomes of singing your place is that the act of allowing those entities to sing through you, or to you, or you to them, causes you to automatically have a more personal relationship with them, which usually results in knowing them by name, keeping an eye on them, and acknowledging them as part of your extended family.

A simple yet powerful way to sing your place is take a walk around where you live and use the various levels of ecoshamanic chanting described in the above section "Chant-song Journeys." Doing this at different moments throughout the yearly cycle of seasons will produce unique song journeys each time, and connect you in special way with your home area.

PRACTICE 33: Blessing and Healing—Blood and Breath

Ecoshamanic chanting can be used as a powerful form of blessing, both on its own and in conjunction with other shamanic tools and/or natural entities and energies. Blessings come in a variety of forms to support, empower, and nourish people, places, circumstances, and special events. They can even appear in physical or metaphysical form, as in "her presence was a real blessing," or when, in retrospect, events that seemed detrimental at the time, such as losing one's job, are often seen later as being a "blessing in disguise." Therefore, in general, blessings can be said to enhance, consecrate, or make something special.

Linguists tell us that the English word *blessing* comes from the Old English *bledtsain*, "to consecrate," and that bledstain originates from *blod*, "blood." From this we see that *blessing* originally meant, literally, "to consecrate with blood," which would be in line with many ancient religious ceremonies, both shamanic and otherwise, as blood has always been valued as the carrier of life. It is a most valued, most holy, and most precious phenomena, not to mention one of the most magical. Although still commonplace in the shamanic world, the use of blood for blessing, in most cases, has now been replaced with the simple sharing of good intentions, or spirit, by use of words or song. But when the magic use of our breath, in this case the ecoshamanic chant, is combined with the powerful magic of blood, we engage and put into service two of the most mysteriously fundamental aspects of human life. Just as the exchange of our breath connects us in the most intimate way to the energies of the flora and fauna that share the atmosphere with us by supplying oxygen for the circulating blood of our body, a blessing of breath and blood circulates a flow of life force between the human organism and what it is blessing. This flow of circulation can be employed in blessing and healing to open blockages, heal relationships, and foster deep connection with the forces of creation.

When we bless or heal something with our chanting, we don't, of course, always need to use blood in conjunction with our breath. Sometimes the words of the chant are enough, and other times we can join the power of the chant with other energies, such as the light of a flame, the healing flow of water, the grounding essence of soil, or the sacred energies created by instruments of music and shamanic tools made from the essences of sacred trees and animals. In this sense, a blessing or healing is an infusion of energy or spirit, and many configurations of energy can be employed, depending on the situation. In the following chapter, I recount my experience with the kawitero who was healing and blessing the children each morning by infusing them with a combination of sunlight, breath, chanting, water, and the essences of flowers and feathers. This is a perfect example of how we can combine ecoshamanic chanting with other energies to create powerful rituals and ceremonies of blessing and healing.

Another perfect example, this time using blood, that I witnessed in an indigenous community and have since incorporated into my work of healing and blessing came as a result of a young woman who was raped while walking on a remote trail from her village to the closest non-indigenous town. Approximately a week after the incident, her mother took her to the kawitero/shaman because the young woman was so emotionally distraught that she had not eaten anything since the tragic event. The shaman decided to ask the fire what to do to heal the woman, and called for a ceremony to take place the next night. During the ceremony, the shaman sang and chanted with the fire and received the message that they should all (most of the people of the village were present at the ceremony) go to the place where the rape happened. In that exact place, the young girl should bury the blood-stained clothes she was wearing during the rape so that the earth could transform the hurtful energy of the experience by receiving the blood of the woman and turning it into life-giving soil. The group should then build a small shrine over the hole and each person would put a small offering for the spirit of the woman in the shrine.

During the construction of the shrine the shaman chanted verses of offering and allegiance to the natural forces of the world, and the people making the shrine all answered the verses of the chant with their own personal verses of response. After the shrine was complete, it was never to be touched again. In this way, as the shrine (made from branches, reeds, and flowers) gradually became cleansed through the forces of wind, rain, and sun, and so slowly decomposed and was given back to the earth, so would the soul of the woman be gradually cleansed and healed, and the traumatic experience would be absorbed by the forces of the earth.

This beautiful and powerful ceremony of blood and breath, combined with so many other sacred energies and essences, was one of the most open and pure responses to a tragic and hurtful action I have ever witnessed, and judging by the face of the young woman, it was completely effective. By sharing her pain with the community and having them chant and offer their energy and time, she didn't have to bear the pain alone and she didn't have to live the rest of her life in shame with the secret. The community, so deeply embedded in the shamanic worldview, completely accepted the healing advice of the fire through the shaman and so thereafter considered the woman completely healed of the event to the point that it never affected her relationship with people in her community, including her future husband. The young woman, with the help of her mother and the community, took responsibility for the healing. They knew that even though the man who committed the atrocity was responsible for the horrible act, they were responsible for the rest of the woman's life, and so they let the authorities deal with the man while they supported and facilitated the healing of the young woman. What a wonderful lesson!

This type of ceremonial response to healing with breath, blood, and natural energies and powers, along with similar proactive ceremonies of blessing, can be employed to heal and bless many different things and circumstances. Along with using ecoshamanic chanting to bless and aid in the healing of individuals and groups, one of the other ways I use it is to aid in the healing of land decimated by industry and greed. Either alone, or preferably with a group of people, singing and chanting your emotions and your healing intentions to the land, while infusing blood, tears, and handmade offerings into the earth through sacred portals dug into the soil, or shrines built on the place of injury, are incredibly powerful acts of healing and blessing that reverberate throughout the entire world and multidimensional cosmos.

PRACTICE 34: Protecting Sacred Places

All of the above-mentioned techniques of ecoshamanic chanting can be used to honor and protect the natural places and spaces that are sacred to us. In fact, these places are perfect to engage in a chant-song journey, to receive a power song or a message from the sacred place, to be the voice of the place as you let it sing through, to bless and heal the place or others, and to maintain your sacred connection to the place and thereby infuse your energy as a way of protecting the place from hurtful hands. By routinely visiting our sacred places through formal pilgrimages or simple periodic trips, we maintain a living relationship with the energy and essence of the place that we carry with us into our everyday lives. In this way, by carrying the energy of the places within us, we become the places, just as the places become us. When they are threatened, so are we. When we protect them, we are protecting that part of ourselves connected to them. This is one reason that makes the connection obtained through chanting with the sacred place so important and vital. The more people that connect to a sacred place, the louder will be the voice protecting it from destruction.

One of the most important strategies currently being used by some of my indigenous friends is protecting the sacred places by inviting politicians and CEOs to develop a connection to them, whether simply at a level of appreciation for the physical beauty of the place or at a deeper level, by exposing them to rituals of connection or the witnessing of the profound connection of the people to the place by way of their devotion, songs, offerings, blood, and tears. There exist few sacred places on Earth that are secret anymore, or that are outside the long grasp of industry. Our sacred places are now basically public places, whether we like it or not, simply because the human enterprise now affects the biosphere as a whole, and no place is an island safe from the effects of environmental catastrophes. The best defense we have now in protecting the sacred places is to go to them regularly and let them sing through us in order to gain their strength, be their voice, and sing their messages to the world.

6 | RITES OF PASSAGE AND INITIATION

The worldview of shamanism considers all of nature sacred and spirit-filled. Very naturally, many of the responsibilities and tasks of indigenous shamans happen during their daily lives in the course of "normal" activities. Since everything that happens during the course of normal activities is just as spirit-filled as the shamanic journey they might take during ceremony or ritual, the two dimensions are not seen by them as separate. This is the main difference between modern urban neoshamanic practices that focus entirely on traveling "out of body" to the spirit world, and the indigenous tribal shamans who work in the here and now. They do this by developing their ability to alter "ordinary" reality by reconfiguring space, matter, and time through channeling their psychic abilities and connecting with tangible natural powers such as sun, water, wind, earth, fire, plants, animals, rocks, etc. What many modern people interested in shamanism have yet to understand is that these extremely powerful tribal shamans are not usually concerned with escaping out of their body; rather, they are engaged in the expansion of what the body—composed of matter, energy, consciousness, and spirit—is capable of doing.

One of the most beautiful and profound examples of this I have ever seen happened once when I was visiting a ceremonial center deep in the Wirrarika sierra. It was dawn on my first day there and I had just been awakened by the sounds of someone building a fire in front of the rirriki (sacred house where offerings are kept), which was next to the little hut I had spent the night in. As I sat next to the fire, I remembered the dream I had in the night. In the dream was an old shaman that I had met briefly a few years before but that had left the ceremony where I met him before I had the chance to find out his name. For the past few years, he had frequently appeared in my dreams in different capacities, and I always hoped to meet him physically again one day.

As I sat staring into the fire and remembering my dream, a few of my friends from the village came and sat next to me, and in the course of conversation I asked them who was the current presiding shaman of the ceremonial center (this duty changes every five years). They told me his name but that he was not in the village that day. Feeling a little disappointed at missing the presiding shaman, my spirits were immediately lifted as a few small children joined us by the fire, but after a few minutes they all got up and ran away to a small hill about forty yards away where a man was standing holding various things in his hands, including his feathered shaman's wands (muvieris). I couldn't see his face, as he was silhouetted by the glow of the soon-to-rise sun behind him, and I asked my friends who he was. They told me he was a kawitero and powerful shaman currently presiding over another ceremonial center close by, but that he lived in this village most of the time. By the time the children reached him, he was already chant-singing to the spirits and waving his feathered muvieris in circles through the air. In the next few minutes I would have the privilege to witness what truly lies at the core of shamanism.

Just as he picked the first child off the ground and held her in his arms, the first ray of light from the sun pierced the top of the hill and he put her directly into it. Then, holding her in one arm, he gave her a small gourd of water from a sacred spring to hold, and five times he placed his feathered muvieris into the water, infused them with sunlight, whirled them through the air while chanting, and dabbed her various body parts with the wet feathers. Then he did the same thing with the head of a beautiful flower, and while chanting he gently sucked or blew his breath into various parts of her body.

The tenderness of the old shaman blessing and healing the tiny girl with sunlight, water, air, flowers, breath, and the powerful chanting in the dawn light on that special little hill touched me in such a profound way that I was moved to tears. It was like something out of a fairy tale. When he was finished with the first child, the second came and jumped into his arms like he had the most special present that child had ever seen! That little boy simply couldn't wait for the old shaman to give him his magic, and this, too, touched me deeply as I reflected on how children of my society are practically forced to leave their video games and televisions behind to participate in spiritual blessings and communions.

As I continued to watch the scene on the hill, I gradually began to fully perceive what was going on, and by the time the shaman was with the fourth child I could actually "see" the luminous energy that he was drawing with his muvieris from the sun, the water, the air, and the flower and infusing into the children at different parts of their body that seemed to be missing some radiance.

I found out later that these four village children were being treated by the shaman for various ailments, and that he performed this type of follow-up treatment regularly at dawn for the children. When the shaman was finished with his work, I couldn't resist going to speak with him, so I walked over to the hill and as I approached him and he turned toward me, I stopped dead in my tracks. It was the old shaman from my dreams that I had met years before! I was so happy that I almost hugged him, but he didn't seem to recognize me, so I held back my mirth and simply asked him if I could meet with him later in the day, to which he agreed. Since that special day he has been one of my chief mentors and teachers, not only of shamanism but of life. It turns out that he did remember me and was not at all surprised that I had "inadvertently" come to his village. That day, knowing that I had seen his work with the muvieris and that it was, of course, no accident that I was there with him, he helped me to make my very first muvieri, which later in my trip was blessed and consecrated in a very powerful and ancient Wirrarika ceremony where the shamans sing and chant for hours with the feathers of the muvieri in order to call the spirits and infuse their energy into the feathers.

The type of activity that the old shaman performed on the children is an excellent example of ecoshamanism in action. Gathering the tangible essences and energies of the natural world, the shaman infused the children in specific ways and in concentrated doses with what their total human organism was lacking, for this shaman could "see" that what is outside and inside are one and the same. It was like he was giving each of them an energetic booster shot of energy from the sun, water, earth, and air, while at the same time mingling his energy with theirs by using his shamanic knowledge. Even after many of years participating in rigorous and sometimes extremely complex shamanic ceremonies and rituals with indigenous shamans, this simple healing practice performed by the old kawitero continues to be a great source of inspiration and awe for me.

One of the things I came to learn later as I watched these children grow up over the years is that this type of activity, along with countless others that the children participate in while growing up in the shamanic worldview, provides the children with an extremely organic basis for perceiving and understanding the world while at the same time preparing them for a shamanic ceremonial life and initiations. The old shaman on the hill had a lifetime's worth of experiences living in the natural world, and over fifty years of shamanic rituals and ceremonies of connection to the sacred places and the fundamental energies of the world. His ability to act as an intermediary between his people and the powers and spirits surrounding them is a direct result of his lifelong dedication to his relationship with the energies of sun, water, air, fire, and earth, and the spirits of the various sacred places that are his main teachers.

In this section of the book it is my intention to offer practices with the power to shamanically introduce us to the fundamental energies and the spirits of the sacred places so that we can be initiated by their power and learn from their wisdom.

SHAMANIC RITES OF PASSAGE

In the modern cultures of the West we tend to view the unfolding of our lives as a relatively uniform and continuous process punctuated at times by secondary changes and events. But in the shamanic world the tendency is to view personal development as a series of leaps or jumps from one dimension of existence to another, even to the point that a person's name and identity can change many times during the course of a lifetime as one evolves from one mode of being to another. This may seem a little strange to us because we don't engage in powerful rites of passage whereby a person is purged, purified, and initiated throughout the various life stages, as is common in the shamanic world.

In the life of a shamanic tribe the important stages in a person's life are marked by activities of inner purification in order to sweep clean the past, disrupt the routine thought process, and remove unwanted distractions so that the individual can proceed unimpeded into a new dimension of existence. The forms of purification can take many forms, including physical processes such as fasting, sweating, exposure to extreme heat or cold, vomiting, pain, or bleeding; cleansing by natural energies such as water, wind, earth, smoke, steam, and fire; or the purification may alternatively or jointly be combined with psychic cleansing by prolonged isolation, repetitive actions, severe exhaustion, or psychic bombardment by presiding shamans, all of which contribute to the diminishment of the controlling side of the initiate's ego in order to become "small" before entering into the new life stage.

This idea of "becoming small" is extremely important for modern people because we have been taught our whole lives to strive to be independent, successful, and "big," and by doing so we miss the flow that is the undercurrent of magic in organic reality. All of the above-mentioned forms of purification, as well as many of the ecoshamanic techniques I am sharing in this book, are designed to foster an entry into the "flowing force" or "stream of power" that spontaneously arises during prolonged entry into heightened states of awareness, peak emotional experiences, and moments of ecstatic bliss, unbearable pain, and especially mystical union. When the controlling aspects of our ego are quieted and we engage the primal flow of consciousness that animates our world, we become acutely aware of our smallness when compared to the incomprehensible vastness of the universe. Touching the stream of universal power goes hand in hand with the ritual purification of becoming small in the face of the great mystery. The relevance of this experience for modern people cannot be overstated, because our culture teaches us to utterly reject the idea that we are no better or worse than all that surrounds us. When we become small and humble, even if it's only during periodic rituals or ceremonies, we allow our grandiose ego to shrink up and move out of the way so that we can perceive life as a magnificent gift and fully appreciate the scope of our time here.

Making the most of our time here is one of the key reasons to engage in rites of passage, because they spur you out of complacency, give you a kick in the butt, and push you to claim your own authentic, unique abilities and creative power.

PRACTICE 35: The Embrace of the Earth

The Embrace of the Earth is a rite of passage ritual that has developed over the course of many years from its original format, created by one of my first non-indigenous shamanic mentors, Mexican researcher and author Victor Sanchez. Although many of the core elements of the ritual have remained intact throughout the years, as with all authentic shamanic practices, this ritual has steadily evolved and been adapted to fit current needs and life situations. In 1999 I began to offer the current version of this rite of passage in a two- or three-day format in order to make it more convenient for people to engage in this important rite over the course of a weekend, as long as they properly prepared for the rite at home in the weeks prior to ceremony.

The key aspects to this rite of passage are the purification, heightened awareness, and visionary experiences fostered through spending one whole night (or longer) embraced by the earth in a gravelike tomb that is dug by hand into the living soil. The experience of ceremonially digging your own gravelike tomb and being buried in the ground overnight has been described by many that have passed through the ritual as a combination vision quest and full-body meditation. It feels like returning to the womb of your true mother to reclaim that mystical union where all of your hurts are purged and absorbed into the immense physical body and energy of the earth, and then being birthed once again into the light of the world to walk a life path infused with the unconditional love and spiritual guidance of the earth.

When performed with proper preparation and in the appropriate manner, the structure of this rite of passage provides an extremely safe and potent opportunity to touch with your whole MBESA an ecoshamanic state of consciousness with the power to change your life. Even if you were to simply prepare for the rite, dig and enter your tomb, and then fall asleep for the whole night, you would still be changed. There is no way that one can pass through this rite without being transformed to some degree. However, if you genuinely enter the experience and follow the time-tested suggestions for distilling the most from the rite, the transformational aspects and opportunities for growth and knowledge are limitless.

The Embrace of the Earth rite of passage is paradoxically very straightforward and extremely complex. The physical side of the ritual is quite simple and once you learn and understand the logistics you can quickly become comfortable and at ease with the physical aspects of what you are doing and how to do it properly and safely. However, on the mental, psychic, and spiritual levels, the range and complexity of possible experiences prohibits one from knowing or predicting what will actually occur in those realms. The best that one can do for another is to provide a time-tested structure for the ritual along with complete and unconditional support. Of course, there is no substitute for experience in this type of ritual, and having someone to guide the rite who has passed through it multiple times is immensely helpful. As with all shamanic activities, except for the general framework, the internal dynamics of this rite of passage are almost indescribable using words. I'm going to try as best as I can to provide as much information in the space allowed, with the hope that these words will inspire people to enter the ritual and discover their own inroads to this powerful and transformative experience of ecoshamanism.

In the course of writing this material it became apparent from the first few moments that my perspective of the ritual, however knowledgeable, in the bottom line is simply one person's perception, and so it felt appropriate and necessary to include supporting material from others who have passed through the rite. In the following sections I will provide both explanations as to structure and functions of the rite, along with comments from people that have passed through the rite. All of the comments were made by initiates that passed through the rite while I was guiding the rite in a group setting at various locations during 2001 and 2002. Some of the comments come from journals written during the actual ritual and others were written in the weeks following it. All are used with permission.

Below is a brief five-step outline of how to physically construct the tombs, followed by a more detailed explanation of the ritual, accompanied by comments from initiates. Please be aware that due to both the physical and metaphysical aspects of this rite, it is not advisable to perform it without a companion or group. First-timers should experience the rite under the guidance and safety of an experienced ecoshamanic practitioner. Please note: When performed as described here, there is no chance of suffocation and you can easily be removed, or remove yourself, from the tomb.

1. The place where you will carry out the rite is extremely important because it is not just the physical location of the rite, it is the co-creator of your experience. Optimally, it should be a place that is far enough from civilization that there are no noises from human activity reaching it and other people are not going to wander into it during the rite. When choosing the site, keep in mind that you will be digging into the ground at least two feet deep, so choose a location that has some type of topsoil or sand, not bare rock. If this will be a group activity, you should test the site beforehand by digging a few pilot holes or even a full tomb to make sure the area will be suitable for the group to dig all the tombs. Be sure to check the area thoroughly to avoid anthills, gopher or other animal holes, snake nests, etc. Also, never perform the rite in an area near to a cemetery or archeological site.

2. Once the site is chosen, you must decide exactly where the tomb(s) will be located and positioned, and where the fire will be. If only one tomb is being dug, I suggest that the tomb face east, toward the rising sun. If there are multiple tombs being dug, place the tombs in circle around the central fire so the positioning of the tombs resembles the rays of the sun. In both cases, the tombs are approximately five paces from the fire, and while lying in the tomb the body of the initiate is positioned with the head in the part of the tomb closest to the fire. The tomb is rectangular in shape and slightly longer and wider than the person going into it. Using a stick, pick, or shovel, mark out the outline of each tomb on the surface of the ground, but do not start the actual digging yet.

3. Once the location of the fire and the tombs is finalized, before any digging is done, the site should be consecrated with blessings and offerings. The best place to do this is in the spot where the fire will be alive and watching over everyone during the entire night. A small hole is dug in the exact spot where the fire will be, and each person going into the earth, as well as the firekeeper(s) places an offering into the hole while saying words of thanks to the place, requesting support and

safety from the land and all the living beings that inhabit it, and briefly explaining the offering being made to the earth. The offering that you give is something deeply personal and should not be taken lightly. It should be something very small physically but very powerful energetically. It should be nonpolluting and symbolic of your desire to merge with the earthbody. One of the most powerful yet simple offerings you can make is your own blood. To do this, prick your finger with a needle or razor blade. While placing a few drops in the hole, tell the sacred place that your blood is your offering of union with the soil and symbolizes your desire and intention of becoming one with the land. Watch as your blood is absorbed by the earth and then cover the hole with soil and tend to your finger.

4. Now use whatever hand tools are necessary to dig the tomb(s). While digging, place the soil to one side of the tomb or in back, but not between the tomb and the fire. Dig the tomb deep enough so that you have a few inches between your face and the roof when the tomb is covered. Be sure to carefully check your tomb for size by actually lying in it. There should be two to four inches' extra space all around your body, but not more or you will lose some of the energetic qualities of the soil encapsulating you.

5. Once the digging is complete, then construct the roof by placing branches or wood planks across the top of the tomb from side to side, not front to back. Once the supports for the roof are in place, the easiest way to cover the roof so that when earth is placed on top it doesn't sift through into the tomb is to place a piece of natural cloth (a hemp or cotton bed sheet works fine) over the top of the tomb, making sure it is large enough to extend at least six inches over the tomb on all sides. For this stage you can also use natural materials such as leaves, pine needles, field grass, etc., but keep in mind that the last step in constructing the tomb is to completely cover the roof of the tomb with soil, so the roof will have to be able to hold the weight of the soil and also keep it from sifting into the tomb from on top of you.

To complete the roof, shovel earth onto it to cover the whole tomb with at least three inches of earth except for an opening just large enough for you to get into at the head of the tomb, where you will enter. This section will be covered with earth (except for an opening for air approximately four by four inches) by the firekeeper after you are in the tomb.

Preparation

During this rite of passage you will pass through five "gates" or stages. The first gate is reviewing and acknowledging your life and what has led you to the moment of this ceremony. During the two-night, three-day version of this rite, the participants tell their life story to the fire and their companions either in one group or separate groups, depending on how many people are participating. Recounting your life out loud in front of a sacred fire and other people, and listening while others do it in front of you, is a powerful exercise that has numerous benefits in terms of personal growth and raising awareness. For the shortened version of the rite, and for those not participating as part of a group, I suggest that you write down the story of your life in the weeks prior to going into the earth. This important step helps you to discover patterns in your behavior so that you can develop strategies to break free from the unwanted ones, and it places your life into a context so that you clearly see where you are in the current moment of your life and how that relates to being buried alive in the earth.

Whether you tell your life story with a group during the rite or you write it down beforehand, the most important preparation for this rite is simply to become clear about why you are doing this, or to at least start the process of this knowing. Some of the reasons may be very apparent, but some may only become clear as you proceed through the process. One of the main tasks of preparation before and during the ceremony will be the finding and clarifying of those parts of yourself and your life to be placed into the forefront of the earth's energy. Below is a short list of circumstances that are appropriate for this rite of passage, followed by brief comments on how to prepare for those that pertain to you:

Obtain clarity and vision in personal matters. This is one of the most readily available gifts of the burial, but in order to get the most from it I suggest that you enter the earth with a short list of very specific questions to pose during your time in the ground. The more to the point the question, the clearer will be the answer. During the days prior to the burial, work on this list and refine it until the time of the ceremony.

Recharge personal energy before or after a demanding task or challenge. The burial into living soil can be a significant activity for preparing energetically and emotionally for a big life event, and/or for recuperating from such an event. The burial places your energy firmly into the reality of the organic world. It cuts through all the technological conveniences of the modern era and allows your energy to mix with the energy of the earth in a pure and intentional way. All that is needed for sharing energy with the land is for you to be relaxed and have an open heart and mind. Make whatever preparations and ask any questions you need in order to promote a peaceful and receptive state of being.

Heal and absorb emotional wounds. Emotional wounds can never be healed by burying them deep inside of your heart or head. They must be brought out and set free. The burial is the perfect place for this, and Earth will accept whatever you need to set free. She won't judge or condemn you, and she will always be there. If you need emotional healing, prepare by writing down and clarifying those specific events that hurt you so that you can bring them out and release them while in the ground.

Mark a significant life change and rite of passage. The Embrace of the Earth rite has proven to be an extremely valuable tool when passing through a significant time of transition in your life. Make sure to spend time alone with yourself and write down what you want to manifest in your new life and why. Then write down the small steps you will take in order to get there. Take this with you into the womb of Earth and use the experience to mark the moment and obtain vision.

Bury the "old" self and allow the birth of the new. Obviously, digging and spending the night in a gravelike tomb does hold implications of the awareness of death. This can be used in a nonmorbid way in order to give renewed energy, urgency, and strength to your actions. Although you are not placed in any physical danger during the burial, the near-death implications of being buried alive will help you to not put off the things in your life that would be better done today.

Experience in a tangible way the profound love and healing energy of Earth. If there were no other reasons for intentional burial, I would do it simply because it is an extremely potent way to feel physically, psychically, and spiritually our profound connection with the organic soil and the spirit of Earth. Prepare to feel this by acknowledging the daily gifts of life Earth provides us with during the days prior to the burial. If you have time, go to a place in nature and talk to the land about your current life.

Aside from the above considerations, it is a good idea to prepare your body for the experience by treating it well in the days prior to the burial. Avoid overeating and intoxication. Try to walk and breathe intentionally and in a way that improves clarity of thought and action. If you have experience with fasting, this is an appropriate supplement to the burial, but keep in mind that whether you have fasted before or not, you will need sufficient energy for the hard physical work of preparing your tomb.

In the days prior to the rite, you will also have to prepare the material items you will need. These include:

- Materials for taking notes

- Clothes and shoes appropriate for the season and for working outdoors (digging)

- Extra changes of clothes and shoes

- Raingear (in case of wet weather)

- Sunscreen

- Hat for sun protection

- Sufficient drinking water

- Work gloves

- Flashlight with new batteries

- A shovel for digging

- Branches or planks, and cloth for the roof of the tomb

- A pick or adz

- Materials for starting a fire and enough wood to keep it burning all night

- Sleeping mat/camping pad or extra blanket to lie on during the night

- Sleeping bag/blanket for warmth

- Pillow, if you want one

- Offerings and personal items (such as photos or sacred objects) to take into the tomb

Keep in mind that from the very first moment you decide to enter the Embrace of the Earth rite of passage, the sacred time has begun. Everything you do from that moment until you come out of your tomb will affect your experience, so proceed with common sense, intention, and honesty. Many questions and fears are likely to be rolling around in your head. That's good. They are all part of the rite. The more unsure you are about the perceived risks, the greater the possibility for growth and the more lasting the effects of the experience will be. Center your attention on steadily using your fears and insecurities to focus on your preparation.

Susan, a forty-two-year-old single mother, came to the burial after a failed marriage and with a lot on her mind. Despite her fears, she prepared very well:

I heard about the Embrace of the Earth burial rite when James was doing a local workshop . . . The timing of it was perfect—one day after the closing of my first house purchased on my own, and my son was scheduled to be with his dad that weekend. I felt God/Goddess was guiding me to the ceremony. I decided to participate in the burial and from that moment the process of preparation began. Since my divorce I've been living with this motto: if you're scared, you've got to do it anyway. Images of me laying under the earth all dark, with worms crawling in my ears, with the roof coming down on me, kept running through my head. I tried using relaxation techniques to pair with the images, but my stomach was still doing flip flops up until the actual burial. In the days prior to the rite I started emailing James with my questions and concerns and patiently, with care, he answered them. Preparations for the burial included physical and emotional/mental work. We had to write our intentions for the burial. I worked and revised my list, trying to get it as detailed as possible, separating what I hoped to let go of and what I wanted to let into my life. The final list included:

What I want to let go of:

- fear that I won't be able to thrive on my own

- fear that others won't be there when I need them

- the idea that I'm a burden when I need help

- not appreciating my strengths

- guilt about having the affair and behaving in a hurtful way

- anger and blame when I'm disappointed that something doesn't go my way

- pain of a failed marriage

- pain of a failed engagement

- controlling to get what I want

- procrastinating

- forgetting my strengths and specialness and instead looking outside myself and relying on others' attention too much to get those good feelings about myself

- sex without true connection to my heart and a partner's heart but with connection to ego

- guilt about putting Tom through the divorce

- a cold heart

- Holocaust hurts passed on from my father's side of the family

What I wanted to bring into my life:

- mark my strengths, my connections, commitments and rootedness in buying my house

- allow myself to grow and nourish my strengths, specialness

- prepare and take responsibilities for the upkeep of my house and a partnership

- trust that I can stand on my own and thrive on my own

- stay connected to myself and God/Goddess in my work and relationships

- open my heart safely

- trust others will be there when I need them

- create a loving partnership with kindness, respect, fun, joy, consciousness, understanding, passion, commitment, and balance of togetherness and aloneness

- to accept disappointments as part of humanness in myself and others

- patience for myself and others

- to appreciate all gifts

- emotionally be present for others

- another child

- to continue success at work

- get my paperwork, bills, and billings done

- forgiveness for when I haven't been the best person I can be, when I didn't walk with God's light, when I've been hurtful

- listen to my guides

I also prepared physically by getting warm clothing and boots and making a meal to share with the group afterwards. I'm usually not that prepared, but I was for this ceremony, marking how important I felt it was but not knowing exactly why. I also wrote a song preparing me for the burial.

Susan had a truly life-altering experience in this rite of passage, in part due to the care and intention she placed on the preparation. She carefully made her preparation lists, and tuned them up until the final moments before entering the earth's womb. This provided her with the clear intention to overcome her fears and allow the energy of the earth to embrace her.

Walter, a thirty-six-year-old survivor of the September 11 tragedy, learned about the rite of passage just a week before he did it, but the circumstances, and his clear intention, came together in a positive way:

I realized I was not living up to my true calling, or full potential. Eventually, I knew I had to quit my job (as an equity options trader on Wall Street) and start on a new path, better for me as well as the planet. The timing of the Embrace of the Earth rite was perfect . . . it was the perfect way to begin and I realized how powerful this experience could be if I allowed myself to just be with the experience. After having worked in the "greed is good" environment where materialism ruled supreme (and the splendor of nature was totally ignored), it was fitting that I would end, and begin, with the earth.

The night before the rite I finally sat down, took pen to paper, and thought about why I was doing this. By that stage, I had already overcome my fear of being enclosed in the tomb. Looking back, it seems so easy and simplistic. I also wrote that I wanted to be embraced by Mother Earth, to return to the peace and tranquility of the womb, preparing to be born anew, reborn full of energy to carry out the new challenges that await me. I also felt I wanted to be nurtured, cared for, loved, and protected. Little did I know that this was to be answered with a powerful vision during my time in the earth. Lastly, I wanted to know and understand my weaknesses—to leave them behind as I entered the world with a new vision, clarity, and understanding.

In Walter's case he was at a natural point of transition in his life and this rite of passage came at the perfect time. More importantly, he seized the opportunity and went into the rite knowing why he was doing it. His experience in the earth was powerful because he jumped right into it openly, intentionally, and with his eyes wide open. But many times it doesn't happen that way. Janet, a fifty-five-year-old restaurant owner, enrolled for the Embrace of the Earth rite six months in advance, but during that time period she cancelled and then reconsidered four times before the big day arrived. Through many conversations with her I felt confident that she was preparing herself in a strong way and that if she could just get herself to actually show up for the rite she would have the experience she needed to continue with her life in a new and clearer way. Many times during the preparation period she actually became angry with me because she resented the fact that I was suggesting she work with the past in order to fully see the present. The past is not just the past, it is happening right now as well. The past is what has made the current "you" and should not be forgotten while preparing for the rite of passage. Here is a section of what she wrote about a portion of the time she spent in her tomb:

> I woke up and didn't know where I was and I couldn't move, I felt trapped and started sobbing loudly. James came to my air hole and shined the flashlight in and asked if I was all right. I told him to get me the hell out of here! He calmly told me that I could come out at any time but wanted to be sure that was what I really wanted and that it was the best thing to do. We "breathed" together for a few minutes and then he talked with me for quite a while as I laid here in this hole in the ground. At first I didn't really want to stay in the tomb, but after talking a while I felt silly about coming out for no good reason. So I told James I would stay a little longer and see what happened. I kept asking myself over and over what am I doing here laying in this tomb? Have I gone completely crazy? Are all these people, including James, just nuts?
>
> Just as I was about to call James again and get out of the tomb, I remembered my notebook that I brought into the grave with me. I turned on my flashlight and began to read the things I had written over the last six months of preparing for this. They saved me. I mean, they actually saved my life because they kept me in the tomb when I wanted to come out, and if I would have come out I would never have had the wonderful and healing experiences I had later in the night and this morning that changed my life. My release of my anger into the earth and my visions of my new life have kept me alive and kicking. My notebook full of shit literally saved my life!

The Dig

The physical aspects of this rite of passage are just as important as the other levels. If we were to hire a machine to come and dig the tombs, we would lose an incalculable amount of insights and lessons that come as a result of digging our own grave. Tina, a forty-six-year-old massage therapist, describes meeting some of her demons while making her tomb:

> As I began to carve my grave out of the earth, I could not separate myself from the journey that had gotten me to that point. I felt so fortunate to have the opportunity to join others in this rare opportunity to enter the earth in a self-made space . . . to lie all night in her embrace.

The first lessons came almost immediately as my attempts to remove the sod revealed how long a day this was going to be! With each pick and shovel and handful of Pennsylvania shale I removed, I began to process the way I deal with the difficulties in my day-to-day life. Sometimes the joy would win but most times I was annoyed at how often I wanted to give up. Then, with the sweat, produced by a hot August sun, pouring out of my body, mixing with the occasional tear of frustration or the blood from a sharp stone, I could feel the resistance drain away. I began to sing!

As my fellow "gravediggers" became more and more engrossed in their own process, I could tell we were all being drawn deeper into the release of any romantic ideas about this experience and closer to the reality of our night ahead . . .

Steve, a teenager that came to the rite, put it this way:

Digging the tombs was great. I don't particularly enjoy physical work, but it always seems gratifying when you're doing it in a positive light. I think the physical side of the ceremony is great for getting you into the right mindset. A lot of the extraneous thoughts you have seem to fade away. You start thinking to yourself, "Wow, I'm really here doing this, it's really happening." It's as though the physical exercise transports you to the "now," the "present."

The digging of the tomb, at many levels, becomes a mirror reflecting the realities of birth, life, death, and rebirth. Many times the insights gleaned while digging the tomb are the most powerful of the whole experience. Ellen, a forty-nine-year-old salesperson, found this out:

The first thing I did was carefully take all the sod off the top and placed it in a special place so I could put it back on exactly as it was when we were finished. It took me a long time and I was far behind the other diggers, but James told me that we weren't done until the last person in the group finished and that even though most of the tomb should be dug personally, the whole group would help each other as a team to get the tombs all ready. So, I wasn't really worried and I kind of took my time, plus it was really hot. As I dug, I started singing a line from Peter Gabriel—"Digging in the dirt, to heal the places we got hurt."

I was digging for a while and getting a lot done. Then I hit my first big rock. I dug the dirt out from around it and could see how big it was. Just as I was really starting to feel annoyed about having to dig it out, I heard James announce to the group something like "While you are digging, pay attention to what is happening. You may meet a living creature, a root, or a rock that has a message for you. We are in the magic time now, everything that happens here has meaning. Pay attention . . ."

Well, I sat down on the edge of my tomb and looked at that darn rock and immediately I knew what it symbolized. It was the enormous weight I had been carrying on my back since

I was a teenager. It was my fear and my insecurity. I dug that big rock out of my grave and placed it with my sod so I could put it back in the earth and bury it the next day. During the digging of the grave I found three more smaller but significant stones, each one perfectly mirroring for me my two children and ex-husband. Right near the end of digging I also found a rock that looked like quartz. I held it up to the sun and I thought I heard it speak to me—"I represent your inner light; keep me close to you during the night and I will keep you safe."

In addition to the offering we make to the land and the fire at the very beginning of the rite, it is also customary to each choose one medium-size stone that was found while digging the tomb and place it in the circle of stones that create the seat for the central fire. In this way, each of the initiates are represented above the ground in front of the fire during the night.

The Fire

The transition from day to night marks the corresponding transition in the focus of the rite's activities. During the day we physically prepare both the tombs as well as our physical body by taking a little food, water, and, if available, a cleansing bath or shower and change of clothes after the tombs are prepared. When darkness begins to fall, we begin to switch from the physically inspired processes to the more numinous levels of awareness as we prepare mentally, emotionally, energetically, and spiritually to enter the womb of the earth during the night. Assisting us in this is the energy, light, heat, and music of the sacred fire. The fire watches over us throughout the night, just as the sun did during the day. Thus the fire becomes our night sun.

In this rite, as in most shamanic rituals, the fire plays a significant role in the proceedings. In another section of this book I have devoted a special section to working shamanically with the fire, but as it concerns this particular ritual there are some important additional aspects to the relationship and interplay between the fire and the initiates that need to be expanded upon.

1: Purification

From the moment that the first human beings discovered how to make fire, up to the present day of our highly sophisticated technologies, the dramatic and, at times, incredible power of fire to consume and transform matter at grand scales is an undeniable display of just how susceptible we are to the powers that rule the earth and the cosmos. The purifying aspects of fire as witnessed in the natural world led to its becoming associated with the inner processes of human purification in shamanic and mystical rites of passage, ritual, and ceremony. But in these traditions fire is not simply used as a symbol or metaphor. On the contrary, connections between outer fire and inner fire are actual tangible experiences of a kind of mystical union that is used in myriad ways to facilitate psychophysical transformation, purification, and, in the case of my Wirrarika shaman mentors, communication and divination.

For these shamans the fire is infinitely more than the physical manifestation of fire that we see in a campfire or harnessed by our stoves, furnaces, and automobiles. To them, and to anyone that has felt a connection to the fire that surpasses the common perceptions of light and heat, the fire is very much a force or presence that is found in all organic life. In this sense the fire is very much alive and carries within it the universal energy of not only our sun but the entire cosmos of constellations in such an immeasurable way that it is truly the spark that animates what we call nature and life. Within this context, the fire carries the spirit of life within it.

This is why shamanic initiations, especially ones with the transformative implications of the Embrace of the Earth, have at their core a significant interaction with fire at many levels. At the level of purification, connecting to the fire "burns off" our masks and layers of protective coverings that we have placed over our true nature throughout our lives. This contributes to the removal of our "thick skin" so that we can truly lay the flesh of our soul bare to receive the embrace of the earth. But just as the physical transformational properties of fire are powerful and destructive, so, too, can be the psychic cleansing involved with purification at a psychological level. However, as painful as these experiences can be, they are simply part of the rite of passage, and they are essential because they accelerate the purging of emotional and mental fixations as well as suppressed bodily urges and physical tensions so that we open the door to our true perceptual abilities.

When I facilitate the Embrace of the Earth rite of passage for people, the energetic exchange with the fire and subsequent purification is always one of the final activities before entering the tomb for the night. The fire is made in a special way and normally the arrival of the fire is welcomed and comforting for the initiates. People have a natural affinity for the flowing energy of fire, and when brought to life in a special and meaningful manner the connection is usually immediate. The task then becomes to take this initial connection deeper, deeper than the initiates have ever gone before, so that the presence of the fire aids in the energetic cleansing before entering the tomb. Depending on the size of the group, this cleansing could take many forms, but in all cases there are at least five specific energetic exchanges between the initiate and the fire in this preparatory cleansing stage of the ritual. It is helpful to view these exchanges as gates or doorways that one passes through, with each successive gate leading to an area of increased clarity or purity of intention. Passing through each of these five gates is most efficient when an experienced facilitator of the rite is present to keep the energy flowing.

The first gate has to do with owning the past and purging any bottled-up past emotions by giving them to the fire. Each initiate is given the opportunity to speak with the fire about their past, how it holds them back, and how they came to be present in the rite. If there is an experienced facilitator present, they can pose pertinent questions to the initiate while they are speaking, if they feel it would help the initiate to get the most from the activity. The most important part of this first step is for the initiate to simply keep talking, especially if they are having a hard time. Some people have no problem talking with the fire, but others simply freeze up, and that's when an experienced ecoshamanic facilitator is indispensable.

What we are trying to do in this first step is open that energetic door with the fire through communication, and there is nothing that we seemingly know better than our own personal story. When the bashful and controlling side of our ego is turned off, the recounting of this story should be something that just flows out of us. It should not require any time to "stop and think." On the contrary, this purging should be one continuous stream of words and energy flowing from the initiate and going into the fire. To foster trust and also to honor the heroic act of people opening up this way, I always begin this first activity with the fire by speaking to the group about the sacred aspects of what we are doing and then having the group make a sacred agreement that nothing said around the circle of the fire ever leaves without permission. The only task of the initiates that are not speaking is to listen in a nonjudgmental way to the person speaking and to "feed" the person speaking with good thoughts and intentions. In this respect, the initiates become for the speaker the extended body of the fire. Tina wrote about this part of the ritual in this way:

> We agree that this is sacred space, and that what is said here doesn't leave. This creates the secure environment to feel comfortable—to be ourselves, to be real. We can't worry about what comes out of our hearts and into the fire . . . the power of the group is that we support each other, facilitate our openness, and mirror our feelings.
>
> The fire invites us to let our energy flow from deep inside, outwards to the flames. We will be doing the same with the earth, letting ourselves become energetically connected. James tells

us that the first door has opened, and we take turns talking to the fire. As I start to talk, I'm not thinking . . . the words just come from within, and I realize that I have to release issues from my past . . . issues about my family, about my childhood and college, and about my career . . .

The second activity in this stage is for each initiate to talk to the fire about their present life. This should happen in the same way—one continuous flow of words from initiate to fire. Usually this second stage of talking about the present is much easier than talking about the past and normally flows without much input from the facilitator.

The third gate is the present moment, sitting next to the fire, soon to go into the earth. One by one the initiates speak to the fire about how they feel in that moment, what they hope to receive from the experience, what they would like the earth to help them with, and anything else they want to say. In this stage it is very important for the facilitator to make clear, from the very first person talking, that now we need to get as specific as we can about our intentions. If the initiates have prepared a list of items to bring up while in the earth, this is the time to read the list out loud to the fire and to add to it or subtract from it. It is very common that after digging the tomb and speaking with the fire in the first two stages it becomes clearer why you are doing this, and oftentimes you realize issues to bring out in the tomb that you hadn't thought of before. Or maybe the core of many issues becomes distilled while talking with the fire. If someone is not being clear in this stage, then it is the job of the facilitator to carefully and compassionately help draw out the initiate from what they are hiding behind so that they can enter the earth with clear intentions.

The fourth stage is the hypothetical future that is made not through asking but by doing. During this stage of work with the fire, each initiate spells out precisely what they want for their lives in the future and also how they plan to get there.

The fifth and final act of cleansing and purification with the fire is the confession. In this case we are not talking about the kind of confession made in a church with the intention of being absolved from some sort of moral sin. This type of confession is purely about energy, not morals. It in no way concerns how anyone else might view your actions. The reason you are confessing is not because you may have done something wrong in the eyes of another person, but rather because the events you confess have left an energetic stain on your true being and this is the chance to invite the purifying fire to help burn them away. For example, many times it is hard for people to truly say goodbye to either a relative or past lover, and so they carry this unresolved issue around with them for the rest of their life. In this moment with the fire, you would say that goodbye. You would use the person's name and talk to the fire, just as if that person was the fire. Another common energetic stain is not saying thanks to someone who has helped you. Now is that time. Say names. Bring out the emotions behind the event. It has been my experience that in this type of ritual, as well as with sustained pilgrimages and vision quests, the more thoroughly you open yourself to releasing the events of energetic blockage in this type of confession, the more profound and useful will be your experiences in the sacred time of powerful ritual and ceremony. If you don't do it, it is like trying to walk with a heavy ball and chain attached to your ankle. By releasing the weight, you allow yourself to soar.

2: Protection

The second significant aspect of the presence of the fire in this rite is protection. What exactly happens to a person engaged in shamanic ritual is a mystery as big as why we are all here on Earth. The process of transformation initiated by the ritual can be directed and structured through conscious control, but the psychophysiology and physics of the rite are not understandable within our current paradigms of science. The only way to safely open the door to such experiences is to travel on paths that others have safely taken in the past and apply the experience and knowledge of those previous journeys. Even when this is done there are still risks, just as there are risks in anything we do in life, but starting off on the journey with a time-tested tool kit is just common sense, and it also fosters confidence for when we come face to face with the mystery and the unknown territory.

The most time-tested shamanic tool of protection is the sacred fire, especially at night. When we invite the energy of the fire by igniting it in the center of our ritual, we have now come under the metaphysical protection of the fire if we feed it with respect and intention and a clean heart. One of the reasons for engaging in the five-step process of cleansing with the fire that I just explained is that by energetically entering into a dialog with the fire, we "feed" it with our hearts and souls and offerings. In return for feeding the fire, the fire protects us with light and a unique quality of metaphysical energy. How this happens is really not explainable, but it is certainly quantifiable. I have seen it happen so many times that for me it is a situation as real as a dog protecting its master from a stranger in the night. The light from the sacred fire blankets the entire circle of the tombs and inside that area of light we are protected, as long as we feed the fire with pure intentions and open hearts.

3: Connection

There is an undeniable connection that can be made to the fire with sufficient intention and experience. The most knowledgeable and influential indigenous shamans I know communicate with and through the fire as part of their core shamanic abilities. When we foster a connection to the fire through passing through the various stages laid out in this section, and we can tangibly see the light of the fire dispelling the darkness surrounding the circle of tombs, as well as feel the flowing energy of security that being next to a living, sacred fire provides, we have an immensely valuable source of inspiration that we can focus on while in the darkness of the womb of the earth. That is one of the reasons the fire is fed and kept alive the whole time the initiates are in the tombs. And because (at least for the first-time initiate) there is a hole for air at the head of the tomb, once in a while the initiate will hear the fire talking or catch the flicker of light and know that the fire is there, watching over them and promising the rebirth and light of a new day.

Connecting to the fire also helps in establishing a connection to the land and Earth itself. This is because the fire is so easy for us to connect to. This can be observed in the way we have "fireplaces" that don't function as a primary source of heat in a home, or restaurant, or lodge, but rather are there because people enjoy the conscious and subconscious presence of the fire. Connecting to this energy and feeling can function as a bridge to connecting to the energy and feeling of the soil. Once you open to the connection of one, the transition to connect with the others becomes more fluid and natural. The other fundamental elements of the world, water and air, can also facilitate this. Susan put it this way:

> James explained the ways of Grandfather Fire and how we can merge the fire inside of us with the sacred fire in front of us. I've had that experience with water when I went to the Smoky Mountains and the power of the Chippewa Falls was felt inside my belly as I stood before it and merged with it, and I have also had a similar type experience with the sparkle of Lake Superior that is known inside my heart. I had never heard anyone explain this kind of connection, especially to the fire, and it was comforting to hear that other people felt these things, and it was very helpful in developing a similar connection to earth energy while in my tomb.

One of the senses that helps us to connect to the energetic essences of the big natural powers is sound. The sound of the ocean, or a river, the wind, or the fire, among so many others, provides us with a jumping-off point to enter into even deeper levels of connection. Also in terms of sound, another important element of this particular ritual is the presence of the drum.

The drum sings the voice of the fire to the initiates during the night in the form of the heartbeat of the earth and cosmos. The facilitator and their assistant, while feeding the fire, will also periodically drum throughout the night. In this case, the cadence of the drum is always the same. It is a simple and slow one-two rhythm resembling the beating of the human heart. Any other drumming styles or rhythms are to be avoided, as they will be distracting to the initiates in the ground. This is not a drum concert. Throw all of your formal drum training out the window; now is not the time for any sort of performance. The functions of the drum in this ritual are to signify to the initiates in the tomb that they are not alone, that they are safe and protected by the fire as well as the human helpers, and to provide a steady audible as well as energetic reminder of the heartbeat of the earth. In the tomb you are a baby in the womb of your mother; you have a heartbeat and so does she. The heartbeat of the drum reminds and connects us to the fact that we live as part of a much bigger body.

For this ritual it is very important that the drum be introduced to the fire and the initiates before they go into the tombs. This can be very simply done by the owner of the drum presenting it to the fire and, while drumming the heartbeat with it, recounting briefly its history and why it is there in a similar but briefer way to how the initiates present themselves. An offering to the fire can also be made for the drum. If the drum was made by the owner, then a few drops of blood saved from the animal whose skin will be chanting can be offered. At many levels, for the ecoshamanic facilitator, the significance and power of working in concert with a drum made from materials obtained by you, and put together by you, become especially apparent at moments such as this, when the connection you have to the spirit of the drum can take the whole ritual and everyone participating to an even higher level.

On Dying and Being Reborn

In this rite of passage we intentionally pursue circumstances that bring out from within us the transformational power that is fostered through metaphorically dying and being reborn. But unlike other spiritual forms of this process, where the metaphor is drawn up through words or commitments of being born again, in this ecoshamanic ritual we actually dig our grave and submerge ourselves in it, thereby facing our mortality with the entire MBESA of our human organism. This is about as close as you can get to the awareness of death without placing yourself in mortal danger or having a physical near-death experience. Plus, in this ritual context you are totally submerged inside of an organic process and provided with the support and encouragement to take the opportunity to make positive use of the experience in a way that improves the quality of your life and happiness. In his book *The Unfolding Self* (Novato, CA: Origin Press, 1998), Dr. Ralph Metzner, an expert on transformative experience, gets right to the point with respect to the implications of the "death-rebirth" initiation:

> Whereas in some Christian fundamentalist circles it is customary for people who have made a commitment to Christ to refer to themselves as "twice born," the original meaning of that concept goes much deeper than simply a profession of renewed faith, however sincere. It refers, actually, to the second part of a death-rebirth transformational process. The rebirth experience, to be authentic, must of necessity be preceded by an experience of metaphorically dying. This first, dying phase is inevitably anxiety provoking and problematical for most people. . . . In the mystery religions of ancient times and in many traditional cultures, "death-rebirth" was and is the name of an initiatory experience. Associated with it are the ritual practices such as entombment, profound isolation, or painful ordeal through which the initiate must pass. Afterward, the initiate customarily adopts a new name, perhaps a new garment, and sometimes a new role in society, all of which express the newly reborn being.

A powerful activity before entering the tomb is the preparation of a short note that will act as your final words of connection to this life. The note is written just as if you knew you were going to die and never see your loved ones again. The note should include anything you want them (or the rest of the world) to read after you are gone. This note is placed under your rock in the fire circle.

The Tomb

The initiate climbs into the tomb and the material world is left behind. A threshold to the shamanic world of nature and spirit is crossed. The immediate and familiar support of family, friends, colleagues, pets, accomplishments, failures, and all the trappings and freedoms of everyday life are severed. As the initiate lies down in the tomb, the tomb becomes a sacred chamber consecrated by the concrete action of the initiate to know both self and world in new and improved ways. Lying in the tomb with the entrance being covered by the fire-keeper, the flesh of the initiate is formally offered to the body of the earth. In these moments, as the last shovelfuls of soil are being thrown on top of the tomb, the exchange between initiate and Earth begins. Flesh begins to become soil and soil begins to become flesh. All begin to come together as one.

The preparations are over, everyone has left, and now it is just you, the earth, and the journey you are about to take, inside and out. Then the firekeeper opens a fist-size hole in the corner of the roof of your earthly cocoon. You are not trapped and you will not die this night. The air hole ensures that fresh, life-giving air surrounds you and is inside of you. The love of the earth is embracing you. The energy of the fire is protecting you. The rest of your life is waiting for you.

The firekeeper puts their hand through the air hole and into the tomb. As you take their hand in yours, the feelings of life and love, companionship and kinship flow between you. And then the hand is gone. The journey begins . . .

From Susan:

I stepped down and into my grave. It felt all cozy. Jim shoveled, and the dirt falling on top wasn't as scary as I thought. It had a rhythm to it that seemed to help me transition into going deeper into the earth, but also deeper into myself . . .

From Tina:

As the last shovel of dirt was piled on the roof and the air hole was finished, I had a rush of anxiety that quickly dissipated by keeping myself "busy." I took my light and began to examine my space. To my delight I realized how intimate a connection I had to my grave. I remembered digging every bit of it. I remembered the rocks like friends: the ones I removed and the ones I had chosen to have stay. I remembered the small roots I had chopped and now saw the dangling ends as a source of wonder and appreciation of the unseen world, so beautiful and efficient in creating and sustaining life as we see it on the surface. I thought about Water and Sun and Air and Earth. Ahhh, the Earth, filling my senses to overflowing . . . I prayed and meditated and began to ask the questions I had prepared. I was amazed at how quickly the responses came! The first surprise was that as soon as I asked a question I had such increased clarity, that a more "proper" question would come to me in a flash. It truly IS about the question because once I asked the one I truly needed to have answered, the answer would come immediately. The questions I thought of, the ones from my head, were not the ones that came from my heart. And although not all the answers were the ones I wanted to hear, the truth held within each one was clear.

I began to get tired as I relaxed into my space. I could hear the drumming and chanting of the firekeeper. Although comforting, I preferred a more quiet experience. I put in my earplugs and fell asleep. Thus beginning the journey of dreams . . .

From Walter:

Well, here I am, lying in my grave. Quite an amazing experience so far. Hearing the sound of the dirt as James and my companions threw the last few shovels full, with just a small hole for air. Looking around my tomb, it's quite fascinating. It's really like another world down here—a variety of textures and colors in the soil, an occasional stone visible, all held together by an intricate network of roots—some tiny, some quite chunky. Holy cow! I just got the heebie-jeebies scared out of me by a tiny bug walking around on the lens of my headlamp, making its shadow appear like a huge monster. Suddenly, I'm not tired at all. After feeling so exhausted from digging the tomb and lack of sleep last night, I feel as if I have adrenaline coursing through my veins. I hear the firekeeper singing and drumming:

We are weavers, we are the woven ones;

We are dreamers, we are the dream;

Spiraling into the center, the center of the flame . . .

I feel quite comfortable, very safe and secure. No sense whatsoever of claustrophobia. One part of me is asking, "What on earth are you doing here!?" The other part is feeling inspired and energized, though starting to feel a little tired now. I'm going to spend some time now reading through my questions . . .

And so the journey, so unique and personal to each initiate, begins as the settling-in process continues and the fears, anxieties, hopes, and dreams begin to increase and dissipate as the passage unfolds. The experiences in the tombs are as unique as the individuals; the lessons as profound as the mysteries of life. At this stage of the ritual it is common to pass through a period of questioning or even rage or feelings of depression. In many cases, but certainly not all, this phase is actually very conducive to later in the night experiencing profound insights and/or visions. This period of doubt is another threshold to cross over once one is actually inside the tomb, and once it is crossed a new hallway opens up in front of you with many more rooms to explore.

From Sarah:

I just got into my grave and all I keep asking myself is what did I possibly do to end up here? And then I feel the darkness answer. *Everything. Everything you've ever done has put you here.* I start to cry. I can't remember one decision I've ever made that was right. I can't remember ever loving anyone with all my heart. No wonder I'm lying in this grave, I deserve it. I always think of myself first. The fire just told me that when all the other people were talking and instead of listening and sending them my good thoughts I just sat there thinking about myself and what I was going to say in front of the other people and especially James. If I tell the truth he will think I'm a failure. If I lie the fire won't protect me. What if I tell half of the truth? You know what, I really don't give a shit. Wow, what an awful realization. Did I really need to dig a hole in the ground for hours, get all dirty and sweaty and smoky, and be surrounded by bugs and worms to realize that? Yeah, I guess so. AAAHHHH! I screamed at the top of my lungs. I DON'T WANT TO BE LIKE THIS ANYMORE. HELP ME. SOMEBODY. ANYBODY!

After yelling and kicking and screaming and crying, I finally started praying. I didn't really know how. The words just started coming. I asked the earth and sky to help me know and understand myself so that I could change from this pitiful selfish person into someone more authentic and caring. I asked the earth to show me how to love. I asked the earth to show me how to live.

After a while I fell into a half-awake, half-dream state. Or maybe I fell asleep and then woke up. I'm not sure. But in that state I felt like I was actually in my grave as a dead person. I felt like I was a dead skeleton and that I was lying in a puddle of my own guts. It felt very peaceful and I wasn't scared at all. It was very matter-of-fact. You are dead and you are lying in your grave. No big deal. When I woke up the next time it was a completely different story. I remembered being a skeleton and was freaked out. I turned on my light and looked all around the tomb. I found the hawk feather that I found in the field when we were digging our graves. That calmed me down as I began to think about how hard we all worked to dig the graves together. I feel better now thinking about that. I actually did help some of the other people, now that I think about it. And I even gave part of my lunch to Nick 'cuz his got stolen by one of the farm dogs. Okay, maybe there is hope for me. Where did I put my notebook with my questions?

In the scheme of experiences common to initiates, Sarah's trials are common to many. Another common feature is being forced to relate to the other beings that sometimes share the grave. This can be very enlightening.

From Kim:

I hear dirt crumbling down the wall and turn on my little flashlight to see where the sound is coming from. (I had thoughts the night before that some animal, snake, mouse, etc. would come crashing through the dirt wall). I will try to sleep after I discover what the dirt noise is. It is an earthworm, very long, I might add. I ask it to please go back for just tonight. Another one pokes its head through a bit later and I ask it nicely also. Thank you, Mother Earth, for beckoning them back. I realize that maybe they are more surprised to see me here than I of them. They are just doing their job. My fear of worms and snakes and mice really doesn't have anything to do with them. They never did anything to me. I projected my fears onto them. I don't feel so squeamish anymore!

Once one passes through these initial phases of the ritual, sleep sometimes comes as one becomes more comfortable with the surroundings and with themselves. From this point the initiate passes through different levels between fully awake and fully asleep. In my experience this is usually the most productive way to spend the first night of this ritual because you get to experience many different levels and states of consciousness. This is also one reason for periods of drumming throughout the night. The external sound of the beating drum facilitates the shift in states of consciousness. Although the experience of sleeping throughout the night in the tomb has its own benefits, shifting between being awake and asleep, and all the levels in between, has proven to be the most useful format for first-time initiates.

At this phase, which could be considered the core phase of the time actually spent in the tomb, perceptual shifts similar to peak-type experiences or even psychedelic trips are often produced. But in this case the psychoactive medicine is the ritual of being buried in the ground, and the trip is guided by the perceptual qualities brought on by the living soil, the mystical energy of the fire, and the heartbeat of the earth.

Common to both psychedelic experiences and the Embrace of the Earth ritual is the moment during the journey when everything seems to hinge on one small decision or single moment—as if the course of one's life would be decided if to turn left or right, go into the house or stay outside, to speak up or keep silent, and so on. In a similar way, I have heard this described many times by initiates to this ritual, and oftentimes it leads to transformative experience.

From Trish:

Oh my god. I have to pee so bad. I HAVE TO PEE. But I can't come out of the grave. I mean, I can come out but it would be such a hassle and I would disturb everyone and feel like such an idiot. But I have to pee so bad it hurts. No, it hurt a long time ago. Now the pain is getting unbearable. I've got to get out. No. Just a few more minutes. Maybe it will go away. It's not going away. OOOOWWWW. I gotta pee REALLY BAD.

So here I am now. It's almost morning and I'm going to write some of what happened to me last night. I think I'm ready. I don't want to forget. I tortured myself for about two hours trying to get up the courage to tell James I HAD to come out of the grave to pee. But in the end I didn't. Just as I thought I was going to explode, I just let it out. I peed myself right here in the grave. I can still feel the release. It was so powerful that waves of colorful purple and pink and peach rainbows flowed over me in my grave. Then I felt both the top of my head and the bottom of my womb open at the same time and a flood of soul or energy or something came pouring out of me and the next thing I new I was flying in the night sky. I don't remember seeing much but I remember flying and feeling the cool air blowing through my hair and my clothes. Yeah, I still had my clothes on! I don't know how long I was flying but when it was over I remember I was looking up at the top of my tomb. Just like I'm doing now. And I was wondering what just happened.

Then I remembered that I peed. But instead of feeling ashamed or angry, for some reason the first thing I felt was proud that I did it. I realized none of the awful things I thought would happen to me actually happened. It was really no big thing. I was a little wet but it is plenty warm in here and I'm not moving around, so I'm not really uncomfortable because of it. Then it hit me. What really happened. I did something I never do. I didn't control the situation, and I didn't wait around for the "right time to come." I just released and did it. Wow, why do I always make such a big deal about everything? Why does every little thing seem so important? Why do I care so much about what people think? How many things have I missed because I felt embarrassed by what people may think if I messed up? Oh my god. Could peeing myself be the most life-changing experience in my life? What happened to me after I released . . . I must have released a lot more than just my water. I must have released a lifetime worth of pent-up stuff that I was too self-conscious to admit. Wait. Now I remember more. As I was flying I saw down below me the circle of graves with the fire in the middle. I saw the energy and sparkly lights of the fire rising up from the flames and soaring into the sky to join with this flowing, multicolored energy of the sky in the stars. Then I saw my grave. I couldn't see into the grave but I knew it was mine. And coming from inside the grave was a bright ray of light about a foot in diameter and it was shooting up just like the fire and joining with the energy of the universe. It was my energy. It was me. I know it was.

I've never seen a bigger smile on a face than when Trish came out of her grave that morning. She was beaming. Her epiphany, aided by bodily function and physical confinement in the grave, contained many of the psychological and visionary aspects common to both psychedelic trips and the severe stress induced in shamanic rites of passage. Even though her stress was considerably self-induced, it still provided amazing results.

However, at this point it becomes necessary to distinguish between the "weird" things that people sometimes see during visionary experiences and those visions that actually promote the authentic unfolding of one's calling in life.

Without going into this topic at great length, which could be a whole book on its own, I invite you, especially with the ecoshamanic techniques I'm presenting in this book, to use this simple criteria when it comes to visionary experiences: if a vision helps you discover a piece of your hidden potential in a way that ultimately improves quality of life for you, someone else, or the planet, use it. If it doesn't, discard it. This simple criteria will help to eliminate many of the questions about seeing and feeling weird things while involved in shamanic, mystical, or spiritual activities. If a vision doesn't help you in some way, what good is it? Why waste your precious time and energy trying to figure it out? Granted, sometimes we receive a strong vision that we just know is important yet we can't quite put it together in any context that makes sense to us. That doesn't mean the vision was empty, it just means that maybe we aren't quite ready to understand what it means. When the time comes, we'll figure it out. But in the meantime, let it go and don't dwell on it. Especially if it is just some sort of bizarre image that doesn't help you with anything. Also, almost always in rites of passage such as the Embrace of the Earth or vision quest, it takes weeks, months, or even years to fully remember and put into place many of the helpful visions and perceptions and even questions brought out by the experience. This is part of the process. Don't fight it and don't hurry it. In summery, lots of "weird" stuff can appear to happen when you are buried in the ground all night in a tomb. If it's just weird, let it go; if it contains some sort of meaning to you, go forward with it.

In the experience of Trish, we saw many items common to transformational and shamanic journeys. It is always amazing how being isolated and enclosed so often leads to out of body experiences (OBE) and flying. During the core segments of this ritual it is common to feel sensations of being out of the body, or looking down upon the graves or fire. Sometimes this leads to a feeling or perception of transition between one level of consciousness to another. Initiates also often describe moving through or down a tunnel that leads to a transition that fosters feelings of serenity, peace, unity, love, or even ecstasy. Some people even describe seeing or visiting with dead relatives or friends. Others receive complex yet meaningful visions about life and our connection to the living earth. Brian, a molecular biologist, received a vision comparable to how he uses his intellect in the "real" world:

> My consciousness was floating above my grave and I could see my body down there as if my grave had no roof. As I watched I saw my body changing, almost imperceptively. As I continued to watch I slowly began to understand what I was seeing. I was actually watching the cells of my body die and others be born to take their place. Consciously I knew that millions of cells in our body die and are replaced each second we are alive. But what I didn't realize until hovering over my grave was that it is pointless to dwell on the fact of my mortality (which I had been doing lately since I had my sixty-second birthday) because since all of my cells are constantly being replaced during approximately every seven years, "my" consciousness has never really been attached to "my" body because I never had just one body. I've had several bodies that have been generated and then died and then were replaced. But my consciousness didn't die with them. I am still the same person I was when I was born. If that's not a miracle, I don't know what is!

Although we might debate certain points in Brian's logic, one thing that is not debatable is how that experience helped him to overcome the feelings of fear about dying that he had been carrying around with him. In this case, Brian's sometimes overly analytical mind melded with the perceptual shifts of the ritual burial to provide him with a vision that affected very positive change in the outlook he had on the rest of his life, and his eventual death.

A similar result is sometimes reported by those who have another type of common vision. Edward describes it this way:

> I had such an incredible feeling of peace in my whole being: my body, my mind, and my soul. I felt like I could spend an eternity just lying there in my grave in that state of peace and tranquility. And then, after what seemed to be many hours (but may have been only a few minutes, I really can't say), I felt like my body slowly but surely began to dissolve or disintegrate into the soil of the bottom of my grave. It was the most curious sensation because as my body fell into the soil I had the immediate sensation that the soil was alive and at one point I could feel the upper half of my body solid as usual but the lower part, the part that was now in the soil, was moving like the soil moves, with all the microbes and tiny life forms that make up the soil. So even as I had the sensation of losing myself into the earth—in effect, dying—the peace I was experiencing and the feeling of being transformed into the living soil made the transition from life to death seem more like a transition from life to life . . . Needless to say, I've come from this experience with new and increased awareness of the living soil I'm walking on, and when I get home I'm going to throw out all of the lawn chemicals I've been using for so many years, and one of my commitments (made at the end of the ritual) is to start a garden and a compost pile with my kids.

By far the type of experience recounted most often by initiates is the "life review." This phenomenon is in many ways similar to that of people who go through a near-death experience (NDE) in which during the course of only a few seconds their lives flash before their eyes like a movie run at super high speed. This type of life review spurred by a NDE often results in an "awakening" inside the person that marks a major turning point in their life, and subsequent changes in lifestyle and a deepening of relationships at a personal level.

Having personally passed through four separate NDEs (two as a result of automobile accidents, one from a rock-climbing incident, and one at the hands of the Wirrarika hikuri) while also having similar experiences while buried in the earth, I can say, at least for me, that there are similarities in the two experiences, but also some significant differences. The NDE life review is super fast, even though while you are living it, it may seem much longer.

Although each of my four life-review experiences that were brought on by NDEs were unique in feeling, in many ways they all felt like a sort of purging of my conscious life experiences before my consciousness would move to another realm or be obliterated. In each case the awareness that the end of what I call "me" was about to happen was undeniably real and the resulting effects (as, of course, I didn't die) were powerful to the point that in each case I came from the experience a changed person with renewed motivations and inspiration.

In contrast, I would say that the life-review experience that happens in the tomb is more comparable to experiences recounted in the last few days or hours of a terminally ill person. In this case, the person approaches death gradually and has the chance (if they take it) to review their life more slowly, to make amends with people, resolve inner conflicts, etc. In fact, sometimes initiates of the burial ritual complain that during a life-review experience they got "stuck" along the way, sometimes in a very uncomfortable spot. This is something I've never heard of during the life review in a NDE. Also, it is often reported during the life review in the burial ritual that life experiences that were apparently forgotten by the initiate were suddenly resurrected, and in most cases the forgotten moments were very poignant to the future growth of the initiate.

From Dave:

I woke up and I felt like I couldn't breathe right. In fact, I think I started hyperventilating. The next thing I knew I was seeing my life flash before my eyes, but it lasted only an instant. When it was over, I felt spent and I just laid there like a wet noodle. I could breathe again and for that I was happy . . . after a while I began to think about what had happened and I felt sorry that the "flash of my life" went by so quick, so I decided to try to consciously make it happen again. I couldn't. But what I did do was start remembering what I saw from the "flash" and then extend some of those memories out into the full drama of what they were about. It was the most incredible experience because almost every one of the moments ended up with me remembering something that happened that I completely had forgotten about. Or I finally realized the complete situation where before I really didn't understand. I also remembered things I had forgotten about my father, but they were mostly good things. And I also remembered things from college, a lot of them were things I did that I had forgotten because I was drunk or stoned. But in each moment I discovered something about myself that I didn't really own up to until now. But now that I know them, I feel different and more confident about myself.

The life-review experience can happen in many different ways while in the grave. Sometimes the experience unfolds while the initiate is asleep or in a half-sleep state. Other times it happens in between moments of being awake and asleep, or even as a kind of dialog between the earth and the initiate.

From Sarah:

Mother Earth, why am I such a selfish person? I always hide from doing things unless they benefit me. I feel resentful for all the crap I've been through. Why can't I be different? I've never truly done anything to help anyone my entire life.

Sarah, that's not true. Don't you remember what you did for Jason (my brother who was four years old at the time) *when you were eight years old?*

No. What do you mean?

Don't you remember when a friend of your dad's came to the Fourth of July party on his motorcycle and he parked it in the driveway? Everyone came out to the front of the house to see the motorcycle but when they all went back to the party Jason stayed near the motor-cycle and he began touching it all over. You saw him doing it while you were standing in the garage. Then you watched as he was about to touch the hot exhaust pipe. You knew he would get burned so you ran over and grabbed him, but as you did your ankle hit the pipe and got burned. You cried out and when your mom came she helped you with the burn but your parents scolded you for touching the motorcycle and you never told them you were just helping Jason. I don't think that was very selfish.

Okay. Well, I forgot about that until now . . .

What about the time in fifth grade? You helped your friend cheat on the test because you knew that her dad was hitting her because of her bad grades. But you got caught cheating and you took all the blame so she wouldn't get hit. That wasn't very selfish.

Oh, yeah . . .

In Sarah's case, she entered into a dialog in which she remembered dozens of events during the course of her life where she actually did something nice for other people but somehow or another got blamed, took the punishment, or came away from the experience with a less than positive feeling. She therefore habitually only associated those experiences with the end result of being hurt, while at the same time she habitually discounted her original selfless action that got her into the mess in the first place. Having spent a significant amount of time with Sarah before the Embrace of the Earth rite, it was clear that she felt like a victim of life's circumstances, and she wore a thick, hard covering to protect herself. After the burial there was a marked difference in her attitude and even in her appearance, as she began to prefer wearing more feminine clothes, and it actually seemed like many years of aging were removed her face.

The question and answer dialog has been found to be one of the best ways to get the most from this ritual, especially for those who are passing through a difficult life period. In the above case the dialog ran its own spontaneous course, but frequently the question and answer dialog is structured by the initiate's preparation of specific questions before entering the tomb and then bringing them in writing into the tomb to use during the night. These questions are of the most personal nature, and experience has shown that the more specific the question, the more specific the answer. Generally phrased questions usually receive general or vague responses.

Throughout the years of listening to initiates describe the question and answer process that goes on inside the tomb, one of the striking parallels is between the outcome of the dialog and the transformational metaphor of passing from fragmentation to wholeness. This is a recurrent theme in shamanic initiations as well as ancient mystical traditions and stems from the idea that fragmented parts of our psyche can be joined together and made whole again, thereby moving a person from a disjointed or confused state of being into a more harmonious and centered perspective. This is a particularly valuable experience especially for our lives in the modern, fast-paced world where we sometimes feel split and scattered and not sure if we are coming or going. Our modern lives frequently ask that we wear many different hats all at the same time, and often these separate roles become at odds with each other and we end up feeling torn and pulled and stretched to the breaking point.

A significant aspect to the Embrace of the Earth rite is that the unique qualities of the soil and being buried in the earth come together to form an experience that is so "grounded" that it directly promotes the gathering up and pulling together of the splintered, fragmented pieces of our psyche and soul. This process is often described as re-remembering who you really are.

From Brian:

And then it hit me—WHAM! My mental masturbation was a direct result of male ego fragmentation. I was put in a situation by society, by my parents, and by my own doing that asked me to be too many people all at the same time, but not one of them was who I really wanted to be. Some of those pieces were me, or included me, but others were just made up. My mind was constantly engaged in a neverending pattern of multi-tasking, to the point that I never stopped to see and feel who I REALLY was! WOW, this is great. I can even see myself multitasking when I am meditating or practicing Tai Chi. I can see how I do it all the way to when I finally fall asleep at night, many times with the help of a pill. However, while realizing this, I can also see back to the time when I wasn't like this. I see a little boy who is intently concentrating on just one thing. I used to concentrate on my toy cars, or my dog, or the tire swing, not all of them at the same time. That is who I really am. That little kid that gets the most out of each situation before moving on to the next. I can feel him inside of me. I can feel the earth pressing my body from the outside so that I feel the center core of my absolute being. I've never felt anything like this before. Thank you, Mother-Father Earth!

Healing ourselves from fragmentation also comes in another manner as we see that the splinters of our lives are not just pieces formed from attempting too many activities, but they also result from intentionally or unintentionally hiding those parts of ourselves we can't face. Without going into a long discussion about Jungian shadow philosophy, suffice it to say that reconciling with the shadow aspects of our psyche is, in many cases, facilitated by the ritual burial experience. This happens in myriad ways but one common component seems to be that being in the grave for an extended period of time places everything in perspective. While in the ground, everything comes together and becomes equal. Everything is equally relevant and irrelevant. There is no one to project my feelings onto, and no one there for me to mirror. My mirror is the earth, and my reflection is the universe.

From Susan:

In my grave there are no opposites. There is no up and there is no down. There are no shadows without light, so shadows and light must be part of the same thing. If I can accept my light, then I must accept my shadow, because they emerge from the same place.

From Dave:

At one moment during the early morning, having spent about seven hours in my tomb, I realized that forgiving my mother was not something I had to do in front of her, face to face. Even though I hope to have the courage to do that someday. What was more important was just the fact that I could see clearly that my resentment and anger towards her didn't amount to a hill of beans because all it was doing all these years was dragging me down. As I lay in this tomb surrounded by dirt and staring up at the planks of wood and dirt, the feelings about her that are usually so close at hand are now very far off, almost like they don't matter or can't touch me. I can't even make myself feel mad at her right now because the whole thing has lost importance. The important thing is what I do when I get out of here. Not carrying around my feelings of a hurtful and neglectful past. I feel like something inside me is different. Less petty. More real . . .

In terms of moving from fragmentation to wholeness, or reconciling with our hidden or shadow sides, the Embrace of the Earth ritual almost always has a positive influence, as these themes are integrated into the initiates' lives after they leave the tomb. The underlying physical structure of the ritual simply perpetuates wholeness and grounding. In some way, the earthy cocoon of the grave compresses our energetic field so that even if we don't have visions or receive answers, we still come out feeling different—more confident, at ease, peaceful. Some describe it as being engulfed in the loving embrace of the earth. Others feel it as overcoming their greatest fears or pulling through a great challenge.

From Ellen:

It's almost time to get out of my grave. For about an hour now I have perceived the light of dawn through my air hole but now there is no denying that the sun has just risen. Rays of light are entering my grave through the small hole. I can hear James and his helpers beginning to get people out of the tombs. I look around my tomb and begin to gather my few items. I feel disappointed. I got no answers. I slept most of the night. No meaningful dreams, no visions. Right now the whole thing feels like a big waste of time. I'm dirty, hungry, and thirsty, and I'm sure we have more work to do. Maybe this would have been better if I had prepared more. If I was more clear. If I had spoken more truthfully to the fire. Probably not. This is how it always is for me. I get all wound up over something and then in the end I just get disappointed. Then I usually hide my disappointment because I don't want others to think I couldn't do it or that I failed. So then I lie. I don't want it to be this way anymore . . .

Ellen tried to hide her disappointment in front of the others but it didn't work. In front of the fire and your companions in this ritual there is only one way you can be: real. So she cried about her disappointment and she talked with the group and the fire and she made a valiant effort in the final activities. A few weeks later I received a note from her:

My time in the womb of the earth was an experience I will never forget, and it has been a gift to me every day since I did it. Looking back, I have never felt so peaceful as that night wrapped in the arms of my true mother. I felt safe and strangely comfortable. My tomb/womb was a miraculous gift from the Goddess. It is permanently etched into my mind. Every rock (even the ones sticking in my back that I hated then but love now); every root; every hue of clay, soil, and mud; every smell and sound I will never forget. My lesson was that I can be loved, that I deserve to be loved, and that I want to be loved. Mother Earth gave me an awesome gift—she woke me up silently and without me even knowing . . .

Emergence

It may sound hard to believe but when the time has finally come to get out of the tomb, most people don't want to leave just yet. After spending the whole night in their cocoon, it has become part of them, or they of it. With the morning light of a new day streaming in through the air hole, the tomb doesn't seem quite so menacing or intense. When leading a group through this rite of passage I always try to feel how the group is doing in the moments right before emergence and weigh that against the experiences of the night. Does it feel like one of the group needs or wants to come out first, or right away? Or does it feel like they want or need to stay buried for a little while longer? Normally it is clear how long to wait. When the time comes I go to the first grave and gently tell the initiate that it's time to emerge. I give brief instructions as to how I will get them out, tell them to cover their eyes, and as a last instruction I suggest that when the passage is made for them to come out, and they are ready, to crawl out of the grave, stand up with their arms and fingers outstretched to the sky, and pronounce, "Here I am, for the first time!" or something similar.

From Walter:

James came for me and uncovered an opening at the top of my tomb. After I finished scribbling down my visions, I stood up and shouted, "This is the first day of the rest of my life!" What a great feeling to come out and be there in nature. I felt like Adam. Not only was this my first day alive, but I also felt like the first person to be alive! I felt emotional, like a happy crying feeling. I sat there for a while, enjoying being alive and not ready to leave my grave just yet . . .

From Janet:

The answers to my questions, my visions, hopes, and dreams came to me during the night in the form of many songs. My latest song came in the pre-dawn light as the little birds began to sing in the trees near to the gravesite and I heard a flock of geese fly overhead. Even though I had a few rough moments during the night and some of my songs were accompanied by great pain and remorse, now that the time draws near to come out I feel like I could stay in here a long time more. Especially if I had a yogurt and some fresh water!

Now I can actually hear the others being taken out of the tombs. Some of them are greeting the sun and singing. I don't feel like coming out. It's so nice and cozy in here. Now that the ritual is over, I wish I could just stay in here and sleep for a few hours. Or is it that I just don't want to face the world just yet? Being with people has never been very easy for me. I need another song. A song of rebirth, of a new life. James just came and I asked him if I can stay a few more minutes. I'm not ready yet . . .

Although in some cases, such as Janet's experience, I allow an initiate some extra time in the tomb, for first-time initiates it is extremely important that they rebirth and emerge from the womb as part of the ritual, and in the company of both the living beings of the land and their human companions. Too many adults of our culture are adolescents in adult bodies. This ritual marks a significant transformation for those individuals, and for the others it is important to simply put the experiences of the grave in perspective and walk out into the world to begin reintegration. At this point in the ritual many possibilities emerge. In the best-case scenario we would have at least the whole day to fill in the tombs, perform a ritual that incorporates submerging in the water of a stream or lake, sharing a light meal, and discussing the trials and tribulations of integrating the experiences of the burial into our daily lives. At the very least we restore the area as close as we can to how we found it and have a brief ceremony and discussion before departing. In any case, the first hour or two after you emerge from the tomb will be very special. Words appear in the air again, hugs are received and given, laughter and smiles are shared, and the eyes of your companions will reflect your journey. You are back in the world of people and the most difficult part of the ritual has just begun: taking your experience with you and not forgetting.

Integration

While integrating back into society you must not let your visions disperse or be rendered useless by letting others suck them dry. While at first it is normal to feel happy about emerging and being with people again, it is important to remember that you emerge from the tomb in a very receptive energetic state. You are like a child again in the sense of being very impressionable and innocent. The ritual time has cleansed away a large portion of your normal defenses and left your true being to shine out ever more brightly. Now the trick is to remain shining. Upon your return home you will probably feel glad but also alienated. You had left home to go find something, and now that you are back you are not the same. While you and your home were once one and the same, now you are different, and so you begin walking in two different worlds. The first world is the sacred ritual time of the ceremony that you just passed through. Your magic time spent with the earth and fire, sun and wind, with your companions and with your spirit. But the second world of "civilized" people and time schedules is calling you back, and you must go. That is the way it is: you go to the rite of passage to submerge in the first world and be born anew into the second. Now your job begins as you walk in the second world and try to balance it with the first. Along the way it will help you to reconnect with the experiences of the rite of passage by periodically going to a quiet place in nature and reflecting about the process as you place your hands into the soil. In this way you can keep the experience close to your heart and also give yourself the opportunity to remember, relive, or integrate any experiences of the rite that may have remained obscure for any reason. Another way to do this is to reconnect with the fire that was present that whole night. Once your visions have been internalized, you walk the world carrying them with you, but now it is up to you to make them manifest in this world. This requires action. It is very rare when a rite of passage provides all the answers or visions that you are seeking; the rite is an ongoing process and it helps you to see what you couldn't before, and spur you onward. Sometimes you will stumble, but it is those moments when the energy of the rite is there for you. The rite has shown you your true potential, and nothing can stop you from emerging.

From Susan:

Reentry into my life has been difficult. I had a long drive home, which helped. I kept yelling out the car window, "Here I am for the first time!" The colors of the trees—bright reds, yellows, rusts—felt like big hands holding me and I had tears in my eyes thinking about how loving and supportive Mother Earth is to us. As I drove into town the first thing I saw was a man throwing his cigarette butt out his car window. I was furious, honked, and yelled at him not to do that. I felt very protective of the Earth Mother and was thrown back into my life right away. I kept thinking about wanting to be back inside the earth.

I've made considerable effort to continue the exercise of the five gates and I've dealt directly with my mom and dad and my ex to realize the dream visions of my tomb. I've been disappointed but also made good progress in some other things in my life. Months later the experience is still very much a part of me, it is embedded in my psyche, and I continue to reflect on the entire experience. It is nothing less than amazing and I can't wait to do it again. I can't say that all of my prayers and questions have been answered; however, I do know that participating in the Embrace of the Earth ceremony has helped me to discover what I may not have been able to otherwise. And that is a great gift . . . THANK YOU!

PRACTICE 36: The Quest for Vision

In the scheme of rites of passage from childhood to maturity, one of the most important procedures for shamanic tribes of North America was the vision quest. In the last thirty years, the vision quest is an activity that has increasingly gained in popularity among spiritual seekers of the United States as well as other Western countries. In terms of eco-shamanism, if performed in a primal way, the vision quest is an indispensable experience of transformation and awareness. In today's modern world where most people miss this type of childhood initiation, as adults it is important that we do it now and not wait any longer.

In the days before the use of medicine plants such as peyote, mushrooms, and datura became popular as a means of accessing shamanic visions, the people of North America relied on induced suffering and hardship in the wilderness to summon up the visionary spirits that would teach them how to live. A young person would travel alone to a remote area where their people knew that the spirits of nature were strong and lively. This could be a dense forest, a mountaintop, a swamp, or any other remote area where the powers dwelled. In this place the young person would stay for several days and nights of fasting from both food and water, and with nothing but a loincloth, to endure whatever Mother Nature and the spirits had in store.

In solitude and outside the sphere of village life, the initiate sat silent and alone, fasting, naked to the elements, and open and wanting to receive anything that would stimulate the mind, body, and spirit. In this place, by design, the initiate has nothing. Stripped of clothes, material possessions, and the protection of family and tribe, the initiate is forced to learn about, and dive deep into, their own physical and psychic resources to deal with the perils of wild animals, storms, hunger, thirst, and boredom. In this position one is completely freed from the normal social concerns of everyday life, and little by little, as the initiate becomes more and more empty of human-centered wants and thoughts, the hidden abilities of the psyche arise and the consciousness of the initiate expands to perceive that consciousness is all around. When this happens, it is the time of vision.

Visions acquired in this manner must not be confused or relegated to internal processes of the mind alone, because what is happening here is an expansion of consciousness whereby the items and energies of the world that are normally seen as "external" to the human organism are now viewed as part of a continuum that includes both of what is internal and external to the initiate. In other words, there is no inside or outside of the head or mind. Both of these realities meet and are bound together by what can loosely be called consciousness. In this visionary state there is little or no perceived separation between different types of living beings. Plants wave and acknowledge the visionary quester, while animals and insects and birds deliver messages. In this visionary state, the lines of nonverbal conversation are open and a dialog between the human organism and the other species in the environment slides open, and the possibilities of communication become limitless.

For adults of modern culture, where everything humanly possible is done to avoid the kind of hardships endured in this type of rite of passage, the decision to embark on a quest for vision is one that is usually brought on by some type of life crisis serious enough to test one's inner strength and determination in such a way that healing oneself is the only solution. Normally when people need help they automatically turn to a counselor, minister, psychiatrist, medium, doctor, or family and friends. But in this case a person must realize deep down that the only way to be healed is to heal oneself. The only way to truly go forward is to leave everything behind and scale the mountain of fears and dreams without someone else holding the safety line. For many people the decision to embark on such a quest is a truly heroic act, because it signifies a departure from the pitiful dependence of believing someone else will solve our problems. Many people that I have worked with in this type of rite, as well as other intense rites of passage, have heroically owned up to their specific life circumstances and taken responsibility for making a better life for themselves. Some have been victims of violence, abuse, or rape. Others have battled depression from loss of a loved one, a miscarriage or abortion, or are in the life and death struggle with substance or alcohol abuse. But many others come to the quest for vision as a result of purely lacking a meaning for their lives. Even outwardly successful people living the cliché of the American Dream oftentimes lack the inner resources and inner spiritual development so common to the indigenous world, where rites of passage such as this provide meaning and guidance from a much larger source of mystery and power than that of the world of purely human concerns. And so the successful businessperson, along with the mother of happy and grown children, will come to seek answers for the biggest of questions in the solitude of the vision quest.

As a practitioner of ecoshamanism, it is often my task to help people make decisions as to which type of rite of passage or initiation into an organic worldview is most appropriate for their current life circumstances, personal history, and physical abilities. Many times the vision quest is initially not the best answer because it is very demanding and is an activity that can be potentially dangerous if not entered into in a proper and respectful manner. It is extremely important, even for those who are experienced with camping in the outdoors, hiking, or mountaineering, to properly prepare for this type of rite, and except for unusual circumstances I greatly recommend that one seek out an experienced person to help facilitate this type of quest. In many cases, especially for those who have lived exclusively in an urban environment, I often suggest that they pass through the Embrace of the Earth rite of passage (described earlier) before undertaking the fasting and extreme solitude of the quest for vision.

In any case, the truth of the whole matter boils down to the fact that what you will receive in any rite of passage, shamanic initiation, ritual, ceremony, or offering will be directly proportional to what you put into it. In this case, there is absolutely no way that talking, intellectualizing, theorizing, or any attempt at influencing with our normal ways of manipulation will have any bearing on the level of transformation you will receive and the corresponding vision you will attain. Only by laying yourself bare, emptying yourself through fasting and solitude, and recounting your problems to a mountain or a spider that is crawling up your leg will you make yourself small and humble and open to receive the vision that will be reflected back to you by the mirror of nature.

There are no shortcuts or magical formulas in these kinds of rites because each individual brings with them their own unique story, needs, and wants. A framework to the rite is used to give the rite a time-tested ritual structure that is proven to be helpful in drawing out the individual's inner perceptions. But aside from this general framework, the rite becomes alive purely with the interaction between the individual and the environment, and the melding of the two. In the vision quest nobody will be there to give you opinions or impose their influence on you. Your councilor is the wind, your supporter the earth, your nourishment the sun, and your only companions are the wildlife. In this sense you transform yourself into one of your ancient ancestors, who lived in a wild and untamed world free of telephone lines, television signals, and high-speed computers.

The first stage of the vision quest is the departure. In this stage you remove yourself from your everyday life and leave behind your family, friends, job, and responsibilities both at the physical and psychological level. When you depart on the vision quest journey, you will never come back to the place from where you left; you cross the border into unknown territory. In this sense, with your very first step you leave your old self behind and begin walking into your new state of being. Sometimes it is helpful to associate this crossing with the symbolism of a doorway, threshold, gate, or passageway. There is a crack between the worlds into which you humbly pass into. Again, there is no magical formula for making this entrance, it is purely a matter of consciousness. Similar to how you can't force yourself to go to sleep, but rather sleep takes you and shifts your state of consciousness, so it is with the departure in the vision quest. It is like moving through the paradox of a "gateless gate."

When you have gone into this crack between the worlds of consciousness and through the gateless gate, you arrive to a new land. This stage is the actual experience of the vision quest as you arrive to the place in the wilderness where you will fast for at least three nights. This is a sacred place far removed from human civilization. In this natural setting, many things will happen to you. It is vitally important to enter into a respectful relationship with the place from the very first moment you arrive. The first thing to do is explain to the land what you are doing and to make a gesture of offering to the place. The most powerful way to do this is with your own blood. This can be simply done by making a small hole in the ground with your bare hands while talking to the land about what you are doing there. Then prick your finger with a needle or razor blade and while placing a few drops in the hole, tell the sacred place that your blood is your offering and that the union of your blood with the soil symbolizes your desire and intention of becoming one with the land. Watch as the earth absorbs your blood and then cover the hole. If you light a fire in the night, it is good to place the fire on this offering.

During your stay in the sacred place, countless things will happen and it is impossible to say what they will include. In a similar way to the Embrace of the Earth initiation, it is common to initially experience periods of intense questioning as to your motives for being alone in the wilderness, fear that maybe you are simply going nuts, denial for the reasons you are doing it, depression or feelings of intense self-pity, and so on. This is completely normal and is just one of the stages that a person of the modern world must pass through in order to become one again with the land and the cosmos. Until you are emptied and freed from these heavy and constricting thoughts and emotions you won't be able to soar. One of the key reasons this rite of passage places you completely alone and fasting in the wilderness is to bring these feelings out and lay them bare before the spirits.

During the three-night vision quest, it has been my experience that, in contrast to what my rational mind is expecting to receive or would consider to be a really huge happening, it is more common to experience many unexpected insights or visions from completely unforeseen sources. For example, on my very first vision quest I can remember that instead of seeing or talking to some sort of wise old spirit being, which would have been congruent with what I might expect or wish to happen, I spent most of the first two days dealing with swarms of both flies and mosquitoes. During that time it seemed like the big deal of my vision quest had been reduced to simply placing myself in a position of being tortured by these aggressively savage little creatures, and I was more than a little perturbed at both the insects and myself for being there. But what eventually happened made the whole ordeal worthwhile. The flies and mosquitoes gave me exactly what I needed in that moment; they pushed my patience and my will to the absolute breaking point. Their bombardment of me was so intense that I "freaked out" so many times that I was physically and mentally exhausted. The resulting shift in consciousness forced me to view the world in a way I had never before. Seeing the world with new eyes is one of the most valuable benefits of the vision quest, and on that day I went from seeing those irritating insects as nothing more than swarms of troublesome and annoying pests to acknowledging them as divine messengers of the spirit. When I finally saw what was truly going on and I stopped both my internal struggle and my outward battle with the insects and just sat there with a feeling of peace and resignation, the insects ceased to be a distraction and eventually a strong wind blew up and they were gone within an hour.

The vision had been gratefully earned, and I was magically transformed from a person easily irritated by trivialities into someone that peacefully receives and acknowledges the gifts of life, which was a completely foreign state of mind to me at that time of my life. The insects delivered this vision and transformation in the most effective way possible. In this sense I was visited by the spirits, just not in any form that my mind would have imagined. The outcome of my ordeal with the flies and mosquitoes was that it affected me deeply enough that I physically and psychically applied the lesson I learned to my everyday life and dealings with people both on an intentional and subconscious basis. After my first vision quest many people that knew me well even commented on the change in the way I handled stressful or potentially annoying situations with much more ease and with a kind of peaceful serenity. And not only did that experience affect my everyday life, but it also raised my level of experiences in other facets of my shamanic and spiritual life.

For example, on my next vision quest it became quite clear after just a few moments in my spot (which was on the other side of the country, in completely different terrain than the first time) that my initial spirit helpers this time would be spiders. During those three days I literally met hundreds of spiders of many different species, and because of my previous experience with the flies and mosquitoes, this time I was able right from the start to make peace with the spiders and just let them walk right over me, under me, on top of me, and even inside of my clothes and blanket. Through the powerful agents of fasting and solitude, coupled with my peaceful attitude of openness and willingness to receive without preconceived judgments, I was able to have remarkable and enlightening conversations with many different and insightful spiders. The spirits of that place had chosen to speak to me through these incredibly interesting and unique creatures, and even though I thought I was as open as possible to receive whatever came, I have to admit that at one point, after consciously realizing that the sheer volume of spiders that were coming to me, one by one, could not be mere coincidence, I felt a peculiar kind of awe that was almost frightful, knowing that I was truly at the mercy of the spirits of those woods and that they were really talking to me in a way that I could understand.

With this type of experience comes a certain level of responsibility in that when you are fortunate enough to receive messages, insights, or visions from the spirits of the natural world they cannot be ignored, even if what they are telling you isn't what you want to hear, or the requests that they are making of you may seem too difficult to accomplish. In a nutshell, if you are not prepared to accept and act on the vision that the spirits of nature may have in store for you, you probably want to reconsider entering into this right of passage. As I progressed through my experiences with the flies and mosquitoes, the spiders, and then on to many other significant connections with other beings and powers, I began to more fully realize what my Wirrarika shaman mentors had been saying to me from the start: the level at which you offer to the spirits corresponds to the level at which you will receive, and the higher the level of offering, the further you will fall if you fail to complete your offering or the task given to you by the spirits during your vision.

This is a vitally important aspect of connecting in a shamanic encounter with spirits that rule and animate the world. You had better listen to all of what they are saying, not just those things you want or need to hear, because they almost always ask something of you in return for their knowledge. This means that when you return from the threshold of the vision quest and step squarely back into your everyday life, you will have to accomplish the tasks given to you, no matter how difficult they may be, because if you don't you might not only lose your chance for learning what they are trying to teach you but you may suffer the consequences that come from being deceitful and selfish enough to ask but not give. This should not be construed as something like the threat of damnation resulting from sinful activity, but rather as a sort of universally karmic response to your actions that will be directly proportional to the level of reality you attach to receiving from the spirits.

For example, for indigenous shamans the whole reality of life, both sacred and secular, revolves around their constant connection to the spirits and powers of their sacred lands and the larger cosmos that supplies them with life. Because of this incredibly deep connection, if they fail in the commitments that they make with these spirits, they suffer dire consequences at both physical and psychological levels. But the rewards of knowledge and life are equally profound. Now, in the case of a modern urban dweller that is dabbling in connecting to the spirits of nature, or is on their first significant quest for a vision in the wilderness, the commitments and the repercussions that may seem either good or bad will be significantly less because their level of connection to the natural world is very superficial due to a lifetime spent indoors, in traffic jams, and in front of the television. They don't equate the sustenance of their life with the spirits of the local land, but rather with their "job" that makes them money in order to live. As this person develops a stronger connection to the organic reality of life by placing themselves in a position to depend on the land for life and to learn through the spirits of nature, and as their attachment to the abstract reality of dollar bills and commercial media lessens, their level of connection made with the spirits of the natural world, and the repercussions of that connection, will deepen.

Basic Structure and Practical Considerations of the Rite

1. Prepare yourself and your equipment

If you are not accustomed to fasting you will probably find this a difficult experience, not only because of the physiological responses of your body but also the disconnection to the regimented psychological schedule that feeding times provide. Because of this it is wise to familiarize yourself before the quest by intentionally skipping meals for a few weeks and by eating light foods such as vegetables, fruits, rice, and fish and skipping heavier foods like beef, nuts, dairy products, and oily or fried foods. It is also good to engage in rigorous physical activity outdoors and to simply pay attention to your physical and emotional needs, and to avoid intoxication by alcohol or drugs.

Only you can decide what is completely essential to take with you on your quest. This will largely depend on your level of comfort and familiarity with being outdoors for three whole days and nights. If you are new to spending time outdoors, it is a good idea to make a few trial runs at sleeping out overnight in a wilderness area that is not far from civilization in order to gain confidence and increase your skills. If you will be questing under the tutelage of an experienced guide, they should be able to provide the necessary list of gear specific to the terrain you will submerged in. Aside from suitable clothes and footwear for the season, a general list of items to include could be:

- Water

- Blanket or sleeping bag

- Firestarting supplies in a waterproof container

- Knife

- Ground cloth or rain tarp

- Writing materials

- Flashlight

- First-aid kit

The trick behind the whole concept of gear in this type of minimalistic rite is to find the balance between what you truly need to bring and what you dare not to. For example, by my third quest I felt confident enough to lay myself as bare as I could so I didn't bring anything except the clothes I was wearing and one blanket for three nights in the mountains of Colorado in October. Needless to say I was extremely cold at night because I didn't even allow myself the company of the fire, but my profound connection to the rising sun in the morning would never have reached the same intensity if I wouldn't have been so cold. More recently I haven't felt the need to be quite as extreme and now I always have the fire for many reasons, including warmth.

2: Choose your place and prepare your safety strategy

If the rite is not being led by an experienced guide, you should scope out your spot ahead of time and make sure that someone responsible knows exactly where you will be. You can even devise a check-up system where you and your supporter leave each other a signal at a predetermined spot close to your questing area that will indicate that you are okay at certain intervals, such as once a day at noon.

3: Embark on the quest

Once you have arrived at your questing area, it is normal to have feelings of having to "keep busy." Generally speaking, there are simply no required activities in this rite; quite the contrary, the lack of activity produces reflection and submersion in the action that is unfolding around you, and the deeper you can dive into that reality and out of your purely selfish concerns, the more profound will be your experience. Beginner and novice questers are encouraged not to engage in comforting activities done simply to keep busy, such as reading, playing musical instruments, making crafts, or any other type of intentional distraction.

Other than gathering firewood in an area very close to your spot during the day, and the making of intentional offerings to the spirits around you, the only other activities I would encourage would be those that connect you directly to the land and that happen spontaneously. These include face or body painting using materials from the land, tree climbing (though not advisable without a guide in case you fall), exposing your naked body to the wind, and talking to and listening to the nighttime fire.

4: Return, slowly

Upon returning to your everyday life, avoid going right into the frantic pace of modern life, especially the manipulating psychological warfare of media and violent movies and television. Also it is a good idea to intentionally avoid any situations that might make you susceptible to manipulating people because your guard will be down and your consciousness will be altered in a way that you might not recognize potentially harmful deceptions. In the best-case scenario, give yourself a few days of transition between your wilderness fast and the urban jungle by staying somewhere halfway in between in order to better reflect and digest your experience.

5: Fulfill your vision and commitments

If you have been blessed with insights and vision pertaining to your life, then you should take whatever steps necessary to begin living congruent to your vision. Any offerings you made to the spirits of the place in order to "pay" for your vision should be accomplished as soon as possible to ensure the balance of a reciprocal and healthy relationship with the spirits.

Additional considerations

If you are not working with an experienced guide, it would be prudent not to choose a place for your quest that is extremely isolated or where you could become easily lost. As long as your spot is completely devoid of human activity, is free from the sounds of the urban jungle, and is in a healthy ecological condition, it need not be so remote as to pose undue risk. The underlying spirit behind the quest is not to see how far you can escape into the wilderness but to encounter it and become part of it. The five basic steps I have outlined are the bare bones just to get you started, and from this structure your personal spirit will meld with the forces of nature to help you create your own authentic experience. In the final analysis it will be your own tears and laughter, hardships and triumphs, intuition and spirit that will ultimately be your most precious guide on your quest for vision.

Initiations into the Powers of our World

PRACTICE 37: The Way of the Hunt

The sheer volume of customs, lore, rituals, blessings, taboos, and techniques of hunting throughout the indigenous shamanic world is immense and could barely be touched upon in the space allowed here. In light of that, what seems most valuable to this book is to contrast the breakdown and deterioration of sacred hunting practices by modern hunters (and factory slaughterhouses) with the highly spiritual concepts of shamanic hunting, and then provide some honorable alternatives available to modern people.

Within the immense variety of hunting practices employed by shamanic tribes there is one common undercurrent to them all: the fallen animal is honored and cherished both for its inner spirit and its life-giving nourishment. The act of taking the life, and the solemn witnessing of its death, is both an affirmation that death feeds life and a ceremony acknowledging the sacred relationship between hunter and prey. To waste any part of the animal is taboo; to not thank the animal by ritually saluting it as well as the larger powers that provide for the essence of the animal is sacrilegious.

In shamanic cultures the hunters are not merely looking for food. The hunt is an intrinsic part of a holistic view of life where everything is sacred and connected. Spiritually preparing for the hunt often comprises weeks of ceremonial duties as well as abstinence from certain everyday activities such as sexual activity and the eating of certain kinds of foods. A feeling of communion and kinship pervades every aspect of the sacred hunt and the usage of the gifts received from the animal. In contrast to the shamanic hunter, it is tragic to see how we "civilized" modern people have somehow lost the inner feeling that what we put into our mouths is sacred, and so we have also lost the attitude that the killing of an animal can be ultimately spiritual if performed in a sacred and life-affirming way. In fact, many modern people tend to see the hunting of animals as something shameful. Yet at the same time they allow the honorless slaughter of millions of animals to go on behind closed doors in order to have food on the table without having to look into the eyes of the animal they are eating. What could be more shameful and cowardly?

One could argue that vegetarianism is the answer, but for vegetarians of Western societies the abstinence from meat is often simply a result of deep-seated feelings of denial and shame for being part of such an aggressive and destructive culture. To think that we become spiritually or even humanistically elevated when we eat beans instead of game is a fantasy exacerbated by sincere, caring people who have been unwittingly trapped by an insane world and as a result are provided with limited access to demonstrations and actions of compassion. Somehow war, and humans killing other humans by the millions, along with billions of animals being killed in factories behind closed doors, have all gotten confused with the ethical and sacred aspects of a hunter ritually taking the life of an animal in the wilderness with respect and supplication for the spirit of life and the nourishment of the physical body.

Another situation that makes a mockery of sacred hunting, and that has been thoroughly confused and twisted, is the debate between anti-hunting groups and the so-called game managers and hunters practicing the degenerated versions of hunting so common today. First of all, the "management" of game is purely the outcome of our industrial way of life that has eliminated all the natural predators and that has gobbled up the land with the asphalt of our modern cities and roads. States now "need" to sell hunting licenses to help fund the preservation of tracts of land because the whole foundation of corporate America is in philosophical opposition to the presence of the sacred hunter, and so won't give up a dime to anything that doesn't increase the profit margin of the corporation.

As far as the anti-hunting establishment goes, one can hardly argue on an ethical basis for the continuation of the current mass hunting practices in the United States. But to simply say that no one should be "allowed" to hunt is simply preposterous and exhibits the cultural blindness that completely denies the manner in which the human body and psyche has been formed. Anyone who steadfastly holds on to the conviction that sacred hunting is evil is not connected in a tangible way to how the healthy life systems of our planet function. What we need is an evolution—or de-evolution, depending on your point of view—in modern hunting practices as a response to the global ecological catastrophes we now face on a daily basis.

In the first place, just as in shamanic tribes, not everyone needs to hunt. The hunter plays just one role of the many needed to maintain a happy, healthy society that lives intimately with its environment. In this day and age, sacred hunting would be better viewed as a privilege and form of initiatory ceremony into the adult realities of life and death, where one experiences the sacredness and miracle of life by intimately knowing in the deepest way possible that act which sustains life. At the same time, the passing of knowledge about the rituals and taboos within the complex of the sacred hunt should be seen as a right of passage and carry with it significant obligations and duties relating to not only the species involved in the hunt but also the land in which one hunts. This last point may be the most important and least understood aspect of sacred hunting, for those who think that hunting should be abolished.

In a world in which everything is dissected into the smallest possible parts, we lose the larger view. The botanist names the plants, the zoologist labels and captures the animals, and the tourist drives by to see what is there, but the hunter sees and senses the unfolding interaction of life unique to the place he is hunting within. There is absolutely no other way to awaken every one of your senses, and even ones you didn't know you had, to the unique level of when your total MBES organism is engaged in the interaction with both the animal and its environment during the sacred hunt. In this respect, the exercise of "hunting" with cameras or video equipment doesn't even come close, because the life-and-death factor is completely missing. Only in the ancient dance of predator and prey can one truly feel this uniquely sacred and spiritual connection between not only the hunter and the hunted, but between the hunter, the hunted, and the living environment that forms the basic and underlying reality of the experience.

It is my dream that people open up to this knowledge because then there wouldn't be a need for anti-hunting groups or game managers. The wasteful and honor-free form of hunting so commonly employed today would become naturally extinct. There would be no such thing as "trophy" hunting with long-range, high-powered rifles. There would be no two-day hunting "season" whereby millions of animals are killed all at once and the surviving animals are psychologically traumatized. Sacred hunters would use common sense and be selective in taking animals from the herd, and therefore they would contribute in a positive way to the self-regulating systems of which they are a part. Every single part of the animal would be respectfully used and honored. Ritual and ceremony relating to specific species and specific locales would be born, grow, and be passed down to the new generations. The living systems of flora and fauna that provide life would be under the natural protection of the hunters, not in the way of armed patrols or fences but simply as a consequence of the reverence and connection to the land and its wild inhabitants.

This seemingly utopian vision of sacred hunting is not a dream. It has happened for millennia in the past and in isolated incidences it is happening right now as well. There are even live models of ancient shamanic tribes that still live the reality of the sacred hunt. My Wirrarika companions are a good, if not perfect, example. Actually, the way they do it is infinitely more sacred and precious than anything I could ever describe in writing, and the truth is that in a cultural context I probably haven't even been able to perceive or comprehend a large part of what they do during the sacred hunt, even when I am right there, sharing it with them. What I do know and take with me from my experiences in this ancient hunting practice is that in terms of sacredness it is beyond anything I have ever encountered in the modern world. Due to the lack of game animals in their home territory (as a result of infringing Mexican poachers and encroachment of cattle farmers on their land), they have to make special arrangements with landowners months in advance, pay them, and travel very far from home just for the opportunity to hunt a sacred animal, such as the deer that they need to complete their long pilgrimage to Wirikuta.

The privilege granted to the hunters by their community to even be in the hunt is enormous, although someone from our culture would question why they would even go through all the trouble when they can more easily raise or buy beef, pork, and chicken for consumption. The answer is found in the sacredness of the hunt and the relationship between the hunter, the hunted, and the spiritual environment that holds it all. There is absolutely no substitute for the connection established between their culture and the cosmos during the hunt for the wild and sacred deer. The sacrifices of time, effort, and prayerful preparation, not to mention the monetary expenses to engage in this event both weeks before and after, are so large that the corresponding sacredness of the flesh, hide, bones, sinew, and antlers of the deer is beyond words.

The most amazing part of their ritual is that the shaman calls the spirit of the deer through an all-night ceremony with the fire so that on the day of the hunt the deer comes to the hunters to offer itself. This type of situation is so foreign to the worldview of modern people that I had a hard time even believing that it could happen. But that all changed when I began to do it myself, not in the same exact way as the Wirrarika shamans, but by also becoming one with the spirit of the deer and of the land where I live. In some inexplicable way, when you truly connect to the spirit of the land and the prey, you become a functioning part of the multidimensional web of life that holds it all. At this level of unity you are not simply killing the deer, the deer is dying for you in a way that fulfills its particular life path. I realize this may be hard to understand, but I have seen it happen time and time again. One example that I can site might make this more clear.

A few years ago, after many years of developing my connection to the deer, I received the silent call from the deer spirit during the time of year I usually make my sacred hunt. This year it happened to be on Christmas Eve. Since I had the feeling that this day was approaching, my equipment for the hunt was already prepared, and I performed my final ceremony and went to my sacred place. I had no doubt in my mind that the hunt would be successful that day; I could feel the unique call of the deer spirit that shared my body and spirit from the many other sacred moments that we had shared together. But I waited all day in the sacred place and the deer did not come. I didn't even have the feeling that any deer were near my area, which was very strange. I was tempted to go look for them but I knew that was not part of the agreement. The agreement was that the deer spirit would offer itself to me if, of course, I respected our sacred relationship with the utmost care.

At this point I was feeling very confused. I still carried the feeling of the now-familiar pull that I always received when the deer spirit is calling me, but now it was dark and the hunting day was over. Well, I had committed to go see some friends that evening, so I put the deer episode behind me for the moment and a few hours later I went to a party. But the whole time I was there I couldn't shake the feeling that the deer spirit was still calling to me. I didn't feel that I had done anything wrong to break my contract with the spirit, but something just did not seem right. I ended up staying until very late at the party, and when I left there was a blinding snowstorm and the roads were treacherous.

I was driving very slowly, carefully, and with complete attention on the small country road when my friend in the passenger seat said "Hey! Did you see something back there? I think I saw a deer lying on the other side of the road." I thought to myself, "Oh, no. I hope a deer didn't get hit by a car." Despite the hour and the blinding snowstorm, I knew that I had to turn around and see if there really was a deer there. I owed it to the deer spirit.

So I found a place to turn around and sure enough, there was deer lying on the side of the road. Its head was up, which gave me a lot of hope because I had helped deer up off the ground that been stunned by car accidents, or freed them when stuck in fences, lots of times before. So I stopped the truck and went out to see if I could help the deer. It was completely alert but it couldn't get up no matter how hard it tried. I surveyed the scene and quickly saw fresh tire tracks in the snow and a splatter of blood on the road where the deer had been hit by a truck. I went over and spoke softly to the deer as I covered its eyes with my hand and gently examined it.

The deer was a doe, about two years old. She had a shattered hip and suffered severe trauma to the spine. She wouldn't walk again, that was clear. If she stayed where she was she would probably be hit by another vehicle or she would freeze to death on the road. It was

1 AM in the morning in the middle of the Pennsylvania woods on Christmas Eve and there was no hope in sight for the deer. And then it hit me. The deer spirit had called me—I had felt it all day—but what I hadn't realized was that this year the deer would find me in a different way. Instead of sending me a healthy deer, the deer spirit was putting me to work by helping one of its children. I knew then that I had to end the suffering for the deer and send its spirit home. So that's what I did. And then I put her in my truck and took her home so I could honor her spirit by not letting her go to waste on the side of the road.

As I followed the same rituals of converting her flesh to food the next day as I would have done if she had come to me during the hunt, I received the clear message that I had passed a test. The deer spirit tested me many times the day before to see what I would do. First with the call, then the fruitless hunt, going to the party when I could have stayed home and felt sorry for myself or confused with the failed hunt, driving by the deer in the snowstorm and having to decide whether to turn back, correctly analyzing the situation and making the decision to do the right thing, the extremely hard moments of ending her life while I held her in my arms and comforted her, and, finally, treating her afterwards with the same respect that I would with a deer that came to me in the sacred hunt.

After that day my relationship with the spirit of the deer and with the spirits of the region of land where I lived rose to a new level, and I actually felt a little bit nervous because I knew that I was being given more responsibility by the spirits. Since then I have been on many more sacred hunts and the deer spirit has provided deer each time, but every year there are many missions and tests that I pass through, and each year our relationship grows stronger and the trust and bond between us keeps growing.

In the following section I'm going to outline an example of the components of a modern-day sacred deer hunt. This hunting ritual is a holistic ritual of initiation to both the realities of the natural world and the magical spirit of the deer. If this ritual is carried out with a high level of attention to detail and with an encompassing attitude of honor, the initiate will come away tangibly carrying both the spirit of the land and the spirit of the deer inside of him or her. These spirits will forever be your companions and allies.

1. Get yourself a portable tree stand specially designed for hunting (see page 64). A minimum of one year is spent constantly visiting and interacting with the land of the hunt. Periods of time are spent silently walking on the ground, sitting up in the trees, and sleeping overnight on the ground or in the trees of your hunting area.

2. During this time period, intense observation of the deer is conducted, as well as the natural environment and especially what the deer are eating and where they sleep. The movements of the deer and any patterns that develop are also noted.

3. A feeling of what the spirit of the deer contributes to the environment is developed and nurtured while at the same time the same question is asked of oneself, "What does my spirit contribute to my environment?"

4. After a significant period (three to six months), a personal relationship with both the deer herd and lone, individual deer is developed to the point that you can recognize each deer by site, mannerism, age, and status. You know where and what they are eating, and where and when they are bedding down.

5. Appropriate steps are taken to ensure complete familiarity with the weapon to be used during the hunt, and skill at using the weapon with 100 percent accuracy must be developed through continuous practice in a wide range of weather situations. As the weeks draw closer to the anticipated day of the hunt, practice with the weapon should include simulating the exact conditions of the hunt. For example, if you will hunt from a tree, practice with the weapon while elevated to the same height. If you anticipate hunting in the extremely cold part of the winter, then practice during the coldest days.

6. Locate a knowledgeable person to help you with the carcass of the deer in the event that you kill one. Self-taught skills are great, but in this case it is extremely advantageous, at least for the first time, to have an experienced guide show you how to work with the carcass. Especially important is the proper removal of the internal organs without ruining any of the meat, and the removal of the hide can be very difficult if you don't know how to do it. Also, just in case your guide is not available during the day of your hunt, you should obtain and study articles on how to field-dress and butcher the deer, and/or visit a deer processing center if it is during hunting season and watch how they do it.

7. For this ritual hunt, there is no better way than hunting from a tree stand because it allows you the most effective way to be extremely close to the deer and therefore ensure a one-shot kill so that you will be close enough to reach the deer before it dies, which is crucial to this hunting ritual. In the weeks leading up to the

hunt, place your stand in an area where you consistently see your herd and practice taking your shot without actually taking it.

8. The actual day of the hunt should be determined not by the calendar but by instinct. Wait until the day comes when you just know that the time has come and you actually hear the deer calling you. As you feel this time approaching you should begin to fast, especially from meat, and perform any other rituals of inner and psychic cleansing that you feel are appropriate so that you are not carrying any unwanted baggage with you into this most sacred event. Although sometimes the call of the deer is crystal clear and so there is no choice as to timing, when possible I usually try to steer the moment to a day of rainy weather because on those days the deer remain active when people usually stay indoors, which means you are less likely to be disturbed by anyone during or after your hunt. If you have conscientiously prepared throughout the whole year, by now you will have the proper clothing and gear so that "bad" weather will not be an issue and, in fact, can be a real blessing.

9. When you receive the call, all your things should already be prepared. When you arrive to your hunting area perform an offering and state out loud exactly what your intentions are and why. Then take the arrow or bullet that you will shoot first and bless it by presenting it to the five sacred elements. Then bless it and your weapon with your own blood (unless you have deer blood from a previous sacred hunt) by pricking or slicing your finger and applying the blood to both the projectile and the weapon.

10. Go silently to your tree stand and wait for your deer. During this time talk softly to the spirit of the deer in a loving and affectionate way so that the deer spirit will not be afraid. Be careful in your selection if more than one deer appears. If there is more than one deer, try to intuit which one is meant for you. If the deer does not come close enough to you so that you can clearly see its eyes, then DO NOT shoot at it. Let it go. But if it does come that close, then carefully shoot into the vitals right behind the front leg. If you have practiced enough, this will be the simplest part of the hunt and the deer should fall immediately or within a few steps.

11. Being as safe as possible, get to the deer as fast as you can. You must try your hardest to reach the deer before it takes its last breath. When you reach the downed

deer, quickly say to the deer, in a calm and clear voice, "I honor your spirit by taking your last breath into mine. With this sacred act I join your spirit to mine. In this way your spirit will continue to live through me and I will forever remain in kinship with the deer of this land." Then *immediately*, before it's too late, put your mouth over the deer's mouth and breathe in the breath of the deer, and breathe out your breath into the deer. Do this multiple times if you are not sure you got it, or you can even push down on the deer's lungs if needed.

12. Once the breath of the deer has left its body and gone into yours, it is your sacred responsibility to continually honor the spirit of the deer in all of your future actions, including the immediate responsibility to take care of the physical manifestation of the spirit you took into your own. This means that you must use all of your knowledge and resources to use the carcass of the dead animal in the best way you can. Following ancient tradition I always dig a hole on the exact spot where the deer died and bury the intestines of the deer, which have the spiral-shaped "nierika" of the deer, in order to give back to the land the essence of the deer that bore it. If this isn't done at the time of the kill it is performed as a separate ritual after the deer has been butchered and at the same time as any other unusable parts of the deer, such as bone or flesh damaged by the arrow or bullet, are also returned to the earth in the same spot along with any additional offerings of thanks to the deer or the land, such as those from friends or family that will benefit from the flesh and carcass of the deer. During the process of removing the deer meat a significant amount of blood can be saved in a special container(s) to be used during rituals and ceremonies throughout the year. Be sure to store the blood in a cool, dark place or in the refrigerator or freezer.

If you are utilizing the flesh of the deer as a significant portion of your yearly diet this hunt can be performed again, but never take more than you will consume in a year. Also, if for some reason you took a bad shot at the deer and it ran away from you, it is your sacred responsibility to find out if, and how badly, you wounded it, and to kill it if necessary. If you are sure you hit the deer but it ran from you so that you no longer see it, the best thing to do is wait for at least half an hour before looking for it. Don't chase after it right away because if it is wounded you will make it suffer even more and you may never find it even though it is mortally wounded. If it is badly injured and does not sense any more immediate danger, it will simply find a nearby place to lie down and die. But remember, in all cases you have to either find the deer by following its blood trail, or verify that you didn't hit the deer by thoroughly searching the area where you shot for signs of blood or hair. This is one of the main reasons for not shooting unless the deer is extremely close to you. The horror of wounding the deer instead of killing it is the worst thing you or the deer could ever experience.

If your hunt was successful, you now have the spirit of the deer alive inside of you. The feelings of kinship and connection to both the deer and the land will be tangible and extremely beneficial to your shamanic path and your life. But remember that the physical parts of the deer are now sacred extensions of the cosmic union between you and the deer, and every single thing you do with the carcass will have meaning and consequences. It is your responsibility and duty to make those consequences energetically positive, which is simple to do if you act with respect in your intentions. With effort you can utilize all the major parts of the deer for nourishment and the making of sacred tools and instruments that will help propel you down the path of organic spiritual enlightenment. When you eat the flesh of the deer you are in communion with the sacred being that gave its life for you. When you breathe through a whistle, shake a rattle fashioned from the bones of the deer, or drum on its skin, you sing to the universe of the union between your spirit and the spirit of the deer that you are honoring by your song. This is one of the deepest types of connections we could ever have, and is one of the true core experiences of shamanism.

SACRED TREES

Trees become sacred in the shamanic world of indigenous tribes for a wide variety of reasons and circumstances, some of which include:

- The essential materials they provide for the tribe. Bark, branches, roots, leaves, sap, flowers, and fruit all play valuable roles in the making of canoes, shelters, baskets, tools, foods, and medicines.

- The fire, the vital heat and energy source, that they created and sustained.

- Special qualities certain species of trees possess that can be extracted and used in healing and purification.

- The physical location of a tree (or grove of trees) on or near a sacred place, such as a spring, well, river, lake, canyon, or hill.

- The association with sacred animals that make their home on, in, under, or around the tree.

- A tree (or species) becoming associated with a particular event, such as a yearly ceremony, ritual, or birthday.

- An individual tree may be somehow distinct or unique from others around it or for its species. It may be unusually large or old, or have an outstanding feature or shape.

- A tree is planted especially to mark a significant event.

For modern people, trees remain sacred if for no other reason than they are indispensable to the healthy functioning of our planetary ecosystem. While most of us readily realize that trees provide the raw materials for building materials, paper products, and myriad other goods and foodstuffs, by far the most important contribution that trees make to the planet are the low-cost health care services they provide to other living beings on earth, some of which include:

- Trees remove gases and particulates from the atmosphere, including carbon dioxide from the burning of fossil fuels in automobiles, electricity generation, and the heating of homes, schools, and businesses.

- Trees absorb many of the chlorofluorocarbons (CFCs) produced by household products and used in refrigerators and air conditioners, which destroy the protective ozone layer surrounding the planet.

- Trees provide shelter and food to animals and birds, and moderate water temperatures in streams and lakes so that fish and other marine life can proliferate.

- Trees fertilize the land and help create topsoil.

- Trees prevent erosion and protect soil integrity through their root systems and by forming windbreaks with their branches and trunks.

- Trees provide the base for many modern pharmaceuticals.

In an age when worth is calculated by money, it's ironic that the almost incomprehensible value of the world's trees goes largely unnoticed by the public. However, in his book *Sacred Trees* (New York: Sterling Publishing Co., 2000), Nathaniel Altman cites an amazing California Department of Forestry and Fire Protection study that calculates "a single tree that lives for fifty years will contribute services worth nearly $235,000 (in year-2000 dollar value) to the community during its lifetime. This includes providing oxygen ($37,000), recycling water and regulating humidity ($44,200), controlling air pollution ($75,000), producing protein ($3,000), providing shelter for wildlife ($37,500), and controlling land erosion and fertilizing the soil ($37,500). No monetary value has been placed on the value of the tree's roles in maintaining rainfall level or providing the shade, beauty, and inspiration that a mature tree can provide. Nor is any estimate given on the cumulative value of the lumber, nuts, or fruit derived from a tree during this fifty-year period."

Although this study clearly excludes many important uses for trees, it makes us aware of the life-sustaining value of trees, both to modern people and our ancestors. No matter what specific quality we focus on, trees have been and continue to be superior allies to human beings, not only at a material or practical level but also in the sense of spirituality and the ability to raise consciousness. When in their presence, we can feel the undeniable atmosphere they create that can have great relevance to connecting with the various healing energies available throughout the natural world.

On psychological and emotional levels trees can be excellent counselors and therapists. For example, the presence of an oak can help foster strength and the "backbone" to face difficult situations, while the feelings evoked by the willow provide vision into the depths of emotional situations. The delicate forms and movements of many trees, such as the silver birch or quaking aspen, are perfect for counteracting the spell created by the one-dimensional visual trance of TV and computer screens. Becoming aware of these types of healing atmospheres created by trees can lead to the acquisition of a whole new set of powerful allies that can lend support to your life or help answer important questions. Sometimes the insights delivered by a sacred tree ally will come in a very subtle way that feels like soft leaves barely brushing the surface of your mind, while other times the message will hit you abruptly like being smacked with a wood bat and you will feel the reverberations to the very core of your being.

When interacting with trees on an emotional-intuitive level, it is important to open to the complete range of feelings being delivered by the tree. Oftentimes we view trees as static and rigid beings that have little to offer our fast-paced lives that rarely allow us to stand still. But this narrow view can be easily expanded once we use the shamanic technique of inverting the world and delving beneath the surface to see from the inside out. In the case of trees, this implies relating to the tree as a being that is not rising from the earth but descending into it. By limiting our perception to always paying attention to the branches and leaves of the tree, we miss the fact that the tree is involved in a whole other world of life and relationships that are happening beneath the surface. The myriad processes going on between the roots, trunk, branches, leaves, and flowers interacting with the living soil and moving air in the creation of the atmosphere and stabilization of the land reveals that the tree is in reality a dynamic, life-giving being that is in a constant state of motion and interaction. So when we approach the energy field of the tree, we must be open and aware of the complete array of tasks and responsibilities it is involved in, above and below the surface, and the corresponding knowledge and intuitive presence it can provide at all levels, not just the levels we may be accustomed to.

PRACTICE 38: Communicating with Trees

Like people and the land itself, trees are keepers of memories and are magnificent story-tellers. They are repositories of large amounts of information and even though their cognitive process may be much different from ours, they imprint and recount the history of where they live and what has happened there over long periods of time. Much like the care lines and creases of the wizened face of an old sage, the outstretched arms and roots of the wise old tree tell the story of countless experiences, triumphs, and turmoil. Whether old or young, our natural connection and affinity for trees enables us to both physically and psychically make contact with them, and the lines of communication can be easily opened with a little effort.

Since there are so many different and unique types of trees, it is important when approaching one to simply start by standing back from it and noticing what it is like and what it is doing. In this way you will have a better idea as to what kind of conversation you could have with the tree and what you may be able to learn from it. For example, if you were to meet a person who is a math professor, you probably wouldn't start a conversation with them about Shakespearean literature. In the same way, a tree that lives alone at the top of a hill won't be as insightful about getting along with others as a tree living in a thick forest or grove. A tree living inside the main courtyard of a monastery may have much to say about the people living there, just as an oak living in the wilderness may have a lot to teach about deer and squirrels and birds.

The outwardly manifesting characteristics of the tree will tell a lot about the internal insights and lessons that the tree may have for you, so it is worth the effort to open up to what the physical qualities of the tree are telling you before going into a deeper conversation. Many clues about the personality of the tree can be found by simply noticing the answers to the following questions:

- What social environment does the tree live in? There are numerous varieties of forests that the tree could live in, or it could live alone in a field, alongside a stream or river, or even isolated in the city. What influence does the tree's relationship with other trees have on its personality?

- What physical environment does the tree live in? Take note whether the tree lives in the mountains or at the beach, in an agricultural field or next to a brand-new housing development. What has the environment of the tree contributed to its knowledge of the world and the lessons it might share with you?

- How has the tree grown? Notice the size and girth of the tree, and the pattern of its growth. What does the tree tell you about its age? Are there any special clues about its life that you can see, like curving of the trunk, growth more toward one direction, attacks by insects, lightning strikes, wind or water patterns? Does it seem like the tree has led a hard or easy life? Is it thriving in its environment or do you think it would be happier living elsewhere? What does the physical growth of the tree tell you about the trials and tribulations of the tree's life and how that might affect its personality?

- What season is the tree in? Be sure to notice if the tree is without leaves, or is flowering or dropping fruit. Does the tree appear to be busy or resting?

- Can you tell what the tree contributes to its community? Depending on the season and location of the tree, it might be very obvious or extremely difficult to visually see what the tree offers to the other living beings around it. All trees provide shelter, shade, and food at varying degrees for many different beings, so it is important to take careful note of these specific qualities. It may take some time or many visits to the tree to accumulate a good picture of what the tree provides its surroundings. Also be sure to look at the bigger picture; for example, if the tree is part of a forest on a mountainside, it is certainly contributing to prevent soil erosion in cooperation with all of its friends and relatives on that mountain. If the tree is located near people or in a special urban or historical setting, it could also be a great source of inspiration and beauty to humans. What does its contribution to the world, whether seemingly large or small, tell you about the tree's personality?

- What does the species of the tree tell you about it? Certainly an oak or redwood tree will have something different to say than a sassafras or a hawthorn. The growth, responsibility, and personality of different types of trees is immensely diverse, and because of this, connecting and communicating with trees is an exciting and inexhaustible activity.

Once you have gone through this type of initial process with the tree, the next aspect of communication can be in the form of an offering from you as you begin to relate to the tree through your words. Even though the communication you receive from the tree will not come in the form of human speech, you can use your own speech skills very effectively to share your energy of the moment with the tree. In terms of moving energy our speech is one of our most powerful tools, and when you talk or laugh or shout or cry during your conversation with the tree, the energy moved is what the tree will feel—not necessarily the meaning of specific words, but certainly the feelings evoked in you by them. That is why, especially in the beginning, it is far more productive to actually use your voice to talk to the tree and not try to do it telepathically. Also, the uncommon act of talking to the tree will loosen you up and shrink your ego by placing yourself on the same level as the tree.

When receiving dialog from the tree be sure to listen at all perceptual levels, because just as we relate to people at different levels, the same happens with trees. Intuition plays a large part here, as does relating to the postures, movements, and language of the tree, both at a sensory level as well as the physically imperceptible actions of the tree that are continuously happening. Interacting with a tree in this way is an extremely enlightening and personal experience, and as you develop your communication skills you shouldn't be afraid to pose relative questions to the tree just like you would a good friend, and like a good friend you should be available to listen to the tree's questions as well. Even though this type of conversation is utterly personal, I have found in my workshops that people sometimes have similar experiences with different types of trees. In order to give an idea of what might possibly be learned or gleaned from a dialog with a tree, I'm going to share a few personal insights and general information about a few specific trees that I have been fortunate enough to connect with during my life. This information is simply provided as an example of how your own relationship could develop with trees of different areas and of varied species.

Ash: Long before I knew the ash has historically been associated with the "world tree" of certain cultures (a great mythical tree that formed the axis of the world by its roots delving deep into the underworld and its branches reaching high into the heavens), I was deeply inspired by the graceful balance of the huge ash trees that lived close to my house as a child. As I learned that the ash was considered to be a magical tree by many ancient cultures of Europe, such as the Druids, Celts, and Vikings, it was even easier for me to encourage my own mystical associations with the ash and appreciate that what I had felt as a youth had been felt many centuries before by people that lived with a deep connection to the land. Most of my more recent conversations with ash trees have been about universal truths and the balancing of opposites. The ash, even the enormous and fully grown tree, has a very feminine way of growth but the buds of the tree are phallic in shape and the flowers can be of either sex or bisexual. The branches of the ash seem to grow in perfect balance, and the message of the ash is usually about living in harmony and about ways of grounding our hectic lifestyles by balancing our lives with experiences and activities that relate to nature and the cosmos.

Aspen, quaking: My first real experiences with the aspen were in Colorado when I first began experimenting with fasting alone in the wilderness. Since aspen trees don't easily tolerate the shade from other trees, they tend to stay in groves of identical trees all intertwined and connected at the roots. So when I began listening to the aspen it was always like listening to a chorus rather than a single voice. The aspen is one of the easiest trees to "hear" and is often referred to as the whispering tree because the stalks of its leaves are perfectly flat and they grow at right angles to the blade of the leaf, which causes them to flutter in the slightest breeze. In my experiences with Wirrarika shamans, especially on pilgrimages, one of the first lessons I learned was to listen to the wind, and since that time I have come to associate the small hanging objects that Wirrarika shamans sew onto their sombreros in order to better hear the messages of the wind with the hanging leaves of the aspen tree that are so obviously in permanent communication with the wind. The messages of the aspen normally have to do with listening intently, especially to silence both internal and external, and the gentle rustle and movement of the leaves is very conducive to producing deep meditative states and chant-song journeys. Compared to other trees, the lifespan of the aspen is short (usually around fifty years), so oftentimes the aspen also teaches us about living life fully in the moment and not wasting time on trivialities and wasteful emotions.

Beech, American: Large beech trees have a majestic appearance, as their trunks rise like a column up to 150 feet. The curves of the branches and shape of the trunk resemble parts of the human body to such an extent that they can feel quite eerie when you are alone in a large forest. With the beech it is very easy to see the spirit of the tree because of its visual appearance. One of the main reasons I became attached to the beech is that in the woods of my youth most of the large trees were covered with poison ivy and sumac in the summertime, but the beech has the remarkable ability to repel ivy and undergrowth so I was able to get right up to the large base of the tree and make physical contact without much trouble. Although historically the beech is often associated with wisdom because it is said that the thin slices of beech wood were bound together to make the first books, most of my lessons from beech are more in the line of confidence and hardiness. Often you will find a beech completely uprooted by a high wind and that's when you realize how few roots they have and what confidence they must have to grow so large.

Birch: The birch tree has many lessons and much wisdom to share. Although the tree appears to be fragile in its slender and feminine pattern of growth, it is one of the hardiest trees and will often grow in places where no other trees can survive. This has taught me not to focus so much on exterior appearances because inner strength can be so much more important. The birch has also shown me many lessons of unselfishness and caring for the needs of others. Because its leaves are small, it is often seen to give light to smaller trees growing beneath it while at the same time protecting them and nourishing them. This unselfish act is not seen in many trees and oftentimes when a birch helps an oak or pine to grow it is often smothered many years later by the same tree it helped. But that is part of its nature, as it also rots very easily and provides nutrients for other plants and trees to grow. Birch is commonly known as the Lady of the Woods; it is called the Cosmic Tree in Celtic Shamanism, and it is said that the Druids used its white trunk to climb to other worlds of consciousness. Not surprisingly, it is under the birch that the hallucinogenic toadstool known as fly agaric is most often found.

Elm: The shadows created by large elm have a magical quality weaving the ground with shadows that seem alive with movement. This interplay between light and shadow, sky and earth somehow lends to feelings of balance and peace. To Native Americans, such as the Winnebago and the Delaware that occupied the area where I grew up, the elm was a sacred tree whose shade was used in large council meetings and treaty signings. Today the elm can be seen lining both sides of stately avenues in urban locations. But whether in the city or the woods, the gracefully drooping elm invokes a uniquely spiritual and peaceful atmosphere.

Hickory: The large shagbark hickory resembles a wise old man sporting a long shaggy beard, and whenever I find one in the woods there is an immediate feeling of friendship and camaraderie that always draws me to the tree to say hello and touch the amazing peeling bark. As a child I always had the irresistible urge to touch, feel, and sometimes peel the shagbark, and even as an adult this feeling has not departed. There is just something so magically alluring about the appearance of this tree that sometimes when I'm out walking in the forest I'll find myself standing next to one without even realizing consciously that I had seen it and walked up to it. When the first frosty days of October come there is a flurry of activity in the woods as the hickory nuts begin to fall and little animals such as squirrels scurry around to collect the precious prize. For me the hickory has always represented the best qualities of strength and fortitude, similar to the life-giving energy of the walnut and oak but somehow in a wiser way that is felt, like the essence of the hickory is like a wizened grandpa or grandma even when an individual tree might be physically younger than the trees around it.

Maple: Anyone who has red maple near them knows of the fiery blaze of red that lights up the sky in autumn. As a child I remember clearly the giant maple near my house that would signal the change of the seasons, but just as clear in my mind are the sugar maple trees that we would tap for the sweep sap to make syrup. This tree, even as much as the apple and peach, made me realize how alive and generous trees really are.

Oak: Even though throughout my life I have had deeper connections with some other trees, the sheer volume of oak trees that have been in the sacred woods of my life and the variety of wildlife that they support, including my sacred deer, make the mighty oak one of my most powerful allies and mentors. With many different types of oak able to thrive in a multitude of environments, the energy of the oak always seems to follow me wherever I go. And so in my adult life, oftentimes surrounded by huge oak trees in the forests where I work with people and constantly learn about myself, the oak represents a doorway into other dimensions of being. For me the oak is like the sentinel standing at the gate to a world of precious knowledge and discovery.

Pine, eastern white: The pine is the tree of light, the tree of the sun. After a night and day of fasting in the wilderness, as the sun is setting and the forest loses its light, I have seen countless times how the pine remains magically lit far longer than the other trees. On one occasion when I was anxiously anticipating the rising of the sun after a long, cold night, a pine cone fell from the tree I was standing under and hit me on the head. In the exact moment that I began to look at the pine cone that hit me the sun came up over the horizon, and in that moment I first realized the depth of the mystical connection of the pine to the sun: the pine cone grows spirally on the branches, imitating the pattern of Earth's movement around the sun. Years later I would learn that ancient people would burn huge fires of pine at the winter solstice in order to call the sun back to be reborn so that the cycles of growth could continue. As a tree of the sun, the messages of the pine are full of light and illuminating perspective to see the whole picture. The pine also teaches us to live lightly, as it sometimes will live and grow on next to nothing, seemingly dwelling on almost pure rock, like the only nourishment it needs is the light of the sun.

Red cedar: The red cedar is one of the most plentiful and familiar evergreen trees of the eastern United States, and has been one of my favorite trees since I was a child.

The fragrance of a red cedar grove is intoxicating to me and immediately transports me back to one of my secret places of power and connection to the animating spirits of the natural world. This is one reason why I often make my prayer arrows from red cedar, especially the arrows used in the sacred deer hunt. I will always remember the time when, during one of the coldest and longest winters of my youth, I spent three whole days looking in vain for my local deer herd. I actually thought that maybe they had all died of starvation and cold because there was simply no trace of them. Then on my way home I found them in the red cedars, the last place I thought to look because it was an area that I in no way associated with food for deer. But there they were, lying under the trees and nibbling on the cedars' precious sprigs of green. The cedars literally saved the life of some of my best wild friends and so hold a very special place in my heart.

Sassafras: The sassafras is unusual because on a single tree it can grow three different shapes of leaves. Usually it grows to little more than a shrub, but it has been known to live up to 1,000 years. Since I had a large sassafras in the front yard as a teenager, it was one of the first trees that I ever connected to in a sort of spiritual way. Long before I found out it was a sacred tree to the native people of the area, who used it in numerous ways, I learned on my own to appreciate the fragrance and special qualities of its leaves and bark. Later in my life sassafras tea and oils became significant items of nature to share with children. Then, as I delved deeper into shamanic teachings, I found an amazing connection between my indigenous shaman mentors and the mature sassafras tree. It is well known in shamanic lore that many times shamans exhibit some kind of physical deformity at birth or that they develop with age. In a profound vision when connecting to the energy of a large and very old sassafras, I distinctly felt a power uncannily similar to an old shaman I know who has a deformed right hand. The next time I saw the old shaman I had another vision—that his hand was a three-fingered sassafras leaf! From then on the sassafras tree has been a constant source of shamanic vision and wisdom for me. The somewhat small and comely sassafras teaches us that potent things sometimes come in small packages, and not to underestimate the abilities of those beings that may seem weird or strange.

Walnut, black: Unlike some other trees such as the aspen that are always in groves, the walnut tends to live alone in the natural world, and the flurry of activity surrounding it gives the impression of independence, like the walnut is the center of its own little universe. From the amount of wildlife that encompasses the walnut it is easy to see how this tree became sacred to indigenous people. One time I counted five squirrels, a chipmunk, two cats, two robins, and a hawk eating a rabbit all in or within five yards of a huge black walnut tree. The growth of the branches of the walnut often reflects the complexity of the relationship between it and the environment. It seems that the walnut is always busy doing something, and maybe it's no mere coincidence that the fruit of the walnut resembles a human brain. My personal lessons from the walnut most often take the form of learning to be more dynamic, to keep moving even when I'm feeling uninspired, and to allow the complexity of the creative process to flow through me so that many can be fed and nourished by it.

In addition to physically and psychically connecting to the unique essence and energy of a tree, we can also learn from it and use its distinctive qualities by incorporating it into shamanic tools, rituals, and ceremonies. This can be done in numerous ways, such as using the wood of a special or sacred tree to make shamanic tools, such as a flute, drum, rattle, wand, or fire. In this way the essence of the tree "sings" in concert with the interaction between the human organism and the forces of the natural world. That is why in many shamanic traditions the flesh of the tree used in the construction of shamanic tools is taken from a live sacred tree, therefore making the tool a living extension of the essence and energy of the special tree and the wisdom of years alive within it.

Once when I was invited to a Wirrarika ceremony there were three young anthropology students there observing, and when the fire maker was arranging the sticks to fuel the fire one of the students commented to me, "Why is that guy using green sticks to make a fire? Those sticks aren't dry enough to light." Of course I just laughed to myself and simply suggested that he remain open to the experience and pay attention. The usage of fresh wood taken from a live tree to make a fire seems like an unusual circumstance since we normally use dry wood that has been aged and seasoned because it burns much better. But in the sacred time of the shamanic world, physics as we know it often doesn't apply as the magical forces of the energies included in the ceremony interact, combine, and come alive.

This is the case when the profound connection of the Wirrarika shaman to the living energy of the sacred fire combines with the living energy of the fresh flesh of the tree in a magical way that allows the shaman to ignite the wet wood, which under normal circumstances would not light.

PRACTICE 39: Rituals with Trees

Many times during my life I have had to hopelessly endure the complete destruction of a favorite forest to "make room" for a new housing development or shopping center, or to supply timber for construction or paper products. Anyone who has had to witness a favorite tree or forest get cut down or bulldozed over knows the sickeningly sad feeling of helplessness that accompanies this experience. If only we could call the trees over and get them to run away or move to a new spot! But unfortunately our large friends are not very mobile and once the survey crew marks out the area to be cleared it is usually a death sentence for all of the trees and plants of the area. But in this age of unparalleled deforestation there are a number of things we can do to help the trees at a practical level that can also lead to heightened states of awareness and shamanic states of consciousness.

While many of these suggestions could be mechanically performed with a minimum of emotion and affection, if accomplished with high levels of awareness and openness both to the sacredness of all life and the personal feelings evoked by the action, these activities can become life-changing experiences of personal and spiritual growth. At the highest levels these actions become ecoshamanic rituals whereby we are transformed into life-giving, life-saving, and life-sustaining co-creators of this living entity we call Earth.

Saving Trees

Although we are often unable to save the large trees we love by physical or legal means, we can certainly save the smaller trees that are their offspring by digging them up and transplanting them before the chain saws and bulldozers come, and we can also save the seeds or take cuttings from the shoots of beloved trees that are marked for a premature death. In terms of deep psychic connection between you and a tree, these activities are some of the most potent imaginable. When you sit with an old tree friend that is marked for death and you tell the tree that you are going to save the life of one of its offspring and raise it as your own, you are demonstrating in the most sacred way possible your respect and your love toward that amazing being. In a similar way, when you transplant and take care of a sapling that otherwise would have been destroyed, you begin a magical relationship with that entity that may last for the rest of your life, or even longer if you pass the custom on to your children.

My first experiences of saving trees was as a child with my father, who rigorously transplanted trees that he knew would be destroyed by the continued construction of housing developments in our area. He saved many wild fruit trees, which were his favorite, as well as other types of trees by transplanting them into our yard and into the other wild areas of our property. Although he didn't emphasize to me the spiritual aspects of his actions, getting our hands into the soil together while saving the trees and then nursing them along until they were healthy was truly a bonding experience for me, both with my father and with the different types of trees and the soil. And I definitely contribute those early experiences to fueling my lifetime connection and fascination with the energy and wisdom of these unique life forms.

Planting Memorial Trees

Planting trees to commemorate and remember important moments, such as the birth of a child, a marriage, a graduation, a birthday, or as a living memorial to those close to us who have died, is a powerful, life-affirming ritual that promotes a real, tangible connection to the way our lives intertwine in the web of life fabric of organic reality.

Creating Tree Shrines

A tree shrine can be a lifetime source of inspiration, healing, and connection to the natural and spiritual worlds. The making of tree shrines is an ancient tradition found in many parts of the world. In some cases specific trees are thought to be connected with, or possess, particular deities or spirits, and therefore are protected by enclosures or marked with ribbon or colored rope around the trunk. Sometimes miniature houses or altar-type benches are constructed at the base of the tree to hold sacred offerings to the tree and its spirit. The trees singled out for this special kind of reverence are obviously exceptional entities that exude a unique energy and powerful presence. Sometimes they are commemorative trees that have been planted for a particular reason and have been nurtured their whole lives with special attention. But it is important to note that most often, at least in my experience, the incredible trees that are most sacred to us are the ones that we find living in the wild where they have naturally grown into the wise old grandmas and grandpas of the forest.

Tree shrines are perfect for signifying commemorative trees and also those uniquely powerful trees that you just know have special abilities. Creating shrines for these special trees, and of course maintaining the shrines, are a continued source of spiritual energy and can also help in protecting the tree, especially when an area of land that is being cleared for construction of housing or commercial buildings is owned by people sensitive to the value of such trees. More than a few times I have seen universities, golf courses, and sensitive landowners building their dream homes rethink the removal of certain trees simply because there was a tree shrine honoring and protecting the tree, along with those people who created the shrine speaking up for the survival and nurturing of the sacred tree.

PLANTS

PRACTICE 40: Working with Edible and Medicinal Plants

As with many of the techniques presented in this book, working with plants on a shamanic level begins with relating to them in the reverse way to how we are normally taught. This means that instead of borrowing someone else's knowledge to learn about a description of the plant from the outside in, you will relate to the plant from your inside out. Deep inside all of us is an instinctual kind of knowing that informs us of how something seemingly outside of us might affect us. This is particularly true when relating to plants, especially those that are edible, medicinal, or poisonous. But this instinctual knowing is only engaged when we let go of our modern patterns of control and open up to touch our primal awareness. Most of us have a lot of work to do in order to open to this primal awareness of edible and medicinal plants. Our educational systems are all but devoid of experiences that promote a healthy interaction with the flora and fauna. And from the time we are born we are given, and many times even forced, to eat foods that are supposed to be good for us. We are taught to suppress our inner knowing and choke down whatever food is put on our plate that is deemed healthy for us by someone else. This continues through adulthood as most people struggle with their weight and so move endlessly from one "expertly" conceived diet to the next. Also, as we learn to depend on the inherent authority of written sources of information and television we are further disconnected to our inner primal knowing.

Because of this human disconnection, many plant researchers working in the incredibly diverse ecology of rainforests are now finding it helpful and productive to follow around our not-so-distant cousin the chimpanzee, as well as other primates and animals, to learn about what their inner knowing tells them about the plants in the jungle. When a chimp, or other animal, significantly alters its behavior, or is seen to not be functioning optimally (does not feel well, stops eating, has diarrhea, etc.), and then begins consuming plants that are not normally found in their diet, the researchers gather these plants and study them in order to take advantage of practical, primal knowledge. In addition to the awareness of animals, another source of primal knowledge is found in indigenous cultures that still rely heavily on traditional plant remedies and traditional sources of sustenance. The way indigenous people relate to plants can teach us a lot about how to start on our own path of discovery in this immense field of knowledge. It is often thought that indigenous people, being scientifically unsophisticated, randomly pick plants and through trial and error eventually find out which are edible, medicinal, or poisonous. But that simply is not the case. The reality is that indigenous people know through careful observation combined with intuition that the major properties of plants can be placed into just a few categories, and all the major plant constituents can be learned simply by knowing these major properties and then using the human senses to quickly gather information about the general uses for any plant.

For example, aromatic plants contain volatile oils, and although there are over 30,000 known volatile oils they tend to have similar effects on the body. If you chew a leaf from a plant and it takes the saliva away from inside your mouth, leaving you with a feeling of "cottonmouth," this is a strong sign of the presence of tannic acid, another common constituent of plants. The astringent effect of tannic acid can be used medicinally in hundreds of similar ways. While developing a primal or shamanic awareness toward plants, the inner knowing of the chimpanzee and the straightforward herbalism of indigenous people are key. But my best suggestion in terms of safety, and also in making a bridge between how we are used to learning and our instinctual ways of learning, is to first seek out a reputable local herbalist to learn precisely which plants in your area are poisonous, and also to learn about the basic properties of plants, such as astringent, mucilaginous, and aromatic. From there, you can safely explore the world of wild plants in a primal way that fosters connection and growth.

It is important to note that here in North America there are few plants that are truly life threatening to a healthy adult. Of course people do die every year from ingesting poisonous plants, but in most cases they are the same few plants. Once you are able to identify these plants it is actually very difficult to significantly harm yourself or another person by ingesting or eating wild plants, if for no other reason than poisonous plants generally taste horrible and it is unlikely that you will eat a sufficient amount to cause harm. However, keep in mind that when we create medicines from plants we extract and concentrate certain qualities of the plants. The leaves, stems, or roots of a whole plant may be harmless but an extraction of one of its chemicals may be very dangerous. These chemical extracts are more properly termed *pharmaceuticals* and represent the specialized world of modern science more than the holistic world of shamanism.

My suggestion is to work on developing a relationship with the incredibly diverse, powerful, and beautiful world of whole plants rather than overly focusing on the individual constituents of any one plant, because learning about the hundreds or even thousands of isolated constituents of a plant may actually teach you less about the plant and not more. Each of the isolated constituents can have many different uses than when they are combined within the whole plant. The whole plant, with all of its ingredients living harmoniously within it, has been birthed naturally from the earth, has evolved through countless generations, and deserves our respect and admiration. It is the characteristics and personality of the whole plant that is truly important at a shamanic level.

The basic procedure for approaching a plant and entering into a meaningful dialog with it is similar to what I have already written in the section "Communicating with Trees." Although significant differences certainly exist between them, both trees and plants are dynamic entities that live their lives in one place but participate in the community of that place in many meaningful ways. At an even more immediate cognitive level than trees, plants are extremely sensitive beings and any good shaman certainly doesn't need current scientific research to confirm that plants can sense and feel not only the environment they live in and the pain of being injured or destroyed, but they can also sense and feel our human emotional states as well. So when working with plants it is important to remain cognizant of all levels of your MBESA. There are many field guides, books, and other resources available that can give you information about how people commonly relate to certain edible and medicinal plants. But although these sources of information can be enlightening and very useful, in terms of working shamanically with plants there is simply no substitute for personal experiences.

In a somewhat similar way to how I have contrasted my personal experiences with animal spirits (in the next section) to the general information provided by books written about animal totems, my personal experiences with plants also differ significantly to the things I read about the same plants in books. That is not to say that one is correct and the other is not, it's simply a matter of your personal perception and relationship with the spirit of a given type of plant. Granted, many of the qualities of certain plants will be felt the same way by most people. But that doesn't change the fact that the relationship you have with a particular plant spirit will ultimately be personal and uniquely dependent on how your MBESA relates to the plant.

To illustrate what I mean about having relationships with specific edible plants, I've included below a brief account of my relationship with four edible plants. I have chosen to include these four plants because they are very common, often misunderstood, and can be easily found in urban areas, especially areas being gobbled up by suburban sprawl. Please remember that these are simply my personal perceptions and relationships to each plant and that yours may be quite different. The important thing is that by forming these kinds of relationships we enlarge our sphere of perception to include the other many life forms around us.

Wild onion: As a small boy the wild onion was the first wild plant I ever ate, and to me it was a miracle plant. It grew profusely in the area where I lived and I pulled it up and ate it so often that the other kids, and even my parents, would often complain about my onion breath. But I didn't care because I loved the taste of it and loved even more the fact that it was just growing wild from the soil of my home range and there for me whenever I wanted during certain months of the year. And the spirit of the wild onion taught me some of my very first lessons in wastefulness, patience, and concentration. You see, at times when the ground is soft, wild onions can be pulled out of the soil quite easily, but at other times the soft leaves of the plant will break off when you try to pull them up, leaving you with handful of greens but no onions. I would always feel bad when I pulled too hard or hurriedly and broke apart the onion from the stalks, and so I learned early on to be very careful and if the onions did not come out with a certain amount of force I would leave them be instead of damaging them.

An interesting thing to note is that I could actually feel the onions' pain and hurt if I accidentally broke off the stems, but when I successfully pulled out the whole plant and ate it, the plants didn't say a word or seem to mind a bit. In some inexplicable way I could feel the spirit of the wild onion harmoniously fulfilling its niche in the world whenever I removed and ate the onions in a respectful way, but when I pulled at them hurriedly or in a damaging way I could feel the disapproval of the plant spirit, and that feeling was not at all pleasant.

This type of innocent and enlightening experience with a plant spirit gives me hope that sharing these types of experiences with people may facilitate some positive change in the state of the world. I have often thought about how to describe "hearing" the onion share its lesson with me or how to label or classify the experience. In the bottom line I have made peace with myself by using the term *shamanic* to describe these types of experiences, simply because the people that have regular conversations with plants are often referred to as shamans.

Getting back to the lessons of the wild onion, this plant spirit also gave to me my first feelings of the cleansing qualities of certain foods. I didn't need anyone to tell me that the reactions of my body to the onions, including the strong taste, the tears streaming from my eyes, the burping, etc., all contributed to a sort of purging that I didn't quite understand but I could definitely feel. This awareness brought about by the wild onion raised my general awareness to my body's reaction to different types of foods, which is something that I contribute to this day as being one thing that has kept my eating habits very healthy throughout my life.

Cattail: Cattails are one of the most easily recognized wild plants in North America. But while most people see marshes or swamps when looking at cattails, and survivalists and Boy Scouts see food, when I see the cattail I immediately see flames. This is because the very first time I ever brought a sacred fire to life without the use of a match or lighter was under the tutelage of an old Lenape shaman who showed me how to use a wooden bow drill and the fluff of a cattail to manifest the sacred fire into our physical realm. Although since then I have found many other sources of tinder, that first experience with the old shaman of making fire from what was just naturally around in that moment was an experience that will last a lifetime. Inside my fire spirit rirriki you can usually find some fluffy cattail down in honor of this plant's sacred connection to the fire for me.

One of the most significant outcomes of powerful experiences with commonly found plants is that after these experiences happen the plant is forever a source of connection to both the planes of the physical world and normal awareness and the metaphysical worlds of altered states of consciousness. For example, the cattail is such a common and widespread plant that almost wherever I go I find it growing.

This means that even at those times when I am not fully aware of it, such as when driving by it in a car or walking by it while engaged in a conversation with another person, at some level my consciousness still recognizes its connection to this plant and so it becomes a frequent and familiar organic companion rather than just one more unknown item in an overly cluttered urban landscape.

Often when I look back on the experience I had with the old shaman and the cattail I get the feeling that he somehow knew I would come to have a very close relationship with the fire when I got older, and that one of the gifts that he intentionally gave me was the use of the cattail in the tinder bundle, knowing full well that for the rest of my life I would be surrounded by the image of burning cattail fluff because the cattail is such a widespread and common plant.

Dandelion: The spirit of the dandelion is under constant siege by the modern world of chemically treated lawns fueled by the perception that "weeds" such as the dandelion should be eradicated at all costs. The extreme lengths that people go through in order to kill such a beneficial plant is so amazing it seems unbelievable. For me, the dandelion has become not only an ally but also a strong symbol of the struggle between the modern world's ignorant disregard for the natural life systems of the planet and the vast minority of people actively trying to promote ways of life in balance with the organic realities of the biosphere. Even though most species of dandelion are not native to the United States, wherever I see the dandelion, whether in suburban lawns or high mountain meadows, I am reminded of the current war being waged on the natural world.

The tenacity of the dandelion spirit feeds my soul with hope and resiliency. This sun-resembling flower is a constant reminder to me that man is not the most powerful force in the cosmos. Seeing the multitude of dandelion seeds being blown and carried by the spirit of the wind displays for me the self-governing activities of our living planet that was here long before man and that will be here long after we are gone. The dandelion spirit inspires me to plant my own seeds of the sun, to fulfill my task of spreading the sacred light. Although I know, use, and respect the many utilitarian aspects of the dandelion, such as eating the greens in salads, making coffee from the dried roots, and the stimulating effect the ingestion of the dandelion spirit has on the human liver, the magnificent dandelion is a plant spirit ally to me mostly because of the inspiration of its tenacity and symbolism as a little sun growing on Earth.

Plantain: In a similar way to the dandelion, the plantain (not little bananas, but the small, broad-leafed plant that can be found growing in lawns, in the cracks of side-walks, and along the roadside) is a completely misunderstood and unappreciated edible plant. Just like the dandelion, the plantain spirit is under constant attack by those millions of people chemically treating their lawns to eradicate them. The ironic thing is that the best place to find plantains are in the very lawns were they are meant to be kept out of. It's as though the plantain spirit knows what is good for us and continually tries to teach us by springing up in the most useful places. If we were a little more attentive to the plantain, we would all know that the pain and irritation of mosquito bites and bee stings that we commonly get while in our lawns can be treated effectively by bruising the leaf of the plantain and immediately applying it to the wound. The leaves and seeds are completely edible, very nutri-tious, and can be infused in oil to be placed on practically anything that itches or needs soothing. Wow, free food *and* healing that grows between the cracks of a side-walk—just imagine how many more miracles we would find if we would look.

Discovering respectful uses for commonly found plants in the area where you live can be a powerful entrance into the world of plant spirits, especially when entering into the relationship in a reciprocal manner by making offerings back to the plant spirits instead of simply taking from them. Forming relationships with plant spirits can also develop at a high level during the making of tinctures, salves, and infused oils for healing, when respon-sibly working with psychoactive plant medicines, and of course when we relate at a spiri-tual level to the plants and vegetables that we eat. The most important thing to be aware of is simply that plants are aware beings whose animating spirits are completely open for us to connect with.

It's not some sort of romantic notion that plants are sensitive beings with whom we can develop real relationships. Plants have a strong emotional reaction when people think about harming or maiming them, and that is why we should be just as respectful when taking the life of a plant as we are when taking the life of an animal. It is amazing to me how passionately people can be toward condemning the eating of meat but how equally insensitive they can be toward the feelings of the plants they eat.

In some respects the eating of meat is actually more "humane" because when an animal is conscientiously and quickly killed for its meat, the animal is dead—its body is a now a carcass with no chance of ever springing to life again. But a vegetable plant—for instance, a head of lettuce torn from its roots—will still be waiting for the chance to receive water and nutrients to keep it alive. In this case, the vegetable is still "alive" and sits in a box or in our refrigerator until we finally kill it, cell by cell, in the process of chewing and digesting it.

It is hard to say exactly what plants feel when we take their life, but they do feel something, and that fact should be considered in our sacred relationship to them. Aside from that we can also develop a more tangible and primal connection to the roles they each play in the great interconnected web of relationships that forms the biosphere. Plants and flowers provide for our respiration and nutritional needs, and they also color our world and beautify our lives. From this perspective, the spirits of all plants have healing and inspirational qualities, whether we ingest them or not.

Animals

Shamanic initiations with animals is a topic as vast and complex as the multitude of shamanic cultures throughout the globe that practice them. The various techniques employed by shamanic cultures to connect with the spirits of animals are used for many reasons, some of which are:

- To petition for success in hunting.

- To acquire the spirit of an animal to increase personal knowledge and power.

- To petition for the animal spirit's protection (either personally or for the tribe).

- To temporarily borrow the unique perception of the animal to "see" in enhanced ways, to spy on enemies, or to obtain spiritual visions.

- To honor and celebrate the relationship between the tribe and the animal kindoms.

- To connect with the spirits of deceased ancestors that have taken animal form.

- To ask advice in the area of expertise of a particular animal.

The question of whether initiations with animals and their spirits is an activity that would have benefit to people of modern society is an interesting topic, and one that I have been exploring for quite a few years. My current point of view is that the answer lies squarely in your personal intention and level of openness to discovering your true potentials. If you enter into shamanic initiations with animals with preconceived and romantic notions, the only thing you are likely to gain is the fulfilling of those notions. On the other hand, if you are willing to accept what the animal spirits have to share with you, even if their messages aren't what you wanted or expected to hear, you are much more likely to have a meaningful and potentially life-changing experience.

I make this point from the outset simply because the most profound lessons that the animal kin-doms have for us are manifested not through our favorite animal, nor the one we would most like to emulate or become, but through the animals that choose to teach us. The fact is that we don't get to choose which animals will be our guides; *they* decide. We might form special relationships, friendships, and partnerships with certain animals, but in terms of shamanic initiation it is necessary from the beginning to drop all of our preconceived notions in order to fully open ourselves to what the animal spirits have in store for us.

Let's face it: if we could pick our animal spirit allies, most people would choose an exotic and immensely powerful or beautiful animal. For example, I have seen on many occasions that people searching for an animal spirit by traveling inside their own mind most often come up with an exquisite eagle, a jaguar, a wolf, a dolphin, a hawk, a leopard, or some other magnificent animal or bird as their spirit ally. And who could blame them? These wonderful beings are symbols of freedom, power, beauty, and grace. However, what is usually overlooked is that these powerful animals spend most of their time at their trade as highly skilled killers. I doubt very much whether any of the nice people involved in these imaginative searches for animal spirits have ever felt the rush of chasing another animal down and killing it, and then eating it raw. Animal predation is not often a quick business; usually there is a lot of thrashing around by the victim, a lot of blood, and often the predator begins feeding even before its victim is dead.

The point here is that for most modern people the actual animals of the animal kin-doms are so far removed from their everyday lives that the images of animals that come quickest to mind are the ones being continually portrayed as glamorous by TV and advertising. When we visit zoos and watch the Discovery Channel, it is easy to see animals from all over the globe and to imagine a connection to some type of exotic animal. But what is far more important than how many animals we can identify in pictures or in cages is the context in which we relate to them, and our personal relationships with them. When we visit with a caged animal we can only see, feel, and sense a very limited portion of what that animal truly would be in the wild. Its spirit is tamed to live in a cage, or else it dies. And when we simply see the animal on television or in print we see, feel, and sense even less. We surely may pick up some idea of what the spirit of the animal could be like, but we have no meaningful interaction with it and therefore no relationship with it since we have not yet taken the opportunity to have the animal spirit teach us.

Wildlife shows and advertising campaigns containing eagles and lions are much more successful than those with groundhogs or robins, simply because they portray the prestigious qualities of success so admired by our culture. But we have to ask, even if it were possible, do we really want modern people interested in shamanism to consult with the spirits that animate cold-blooded killers like the eagle or jaguar? For the well-being of the world, wouldn't it be better for an army general to consult with a tree sloth, or a Wall Street trader to seek advice from a mourning dove? Surely if there is a balanced force in the universe manifesting its power in the cyclically stable organic reality of earth's life systems, it would choose to send the orderly knowledge of ants to the hoards of road-raged highway commuters instead of the energy of a herd of stampeding bulls. If there are animal spirits in the world available to guide us, wouldn't they send the spirit of a koala bear to the CEO of an overly aggressive timber company, and the spirit of a kangaroo to a neglectful mother?

Well, I'm here to tell you that there *are* these kinds of spirits available to help us, it's just that we've completely alienated ourselves from the levels of awareness that allow us to perceive them. Part of this is fairly easy to resolve because it is simply a matter of physical location. For those of us who are trapped in the urban grid, or have been molded into a human resource by corporate America, the first step is to simply get out into the natural world and re-acclimate ourselves with the organic reality of life. When you get out of your indoor environment and actually see and feel the wild animals of the world, you are stepping out of the confines of your own mind and making contact with the energies and spirits that animate the world. They are real and tangible. You can touch them and feel them and interact with them. And most importantly, they have the power to teach and guide us. In terms of shamanic experiences, these encounters with animals can be the catalyst for modern people interested in shamanism to move from the imagined connection with animal spirits to tangible and empowering relationships with them.

Concerning Animal Totems

Shamanic totems are naturally occurring sources of energy that assist in transforming consciousness and inspiring creative solutions to challenges. The animating spirits of animals, along with the symbolic and archetypal images they inspire, are naturally and perfectly suited to help guide and nurture us throughout the many stages of our lives. Through intimate association with these naturally occurring phenomena we learn important lessons, receive protection and direction, and foster strong bonds with the forces of nature and spirit that transcend the myopic view of exclusively human events and concerns.

Much has been written recently about the powerful benefits of finding and choosing an animal totem, and for this reason we now have many modern people interested in shamanism running around with the totem names of Hawk, Eagle, and Bear, among many other powerful animals, attached to their name. It is actually quite amusing and humorous to meet many of these people, often also calling themselves shamans, because if they actually belonged to a shamanic culture they almost certainly would be given a name that more closely resembles their true animal totem rather than the glamorous totem they chose for themselves.

One of the most grounding and basic lessons of the shamanic worldview is that it is brutally frank when it comes to interpersonal relationships and there is simply no way to pretend to be what you are not. If you were to introduce yourself to a shamanic culture, for example, as "James Medicine Eagle," but as people get to know you they see that your mannerisms more closely resemble a turtle than an eagle, you will most naturally be called "Turtle" no matter if you prefer to be called Eagle or not. If you have a habit of talking too much, you are likely to be associated with a noisy bird such as a "Blue Jay" or to be named "Running Mouth" or something similar. Think about some of the most famous indigenous people of North America, such as Sitting Bull, Rain in the Face, Crazy Horse, Black Elk, Fools Crow, and Lame Deer. This type of naming is not for making fun of a person; on the contrary, it is the most honest and efficient way for the spirits to name you. And, if you are able to handle it, you can use the insights provided by the name that others give to you as an opportunity to see yourself in new and improved ways. When you accept the animal (or any other type of totem) that others see in you and embrace those qualities, you are being true to your nature and opening to personal growth and discovery. Which is also to say that as you grow, your name will most likely change or expand to accommodate your personal transformations once they manifest significantly enough to be noticed by your companions.

For example, the first animal totem acknowledged in me by others significantly enough to inspire a name was the mountain goat. At that time of my life I had a passion for climbing, scrambling, jumping, and literally running down steep rocky mountainsides, and fortunately I also possessed the physicality and dexterity that enabled me to do it without injury. Although much to my chagrin the name "James Mountain Goat" eventually became reserved for formal introductions, while the shortened version of "Jimmy Goat" was used most often by my close companions, the name itself was both enlightening and empowering to me at that time of my life, even though it wasn't by any means glamorous.

By acknowledging the animal totem of the mountain goat inside of me I opened up to discovering that this animal totem extended far beyond the physical prowess displayed by both of us on the rocks. By searching out the mountain goat spirit, I learned that it prefers to spend its time in high places inaccessible to others, and to tread dangerous and precarious paths. When I carried this totem most strongly inside of me I was in my early twenties and I was a true searcher and seeker. My journeys to find myself and my place in the world and cosmos often led me into precarious situations, sometimes on the treacherous paths of plant medicines, always seeking a higher understanding, but often at the risk of falling from a deadly height. As I spent time in the mountains with the mountain goat I learned about its thick coat, something I also needed, both physically and psychologically, to propel me on my journey of discovery. And the dangerous and mystical horns of the goat I found to be within myself also, and to be a great source of both power and mystery, as the mountain goat has been known to kill even grizzly bear at need, and to let its magical horns guide it in the blinding snow when all other senses fail.

The spirit of the mountain goat still lives inside of me and I consider it a personal totem even to this day. My many encounters with this spirit on the sheer and dangerous cliffs of the Rocky Mountains are permanently etched into my being, and I call on them when needed. But as I have matured there have been many other spirits that I have allied with, as my circumstances have changed and my life has unfolded. When dealing with animal spirits and totems, one must always be aware of new opportunities and when a shift or change in your dominant totem is necessary. In my case it was the mountain goat that eventually led me to the elusive bighorn sheep. This new animal spirit in my life marked a shift from my almost reckless excursions on the edge to a somewhat more cerebral period where I still lived with the bighorn above tree level, and therefore away from mainstream society, but in a more comfortable way that allowed me to graze on the tender shoots of human words and meditations. Within the spiraling form of the adult ram's horns I perceived a new cycle beginning in my life, and so the bighorn was a more temporary, although very significant, totem for me.

In my case dozens of animal spirits have come and gone, some staying with me to this day and some merely touching me briefly in a time appropriate for both of us.

PRACTICE 41: Receiving Animal Spirits and Totems

Modern neoshamanic techniques employing guided imagery using animals have been shown to raise awareness of our relationship to the animal kin-doms. However, classic shamanic practices that make tangible contact with the multidimensional realms rely much more on the shaman's actual knowledge of an animal than on what he imagines about it. Although an animal that "comes to mind" may indeed have significance to you or your current life situation, if you have never actually met the animal or been in its presence in the wild, your perception of the animal is limited to what books, photos, or television shows have shown you or told you about the animal, and these impressions may be completely different to what the real-life animal may have in store for you.

The way to receive a visit from the spirit of an animal is to become part of the environment where the actual animal that contains the spirit dwells. The more you become part of that environment, and the more time you spend with and around the animal, the deeper the spirit of that animal will affect your MBESA. For example, a chance encounter with an animal while on vacation somewhere could certainly affect you as the spirit of that animal makes contact with your MBESA, but living for a significant period of time in that environment and making contact on a daily basis with the spirit of that animal will place you into an interactive relationship with what animates that spirit. At this level you are becoming familiar with not only the spirit of that particular animal but also the living environment that sustains and nurtures it. By submerging your MBESA into the living world of the animal you are knocking on the front door of the house of the animal spirit and asking to come inside.

Once you knock on the door, if the spirit lets you in, it is up to you to make use of the knowledge that will be shared with you. In a similar way to being buried in the earth, there is no way that you will come out of the house of the animal spirit unaffected, but the depth of the knowledge that you acquire while in the house, and what you do with the knowledge after you leave, is completely up to you. At one extreme you could simply be touched by the spirit and mildly feel the encounter for a few days until it dissipates as you go about your life relatively unchanged, or on the other hand, you could carry your experiences with you, embody them, and in this way call on the spirit of the animal while you engage in the world of everyday life.

I'm going to provide some examples of how to carry on a long-term relationship with an animal spirit, but first I want to illustrate in more detail what some of the practical possibilities are with regards to working with animal spirits. I use the word *practical* because if you are going to knock on the door of an animal spirit's house, you first have to find the door. From a purely practical standpoint, finding the doors to the animal spirit houses that are already around us, or near to us, is the most natural first step. If you live in a neighborhood filled with the houses of squirrels, chipmunks, robins, skunks, and owls, even if you have never interacted with these spirits, your MBESA is already at some level accustomed to the natural environment where these spirits live. It will be much more practical, especially in the beginning of your shamanic apprenticeship with animal spirits, to work with these spirits, rather than with those in an unfamiliar landscape where you will need much more time just to acclimate to the environment of the animal spirit you hope to work with. In other words, if you have lions and zebras in your neighborhood, then work with lion and zebra spirits first; if you live with sea turtles, dolphins, and seagulls, work with them. Look at your initial relationship with the animal spirit as an apprenticeship. If you view it in this way you will necessarily need to live in the area of your teacher and to spend significant time with them. It's that simple.

Working with the animal spirits that naturally occur around us is also significant to raising awareness of our local environment. There is no better way to tune into what is going on within the organic reality of where you live than to tune into the spirits of the animals that live there. I realize that for many people interested in shamanism the animals that are common to where we live are considered just that—"common"—and so are often overlooked when it comes to tapping into their magic and mystery. But from over twenty years of working shamanically with both animal spirits and human beings, I can tell you that animal spirits come to people as the people become open and ready to receive them. If you live in the city, the spirit of the city squirrel may be much more approachable for you to work with on a daily basis than the spirit of a deer living in a secluded place in the mountains. There is a reason why you both live in the city, or the suburbs, or the country. And by already sharing the everyday sights, sounds, and smells of the area where you live, you already have much in common with those beings that you share your neighborhood with. What you consider to be familiar can tell you a lot about who you are.

To illustrate what the animating spirits of "common" animals to North America may have in store for us, I'm going to share what a few easily found animals, birds, and insects that I have apprenticed with over the years have shared with me.

Turkey vulture: This spirit has provided me with companionship, vision, and countless lessons. Although I had seen vultures my whole life, the animating spirit of this totem didn't reveal itself fully to me until I was ready. One day I was sitting quietly in the sun on a large boulder that was on the side of wooded mountain near to my house. I was close to the top of the mountain, where it was common to see vultures flying and roosting. I noticed movement in the boulders a few yards from me and I began to intently stare in that direction. After a few minutes I saw two small heads pop up from behind one of the boulders, but I couldn't tell what kind of beings they were. So I very slowly and stealthily made my way closer until I could clearly see two magnificent baby birds covered in white downy feathers sitting in a crevice at the top of a large boulder next to me. They saw me, too, but because I moved silently and didn't look directly at them, but rather out the corner of my eye, they stayed put and were not alarmed. A few minutes later the mother vulture came flying down and landed in a tree a few yards away. This is when my silent conversation with the vulture spirit began and my relationship to these birds escalated to a whole new level. It would take many pages to describe what happened that day but the outcome was that the mother bird made it very clear to me that my meeting with her and her family was meant to be and that they were going to be my teachers and companions for many years, as long as I showed respect, manners, and a commitment to come frequently to receive my lessons and apply them to my life. During that first year with the vultures I visited them at least three times a week, often more, and I learned a great deal about both them and myself. They provided me with companionship during a difficult life stage and it was comforting to be able to go and visit them and be part of the secret little world of this new family hidden in the boulders.

Even though the vulture is an incredible and graceful flyer, one of the first and most lasting lessons from this spirit was about grounding myself. This has been one of the greatest gifts from the vulture and one of the reasons it is so easy for me to look beyond the seemingly homely appearance of the bird and accept the profound lessons it has to share. The surprise at finding my first two vulture friends as babies on the ground is extremely significant to what this spirit has to teach. Since these vultures lay their eggs on the ground, instead of in a nest high in a tree, they begin their life in physical contact with the energy of the earth and soil and therefore view the world from the perspective of terrestrial creatures. This provides them with a unique view of the world once they learn to fly, and is part of the reason why the dual vision of the vulture spirit is highly prized in the shamanic arts.

During my lessons with the vulture I have been able to explore the unique vision of the vulture spirit that is derived from its dual life as a member of both the societies of land animals as well as birds of flight. The vulture is born on the ground and spends approximately its first three months in and around the small cave or fallen tree trunk that is its den. Throughout its life the vulture spends a significant amount of time on the ground feeding on carcasses, since its feet and legs aren't strong enough to pick up and fly away with its food. But the vulture is also highly skilled at soaring on thermal currents rising into the air and can fly for hours without once flapping its wings. These two very special traits set it apart from other large birds such as the bald eagle, which spends almost no time on the ground and feeds primarily on fish. By learning about and contrasting the differences between these two types of large birds we can see clearly the unique qualities and energies of these two totems and how having each of them in your life will lead to significantly different experiences.

Another unique characteristic of the vulture spirit is its role as a purifier and recycler. Unlike other raptors, the vulture rarely if ever kills its own food, but rather dines on the corpses of dead animals. Its unique body chemistry and immune system allows it to consume bacteria harmful to other animals and thus helps to clean the environment and prevent the spread of disease. Shamanic cultures, always very practical and keen observers, notice the purifying qualities of the vulture spirit and the dual nature and vision of the bird, and therefore use the feathers of the vultures in various ceremonies of purification and vision.

In my case, the vulture spirit has guided me to purge certain wasteful actions and thoughts from my life and develop a more pure and grounded yet expanded view of the world and my place in it. Anyone who witnesses the vulture spirit face the sun each morning and unfurl its wings to collect the energy, heat, and purifying qualities of the sunlight will no doubt be touched by the unique and powerful spirit of this totem.

Woodpecker: The spirit of the woodpecker for me is one of awareness, for several reasons. When I first began to learn from the woodpecker it was due to my relationship with the deer totem. I started to notice early on in my work with deer that on many occasions when I would see and be with wild deer in the woods there would also be a woodpecker working near by, but when the deer were not around many times the sound of the woodpecker would be missing as well. When I finally began to put two and two together, what I realized was that the deer often look to the woodpecker, as well as many other creatures, to know that the "coast is clear" and all is well in the woods. In an area where woodpeckers live it is quite common to hear their rhythmic pecking in the treetops, but if they are disturbed by, say, a person walking through or maybe a prowling cat, they won't be working and their unique sound will be missing. For the deer, the sounds of the woodpecker working is therefore one sign that the woods are clear of intruders. The rhythmic sound of the woodpecker working also raises awareness to the sounds of the woods in general because by tuning into it you normally will notice other more subtle sounds as you concentrate with your ears. The woodpecker is also great for raising awareness when you try and find one, because although the sounds of the bird working may seem very loud in a quiet wood it is oftentimes difficult to actually spot the bird, and finding it can be quite challenging at times. I have also learned a great deal about trees while searching for the forest drummer.

I have also found the woodpeckers that live near to my home to be quite tolerant of, and even friendly, to me once they get to know me. They are often my companions when I sit outside quietly reading and once they are accustomed to my presence they will continue working in the trees just above or around me even while I move around. Whether deep in the woods or in my backyard, the drumming of the woodpecker has become a comfortable and welcoming sound for me. The woodpeckers' drumming is very simple and rhythmic, and I emulate it when drumming during rites of passage and ceremonies where a familiar and soothing cadence is desirable. The up and down flight of the woodpecker as it flaps, then glides; flaps, then glides also corresponds to the easy beat of its drumming, as does its black and white coloring. I often use the black and white feathers of the woodpecker to raise awareness of the dualities carried within all of us but that come together to create our own unique balance and rhythm. The tail feathers of the woodpecker I also use to support the work of other shamanic objects, including other feathers, just as the woodpeckers use them to help support and stabilize themselves vertically on the tree while working.

Rattlesnake: My initiation into the diverse magic of the snake spirits came in the form of sunbathing rattlesnakes, which are numerous in the mountains where I live. These snakes taught me silence and watchfulness and to be aware of even the slightest vibrations in the environment. While carefully lying in the sunlight on the same warm boulders as the snakes I first discovered how to draw the soothing and grounding radiant heat from the rock into my body and energy field. By emulating the snakes I learned to feel the subtle vibrations in the rock and soil caused by the movement of wildlife, and especially people. Translating these techniques to the sphere of human affairs has optimized my sense of intuition as long as I remain open and clear of extraneous ego-related concerns or motives.

During certain rites of passage and initiations I have been keenly aware of the snake spirit through the feeling of shedding skin and the invigorating sensation of rebirth associated with the leaving behind of the old covering to reveal a new and more sensitive me. Through fostering a relationship early in my life with the rattlesnake I could see from a young age the correlation between the rattlesnake skins I would sometimes find and the changes and transitions my own body and mind was going through. Looking back at my childhood I can also now see a distinct correlation between the times I found the shed snake skins and the transitions I was making at those times. I have no doubt that the spirit of my snake totem was sending me messages even back then. Unfortunately the destruction of habitat by unchecked urban sprawl and irresponsible use of pesticides, coupled with insensitive belt and shoe makers that buy skins from hunters, has seriously endangered the rattlesnake population. Contrary to popular belief, rattlesnakes rarely bite human beings, and it's a tragedy that many types of rattlesnakes are now in danger of becoming extinct.

Butterfly: Although the life cycle of the butterfly clearly represents the transformative process so looked for by those interested in shamanism, my experience with the butterfly spirit has been slightly different. For me the skin-shedding rattlesnake has accompanied me more often during times of heavy change, while the butterfly spirit has arrived on many occasions to announce the coming of a vision, whether transformational or simply utilitarian. For example, there have been times in the wilderness, and especially during pilgrimages to sacred places, when I wasn't sure exactly which way to go or what trail to take, but then the butterfly spirit would come and beyond a shadow of a doubt I would know exactly which way to go, even if it wasn't the same direction as the physical butterfly was traveling. On the other hand, I have also had experiences when the arrival of the butterfly spirit directly preceded intense transformational experiences and visions, especially during vision quests when I had been fasting for a number of days. The butterfly totem is not one that I associate with on a daily basis during the course of my everyday life. It is more of a relationship that has grown and evolved as sometimes does between old schoolmates or good childhood friends, whereby you may now live far apart but you still get together or talk once in while or on very special occasions, and you would be there in a heartbeat for the other person if they really needed you.

Spider: I find myself constantly surrounded by different kinds of spiders. Many years ago during one of my first vision quests I was visited by so many spiders during a three-day period sitting under a large oak tree that I stopped counting them after a hundred. This was my initial (conscious) visit by the spider spirit, and during one of those nights I made an agreement with the spider spirit never to harm a living spider in return for their protection and knowledge. Unfortunately this often drives my friends and companions crazy when they come to my house because although once in a while I may accidentally suck one into the vacuum cleaner, I don't knowingly disturb spider webs, and I let the daddy longlegs stay, even in my bedroom.

Spiders are amazing beings and I feel honored to have a close connection to them. I associate my spider totem with the time of my life when I received the message from the earth and fire to begin writing. Although this message didn't come directly from the spider spirit, it was in that time that the spirit first came predominantly into my life and I see clearly the correlation between webs created by words and those created by spiders. My encounters with spiders, especially when watching one of the orb-building spiders at work making a web, often provide the type of sheer awe that inspires my creativity while at the same time invoking a feeling a humbleness inside of me. Although my writing usually resembles the untidy web of the daddy longlegger, the presence of the orb builders keeps me striving to improve. In all cases, my almost daily witnessing of the agility and balance of the spider inspires an almost subconscious emulation of the spider spirit during the course of my day that significantly affects the way I relate and react to the world around me.

Blue jay: I owe my connection to birds to the spirit of the blue jay, and although this totem is not as strong inside of me as it once was, I will be forever grateful to its spirit and consider myself part of its family. Until my initiations with the blue jay spirit I didn't have much interest in the "common" birds of my area, such as the robin, starling, or wood thrush, choosing instead to tread the conventional path of getting excited only when a magnificent eagle, owl, or hawk would appear. But all that changed when the common blue jay opened my eyes to the secret world of song and flight that goes on from dawn to dusk every day all around me.

What happened to me was that I was fortunate enough to live for a three-year period in a large forest of almost exclusively oak trees, which is a favorite habitat for blue jays, and during that time I communed on a daily basis with several families and generations of blue jays. At first I was a little annoyed at the jays because they can be loud, overbearing, territorial, and even dangerous to other birds. But as I got to know these birds, and watch as they mated, took care of their eggs, raised their children, and protected their homes, I was awed by their skills and began to understand the complex system of communication that they use extremely well but that has often been misunderstood and so has labeled them the "loud mouth."

To really appreciate the spirit of the blue jay you have to spend time with its entire family. The flurry of activity surrounding a household of blue jays is enormous, and because they are always flying to and fro, watching over their territory and sending messages back and forth, the blue jay will be at once your trusted friend when you are treading lightly and your nemesis that will set the whole forest at attention if you cause undo attention to yourself by being noisy or clumsy. Along with squirrels, the blue jay will be the first to sound the alarm to the rest of the woodland creatures that you are in the woods, which can be frustrating until you learn to walk quietly. But once you fully understand the role of the jay you come to respect them for their dedication and loyalty, not to mention their fearlessness. Blue jays will often team up with their cousins the crows and chase off large hawks and other birds of prey such as owls and even eagles.

Having the blue jay spirit as a personal totem is kind of like being friends with an aggressive manager or leader. If you're not friends with them it is easy to dislike them, but if you are friends you gain an important ally and the strength that comes with it.

Dog: My relationship with the spirit of the domesticated dog is sometimes unbelievably painful and other times magnificently rewarding. The spirit of the dog tears me in two unlike any other animal spirit because I am not a fan of man's subjugation and domestication of animals in order to serve our overly consumptive needs, and the tendency of our modern culture toward autonomous individuals and away from functional communities. In the case of the domesticated dog, as well as cat, it is extremely sad to see so many lonely people (including myself in certain times of my life) replace the dynamic relationship of people in a community with the comfortable but socially withdrawn affection of a beloved and totally dependent "pet." On the other hand, the love and devotion, when reciprocal, can be rewarding and nurturing for both pet and master. So in the final analysis I tend not to make sweeping judgments with regards to pet ownership except in those cases that are obviously cruel or neglectful.

In my case, many years of living on the fringes of society left me in some ways maladjusted socially, and so when I tried to reenter mainstream society my faithful dog ultimately remained my closest companion and confidant. But I must note that even though he was a domesticated German shepherd, his life with me on the fringes was very much wild and he basically stayed with me because he chose to, and not because I forced him. During most of his life he didn't even wear a collar and was never on a leash. But because of this it was equally difficult for him to come with me back to civilization. Watching him go through this was one of the most enlightening periods for me with the dog spirit because here I had a dog that basically gave up his freedom to be with me, rather than the normal situation with domesticated pets where they really don't know any other kind of life than the obedient and stifled pet. In the case of my basically free dog (his name was Aragorn), I would say that connection to his dog spirit had more positive effects than anything else, but in general, domesticated animals who have had their spirits broken or tamed into obedient servants don't make for powerful shamanic totems because they reflect the world of human concerns as much or more than they represent their free and powerful ancestors.

Aragorn saved my life more than a few times and for that I will be forever grateful. In his honor I work with my local German shepherd rescue as a foster parent to at risk and abandoned dogs. As rewarding as this work is, it ultimately reinforces my basic underlying feelings that humans have violated the fundamental laws of the universe by domesticating animals. I say this with a love for these dogs full in my heart, and every time I bring into my home a new foster dog, traumatized by man's uncaring and cruel treatment, I look into the eyes of the dog and I apologize to the dog spirit and offer my help to try and bring back the sacred balance that has been so tragically lost.

Deer: People often question how I can rescue domesticated dogs from being euthanized but then turn around and once a year kill two wild deer. They ask this question because they lack the understanding of the differences between animal cruelty and the fulfillment of an animal's natural life cycle. The wild ancestors of the domesticated dog were predators, and by reducing their naturally carnivorous hereditary traits to sitting pretty for a bowl of dog food we have cruelly exploited the spirit of these amazing beings. For various reasons I feel personally obligated to devote a portion of my energy to this situation, and so I rescue dogs. On the other hand, with the white-tailed deer we have a species of animal that is born to be prey for carnivores. That is one of the deer's most basic functions in the ecosystem. But in most places humans have totally eradicated the natural predators so now we have state governments and local municipalities slaughtering deer in the cruelest ways imaginable because there are too many and therefore have been labeled "pests."

Because of my spiritual connection to the deer this situation is completely intolerable for me, to the point that I have no qualms about breaking the so-called rules when it comes to deer "management." Deer are remarkable, gentle, wise, aware, resourceful, graceful, tough, sweet, playful beings that deserve our respect. When I fulfill my carnivorous traits and respectfully fulfill the deer's niche as a prey animal by engaging in a sacred hunt, I merge and flow with the life-affirming cycles of the natural world while at the same time I disavow the cruelty of factory-raised meat and industrial agriculture by putting wild venison on my table instead. The spirit of the deer lives inside of me because I honor it and cherish it and have a reciprocal relationship with it. The deer spirit is begging for us to change our ways, to bring back its natural predators so that it can fulfill its niche in the balanced systems of the earth's body instead of being miserably mowed down by cars or captured in nets and killed without dignity or appreciation.

I have lain in the same beds with deer, have warned them to run from the road or from the cruel netting parties, have sat in trees while baby fawns chased each other around below me, have woken up from a nap in the woods to have a deer standing above me and gently staring into my eyes. And I have taken the spirit of the deer into my breath and made its flesh a part of my own. But aside from all the wonderful and profoundly sad experiences I have shared with the deer spirit, the most important lesson I have learned has more to do with man than it does deer. This is because the deer spirit has opened my eyes to the cultural differences between the irresponsible, cruel, immature, and wasteful consumer society and the respectful, mature, and reciprocal nature of shamanic societies. To me there could be no better symbol or example that exemplifies what can be learned from living within a shamanic worldview than the striking difference between how the modern society that I was born and raised in, and the shamanic way of life that I have adopted, relate to and treat the white-tailed deer.

Wild turkey: The wild turkey is a shaman of the woods and a master of disguise and escape. Unlike the hideously tortured domesticated turkeys of our factory slaughterhouses, the wild turkey can run incredibly fast and can take off flying very quickly when it senses danger. The flight of the wild turkey is designed for quick getaways and they can reach speeds of fifty miles an hour for short distances. I call them a shaman of the woods because many times I have seen them mysteriously disappear in the blink of an eye and somehow dodge the bullets of hunters trying to bag them.

In a similar way to the butterfly, the spirit of the wild turkey usually appears at very auspicious times for me. In the early part of my relationship with this spirit it would seem to come to tell me to pay attention, and like a wizened old shaman its advice has never been subtle. I remember the first time it touched me strongly. I was sitting fairly high up in a large pine tree overlooking a ravine with a stream at the bottom. I was in the tree for a long time, waiting for the deer spirit to come, and I fell asleep. Next thing I knew I was startled awake by a loud crashing sound and I nearly fell out of the tree. Now fully awake, I looked frantically around for the source of the noise but I couldn't see anything around me that was unusual. So I stayed in the tree and after a while I fell asleep again, only to awake again to another loud sound, this time coming from directly above me. As I looked up I saw a large wild turkey taking off from the branches above me and flying away. The turkey had landed right in my tree while I was asleep and then when I woke up and fell asleep again it took off, waking me up once again. When I came down from the tree I noticed that in the snow all around my tree there were fresh deer tracks. The deer had come while I was asleep. I didn't realize it at the time, but now after many years of experiences with the turkey shaman I look back on that experience and know that the turkey spirit came to wake me up so I wouldn't miss my lesson with the deer. Hundreds of lessons later, whenever the wild turkey spirit visits, I get ready for magic to happen.

Please note that the above examples of my personal contact and relationship with commonly found animal spirits in the places that I have lived have been provided simply to illustrate a few of the infinite number of circumstances that could arise during your personal explorations into the world of animal spirits. Your own personal relationship may be strikingly similar or totally different.

PRACTICE 42: Fashioning an Animal Jicara

A powerful shamanic technique for employing the unique energy and essence of an animal ally is to fashion a jicara that is infused by the spirit of the animal and by the living entities that support the animal. The word *jicara*, in this context borrowed from the Wirrarika language, refers to a bowl used to hold sacred items. But in this case, even though the jicara exists in physical form, the objects being held by it come together to form something much more than the physical items themselves. The items contained by the jicara are the embodiment of something truly undefinable. I'm going to call the undefinable aspect of the jicara its "spirit," simply due to the fact that the word *spirit* is commonly used to refer to a type of invisible animating force.

Although the jicara has a physical manifestation, it is not a static object, form of art, or some type of novelty item or trinket. On the contrary, when the jicara is fashioned from the living energies offered to you by a particular animal spirit, the jicara is alive with that spirit and can be worked with just as if the actual spirit of the live animal was in your hands.

Fashioning an animal spirit jicara begins with the bowl. The physical shape of the bowl helps create a spiraling vortex that acts as a womb to hold the spirit of the animal. The bowl is usually a gourd or made of clay and should be fashioned by you or acquired from someone close to you that has a genuine love for the materials of the bowl. The jicara will not be fully activated until the bowl is consecrated with the blood of the animal in the presence of the five life-giving energies of the world—earth, water, air, fire, and spirit.

Since consecrating the jicara with the blood of the animal means that you will need the physical body of the animal in your hands it will probably take you some time, maybe even years, in order to make this happen. This is simply part of the process, and in the meantime you will begin to work with the animal spirit in order to establish your connection and initiate your relationship. This implies seeking out the physical manifestation of the animal and spending time with it, watching it, studying it, talking to it, learning everything you can about it. During this time you will be collecting experiences, some of which will play a part in the formation of the jicara.

As you have more and more experiences with the animal you can gradually begin to collect the essences for the jicara by obtaining specific items infused with the energies that support the animal. These items can include living energies from the animal's habitat, foods that it eats, items from other animals that are its ally or enemy—in short, anything that you deem significant to the animal through your actual experiences with it (not what you have read or been told about it) can potentially be used to form the jicara. The decision as to what or what not to use is purely personal; however, the more significant to the animal the items are, the more power the jicara will hold.

To illustrate what might be included in a jicara, here is a list of things that form my current jicara of the wild turkey spirit:

- One fully feathered wing from each of the last two wild turkeys that have given their life to me and that I've eaten. The feathered wings hold the key to the turkey's ability to mysteriously disappear, blend into its environment, and escape powerful entities that want to devour it.

- Drawings on the outside of the bowl depicting various significant events I've shared with the wild turkey spirit.

- Important foods that I've seen the wild turkey feeding on—acorns, crabapples, red cedar, blackberries, crickets, grasshoppers.

- Items from the wild turkey's predators—red-tailed hawk feathers, red fox teeth, two bullet shell casings blessed with deer blood.

- Items that form the wild turkey nest—oak and tulip tree leaves, poison ivy, and sumac vines.

- Miscellaneous items: I put soil from under a wild turkey nest into the bottom of the jicara to stick feathers into and to drip sacred blood into; apple tree twigs from the orchard I often find the turkeys in; a small piece of deer hide because for me the two are connected; a small Huichol yarn drawing of the sun to honor my Huichol shaman mentor's connection to the turkey, which is a bird of the sun; small personal items from moments when the wild turkey spirit aided me in the course of my everyday life or during specific ceremonies and workshops.

This particular jicara is an active participant in my life, especially in the spring and fall when I renew the jicara with offerings and ask the turkey spirit to share its flesh with me once again. The items in the jicara sometimes change as my knowledge of this spirit evolves and grows, and also when I add items from personal experiences that the wild turkey spirit has influenced in some way. These types of periodic additions keep the jicara alive and the relationship with it active. As you acquire new experiences associated with the spirit of a particular jicara, the power becomes cumulative. The jicara grows from infancy to maturity as your relationship with the animal spirit deepens and intensifies.

PRACTICE 43: Using the Power of the Jicara

The energy of the jicara, in no way imaginary, can be used in many practical ways. All of the energies and essences included in it are real and tangible, and most importantly they have be collected and honored by you through your hard work, time, and effort. All of the things that comprise the jicara, and the countless individual moments you experienced while fashioning the jicara, make it a living extension of both the animal spirit and yourself. That is what gives the jicara the power to aid and support you. Each animal spirit, and therefore each jicara made to hold an animal spirit, has unique qualities pertaining to both the spirit of the animal and the person who fashioned the jicara. To continue with my example of the wild turkey jicara, here is a list of items and/or circumstances in which I have employed the wild turkey jicara or it has voluntarily helped me with. Please be aware that your connection with this same spirit could be much different and I'm including these personal examples simply to help illustrate the kind of circumstances in which an animal jicara may be employed.

- Since for me the wild turkey is a bird of the sun, I use the feathers of the jicara during sunrise ceremonies and in moments during other ceremonies, rituals, or healings to infuse the light and energy of the sun into circumstances, objects, or living beings.

- I use the jicara to petition the spirit of the wild turkey to offer itself to me once or twice a year in the form of a live bird to consume and also to renew my jicara with fresh feathers and blood.

- Since the wild turkey jicara is active in my shamanic work, I consult with it before and during many different kinds of situations. Sometimes this is done by talking directly to the jicara while it is sitting in its special place in my house and by merging my awareness and consciousness with the spirit of the jicara to receive its unique perspective. The best way I have found to initiate this merging is by first activating memories of specific moments with the wild turkey, seeing the particular event like a movie in front of my eyes, and then reliving the event with as much of my MBESA as I can in that moment. Through reconnecting with the physical essences of the items that the jicara is holding I infuse the energy of the wild turkey spirit into my conscious awareness. It is important to note that this technique is completely the opposite of imagination. By having a tangible connection at the most intimate level with all of the components of the jicara and to the wild turkey, all of their essences are available to me at all levels of my awareness—mind, body, environment, and spirit. I am in no way imagining my relationship to the wild turkey spirit; I have tangibly developed it over long periods of time.

- I also use memory, not just mental but also bodily memory, to evoke the power of the jicara when I am not physically near it. Since I have such a tangible connection to the jicara I can easily connect to it at any moment I need to. For example, sometimes when I am away from home writing, as I am in this moment, I connect with the jicara to obtain help with my writing. The energy of the jicara contains the grounding qualities of the earth and the patience of the hen that sits on her eggs for up to a month. Connecting to this energy of the jicara keeps me in my chair writing at times when I need help to stay seated and focused on what I'm writing. The wild turkey spirit also does a lot of scratching and digging in the earth to find things, and when I connect to that movement of the turkey it helps me to keep digging into the concepts and ideas I am trying to convey. When I connect to the wings of the jicara, sometimes I feel the light of the sun and that gives me inspiration; other times I can feel the wind created by the forceful flapping of the wild turkey as it takes off from the ground in flight, and that invokes in me a state of mind where everything falls away except what I am doing with the words I am writing.

- When traveling to places where I have a greater chance of being singled out and taken advantage of because of my appearance or nationality, I ask the spirit of the wild turkey to help me blend in and walk unnoticed. Sometimes I will take an item or two from the jicara with me when traveling to especially dangerous places, like the inner cities of third-world countries where I could be easily singled out.

- Since the wild turkey is a bird that lives in a flock, and I tend to be a solitary person, I sometimes use the spirit of the wild turkey jicara to help me when I work with groups of adults, children, and also in my personal relationships.

The most important aspect to working with an animal spirit through a jicara is the collecting of the items and experiences connected with the animal spirit that you fashion the jicara from. Once the jicara is consecrated and fully awakened with the blood of the animal, you will be taught by the jicara itself how to use it. But getting to that point is the biggest challenge and implies a lot of work and commitment. The only way you can collect the essences and energies that sustain and nurture your animal spirit is if you spend significant time with it while learning all you can about it.

Some people get squeamish or even offended by the idea that the jicara has to be activated with the animal's blood. So let me just say that this absolutely necessary step should not be a source of preoccupation while you are collecting your experiences with the animal spirit and fashioning your jicara. When the animal spirit you are working with realizes a significant connection to you, the spirit will send you the physical manifestation of its spirit in the form of a flesh and blood animal. I have found this to be true in every single case during my many initiations with animal, bird, fish, reptile, and insect spirits. Even though with my example of the wild turkey I do personally take the life of the physical turkeys I use for my jicara, that is only my personal situation with that particular spirit. With the exception of the wild turkey, white-tailed deer, and a few species of fish, the rest of my many animal spirit jicaras are consecrated with the blood and body parts from animals that I find already dead in the moment and place appointed by the spirit of the animal. For example, the most recent jicara I made was for the red-headed woodpecker spirit. I would never think about taking the life of such a bird. But when both the spirit of the bird and I were ready, I found waiting for me the body of a red-headed woodpecker lying under its favorite dead tree—the same tree that I sat under countless times while watching and listening to the woodpecker work. Again, the only way you will be able to collect this most important essence is if you are in intimate contact with the environment of the animal.

Let me be clear that due to the catastrophic circumstances currently being faced by animal spirits throughout the globe I do not condone the hunting of any predatory animal, and with prey animals I only suggest the form of hunting I described in the section "The Way of the Hunt," in which you aren't even actually hunting the animal but rather you are putting yourself in a place to receive the animal if the spirit of the animal decides to grant you its flesh and blood. In all other cases, which comprise the vast majority, you are rewarded with the body of an animal by the animal spirit because of your perseverance and commitment to that spirit. You will find this offering to you from the animal spirit when you are ready to receive it.

Sometimes the spirit of the animal will even fool or test you to see if you are ready. I remember the first time the turkey vulture spirit sent me a physical bird. The old male bird was still alive but couldn't fly. I spent the whole day with him as he slowly made his way hopping down the rocky slope of the mountain. Both of us knew that we were meant to be together in those moments in time, and he showed no signs of being afraid either of me or his upcoming physical death. On the contrary, he was very lucid, fearless, proud, and wanting to share with me. I had a host of amazing experiences with the old bird during the course of two days and nights, but when he finally laid down to rest for the final time I was extremely emotional and I didn't know what to do. I didn't know if I should bury him or leave him be. I felt like I wanted to remember him by taking some of his feathers, but I just couldn't do it in that moment. So in the end I decided to leave him, and when I got home and calmed down I would either come back with a shovel or bring a bag and either take the whole body or just some of the feathers and blood. Well, wouldn't you know that just a few hours later, when I realized that I needed to go back for the body of the bird, I arrived and the bird wasn't there. He had definitely died but I looked every-where and he just wasn't there. But the most amazing thing was that just a few yards from where I am sure the old bird died I found the den of a female vulture with one egg inside of it. Now that I intimately know the spirit of the vulture after many years of working with it, I look back on that day and know that the vulture spirit tested me; I wasn't ready yet, and so the spirit guided me to the female bird and the egg as a gesture to keep learn-ing—which, of course, I did.

The hard truth is that if you can't work with the dead body of your animal spirit ally, then you have not yet accepted the organic reality of the world at a deep enough level to relate to the spirit of the animal in a shamanic way. It makes no difference if you are a veg-etarian or an animal rights activist, because this has nothing to do with eating meat or cru-elty to animals. If you can't take and use the physical manifestation of the animal's spirit, whether it be wings, antlers, claws, tails, or whatever else from the dead body of the animal that is naturally offered to you in the form of its corpse, you are still trapped (as I once was) by the modern idea that death is sad and to be avoided and denied. Only when you can look at the beautiful body of the dead animal that the spirit of that animal gave to you as a treasured gift, which was given in order for you to learn and to take your knowledge of the animal spirit to the next level, will you be able to thank the spirit by consecrating and acti-vating the living spirit of your jicara with the flesh and blood of the animal it contains.

Aside from the uses of the jicara I've listed above, another powerful way to use it is during rituals or celebrations with other people when there is sacred dancing or singing involved to celebrate the large web of life we are connected to. In this way, the spirit of the animal jicara is evoked and embodied through movement in the form of a dance of the animal spirit).

THE FUNDAMENTAL ENERGIES OF THE WORLD

In chapter 3 of this book, the first experiential section, as a form of ecoshamanic counterpractice I introduced the theme of relating your personal self to the five fundamental elements of the world. I did this because for most people relating to the elements is not a form of common awareness, and until we can accept the idea that our relationship to the elements can directly effect the quality of our lives we will not be able to see past this concept as merely an abstraction or metaphor. But once we gain the understanding and the corresponding momentum provided by this knowledge we begin a magical journey into both the subtly illuminating and physically powerful interplay between the elements, the world, and our personal human organism. In the previous section on counterpractice the goal was to make a first approach to relating to the elements on a personal level. Before proceeding with this section, it would be a good idea to go back and review that material because it will help you in gaining the momentum needed to go further and deeper into this next section.

The bulk of the material in this section will relate to communing with, and learning from, the dynamic interplay of the sacred elements in their physical form. Becoming initiated into the physical manifestations of the core spirit of the various elements, described here as the fundamental energies, is the only way to truly develop a practical and authentic relationship with them. But before we get into that I believe it is important to further the foundation of our understanding about these subtle fundamental energies so that we can be as prepared as possible for our shamanic encounter with them.

Before identity, before physical form or corporeal movement, before the nurturing and life-giving interaction between them, the fundamental energies exist as a form of primordial soup that at its core holds a subtle but very real luminosity. But to say that at this level of perception the fundamental energies are luminous is only a play with words because their luminosity is not something that we can readily see with our eyes. They are known to us in this way only as a phenomena that we can somehow be consciously aware of, but not by way of our five dominant senses. They are simply the underlying energies from which all other energies arise.

As this underlying phenomena gathers form and complexity it comes within reach of our sensory perception, and the fundamental energies begin to be perceived as "lights" of various colors. Some shamans describe these lights as corresponding to the colors that we see in the energies as they become manifest in the physical world. For example, earth is green, fire is red, water is blue, air is yellowish, and spirit/space is white or colorless. But this is not always the case because the fundamental energies are, at this level of our perception, readily perceived as mixing and flowing together. Often they are viewed as more of a rainbow of intermingling light from which somehow you just know through your silent knowledge that from this mixing rainbow of light comes forth the gradual solidifying of the fundamental energies into their physical forms.

As our perception moves from the subtle forms of these energies toward their physical forms we perceive them as the raw elements that make up and sustain the physical world. At this level of perception we easily see how the fundamental energies are constantly flowing and mixing together, even though they seemingly have very different physical forms.

By attending to the constant interaction between soil and river, rain and sky, fire and air, wind and soil, ocean and sky, and so on, we are also witnessing the interaction of the underlying primordial energies that directly connect us with the numinous aspects of both the cosmos and our human organism. During the course of our everyday lives it is easy to lose touch with the numinous dance of the fundamental energies as they flow through our bodies and connect us to the very fabric of our environment. But during shamanic practices we reconnect to this most basic yet profound reality of life.

For modern people accustomed to indoor plumbing, central heating, air conditioning, and supermarkets, an important step to shamanic practices related to the fundamental energies is to engage in initiatory experiences with a wide variety of their physical manifestations. By interacting physically with the energies we open the door to also mingling psychically and spiritually as well.

Interacting with the physical qualities of the fundamental energies is a process that begins with actually going to where the different physical manifestations occur naturally or, in some cases, are gathered by man. For the most part this means departing from our indoor environments and getting into the "wilds" of nature to feel the various expressions of water, air, earth, fire, and the spirit of the space/place that holds it all. Once we get our-selves into the various forms of these energies we can begin to be shamanically initiated by them. Below is a chart expressing some of the physical forms that the fundamental energies express to us.

Energy	Physical Form
Fire	single flame (candle, match, etc.), cook fire, bonfire, sacred fire, stove (wood) fire, gas appliance fire, combustion (automobiles, etc.) fire, forest fire, solar fire
Water	rain, stream, river, puddle, pond, lake, sea, ocean, swamp, spring, dam, tap water
Air	breeze, wind, gale, directional (E, W, N, S), temperature (cold, cool, warm, hot), odor (pleasant, foul, informative), medium for sound, speech, communication, breath
Earth	soil, sand, rock, valley, hill, mountain, cave, grassland, shrubland, savanna, chaparral, deciduous forest, deciduous monsoon forest, tropical savanna forest, northern coniferous forest, tropical rain for-est, temperate evergreen forest, temperate rain forest, tropical scrub forest, trade wind desert, high altitude desert, rain shadow desert, midlatitude desert, coastal desert, monsoon desert, polar desert

Most of us have already been thoroughly initiated by the shower of tap water and the fire created by an automobile engine. I have included these types of forms merely to show the contrast, and similarities, between the forms. However, even with the forms we are most familiar with, it is important to realize the depth or shallowness of our perception. For example, for nearly our whole lives we have seen the flame of the cooktop on a range that cooks our food, but in what way have we perceived the difference between that controlled blue gas flame and the wild dance of the multicolored wood flame of an outdoor bonfire? What does each of those forms of fire have to offer us, and at what levels are we open to receive? It is from these types of differences between the forms, and the relationships we have to all of the different forms, that we begin to see how much we have to learn about such fundamental phenomena. When we attend to just how many physical forms the fun-damental energies express to us we get the idea of how immense and pervasive they really are, and we also get a glimpse of how big the project of knowing them could potentially be.

The above list is certainly not a complete accounting of the physical forms of the fun-damental energies, especially when you consider various forms that exist when the energies are mixing, even just at the level that we can perceive, such as smoky air, bubbled water, muddy soil, and so on. It would be virtually impossible to try and describe shamanic practices with all the various forms of the fundamental energies. But what I can do is suggest certain time-tested practices that I am aware of, and from these you can develop your own authentic practices that are infused with your own personal energy and life force. As you become initiated into working with this process and become proficient with it, you will discover that you are using the similar qualities of your human organism to relate in the deepest way possible to the fundamental energy you are working with.

For example, our human organism readily connects with the energy of water because our body is approximately two-thirds water. The complex systems of our body manipulate the qualities of this fundamental energy in miraculous ways. The natural areas where we go to become initiated by the energy of water also manipulate it and express it in many different ways. Listed below are some of the forms and qualities that you might find expressed by the various manifestations of the energy of water in nature.

Water Form	Potential Qualities
Stream	Delicate flow, winding fluid motion, graceful or dainty song, shallow depth, clear appearance, light and youthful wisdom, creative, joyful
River	Mixing of calm near shore and powerful and even dangerous currents in the middle, potential for soft or roaring song, hidden knowledge and mysteries, longer and deeper memory, more extensive experience
Pond	Calm, reflective, soothing, nurturing, safe yet mysterious
Lake	Expansive, filled with hidden power, capable of displaying many emotions, supports many forms of life
Ocean	Awesome, very approachable and knowable at a shallow level but also deeply secretive, incomprehensibly diverse in the amount of life it supports, vast, ultimately powerful

Of course the qualities of water on this list are general, and every body of water will have its own unique qualities and personality. The same can be said for different areas of land, the varied characteristics of air in different locations, or the diverse qualities of fire brought forth from the flame of various materials. In every location and circumstance there will be similarities and differences in energy, and that is what makes experiencing a shamanic connection to the fundamental energies such a rich and magical journey of wonder, discovery, and knowledge.

WATER

Wherever you discover water you discover life, and water is always at work creating conditions supportive to life. Water naturally works to neutralize soils, metals, and minerals that are too acidic or too alkaline in order to provide a healthy environment for abundant and diverse life. All over our planet water is in a constant state of motion creating, protecting, energizing, nourishing, and sustaining life. Water structures our world through the never-ending assimilation of whatever it comes in contact with: wood, rock, plastic, glass, all eventually are dissolved as the molecules in water push apart atoms, envelop them, and then add them to the liquid solution. This universal solvent also works inside living beings as it makes cellular molecules soluble for transportation within the live organism.

Exactly how and where living things obtain the energy to become "alive" is a question that as yet eludes even our modern science. However, what we do know is that it is in the watery creation of protoplasm that we find life being born from nonlife. Modern science therefore provides us with three basic assumptions about protoplasm:

- It is believed that protoplasm was the first life form created on Earth.

- Protoplasm is comprised of approximately 75 percent water.

- Protoplasm occurs only in animal and plant life, and all animal and plant life contain protoplasm.

While the creation and existence of protoplasm may continue to mystify us, other important aspects of life-giving water are well known, even if we don't acknowledge them on a daily basis. A perfect example of this is the hydrologic cycle. One of the most amazing discoveries I have made while working with indigenous shamans is how their actions within certain rituals, as well as their everyday awareness, is so intimately connected to the hydrologic cycle of water. I will delve into this more specifically later in this section, but for right now it will serve us well to reacquaint ourselves with this sacred cycle.

Like most other terrestrial animals and plants, human beings absolutely need fresh water to live; however, drinkable water is the most rare and therefore precious form of water on the planet. Most of the world's water, more than 97 percent, is salty and toxic to terrestrial life. Life may have evolved out of this great expanse of salty water, as the salty taste of our bodily fluids will forever remind us, but we cannot live on salt water. Our lives are possible only due to the hydrologic cycle whereby the salty water of the world's oceans is miraculously transformed through the interaction of water with air, sun, and earth into fresh, drinkable water.

This sacred interaction begins as the energy from the sun causes water in the ocean and on land to evaporate. This water vapor rises into the atmosphere, condenses in clouds, and then falls to the ground as rain and snow. Eventually this water either evaporates back into the atmosphere, seeps into the ground, or runs off the surface and into rivers and lakes that journey back into the ocean.

PRACTICE 44: Initiations with Living Bodies of Water

Water initiation is a matter of experience. The only way to realize a full MBESA with a body of water is to submerge yourself in it, connect with it, and become it. Becoming the water is not difficult if you go into it with an open mind and heart. The fluid makeup of our body, the permeable quality of our skin organ, and the personal energetic vibration that we emanate all have the capability to combine with the amazing potential of living water to produce an ecoshamanic connection beyond words.

The structure and essence of water allows it to metamorphose into different states as its three-dimensional microstructures form and dissolve millions of times a second. As water flows it picks up, carries, and distributes information as it responds and changes with its environment. For example, if we pour water through our hands the water dissolves and picks up physical elements on our skin as well as the vibratory pulse of our being. The water is changed; it now contains part of us. And it will change again as soon as it touches something else. The same can be said for us. When we are submerged in a body of water, the water transmits physical and vibrational information to our human organism. We are affected by the numerous unique qualities of the water: the flow, the temperature, the nutrients, minerals, salts, as well as the particular feeling and energy being exuded by its fluid body. We are changed; we have now become part of the water, until we leave the water body and are then affected by something else.

However, for both the water and for us, the story doesn't end there because we both have a memory. Water affects and is affected by everything that it meets, and it will carry both a physical and vibrational memory of its encounter with us, maybe at a very subtle level, but it will carry it just the same as we will carry the memory of the water within us at different levels. This is one of the core reasons to work with water at an ecoshamanic level. Once we become the water we are never the same, and the more experiences we have with the myriad personalities of water, and the deeper we can dive into those experiences, the more we learn from placing ourselves directly into a natural form of wisdom that contains the energy and vibrations of both the earth and the cosmos. Below is an example of how to engage in an ecoshamanic practice of relating to the fundamental energy of water:

- Approach the water and assess its physical and subtle characteristics. Is it calm or raging, shallow or deep, does it appear safe to enter, are there rocks or boulders visible, how does it smell? Sit or stand quietly next to the water and soak up the unique qualities being exuded by the water; listen to its unique song. The water is a singing shaman that specializes in chanting and shapeshifting. Listen, watch, and learn.

- Use your mind to compare your emotional state to the water and relate the qualities of this body of water to specific past experiences where your emotional being mirrored the feeling of this body of water.

- Relate at a physical level by using your bodily memory of times past to remember physical experiences that share similar qualities of this body of water.

- Contemplate the environmental situation of this body of water. Where did it come from and where is it headed? What are the physical threats you can see or otherwise know about that jeopardize the health of this water? Is there anything you can see, determine, or know about that actively protects this body? What do you notice about the overall health of this body?

- Touch the water and notice how the interconnectedness of the whole body means that by touching one area of water you affected the whole body at a subtle but real level. At the same time realize and feel that the touch of the water has subtly affected your entire organism as well.

If safe, enter the water and open yourself to the total MBES experience of now being a part of the body of water. Feel the vibration of the water body influence your water body. Be aware of how your movements and vibrations affect the body of water. Listen, smell, and taste the unique qualities of the water. Fill your mind with the water. Let the water infuse your organism with its unique memory and luminous energy. Absorb and reflect the water with your whole MBESA. Stay at least half an hour in the water unless it is unbearably cold, but 2–4 hours spent in and around the body will be best. To truly gather a deep feeling of a particular body requires many visits throughout the seasons of the year; however, even one significant encounter with a body can provide incalculable benefit and knowledge. If you are new to working with bodies of water, refer to the chart on page 281 for general qualities to focus on relating to the specific personality of the body.

This type of practice can be done with any body of water. Be sure to take as much time as you need. In ecoshamanic workshops where we have ideal conditions we sometimes spend ten days or more in and around certain rivers and ocean areas in order to deeply explore the unique qualities expressed by the fundamental energy of water in those locations.

PRACTICE 45: Ritually Honoring the Hydrologic Cycle

The importance of healthy water to human beings cannot be overstated. Anyone who has ever been truly thirsty and without fresh water, or who has watched the crops that feed their family die from lack of water, knows firsthand about our complete dependency on this sacred fluid and the deep feelings of helplessness and despair when there is a shortage. In shamanic cultures where a significant part of the tribe's sustenance is dependent on timely delivered and adequate amounts of rainfall for the healthy growth of their crops, many elaborate and powerful ceremonies and rituals exist to call and honor the sacred and life-giving rainfall.

Even though most modern people of so-called first-world countries don't normally experience water shortages as much more than a temporary inconvenience, this doesn't change the level of dependency we have toward the sacred fluid of life, and one of the more profound ways for modern people to connect in a shamanic way to the spirit of nature is to develop a sacred relationship to the life-giving cycles of water. This process begins by collectively learning about the intricacies of the hydrologic cycle (described earlier in this section) and getting yourself physically in touch with various bodies of water in order to raise the consciousness of your total MBES awareness toward the flowing cycles of water.

Once you begin to have a conscious awareness of the sacred role the hydrologic cycle has in your life, many significant opportunities arise for furthering your knowledge and also responsibly honoring the cycle. By engaging your intuition and creativity the waters in your life can guide you in developing your own rituals and ceremonies of heightened awareness toward water. Below is an example of an ecoshamanic ritual involving the hydrologic cycle. It involves making a pilgrimage that transforms the pilgrims into active participants in the great cycles of water.

The first part of the ritual involves making a significant and meaningful encounter with a substantial body of water near to your home. Follow the procedure "Initiations with Living Bodies of Water" on page 283 to accomplish this. In addition to the basic procedure outlined in that section, you also will collect a quantity of water (12–64 ounces) in a sealed container to take along with you on your pilgrimage. Gather the water into your container during a moment of deep connection with the body of water, and using words or chanting communicate to the body of water that you and it are one and that by taking this water you are both symbolically and physically entering both your body and the body of water into the hydrologic pilgrimage you are embarking on.

The sacred water you have collected is already infused with the energy of the place you collected it from, but from now until you get to the destination of the pilgrimage it is your responsibility to infuse both the water in the container and the water or your human organism with the energy of the places you travel through, and also the energy of the sun, so that when the waters reach their destination they will be fully charged, in a similar but more concentrated way than if the water were to flow there on its own.

The destination of the pilgrimage is very important, and in most cases it will be the largest body of water that the water in your container was headed for, or where it came from, depending on which direction you travel. For example, if you took your water from a nearby stream, that stream will eventually flow into a larger stream or river, which will then flow into an even larger river, and so on, until it reaches either a great lake or an ocean. In this case your destination will be the lake or ocean. If you live at or near the shore of a large body of water, you will simply do this process in reverse. Instead of following a river downstream, you will begin at the lake or ocean and follow a river upstream until it branches out to become a smaller stream, and your destination will be a special place where that stream provides life to its home area. In this ritual both directions are equally valid, and besides logistical considerations it makes no difference which point you start from.

Once you have your water collected and your destination planned, begin your journey as the water. During your trip make a conscious effort to embody the fluidity of the water in your thoughts and actions. Along the way stop periodically to infuse your water with the various energies of the land you are passing through: crush small bits of leaves, bark, feather, stone, soil, hair, grass, bone, etc. into the water while being aware of the energy of these items also infusing your being as you rub them through your hands or over various parts of your body. Try to make a connection to how the water in the stream, river, and ocean become infused with the same energies, as the rain hits the flora and fauna and delivers tiny fragments of these energies into the larger body of water while it flows across and under the land until it joins the larger body.

In this pilgrimage you are literally taking the place of the various processes of runoff, percolation, transpiration, condensation, and precipitation by moving the water yourself. To connect with the shamanic journey that this movement implies, it is necessary for you to convert your perception so that you connect with and relate to the water, and the natural journey the water would have made without you, in the deepest way possible. During your journey use whatever means appropriate in order to do that. Some examples are to sit in the sun with your water for periods of time, bring along another container to periodically pour the water from one vessel to the other in order to infuse the local qualities of the air of various places into the water, dip rocks or twigs or other natural items along the way into the water, set the container of water in the sun with the lid off and acknowledge the water's connection to the sun and air through evaporation, and dip your fingers or sacred objects into the water container and intentionally fling droplets of water into the air while connecting to the sacred motion of rain.

When you reach your destination, complete the first half of the trip by ceremonially giving the water to the fundamental energies just as if the water would have made the trip itself. The energy of fire can be invoked either by making a small ceremonial fire, using candles, or using solar energy if the sun is visible.

With your container open, use your fingers or a ceremonial staff to deliver water into the air, into the ground, into the destination body of water, and into the fire energy. The whole time you are doing this talk out loud or chant about the roles you have undertaken in this hydrologic pilgrimage in order to learn about the fundamental energies, especially the water and its interaction with the other energies. Talk or chant about the various parts of your journey as you offer water to each of the fundamental energies.

When this is done, save some of the water from your container and give the rest to the destination body of water. Now is the time to have a meaningful encounter with this body of water in a similar way as you did in the beginning of the pilgrimage. Entering the water in this stage almost always invokes a deep sense of joy and harmony that may be expressed in many ways. During pilgrimages to the ocean with my Wirrarika companions, sometimes there are great amounts of excitement and innocent, childlike laughter while entering the water, and other times the mood is very somber while the incalculable importance of the water sinks into the hearts of the pilgrims.

When the moment feels right, collect water from this body for the return trip in its own container. Follow the same process of infusing energy into this water on your trip home, paying attention to the fact that this water is both different and the same as the water you still hold in your first container.

When you return, ceremonially give the water to the fundamental energies living in your home area while talking or chanting to the energies about the hydrologic process and pilgrimage you are living. Say or chant anything else relevant and give most of the rest of the water to the original body of water. At this point mix the two remaining portions from each stage of the pilgrimage and keep it to use in ceremonies throughout the year and/or for use in your shamanic temple or water rirriki. This sacred water is charged with energy and consciousness, and should be treated respectfully and kept in a special place. Water from other pilgrimages and sacred bodies of water that you connect with can be added to this water as both a symbol and a physical affirmation of your connection to the sacred fluid of life.

SOIL

The thin layer of soil—comparable to the skin of a giant tomato—that covers the outer layer of our immense planet Earth provides for the growth and renewal of all terrestrial life. This precious layer of life sustains life because it is alive. The awe and wonder triggered by gazing into the staggering number of stars in the heavens on a clear night does not even begin to compare to the number of life forms that we can place in the palm of our hand when we hold a handful of fertile soil.

From Peter Warchall's article in *The Fatal Harvest Reader* (Sausalito, CA: Foundation for Deep Ecology, 2002):

> One teaspoon of rich grassland soil can contain 5 billion bacteria, 20 million fungi, and 1 million protists. More microbes live in a teaspoon of earth than people on the planet. In one square meter, the top few centimeters of topsoil might contain galactic numbers of the above microbes, but also 1,000 each of ants, spiders, wood lice, beetles and their larvae, and fly larvae; 2,000 each of earthworms and large myriapods (millipedes and centipedes); 8,000 slugs and snails; 20,000 pot worms; 40,000 springtails; 120,000 mites, and 12 million nematodes.
>
> Soil is literally alive with a networked complexity greater than that of human brain tissue. Besides growing food, soil's powers include influencing greenhouse gases in the atmosphere,

the creation of more soil from bedrock, and the purification of all the freshwater on and in the planet's surface. If anything, the mother of all things has achieved an enhanced status. "Her" planetary tissue is the heart of the biosphere, lithosphere, atmosphere, and hydrosphere of the planet.

Even without microscopes it wasn't difficult for our ancient ancestors to recognize the life-giving fertility of the soil. Careful observation is all one needs to witness how life that dies creates more life—how death transforms into life and then dies once again. How leaves, stems, and branches, as well as whole plants and trees, eventually become compost for the seeds of the same plants and trees. How water and worms, wind and bone combine to form the fertile soil from which all terrestrial life is born.

For all the technological advances of modern man we still live by the same fundamental truth as our ancient ancestors, even if we don't attend to it as they did: what keeps us alive was once alive itself, and everything that we eat from the land is alive because of the thin layer of teeming life that we call soil. Every bit of the nutrition that fuels our body, including the sugars, fats, and enzymes, is built from the dead carcasses of other living beings. And nowhere is this more readily seen than in the incredibly diverse composition of the sacred soil itself.

PRACTICE 46: Communing with the Living Soil

As a catalyst for personal and spiritual growth, and as a gateway to shamanic experience, the living soil created by the interaction of the fundamental energies offers us the opportunity to join with the body of earth in a sacred communion with life. Earlier in this chapter I described at length one of the potent rites of passage and initiations into earth energy, the Embrace of the Earth ceremony. Because the structure of that ceremony is appropriate for a rite of passage, and the implications of that go far beyond simply tuning into the fundamental energy of earth and soil, I included it in the beginning of the chapter instead of here in the section on earth energy. However, when dealing with rituals such as submerging yourself into the living earth or flowing water, it is important to remember that this type of experience can be performed in many different ways and with various intentions and outcomes. I bring this up here simply to state that whether you have performed the Embrace of the Earth ceremony or not, the act of submerging yourself in the energy of the living soil is a beneficial activity no matter how you specifically do it, and I invite you to explore your connection to the soil in this way by whatever means feel appropriate to you.

I know of many people that have taken certain aspects of the Embrace of the Earth ceremony to create other earth energy rituals that they can perform in a more simplified way.

In my opinion, the complete Embrace of the Earth ceremony, when led by an experienced ecoshamanic practitioner, is an invaluable tool with the power to help people in
numerous ways, and is an indispensable rite of passage for people learning the shamanic
arts. But for most people, including myself, one time in the ground is simply not enough,
and so for those who have experienced the Embrace of the Earth ceremony it is very
common to either go through the ceremony multiple times or spend the night in the earth
during more simplified versions of the ceremony. I have personally spent the night in the
ground dozens of times, sometimes as part of a larger ceremony and sometimes on my own
in the wilderness. There are numerous reasons for burying yourself in the earth, many of
which I have pointed out earlier in this chapter. But in terms of rituals designed for simply
communing with the fundamental energy of living soil, the burial rite can be performed
much differently than the Embrace of the Earth ceremony, which imparts a much wider
scope of shamanic experiences.

Since the personality of the living soil can be much different place to place, burying
yourself in various geographic areas, where the flora and fauna of each place has its own
distinctive qualities, will provide you with a wide variety of enlightening experiences.
Although being in touch with the enormous energy of the earth at a core level will always
feel similar when burying yourself in the ground, there are distinct perceptual, visual, psychological, and emotional experiences that arise between, for example, being buried in the
soil of an inland pine forest and the sand of coastal beach or burying yourself in an arroyo
near the top of a tall mountain or in a cave of a deep canyon. The differences in content
and flavor between the experiences that can arise as a result of communing with the soil of
these uniquely individual places is striking.

Each place where you bury yourself will be alive both physically and spiritually in its
own distinctive way. The most important aspect of jumping into the shamanic experience
of connecting to the unique forms of life comprising the soil of each place is to get the
controlling side of your ego to "become small" while at the same time allowing your energetic body to "become big."

The experience of shrinking your ego through the process of various personal rituals
with the powers of nature becomes decidedly easier the more you do it. For people without personal experiences of connection to nature the idea of becoming small could sound

completely absurd, but for those who know this feeling it not only becomes something completely natural but also something that is looked forward to or even craved. This is true even for people that have no interest in shamanism. Millions of people that simply go for walks in nature or, at the other extreme, spend weeks at a time clinging to a sheer mountainside during a rock climbing adventure, feel the impact of their ego becoming small in front of the huge mystery that the mirror of nature provides for us. For those of us compelled toward the deeper shamanic aspects of this, many techniques and rituals can be employed, including all of the techniques listed in this book, but in the bottom line it is a purely personal matter and for that reason I'm not going to introduce a specific formula for this ritual.

The best suggestion I can give for how to shrink your ego before entering the living soil is to experiment with different techniques and see what works best for you. In my case, some of the things I always do before entering the ground are fasting, intense physical labor (such as digging my tomb), making a sacred fire from materials of the area I am being buried in, ritually calling to and connecting with the fundamental energies through chanting and use of the feathered muvieri, and, lastly, psychic purification of energetic confession with the fire and energetic/bodily purification through contact with the smoke and heat of the fire. Of course, depending on the specific location I will perform other actions appropriate to the energy of the place. For example, if I am near the ocean or surrounded by a specific species of tree or plant or under a specific range of mountains, I would perform specific actions to connect with and honor these prevailing energies of the area in order to become small within them.

Logistically speaking, this form of ritual—whereby we intentionally submerge our total human organism into the larger energies of the land—does not need to be the same as described in the Embrace of the Earth ceremony. In the section on the Embrace of the Earth ceremony I described the ideal conditions that I try to achieve each time I lead a group in that powerful rite of passage. In that ceremony it is an indispensable requisite that the initiates be placed into the soil deep enough so that the eyes are 4–6 inches below the surface. But for the technique being described here, that doesn't necessarily need to be the case. I would suggest that whenever possible a tomb similar to that described in the Embrace of the Earth ceremony be used simply because of its efficiency, but when exploring a variety of different terrains it will not always be possible to do it that way.

Simply use your common sense and intuition to come up with the best way to submerge yourself in the energy of the living soil for the particular place you are in. For example, in areas where the land is prohibitively rocky, to dig very deep you could simply dig as far as you can and then construct a cairn-type mound of rocks to lie inside of. If you are in especially wet soil or sand you can dig down until you reach water and then construct a floor of wood or rock to keep you from lying in the water. In any case, the idea is to lie on, or preferably in, the soil, and then have a cocoon of soil, rock, sand, etc., from that area surrounding you. However you accomplish this is completely up to you, but take note that simply lying on the ground without the natural cocoon surrounding you is not the same experience. At all costs make sure you are surrounded and engulfed by the soil of the area, even if it means constructing a natural cocoon above the ground you are lying in.

It has been my experience that if you are only going to stay a few hours in the tomb or cocoon, it is more effective to do it at night because it is easier to become small in the face of mystery when it is dark. But if you are going to spend longer periods, or even come in and out of the tomb, then by all means explore the full range of conscious-altering experiences during different times of day and night. By far my favorite time is sunrise, and the two hours following, after having spent the whole night in the tomb. If the part of your ego that wants to control everything has been shrunk, your total human organism will feel the awakening that the energy of the sun brings to the land, and the living soil will deliver messages to you so that you will never be the same. Each time you bury yourself in this way and in various locations you will receive unique messages and become initiated into another aspect of ecoshamanic knowledge.

PRACTICE 47: Connecting to Grandmother Growth

The enormous star that provides for life on our planet is perceived by us as an identifiable object in the sky, but it is also engaged in an active and unfolding process, as is the evolving Earth and our living human bodies. This unfolding life process found so intimately in our personal body and so unfathomably gigantic in the reality of expanding and contracting galaxies and universes is more primordial than the identifiable but fleeting objects that we readily perceive, and that is why, for shamans, the fundamental creative energy of the process we call fire is often referred to as the father of our sun, or our Grandfather, and the unfolding process of life as the mother to our earth, or our Grandmother. This manner of intimately referring to such grand and seemingly eternal mysteries with names that imply kinship is one way that shamanic cultures acknowledge and show respect for the interconnected web of life that we are all a part of.

When working with the fundamental energy of life manifested by the fertile and living soil, we place ourselves directly into the hands of the grandmother of growth, who can teach us and initiate us into the mysteries of fertility, growth, death, and rebirth. The initiation I'm sharing here with Grandmother Growth begins by making compost. Compost is produced when organic matter is broken down by bacteria and fungi. I'm not going to get into the specifics of the different methods of making compost; that material is easily found elsewhere. The important thing here is that you simply do it. This step will take from eight weeks to a year, depending on the climate and the process.

Composting tunes us in to the microbiological world and teaches us about growth from decay. On a shamanic level, you are taking many diverse forms of normally discarded energy and combining them to create a supercharged mixture of teeming life that can be used as a sort of "magic potion" to aid the growth of all green things. By making and using this potion you enter into the cyclical reality of organic life, becoming a co-creator with Grandmother Growth. And by using organic energies from your home that would normally be thrown into a landfill, you honor the Mother Earth and reduce pollution at the same time. By physically adding and mixing the ingredients of your potion you automatically infuse some of your own energy into the process, but to really connect with it, and to make it infinitely more than a simple exercise in gardening, make it an extension of your MBES organism by relating to it on various levels. This is done during the months of making the potion by intentionally and continually pouring your energy into the potion through talking, chanting, singing, blessing, and making offerings to the energy of Grandmother Growth that is giving life to your potion.

Once your living potion is ready, the second step of your initiation is to grow plants that will bear something edible for you to eat. Grow organic seeds or seedlings of heirloom plants from soil that is mixed and infused with your living potion. Do not concentrate too much on what you might receive from the plants in terms of fruit or vegetable, but rather on a daily basis focus on the unfolding of life and all that the life of the little plants signify and symbolize. As the plants grow, continue to pour your psychic and emotional energy into them as well as keep them physically healthy through your care and attention.

When and if you have been blessed with some kind of food from your plants, take a portion to eat, a portion to dry and pulverize to use later as offerings, and a portion back to the compost pile to bless and begin your next cycle of growth and learning with the soil and Grandmother Growth.

AiR

We are so completely submerged in the fundamental energy that materializes into the substance called air that it is hard to actually say where our human organism ends and the air begins. In every moment of lives, from the minute we are born to the moment of our death, we constantly and automatically take in the air that is surrounding us and deliver it to the innermost regions of our body. This action is so basic and pervasive that it could be seen as the central activity of our existence. And it is this very act of sharing in the sacred atmosphere of our world that connects us in the most tangible way possible to the numinous aspects of this invisible life force that surrounds us.

The fundamental energy of air clearly demonstrates to us that we are certainly not the completely independent and autonomous beings that we oftentimes feel that we are. In every moment we are sharing the living air of our breath with everyone around us, and also with all other breathing beings and green plants. In addition to that, with every breath we take we also draw in and release atoms that were once parts of trees, rocks, birds, and even dinosaurs and our deceased relatives. Because all aerobic life shares the same air, and because even though the air is constantly changing as minute parts are added and taken away, there are inert atoms that don't change, and so the invisible life-giving air also connects us in a tangible and most magical way to both the ancient past and the distant future.

PRACTiCE 48: Initiations with the Cardinal Directions

The movement of air—what we are used to calling wind—is explained scientifically by differences in atmospheric pressure, which are primarily caused by differences in temperature due to the variation in thermal properties between land formations and bodies of water. Large wind types, such as prevailing winds and seasonal winds, are greatly modified by Earth's rotation. The local winds are caused by daily changes in sunlight and temperature occurring over the landscape of mountains, plains, and valleys. While these scientific observations of wind formation may seem to contradict the shamanic view that the movement of the earth's air is somehow alive and can be communicated with at a variety of levels, upon closer inspection, and with a heightened awareness of the living entities that the air is in constant contact with, the scientific explanation of wind actually adds to the understanding of how shamans use the wind.

As the great, flowing matrix that connects all terrestrial life, the air, and especially the movement of air, is a complex, naturally occurring transportation system of local breezes, interstate winds, and international jet streams. The more we know about how and why wind is formed at both a local and global level, the easier it is to see why shamanic tribes, completely submerged and dependent on a holistic view of organic reality, looked to the wind for information, inspiration, and as a tangible expression of the great mystery of life and the cosmos.

Whether speaking scientifically or traditionally, the wind is named from the direction it is blowing. The north wind blows from the north and the west wind blows from the west. Here in the Northern Hemisphere the winds of the four cardinal directions have been traditionally associated by native cultures as the specific qualities that the wind of each direction possesses relative to the location of the tribe. This local awareness of the wind is extremely important to shamanic practices, and the awareness of this is especially valuable to modern people interested in shamanism, because many contemporary people teaching and writing about neoshamanism tend to express the qualities of each wind direction without regard to specific location. But that way of generalizing does not promote direct communication with the unique qualities and personality of winds that have the power to inform and communicate with us in an immediately tangible way.

For example, I have seen it written in various places that the "south wind" is the "fiery wind" related to the element of fire. But this sweeping generalization would hardly be applied by a shaman living on the north shore of one of the Great Lakes, where the southern wind would always be coming off the water and the element of fire would more properly correspond to the east, where the sun rises. In any and all cases I tend to avoid non-localized generalizations when it comes to classifying wind qualities, direction, energy, etc. because each geographic area has its own unique personality. An east wind in New Jersey will contain much different information and have a much different personality than an east wind in Texas, Seattle, or Chicago.

One of the most enlightening aspects to working with the wind is the sense of direction it can instill into your consciousness. In our insulated and air-conditioned indoor environments, most of us are hard pressed to locate the cardinal directions in relation to where we are sitting. This is why, as a first step to working with wind, I suggest that you find for yourself a place outdoors that is free from obstructions and from where the wind can blow in from all directions. This place could be the same as the location of your ecoshamanic temple, a flat place free of buildings, or the top of a hill or mountain close to your home. In any case you'll want to hang up something that will blow easily in the wind in order to point out the direction of the wind for you. Ribbons work well. But remember that once you determine the directions, the cloth will be streaming in the opposite direction from where the wind is blowing.

The next step is to align yourself with the four directions one at a time; if you don't yet know where the sun rises or sets in relation to where you are, you can of course use a compass to determine the cardinal directions of north, south, east, and west. Now proceed with this in relation to where you are by acknowledging the terrain that a wind from each direction will pass through before it reaches you. While facing in each direction, extend your sight and use your memory to picture all that you know about what lies in each direction, from right in front of you to as far away as your knowledge of the terrain allows. Do not use imagination—if you don't know exactly what lies in a particular direction, don't fret, that's part of why you're doing this exercise.

Connect with the terrain in each direction, using whatever means feel appropriate to you. Some suggestions are to sketch the terrain of each direction, chant or talk out loud following the terrain outwards from your body to the horizon and identify all the beings and geographical formations in your perceptual field; walk for long distances in each direction to see what is there; and use topographical maps to raise your knowledge of what lies far away in each direction. If you are very familiar with the land for a wide area around you, you can move to the next step right away, but for most people this first step of becoming aware of the actual terrain the wind covers in each direction before it reaches your location may take several weeks or months to accomplish.

Now to infuse the essence and energy of the terrain of each direction, stand facing one of the cardinal directions and look out over the land. Take as long as you need to let the terrain in front of you imprint onto your total MBESA. Then raise and spread your arms at shoulder level like the open wings of a bird with your palms facing out. With your arms extended out from your sides, slowly bring them together as you do two things simultaneously: one, breathe in deeply through your nose so that your lungs are full at the moment your palms come together in front of you; and two, as your arms are moving together and you are breathing in, draw as much of the feeling, energy, and visual-physical qualities of the place and direction in front of you together with your palms. With your arms and hands now forming the shape of an arrow pointing out from your chest, and the essence of the place in front of you now captured between your palms, quickly draw your hands into your chest as if you were stabbing yourself with a dagger. At the same time breathe out strongly through your mouth. This action of stabbing your chest with the energy of the place and exhaling deeply is like trading the air in your chest for the energy of the place. After you do this don't linger; either do it again, turn to another direction, and repeat the process, or turn away and leave the place.

This technique of drawing in the essence and energy of the four directions can also be used when saying goodbye to a special place that you won't return to for a while and that you want to imprint into your being so as to not forget the feeling of the place. The main goal here is to imprint both the physical and the numinous characteristics of each direction into your being so that you can carry that awareness with you during the course of your day. Try at various times during the day or night to align yourself with the cardinal directions in the various places that you go. By visualizing (not imagining) the terrain in each direction from where you are in various moments, you shift your consciousness away from the purely human concerns that occupy most of our time and instead expand your horizons so that you place your life and your actions into a more organic and holistic version of reality. Also, by ritually aligning yourself to each direction and making a cognitive map in your mind as to the geography of the land in each direction, you raise the moment to moment awareness of where you are in relation to the natural world. By doing this you foster a much greater sense of place and a corresponding shift in consciousness related to being connected to the organic reality of life where you live.

PRACTICE 49: Communicating with the Winds

Now that you have a place where you can work with the wind in a way that you are familiar with what lies in each direction, you can begin to learn more easily how to "read" the wind and use this knowledge in a practical way. I use the analogy of reading because I have found that the process of learning to gain knowledge from the wind is in some ways similar to how we learn to read. When learning to read we have someone there to explain to us what the letters and then words mean. We start with easy words and phrases that convey simple messages. In this way we slowly develop our skills until we can read about complex concepts, intricate storylines, and detailed technical manuals. If we were to put a mystery novel or a car repair manual in front of a person that can't read basic words, they would have no chance of understanding it. Similarly, to understand how to read the wind we need to start with someone teaching us the basic words and phrases and then slowly develop our skills through repetition and practice.

In this case, the "someone" is not a person but rather the immediate terrain surrounding us that we are familiar with. This is why I suggested acquainting yourself with the terrain of the four directions surrounding you as part of being initiated into the fundamental energy of air. The first thing we need to do is learn to understand the meaning of messages delivered by wind traveling through areas we know in order to be able to identify what we are feeling. This is like learning the meaning of words before actually reading. For example, if I live on the East Coast and the wind is blowing from the east, I will feel the qualities of the air blowing across the ocean, and once I can identify the feeling of wind coming across the ocean I can now read that word wherever I am. The qualities of that wind are unique, just as the letters of a word, and I would never confuse it with the qualities of a wind coming through a desert canyon or off of a snowcapped mountain, just as I would never confuse the letters of the word *ocean* for the word *desert,* because I know how to read.

The drastic differences between an ocean wind and a desert wind are similar to differences between the simple words of *cat* and *dog.* Just as it took us many years to become literate with words, it will take many years to learn to read the language of the winds. Once you begin the adventure of being aware of the qualities of wind, you can discover new words wherever you go. But it is not necessary to wait to travel because you can start learning by simply working from your home spot and discovering the words of different winds as they come to you. Whenever there is significant wind simply go to your spot, determine where the wind is coming from, and remember the geography of that direction as you feel the qualities of the wind. In this way the land becomes like your human English teacher because the land shows you its qualities (various circumstances happening in different types of forests, plains, lakes, rivers, mountains, etc.) like words, and then the wind blowing across the living terrain forms the words into sentences. When this happens for you, then windy days turn into reading lessons. Start by reading the book of the spot that you intimately know, and then increase your vocabulary by going to reading lessons in different places with varied terrain.

Now, in order to explain the finer details of reading the wind, it becomes necessary to move away from the reading analogy because reading the wind is infinitely more than a process of deciphering markings of ink on a flat surface. For this process the word *communicating* is a more proper term, because at this stage your human organism enters a dialog with the air at many different levels. Receiving the many qualities of sensory stimulus such as temperature, strength, smell, humidity, taste, sound, and spatial orientation is key to this, but what also happens is that your organism becomes aware of reciprocating with the air. This happens as the wind takes minute fragments of your skin and hair to join in its body, as you trade air and internal molecules from the deepest regions of your body through the magical act of respiration, as the heat energy from the internal factory of your metabolism is given off into the air, and as your emotional field projects itself into the atmosphere. In this way ecoshamanic communication with the wind transcends the one-sided experience of simply feeling the wind as it touches you and becomes a multidimensional interaction with the power to increasingly inform you as your skill level increases, and at the highest levels will also include both your psychic abilities and metaphysical energy.

PRACTICE 50: The Breaths of Power

One of the most beneficial aspects of working with the wind, or any of the other four fundamental energies, over long periods of time is that the experiences have the power to stay with you so that you can use their benefits at a later time. I'm going to delve further into this topic during the next section on fire, but for now I just want to bring light to the point that when you connect to the qualities of the winds, such as the way described in the last practice, *all* the various levels of your consciousness are affected. Because of that, the knowledge of the experiences are imprinted on you and you can draw from their knowledge afterwards in much more powerful ways than experiences that affect a narrower band of your total consciousness, such as reading a book, listening to a lecture, or watching the television. Ecoshamanic experiences that utilize all of your potential, to the point where you expand the limits of what you previously thought you were capable of perceiving, while at the same time expanding your consciousness to include a reciprocal communication between your total organism and what you previously perceived as the "outside" world, are what give ecoshamanism its transformational power and practical usefulness.

With respect to experiences with the wind, the utilization of our breath is a powerful vehicle that allows us to claim and put to use the knowledge and power delivered to us through our communication and relationship with the winds. Once we live tangible experiences of communication and connection to various winds as described in the previous two practices, it is possible to relive and draw upon those experiences through the magic of the circulating qualities of our breath. Honoring, embodying, and employing the spirit of the four winds—the north wind, east wind, south wind, and west wind—is one of the most common aspects of shamanism shared by indigenous cultures throughout the world.

The more lived experiences you have with the wind, the greater your ability will be to use your breath in this technique.

The basic formula for transforming the four winds into breaths of power is: lived experiences of intentional connection to the four winds + specific forms of inhalation and exhalation that enable you to invoke the power of the four winds from inside your human organism = the intentional deployment of each of the four winds in order to gather energy, recover energy, expel foreign energy, clear energy, and use in many forms of physical healing and psychic healing (depending on the skill of the healer).

There are a total of eight breaths corresponding to the four directions during inhalation and exhalation. The first part of the formula is purely personal because this technique relies solely on one's personally lived experiences with the four winds and on the qualities of those winds in the locations where the experiences happened. There is no way for me to say which winds you will draw upon for use in various situations. As I explained in the previous section, depending on the experiences of the individual, knowledge of the west wind for a person whose experiences come primarily from Texas will be significantly different from someone who works with the wind near Lake Erie. Each of our experiences with the four winds are unique, so it will be simply a matter of practice and proficiency in accessing and employing the winds that will determine which winds we call upon in each situation.

The second part of the formula is the actual breathing techniques that channel the energy of the lived experiences so that you can use them. The breaths of power are grouped in two: inhalation and exhalation. Each of the two groups have four positions corresponding to the four wind directions.

Inhalation Breaths (drawing in, recovering, compressing, collecting, remembering)

East: Exhale straight ahead, turn your head to face east (chin over right shoulder), and inhale deeply through the four directions—chin arcs down through the south (chin almost touching sternum), arcs up through the west (chin over left shoulder), arcs up through the north (chin high above center), and arcs back down to the east (chin over right shoulder); now, with your lungs full of air, move head back to center and exhale.

South: Exhale straight ahead, lower chin to southern direction (chin almost touching sternum), and inhale deeply through the four directions—chin arcs up the west (chin over left shoulder), arcs up though the north (chin raised high above center), arcs down through the east (chin over right shoulder), and arcs back down to the south (chin almost touching sternum); now, with lungs full of air, move head back to center and exhale.

West: Exhale straight ahead, bring head to the west (chin over left shoulder), and inhale deeply through the four directions—chin arcs up to the north (chin high above center), arcs down to the east (chin over right shoulder), arcs down to the south (chin almost touching sternum), and arcs back up the west (chin over left shoulder); now, with lungs full of air, move head back to center and exhale.

North: Exhale straight ahead, bring head up to north (chin high above center), and inhale deeply through the four directions—head arcs down to the east (chin over right shoulder), arcs down to the south (chin almost touching sternum), arcs up to the west (chin over left shoulder), and arcs back up to the north (chin high above center); now, with lungs full of air, move head back to center and exhale.

Exhalation Breaths (pushing out, expelling, expanding, infusing, disregarding)

East: Inhale straight ahead, bring head to east position (chin over right shoulder), and exhale deeply though the four directions—chin arcs down through the south (chin almost touching sternum), arcs up through the west (chin over left shoulder), arcs up through the north (chin high above center), and arcs back down to the east (chin over left shoulder); now, with lungs empty, return head to center and inhale.

South: Inhale straight ahead, lower chin to southern direction (chin almost touching sternum), and exhale deeply through the four directions—chin arcs up the west (chin over left shoulder), arcs up though the north (chin raised high above center), arcs down through the east (chin over right shoulder), and arcs back down to the south (chin almost touching sternum); now, with lungs empty, return head to center and inhale.

West: Inhale straight ahead, bring head to the west (chin over left shoulder), and exhale deeply through the four directions—chin arcs up to the north (chin high above center), arcs down to the east (chin over right shoulder), arcs down to the south (chin almost touching sternum), and arcs back up the west (chin over left shoulder); now, with lungs empty, return head to center and inhale.

North: Inhale straight ahead, bring head up to north (chin high above center), and exhale deeply through the four directions—head arcs down to the east (chin over right shoulder), arcs down to the south (chin almost touching sternum), arcs up to the west (chin over left shoulder), and arcs back up to the north (chin high above center); now, with lungs empty, return head to center and inhale.

While you are using the breaths you are moving energy with your physical movements and conscious intention. Even though you are inhaling and exhaling through all four directions, you focus on one direction by starting and finishing the circular movement in that direction so that your full MBESA is concentrated on your lived experiences with the land of that direction throughout the movement. Focusing on that direction implies the summoning and deployment (either in or out) of the energy of that direction's winds that have been collected by your total MBES organism during your initiations and experiences. For example, one of the southern winds I can readily summon is the extremely powerful and magical wind of my sacred place in the desert of northern Mexico. To me this is a southern wind, because this sacred place lies far to the south of where I live. To draw in the wind of this place I focus my total attention (MBES) on my lived experiences of the winds in that place as I perform the southern inhalation breath multiple times. In doing this I activate the power of that place inside of me for whatever purpose I need. Since this is a place of vision, I would only summon this wind if I needed a vision or advice in a serious matter. In the case of an exhalation breath, if I needed a strongly cleansing wind for myself or for a client, depending on the quality of wind I needed I might summon and deploy a wind from a sacred place to me that is high in the mountains of Vermont, to the north. For this I would use the north exhalation breath while activating that strongly cleansing wind that lives inside of me through my many potent experiences with the wind of that place.

Although the movements and the breaths are imperative to help summon and focus the various winds, it is your lived experiences with those winds that is the key to using them. Once you have lived experiences with different types of winds from various geographic locations, you have an extremely practical tool that is always available to you. By using the previous two practices with the wind continuously over the course of a few years you will have collected a repository of winds at your disposal.

FIRE

Our mastery of fire was one of the most significant milestones of the human race. With the control of fire, our species was able to leave the warm equatorial zones and, carrying the sacred flame, spread out across the globe, even into the most barren and cold areas, such as the Arctic regions, the Himalayas, and the Andes. Fire was the inseparable, invaluable, and magical companion for our hunter-gatherer ancestors, and as they evolved so did their abilities and techniques for mastering and utilizing the sacred flame. Beyond the life-sustaining warmth provided by the fire, with the magical light of the fire our ancestors could remain active after dark, and eventually they developed many ways of making torches and lamps by using pitch and animal fat so that they had light even after the sun went down, and could bring light to even the darkest caves. The nightly fire also significantly shaped the social behavior of our species, as it gathered families and communities together for warmth, light, protection, and the cooking of food. Through learning to use the sacred fire to cook food and smoke meat they made the meat of the animals they hunted more digestible and palatable, but more importantly they could now preserve the meat and cook plants to eat that were formerly inedible, thereby reducing the chance of starvation. And with the help of the fire they also learned to make more efficient tools and weapons. As the control of fire became more refined, such as by blowing the flame through pipes of reed, the people created bowls, cradles, and canoes from wood.

While people eventually learned to efficiently cultivate crops and enslave animals, the fire was still a center point of daily life, as most single homes contained a central hearth or fireplace, and the homes of the rich and the palaces of rulers even contained movable stoves and central furnaces that provided heat for several rooms at a time. Ancient people also developed more sophisticated means of using fire to draw back the night. Candles and lamps of vegetable and animal oil became increasingly more efficient, until the eventual use of kerosene and gas.

The use of fire was also essential to the development of pottery, and, later, metalworking. At this point in our long history with fire there is a significant change because we became more demanding of the fire; instead of simply controlling it and moving it around to serve our needs, we finally got to the point where we felt the need to significantly intensify it in order to do more work. People developed the bellows in order to force more air into the fire, and from their hunger for even hotter temperatures to liquefy metal they developed the first blast furnace and the use of wood charcoal. This significant step would eventually reach its pinnacle in the Industrial Revolution and continue even to this day, as fire still forms a central part of our technological existence.

Historically speaking, there are thousands of moments in human history when the fire significantly changed the course of human events. But none is more significant than when humans took their scientific knowledge and broke the natural cycles of the earth by burning oil and gas found deep underground and underwater, materials that have no natural business being on top of the land. For the overwhelming portion of our time on earth we have used the "young" and cyclical materials that we found around us—animal fat, dung, straw, and wood to feed our fires. But in the blink of an eye we have become completely dependent on feeding our fires with ancient fossil fuels that are a result of millions of years of accumulated energy that is finite, which means that during the lifetime of our species they will never be created again and they will, of course, run out.

Digging and drilling beneath the surface of the earth to forward a civilization completely dependent on the use of petroleum for fuel and the making of chemicals is probably the largest mistake our species has ever made. This book is not the place to go into the vast amount of tragedies that this one action has spawned in just the last century of our existence on the planet, but the point I do want to make here is that, on the most primal level, the pathological actions of our society are in many ways related to the loss of awareness to the sacredness of fire. And because of this the fire itself offers a way to alter our consciousness when we cross the threshold of knowing that a healthy relationship with the fundamental energy of fire can lead to a healthy relationship with the world and also with our personal human organism.

PRACTICE 51: Sacred Fire Initiation

One of the most profound differences between the indigenous so-called fourth world peoples of the world and the economically dominant "first world" is the relationship that each has with fire. On one hand, the people of the fourth world relate to fire as a finite tool of subsistence, making their fire with whatever wood, dung, or other naturally cyclical material they can find at hand. On the flip side, the people of the first world treat the fire as an infinite resource as they unceasingly drill and mine fossil fuels from under the ground to feed complex machinery and furnaces. While this disparity in ecological sanity is enormous, the gap is even greater between first-world consumers and shamanic cultures that consider the fire to be sacred, just as our ancestors once did. One of the most tragic circumstances of the petroleum-fueled life of modern people is the loss of the sense that fire is a sacred fundamental energy of the world. Aside from the occasional moments when one seeks to create a special mood by lighting a candle or using a fireplace, the handling of fire for anything other than the extraction of energy to do work is almost totally nonexistent in our culture.

But there is a whole other world of relationships that we as human beings can have with the fire if we are open to making the effort. An initiation with a ceremonially induced fire is an extremely potent and worthwhile ecoshamanic activity. In this form of initiation there are five main goals:

- To place your total MBESA in direct contact with the fundamental energy of the fire for an extended period of time, which requires a significant commitment to the initiation process.

- To learn the first steps of how to create your own authentic personal rituals of inducing and sustaining a sacred fire.

- To feel the differences in the energy and mood of the fire as you provide the fire with different types of food (both physical and emotional).

- To obtain a merging of your perception with the fire so that the fire can provide you with a vision(s).

- To realize an experience with the fire at a deep enough level that the energy of the fire will travel with you in a way that you can draw on it to give you strength for a long time to come.

This initiation with fire begins by committing at least three consecutive days and nights to spend with a wood fire built on the ground, not in a fireplace, hearth, or any other type of restrictive container or stove. The location of the fire is extremely important, as the spirit of the land and the particular essences of the immediate area you are located will be co-creators of your experience. During the course of this book I have explained what I am implying by the "spirit" and "essence" of place. If you have experienced the previous ecoshamanic practices I have described, then you will have a good idea what place will be right for this initiation, but if not, review the previous material and use your own guidance. In all cases be sure that you do not conduct this initiation on park land where fires are prohibited. Rangers that come and put out your fire will probably not be a part of the vision you were seeking.

In a similar way to the "Quest for Vision" practice described earlier, take with you only the items you truly need and make sure you have planned some commonsense safety measures, such as telling others where you are going and for how long, and/or devise a system so that someone can check on you each day without interfering with your work. Fasting is suggested during the initiation but not mandatory; however, keep in mind that your human organism will more readily connect with the process of expansion if it is not already busy with internal processes such as digesting and metabolizing food.

Once you reach your place, the first order of business will be to make your offerings to the land and prepare the seat for the fire. Review the section on offerings if you are not familiar with this topic, but in addition to any other offering I suggest an offering of your own blood, as described on page 219.

The rituals surrounding the preparation, ignition, and maintenance of the sacred fire vary greatly from one shamanic tradition to the next. I'm going to describe one way to go about these processes, a way that has evolved from thousands of experiences with indigenous shamans, workgroups, and my own personal initiations and ceremonies with fire. Please keep in mind that my suggestion is to always stay true to your own inner guidance in developing and employing rituals and ceremonies, especially when dealing with metaphysical powers in a shamanic setting; however, the way of relating to the fire that I am about to describe contains ancient and time-tested formulas that are successful at merging our human consciousness with the fire, and I invite you try it this way whether or not you have previous experience with the fundamental energy of fire.

The first step is to clear a small area where the fire will sit. Since you will be with the fire for three whole days, you want to keep the fire to a reasonable size so that you don't need a truckload of wood. If you clear a circular area thirty inches in diameter and make a seat for the fire eighteen inches in diameter, that should work nicely. "Clearing the area" implies removing all vegetative matter, and anything else that might be there, so that you have nothing but soil under and around where the fire will sit.

To make the seat for the fire you collect stones, preferably the size of your heart (fist), and place the stones in a circle inside of the area you have cleared. This formally delineates the space for the sacred fire to manifest and also solidifies the fact that you are ritually inviting and calling to the spirit of the fire to join you.

Next, place the pillow for the fire, a large-diameter log, inside of the stone circle and position it on the eastern side of the inside edge of the circle. Resting on this pillow will be the arrows of wood that will be the food of the fire. The sticks used to the feed the fire are called arrows because they point to a specific direction both physically and symbolically, and they are the vehicle of flight that delivers your messages to the spirit. All of the arrows rest on the pillow and point in the same direction toward the rising sun. Each time you give wood to the fire, place the food in the same direction on the pillow. In this way you are continually focusing your attention to the sun, which is the fire that gives life to our planet.

How you actually ignite your fire will depend entirely on your skill and relationship with fire. If you are not experienced with starting a fire, I suggest you practice making a wood fire a few times before embarking on your fire initiation. In all cases, whether experienced or not, remember that this fire is fed exclusively with wood sticks placed only in one direction; placing them across each other would introduce an opposing and distracting force to the ritual. Making a quick and hot fire by crisscrossing sticks of wood can work well to maximize the efficiency of oxygen and fuel when making a fire for cooking or in a survival situation, but this is a sacred fire that is being induced into being for completely different reasons. The flame of the sacred fire is brought to life by a mixture of physical realities and metaphysical inputs. So in this case please throw out all of your purely logical and scientific formulas and make the fire with your heart and not your head.

Start by placing very dry and thin-diameter sticks as the first layer of arrows, and then slowly add larger diameter sticks until the fire is established. If there are pine trees in the area you are working, the dead, thin, lower branches are perfect for this. I usually carry a small supply of this type of tinder with me, and also some resinous wood that is close friends with the fire and so ignites very easily. If you have trouble and need to use some sort of fire-starting material, that's okay, because this is a fire initiation ritual, not a course in survival fire-starting.

As soon as your fire comes to life, start talking to the unique energetic phenomena that is front of you. I refer to the fire as Grandfather for reasons I already stated. Although the visions delivered by the fire don't seem to have a relation to the fire being personified as "male" energy by the name Grandfather, I find it extremely useful to name the fire in this way as a form of both respect and personal human connection. In a world which is sometimes so very confusing, it is comforting and empowering to refer on a personal level to

Mother Earth, Father Sun, Grandmother Growth, and Grandfather Fire not as purely a form of delineation but rather as way to personally identify with the enormous powers that they imply.

Once your journey with the fire has begun, your main task until the end of the ritual will be to feed the fire. On a physical level you will have a considerable amount of work to do in gathering wood and keeping the fire alive for three whole days. But that is only one of the ways you feed the fire. The second way is by feeding the fire with your energy through talking and singing your emotions, troubles, dreams, and any and all of your triumphs and failures. In this initiation you are encouraged, by whatever means necessary, to share your uniquely personal energy with the fire and to purge your organism to become transparent, so as to merge with the fire. You are encouraged and required to talk, sing, drum, dance, cry, laugh, shout, get angry, feel sorry, happy, proud, hurt, and whatever else comes up as you vocally release your life into the fire until your words are nothing but gibberish and so lose all meaning and motive. The more you can verbally, emotionally, and energetically give to the fire, the more transparent you will become and the more you will lose touch with your culturally one-sided view of the world, which will enable you to receive from the fire a novel form of energetic imprint that is not culturally based but cosmologically alive.

It is necessary to spend at least three days and nights in this task, and longer would be even better because our patterns and habits are so deeply ingrained into our being. But with the light of the fire reaching into our mind through the shining glow of the flames, and the energetic heat of the fire radiating into our body, we can burn away our predetermined image and become psychically renewed and initiated into a numinous form of consciousness that is the basis for shamanic enlightenment. As we remain seated with the fire over long periods of time we move away from our culture's fascination with accumulation and move toward the shamanic initiation of emptiness, from where we can then be filled with the organically pure spiritual energies, such as that of Grandfather Fire.

During your initiation you will undoubtedly have ups and downs, moments of complete clarity and others of confusion and despair. The most important thing is to simply keep going and stay with the fire until your time is up. Once you have engaged the process of purging for a period of time, experiment with your connection to the fire by feeding Grandfather Fire different types of food and learning about how this affects both him and you. Explore the quality of flame induced by different types of wood, leaves, bark, pine

needles, etc. Look deeply into the fire and feel which quality of flame you resonate especially well with, which flame calls more to you and inspires something from deep inside of
you. You may find that the quick flash of dry leaves may ignite a spark in your mind, or the
slow, smoky burn of green wood shifts your consciousness to matters of mystery and deep
contemplation.

In the beginning, and even periodically while traveling to new geographic regions, it is
good to experiment with the energies of different foods for the fire. But personally, I prefer to feed the grandfather with straight, medium-diameter arrows of wood that I make
from the fallen branches of live trees that I know or have just taken the time to properly
meet and communicate with, so that I'm sure exactly what sort of living energy created
the food that I am feeding the fire. Whenever possible I also like to take the extra time to
connect with, or at least acknowledge, the spiraling shape of the galaxy found within each
piece of wood I give the fire by looking deeply into the growth rings. Doing this adds
another dimension of awareness to the connection between the cyclical act of feeding the
fire and the cyclical reality of life on our planet.

But whatever you feed the fire, make sure you remain aware and ready, especially after
successfully completing a significant amount of purging, for the moments of conscious
merging between your inner fire and the fundamental energy in front of you. At the most
basic level our human organism is comprised of living cells that extract energy from fuel
like minute stoves in order to live. The fire inside of you and the fire in front of you are the
same in the fact that they both need oxygen and fuel to survive. And both of these fires
only exist because of the ultimate source of energy that provides both the fuel and the
oxygen: the sun. The complexity of our human organism is therefore not so different from
the purity of the flame, and when the magical phenomena that we call human consciousness can purify itself to the same level as the sacred flame, we are able to somehow touch
the unfathomable but decisively informative nature of our universe.

When this level of purity of consciousness, and the corresponding merger of inside and
out, becomes real for you, you have now entered into a shamanic connection that cannot
be described by words, and you will no longer have much use for books on shamanism or
personal and spiritual growth. These types of experiences beyond words take on a life of
their own and create their own momentum that you can feel inside of you and carry with
you. Sometimes their power arises again just when you need it the most. I have had more
than a few life-threatening occasions and accidents that I have "miraculously" come

through because of the spontaneous reliving of my connection to the immense power of the fundamental energies and the reality-altering effects that come with them. But I have also found that pursuing this form of shamanic connection can influence even the smallest and seemingly most trivial aspects of life as well, and even in the first years of shamanic initiations they can spontaneously arise to help you when you least expect it.

For example, when I first began sharing my ecoshamanic work with people (and at the time I only had about five years of serious work with the fire), I was speaking to a group of around fifty people in a prestigious center for workshops in Washington, D.C. I was in the middle of my presentation when all of a sudden I went completely blank. Somehow I had forgotten what I had just said, and also what I was about to say, and I found myself staring blankly into the crowd of faces intently watching me. Well, a few eternal seconds went by and I was just about to apologize to my audience and attempt to regroup my thoughts when the most amazing thing happened. In that moment I was transported back to a strong experience I had with the fire about a year earlier. I could see, feel, hear, sense, and somehow even taste that exact moment in time again; it was like I was actually there. But more importantly, in the moment I was reliving, I was in the midst of a primal connection to the fire in which both the body of the fire and my own human organism were the same white-light energy. The moment I realized this, as I was standing there in front of that important audience of people, I felt the consciousness of the white light radiate through my mind, and the next thing I knew I had completely restored my previous train of thought and continued with the presentation in an almost seamless manner. Because I have had countless experiences like that since then, and I have actually since learned to cultivate similar states at will, I know now that the energy of the sacred fire has the ability to not only psychically alter our state of consciousness but also to imprint the "memory" of shamanic moments of connection in way that can be accessed in a practical way at a later time.

After my presentation had concluded I casually talked to some of the people in the audience, and when nearly everyone had gone a woman came up to me and asked me "where I had gone" during those few seconds of hesitation. She said just before I started to speak again, she thought she saw a whitish glow that radiated first from my eyes and then from my whole body for just a split second. At first I was amazed that she had perceived what I had thought was simply going on inside of me, but after a few minutes of talking with her I realized that she also had similar experiences of connection to the fire and so it seemed to make sense that she would have perceived it. Needless to say, I was impressed with this occurrence, and when I told her what had just happened to me a feeling a mutual camaraderie overcame both of us, and I know for sure that our meeting inspired us both to continue to explore the practical aspects of our shamanic connection to the sacred fire.

PRACTICE 52: Taking Care of the Sacred Flame

Once you live experiences such as those described above in the Sacred Fire Initiation, the energy of the fire will become a light that guides and protects you. And you can significantly deepen your awareness of your connection to the altered states of consciousness induced by the energy of the sacred fire through a daily ritual involving the single flame of a candle.

Of course there is no substitute for renewing your connection to the fundamental energy of fire by periodically merging your consciousness with the psychic flames of a sacred fire, but another potent form of initiation is to enter into a sacred relationship with the fire in which you continually provide food and demonstrate your solidarity with the fire through a specific ritual performed each morning and night.

If you get into the habit of lighting a special candle as you soon as you wake up in the morning before you do anything else and connect to the light and energy of the flame in a similar way as you did during your fire initiation, and then do the same thing immediately before you go to sleep at night, you become initiated as a keeper of the sacred flame. Keepers of the flame include all the people past and present that hold the fundamental energy of the fire to be sacred and know that a primal connection to the fire creates holistic states of consciousness with the power to advise, heal, and nurture us on our appointed path.

It is best to ask, during a moment of connection to the sacred fire, how long your initiation of taking care of the sacred flame should last, because I can't tell you. What I can say is that I know authentic, indigenous fire shamans that have on rare occasions taken a modern person as a sort of apprentice, and this type of initiation typically lasts for a period of five years. Of course, in our modern world it will at times be difficult to logistically accomplish this. For example, in most of the hotels that one might stay in while traveling, even a candle might trigger the fire alarms of a sprinkler system, so it becomes necessary to go outside to your car or find some other location nearby to fulfill your daily obligation with the flame. But in my experience these situations are easily solved, and when you have become accustomed to being with the flame each morning and night, the momentum of all those experiences somehow creates the appropriate circumstances for the continuation of the flow. And if for some reason you are denied the opportunity to be with the flame, you find that you miss it terribly and that you can't wait to be near it again.

Through keeping the fire alive by bringing it to light and feeding the flame with your daily meal of sharing your thoughts, your problems, and your emotions, you create a relationship with a pure source of spiritual energy that can't easily be taken from you, that won't judge or punish you, and that will be there for you in your darkest moments and most joyous occasions. And the energy of the fire contained in the flame of the candle can be your close companion as well. For example, since I now have many years of connection to the fire, for me it is extremely difficult, and normally I won't even try, to work on my writing without the presence of the fire. Whether it be in the glass-front woodstove that sits in the middle of my office in the cold months, or a simple candle sitting on my desk in front of me, the dancing flame of the first shaman, Grandfather Fire, is something that I automatically look to in between thoughts, when I get stuck, or simply for the energy and light of creativity that he inspires and projects. And in any moment by focusing my attention on the flame I can reconnect with the unique energy and power of any of the sacred fires I have merged with in the past. If there were just one reason to commit to an initiation of keeping alive the sacred flame, this last reason would be enough for me.

SPIRIT/SPACE/PLACE

The last initiation into the fundamental energies of the world will have to do with the spirit of place and space. This for me is by far the most difficult "energy" to write about simply because the spirit reveals its informative abilities to each person in a unique way, so all I can do is present material that contains common threads of knowledge in a way that proactively invites you to explore your own unique connection.

An in-depth discussion about the various concepts of "spirit" is more than what is required here, so let me be clear that what I am specifically referring to in this section is the experience of shamanic initiation that can happen with the spirit of certain places. So this refers to the collective spirit of a natural place, not the spirit of an individual human being, animal, tree, plant, or insect. Some may liken this phenomena of spirit to the pre-Christian European concept of the *genius loci,* the local spirits that inhabit a particular area such as a hill, valley, forest, spring, or lake. While the genius loci view of spirit has its roots in polytheistic animism rather than tribal shamanism, this view is still far closer to the spirit of place that I will attempt to convey than the spiritless correspondence to place offered by transcendental monotheism.

For people that live without a sense of the numinous and informative qualities of nature, the idea of a place having spirit is usually categorized as some sort of "supernatural" hogwash, or it might be said to be "all inside the head" of a person that claims to be able to communicate with the spirits of the land. But ironically, and at the same time tragically, it is only when we lose our sense of the sentience of the land that anthropocentric consumerism can become the dominant worldview, or the idea of God and spirit can be relegated to some supernatural place such as heaven. When we take the spirit from the land, and/or put all other forms of life beneath us, then the sense of the divine must relocate to either a supernormal space such as heaven above or to the only other place it can go—inside of the human mind.

But for people connected to the numinous forces of nature, forces that have the power to either sustain or extinguish human life, the sacred landscape is animated by living spiritual essences that share the world with us. When the shaman does his work of healing and balancing he doesn't pray for miracles from heaven or journey somewhere inside of his own mind, the shaman expands his perception and sends it out into the energies of the sacred landscape that shares the dream of life with him and his community.

In this way the shaman is never alone because wherever he goes, even to the most desolate and inhospitable places, he is exposed to the spirits of the place that watch him on all sides. But because of this the shaman also knows that when one resides in a place for a period of time, with respect and reciprocity he can become friends with the spirits of the place, and after many months or years of taking the place into his own flesh and infusing the place into his mind, he can join and merge with the spirit of the place so that he becomes the place, just as the place becomes him.

The amazing journey that awaits modern people in this form of initiation is the twofold shift in consciousness that leads to direct perception of the spirit of the land as one and the same as your own spirit. The first shift is when you can experience the land—let's say, for example, a forest—perceiving you, instead of you simply perceiving the forest. At this level you have added to your perceptual experience the reverse of the limited view of reality that you had before. Now when you walk in the forest you are aware of the forest being aware of you as well. In this way none of your actions go unnoticed and you are accountable to the spirit of the place for what you do.

The second shift in consciousness is experienced much later as you come to feel that you are a part of the forest. When this happens your experience of the forest is the forest experiencing itself. This depth or expansion of consciousness was, and still is, a common experience to indigenous people and shamans who dwell not just physically but also psychically in the land where they live. This is not supernatural, it is completely natural. It is simply a matter of our sentient human organism feeling continuous with the body of the land. This is precisely why shamanic tribes have developed differently according to their local surroundings, while also sharing many of the underlying and basic truths. Each large geographic area, and each smaller bioregion, has a unique spirit that the local tribe is connected to and that informs them about their world. But just as the "individual" members of the tribe are continuous with the larger body of the local land, the local land is also continuous with the larger geographic area, and the larger geographic area with the world as a whole. When you gather tribal people from different parts of the world, who all live embedded in the spirit of the land, together in one place, you feel the same spiritual rootedness among them all, and you will also feel the unique spiritual qualities of the land that each is a part of.

PRACTICE 53: Initiations with the Living Spirits of Place

In the vast regions of macrocosmic space, we perceive galaxies, solar systems, planets, and stars as localized places that we can name, map, and therefore delineate and define. On the terrestrial landscape of our home planet, we perceive and recognize places as localized and identifiable areas such as mountains, cities, lakes, roads, houses, valleys, and buildings. Each of these places has a boundary, whether it be clear to us or somewhat vague, that assigns to it certain characteristics and size. Even though the border of a natural place such as a hill or forest might be debatable and not easily defined, we still nonetheless would all agree that the "place" exists, especially if we were to go to the "center" of the hill or the "center" of the forest. But since the hill or forest, mountain or desert can't be specifically delineated because nature simply doesn't create things with a ruler or a protractor, to find the exact physical center of one of these places would be a completely abstract exercise.

Now if we were to turn our focus away from the purely physical center and instead speak on a metaphysical or spiritual level, we could say that if we were to find the "center" of the hill, forest, mountain, or desert, we would encounter the core essence or spirit of the place. In this case, the center is simply a metaphor, but it is an important metaphor that can assist us in encountering the spirit of a place. For example, if you were standing on a high mountain ridge overlooking a forest in the valley below, you may or may not be able to discern what you might guess to be the physical center of the forest, but if you were to journey into that forest and explore it for a long enough period of time, you would eventually be able to say where you feel is the "center" of the forest, or at least the center of a particular area of the forest. This metaphorical center, which could be described as the metaphysical center, is simply the core feeling or spirit of the place that is completely perceivable to us, and which will be different in every place we go.

As complex organisms of this world, we humans have the ability to feel the spirit of a place, the tangible mixture of the essences and energies, as I described previously in the section on cognitive mapping. We can say that the spirit of a place is alive and manifested by these energies and essences simply because if, for example, a particular forest is clear cut, the spirit of that place, which we could clearly feel previously, ceases to exist in the same form as it did when the essence and energy of the forest was physically alive. When the small ponds that I knew as a child were drained and excavated in order to build houses on that area of land, the spirit of those ponds died right along with the life that they supported. Granted, the spirit of those ponds touched me, as they did many other animals and plants, so in some way those spirits still live on in different form, but not in the way that they used to when the ponds were alive.

Becoming initiated by the living spirits of place involves finding the metaphysical center of the place, and when you find it, feeling the spirit of the place being aware of you, and you of it. This is what I described earlier in this section as the first shift in consciousness, and this shift is extraordinarily significant simply because at this level perception is no longer a one-way street but rather a two-way interaction that can lead to actual communication. I have no grandiose ideas that many people living in modern society, or even on the fringes, will ever make the second shift in consciousness, where one feels the local place experiencing itself, at least not in the way that would be as informative as the way we feel our own physical body. But let me be clear, this second shift that I speak of is at a level of shamanic transformation beyond anything anyone could ever write about and is certainly not the goal of the initiations in this section. I am mentioning the second shift merely to put the first-shift initiations into a larger context for reasons of understanding.

I do believe that many people, especially those I know that have dedicated their lives to protecting certain places on Earth, can feel the second shift as something on the edge of their awareness, and even that small taste is powerful enough to excite the psychically and bodily felt knowing that they are part of the land feeling itself. But please note that these special people can sense the second shift only through having felt the first shift in consciousness in a profound way for many years, and it is the first shift, with all of its lessons, both joyous and painful, that is so vitally important for people to experience, because when you are aware that the spirit of a place is aware of you, then everything changes. Places in the natural world cease to be simply huge numbers of diverse life forms gathered together in an identifiable location, no matter how miraculous that in itself may be, but rather natural areas are felt as entities imbued with their own unique form of sentience that is filled with the same form of spiritual essence that flows through our own human organism. At the shamanic level, these spirit-filled places house the world's most knowledgeable metaphysical teachers that are ready, willing, and able to instruct us about the informative nature of the universe.

The first step to meeting these teachers and beginning the initiations is to go and find them. You can start with your home bioregion, by identifying the various areas that comprise it and then embarking on the journey of searching for the metaphysical center of each area. Ask yourself, while walking through an area of forest, grassland, or chaparral, "Where is the spiritual center of this place, what does it feel like, and how does the spirit of this place manifest to me?" You may find the answers to these questions quickly, if you are humble and the spirit of the place is open to receive you, but you may also encounter resistance to your search which, for one reason or another, is not immediately welcomed by the spirit. You may be dragging around a huge ball and chain of tangled emotions or self-inflated concerns that don't allow you to move fluidly through the psychic space of the area. Or the spirit may be occupied with life and death issues or recently been attacked and seriously wounded. So it may be that the spirit of a place doesn't reveal itself to you for many days, months, years, or even maybe not ever.

But when you find it you will know. It will touch you and you will be changed. You feel it aware of you and watching you. And like a wild animal that stops and stares at you, wondering what you are doing, your next move will determine the spirit's response. Since you are a human being, the spirit will want to know what your intentions are—whose side you are on. From this moment on, you will have to prove to the spirit with your actions that you are there to learn and not destroy, to reciprocate and not steal. This probationary period is not usually a big concern because once you feel the presence of the spirit and make the first shift in consciousness so that you feel the spirit is aware of you, it is not likely that you will intentionally harm the place. But the spirit might not know that and so it is best to demonstrate through your actions and over time that you are friend, not foe. This is easily done by conscientiously performing any of the practices, ceremonies, or rituals described in this book. Work with the trees, the animals, the plants, and the fundamental energies of the place; spend time there, make offerings, look after the land, and be initiated by the spirit that resides in that unique place.

At some point, nobody can say when, you will feel completely at home in the place. From now on you will always feel at home in similar areas, and the spirits of other areas like this one will be easy for you to locate and learn from. This is not metaphorical but utterly tangible. For example, the first area I was initiated into as a child was a midlatitude deciduous forest, and during my life I have always kept in contact with the spirits that dwell in this type of forest, so wherever I visit this type of forest, whether it be in the United States, Europe, or anywhere else, I always feel comfortable and at home, especially when compared to other types of areas that I have not yet been initiated into, such as a tropical savanna forest or a polar desert.

While exploring the vast range of possibilities encompassing the project and practices of ecoshamanism, it is my feeling, and suggestion, that we become formally initiated into many different types of areas and ecosystems. The more areas we can feel completely at home in, and connect to the spirit of, the better off we will be. To me, being initiated by the spirits of diverse areas is one of the most enlightening and rewarding aspects to shamanism. Many blessings on your journey!

7 | A DREAM IN THE SERVICE OF LIFE

Through critical assessment, the sharing of personal experiences, and suggestions for action, this book has attempted to put you in contact with the knowledge that shamanic practices, which are designed to shift our consciousness into awakening to the reality of being immersed in a sentient world, can lead to a new and improved worldview of holism and symbiosis. Experiences with the alive and aware landscape can serve to summon back into the animate earth our sense of the sacred.

While many "forward" thinkers have proposed that humanity is moving from the industrial age to the age of information and electronics, the sad truth is that the latter is simply an extension of the former, and so our culture continues down the same destructive path it is now on. The only viable future for humanity, whether the first-world conglomerates and their governments like it or not, is not simply a more technological mindset, nor the postmodern deconstructionist view supported by some current factions of philosophers, but rather a holistic worldview that features sustainability and appropriate use of technology to preserve the planet's ecosystems.

Concerning the current state or future of the world, one doesn't need to enter into scientific or philosophical debates, or feel confused as to which "expert" to believe in. Simply talk to the elders that are around you. Ask the people that have lived in your area for the last seventy or eighty years about what changes they have seen in the course of just one human lifetime. Talk to them about the changes in their neighborhood and community; about how people used to treat each other; about how people communicated and entertained each other; about the relationships with the land, water, air, and other species. It doesn't take a genius to look at the rate of change in just their lifetime and project what little will be left for the children of the coming decades if we continue down this same path.

But this is not the time for guilt. Feeling guilty is draining and depressing; it is better to learn from experience, then act, take a stand, and make a commitment for change. And that is how I would like to end this book: with an invitation, a challenge, and a commitment.

My invitation is for you to explore the projects, practices, and counterpractices of ecoshamanism; to join in the consciousness-raising movements inspired by the psychic correspondence of flesh—that when we feel our flesh as the flesh of the world, we feel the world feeling itself. When our respiration is perceived as a process of the air touching itself, or when the hydrologic cycle is felt as the oceans running through our veins, we become informed by an infinitely larger system than when we remain trapped inside the narrow limits of self-centeredness. That is good medicine for the modern age.

The challenge I would like to offer is one of cooperation toward advancement. If the projects and practices laid out in this book touch you even in a small way, then take the challenge to share them, advance them, create new ways to use them, deepen them, and expand them. The project of ecoshamanism is enormous, and it is my sincere hope that people with many different specialties, talents, and interests will add their own unique flavor, perspective, and wisdom to what I have written here, and take this project, these ideas, and these practices to ever higher levels for the benefit of the world, humankind, and personal fulfillment. The truths are universal and can't be owned by any one person or group of people. The informative spirit of nature is weblike, with each part connected to each other, so the more we cooperate and share, the more we will learn and grow.

The commitment I would like to introduce is modeled from the Wirrarika tradition of the Jicareros. Inside this tradition is the wisdom of the elders. A moment ago I spoke about the wisdom of talking to the elders of our local areas because they can provide for us a real-life perspective as to where we were, where we are, and where we are heading, and we would be sorely remiss if we neglected their unique perspective. But we would also be remiss if we neglected the perspective of ancient nature-based cultures that even to this day still live deeply embedded in the sentient community of life that acknowledges reciprocity as the fundamental law of the universe. These indigenous people are also our elders, for unlike the modern consumer culture, which in terms of history is but an infant, these cultures have ancient roots that spread deep and far into the psyche of the earth. But the Wirrarika have more than just perspective that we can draw from, they have a shamanic system of commitment that provides their entire spiritual and cultural tradition with an efficient and time-tested method of checks and balances that we can use as a model for deepening our own relationship to the making and following through with commitments related to the spirit of the earth.

Commitments give power to our actions. Before there is commitment there is hesitancy, the chance to draw back or walk away. But once one definitely commits, especially in matters of spirit, the ball starts rolling much faster, and out of nowhere things appear that can help you. This is what I have learned from my shamanic initiations and pilgrimages to sacred places. I would never have written my first book, let alone several, if it were not for the vision I received from a sacred place and the subsequent commitment I made to that place to share what I had learned.

The Wirrarika system of commitments regarding the Jicareros that I am presenting here as an example not to copy but to be inspired by works something like this: The elders of the ceremonial center use dreams, visions, and special ceremonies to guide them in choosing which people of the community will hold the jicara (see page 271 for details about jicaras) of each of the thirty or so main deities. These deities include the spirits of nature that give them life—the sun, fire, rain, and corn, along with many sacred places and ancestral figures. The current keepers of the jicaras pass their jicaras to the newly appointed keepers every five years. Which means that for a full five years, each Jicarero is responsible for embodying the spirit of the jicara they hold in every ceremony, ritual, and pilgrimage. But even more importantly, the person in charge of the jicara becomes the spirit of the jicara even in everyday life.

The keeper of the jicara takes the name of the jicara and in every way is related to by the community as the spirit of the jicara in human form. This is such an immense task that it completely changes the life of the person. In the beginning of the five-year period it is common for the new Jicarero to feel trapped by the obligation and maybe even feel resentful for having been chosen. But I have never met a Jicarero that, after completing the five-year term, did not feel sad to pass on the jicara. After five years of serving the community, the group of thirty Jicareros become a close-knit unit, a microcosmic model of the universe, that is now fully initiated into the shamanic tradition of their culture. They feel the strength and the pride that comes with knowing that their tradition is based on reciprocity and balance between humans and the spirits of nature. They will pass on their jicaras to a new group that will carry on the tradition of reciprocity and balance.

Once a person has completed the five-year obligation as a Jicarero, their status in the community is much different. Some will later be elected as leaders, some will simply go back to their humble lives in a transformed state, and those that are to become shamans will usually go for another five years of embodying a different jicara. But no matter what they do afterwards they will always feel the mystical union of their spirit to the spirits of nature that the five years of shamanic initiation provided them, and they will feel honored in having completed their sacred obligation to both their community and the powers of the world that sustain it.

In a similar way to the tradition of the Jicareros, I feel that we can channel our calling for shamanic experiences, and the desire and necessity to heal our relationship with the natural world and the condition of humankind, in a way that will empower us and give strength to our actions. I believe this happens most effectively through making a shamanic commitment or pledge to a specific dimension of the natural world. Just like the tradition of the Jicareros, we can begin a tradition of pledging a period of time to the spirit of our local water or air or a sacred piece of land. Since our lives and educations are more special-ized, we could also make a pledge in the direction of our specialties, such as economics, education, business, or law.

But let me be clear. The kind of pledge I'm referring to is a pledge with the power to radically change the collective dream of industrial-consumer culture, and this can only be initiated in conjunction with deep revelatory experiences such as the ones I have laid out in this book. I believe the enlightenments of ecoshamanic practice can be the catalyst for peo-ple to change the dream. The collective dream of our present culture is one that pits humanity against its earthly condition. But the dream of ecoshamanism is the dream of Earth itself. The dream of Earth was unfolding for billions of years before the dream even included human beings. But since modern humans have entered the dream of Earth, we have turned it into a nightmare by drilling, digging, burning, stripping, and engaging in every other form of unsustainable processing of Earth's body that we can think of.

To rejoin the collective dream of humanity with the unfolding dream of Earth, we must start at an individual level with the things we do every day. Once we have touched the dream of Earth through shamanic experiences, we can apply those experiences to our daily lives in order to change the dream. For example, our revelatory experiences will help us make changes so that schools will teach reciprocal relationships with the planet and its species instead of how to extract and process natural resources as quickly as possible to sell through the consumer market and then throw into the landfill. The legal system will include rights for other species besides humans and also for the sacred soil of our home bioregions. Businesses of every kind will be responsible for their own waste; if the products and actions of the business are not self-sustainable within the bioregion, the business will be phased out. Economics will not be seen in just the light of a global or national economy but rather at the local and regional level, where communities become self-sustainable and reacquainted with the sacred land where they live.

As you can see, I'm not concerned with simply making minor adjustments to the current dream, but radically changing it so that humanity rejoins the dream of Earth and all its other species. The only thing I know of that has the power to do this is the alteration and reconfiguration of human awareness through the deep shifts of consciousness that take place during ecoshamanic practices and the resulting commitments that come from those states of consciousness once a person realizes a reciprocal relationship with other life forms, including the collective spirits of place.

In this way the pledge of commitment comes from the experience of unity with the field or web of energy and consciousness that is the reality of our universe. This experience of unity is the only thing with the power to change the dream. By unifying with the awareness of this power we can then use our specific knowledge and talents to make a commitment to the local watershed, a specific area of land, and with the way we support ourselves, in order to affect change in our daily lives and in our communities, and by doing so we join with the dream of Earth in the service of life.

# BIBLIOGRAPHY

Aberley, Doug, ed. *Boundaries of Home.* Philadelphia: New Society Publishers, 1993.

Abram, David. *The Spell of the Sensuous.* New York: Vintage Books, 1996.

Adams, Carol, ed. *Ecofeminism and the Sacred.* New York: Continuum Publishing, 1993.

Adler, Margot. *Drawing Down the Moon.* New York: Penguin Books, 1986.

Altman, Nathaniel. *Sacred Trees.* New York: Sterling Publishing Co., 2000.

Andrews, Ted. *Animal Speak.* St. Paul: Llewellyn Publications, 1993.

Benitez, Fernando. *Los Indios de Mexico.* Mexico: Biblioteca ERA, 1968.

Berry, Thomas. *The Dream of the Earth.* San Francisco: Sierra Club Books, 1988.

Campbell, Joseph. *The Masks of God: Primitive Mythology.* New York: Viking/Compass, 1969.

Clinebell, Howard. *Ecotherapy: Healing Ourselves, Healing the Earth.* Minneapolis: Fortress Press, 1996.

Deloria, Vine. *God is Red: A Native View of Religion.* Golden, CO: Fulcrum Publishing, 1994.

Diamond, Irene, and Gloria Feman Orenstein, eds. *Reweaving the World: The Emergence of Ecofeminism.* San Francisco: Sierra Club Books, 1990.

Elgin, Duane. *Voluntary Simplicity.* New York: William Morrow, 1993.

Endredy, James. *Earthwalks for Body and Spirit.* Rochester, VT: Bear & Co., 2002.

Fisher, Andy. *Radical Ecopsychology.* Albany: SUNY Press, 2002.

Flaherty, Gloria. *Shamanism and the Eighteenth Century.* Princeton: Princeton University Press, 1992.

Foster, Steven. *The Book of the Vision Quest.* New York: Fireside, 1992.

Friedel, David, Linda Schele, and Joy Parker. *Maya Cosmos: Three Thousand Years on the Shaman's Path*. New York: William Morrow and Company, 1993.

Geldard, Richard. *The Spiritual Teachings of Ralph Waldo Emerson*. Great Barrington, MA: Lindisfarne Books, 2001.

Gerber, Richard. *Vibrational Medicine*. Rochester, VT: Bear & Co., 2001.

Glendinning, Chellis. *My Name is Chellis & I'm in Recovery from Western Civilization*. Boston: Shambhala, 1994.

Goldstein, Eda. *Ego Psychology and Social Work Practice*. New York: The Free Press, 1995.

Grim, John, ed. *Indigenous Traditions and Ecology*. Cambridge, MA: Harvard University Press, 2001.

Grinberg-Zylberbaum, Jacobo. *Creation of Experience: The Synthergic Theory*. Mexico: Instituto Nacional Para El Estudio De La Conciencia, 1988.

Grof, Stanislav. *The Adventure of Self-Discovery*. New York: SUNY Press, 1988.

Highwater, Jamake. *The Primal Mind*. New York: Harper & Row, 1981.

Hillel, Daniel. *Out of the Earth: Civilization and the Life of Soil*. New York: The Free Press, 1991.

Hillman, James, and Michael Ventura. *We've Had a Hundred Years of Psychotherapy and the World's Getting Worse*. New York: Harper Collins, 1992.

Hutton, Ronald. *Shamans: Siberian Spirituality and the Western Imagination*. London: Hambledon and London, 2001.

Jamal, Michele, ed. *Shapeshifters: Shaman Women in Contemporary Society*. New York: Arkana, 1987.

James, William. *Varieties of Religious Experience*. New York: Simon & Schuster, 1997.

Jensen, Bernard, and Mark Anderson. *Empty Harvest: Understanding the Link Between Our Food, Our Immunity, and Our Planet*. New York: Penguin Putnam, 1990.

Jung, Carl. *Man and His Symbols*. New York: Dell Publishing, 1964.

———. *Memories, Dreams, Reflections*. New York: Vintage Books, 1963.

Kalweit, Holger. *Dreamtime & Inner Space*. Boston: Shambhala, 1984.

———. *Shamans, Healers, and Medicine Men*. Boston: Shambhala, 1987.

Kanner, Allen D., Theodore Roszak, and Mary E. Gomes, eds. *Ecopsychology: Restoring the Earth, Healing the Mind*. San Francisco: Sierra Club Books, 1995.

Kellert, Stephen, and Edward Wilson, eds. *The Biophilia Hypothesis*. Washington, DC: Island Press, 1993.

Kimbrell, Andrew, ed. *The Fatal Harvest Reader: The Tragedy of Industrial Agriculture.* Sausalito, CA: Foundation for Deep Ecology, 2002.

LaChapelle, Dolores. *Sacred Land, Sacred Sex.* Durango, CO: Kivaki Press, 1988.

Macy, Joanna, and Molly Young Brown. *Coming Back to Life.* Gabriola Island, BC: New Society Publishers, 1998.

Mander, Jerry. *In the Absence of the Sacred: The Failure of Technology & the Survival of the Indian Nations.* San Francisco: Sierra Club Books, 1991.

Marks, William E. *The Holy Order of Water.* Great Barrington, MA: Bell Pond Books, 2001.

Maslow, Abraham. *Religions, Values, and Peak Experiences.* New York: Penguin Books, 1964.

Maybury-Lewis, David. *Millennium: Tribal Wisdom and the Modern World.* New York: Viking, 1992.

Merleau-Ponty, Maurice. *Phenomenology of Perception.* London: Routledge Classics, 1958.

———. *The Visible and the Invisible.* Evanston, IL: Northwestern University Press, 1973.

Metzner, Ralph. *Green Psychology.* Rochester, NY: Park Street Press, 1999.

———. *The Unfolding Self.* Novato, CA: Origin Press, 1986.

Milbrath, Lester. *Envisioning a Sustainable Society.* Albany: SUNY Press, 1989.

Miller, John. *Egotopia: Narcissism and the New American Landscape.* Tuscaloosa: University of Alabama Press, 1997.

Narby, Jeremy, and Francis Huxley, eds. *Shamans Through Time.* New York: Tarcher/Putnam, 2001.

Nicholson, Shirley, ed. *Shamanism: An Expanded View of Reality.* Wheaton, IL: The Theosophical Publishing House, 1987.

Orr, David. *Earth in Mind: On Education, Environment, and the Human Prospect.* Washington, DC: Island Press, 1994.

Pinkson, Tom Soloway. *The Flowers of Wirikuta.* Rochester, VT: Destiny Books, 1997.

Ripinsky-Naxon, Michael. *The Nature of Shamanism.* Albany: SUNY Press, 1993.

Roszak, Theodore. *The Voice of the Earth: An Exploration of Ecopsychology.* New York: Touchstone, 1992.

Sessions, George. *Deep Ecology for the 21st Century.* Boston: Shambhala, 1995.

Shepard, Paul. *Nature and Madness.* Athens, GA: The University of Georgia Press, 1982.

———. *The Tender Carnivore and the Sacred Game.* New York: Scribners, 1973.

Shi, David. *The Simple Life: Plain Living and High Thinking in American Culture.* Athens, GA: University of Georgia Press, 1985.

Snyder, Gary. *The Practice of the Wild.* New York: North Point Press, 1990.

Soule, Michael, and Gary Lease, eds. *Reinventing Nature?* Washington, DC: Island Press, 1995.

Strassman, Rick. *DMT: The Spirit Molecule.* Rochester, NY: Park Street Press, 2001.

Suzuki, David. *The Sacred Balance.* Vancouver, BC: Greystone Books, 1997.

Thomashow, Mitchell. *Ecological Identity.* Cambridge, MA: MIT Press, 1995.

Tucker, Mary Evelyn, and John Grim, eds. *Worldviews and Ecology: Religion. Philosophy, and the Environment.* Maryknoll, NY: Orbis Books, 1994.

Turner, Jack. *The Abstract Wild.* Tucson: University of Arizona Press, 1996.

Van Matre, Steve. *Earth Education: A New Beginning.* Greenville, WV: The Institute for Earth Education, 1990.

Worldwatch Institute. *State of the World 2003.* New York: W. W. Norton & Company, 2003.

———. *Vital Signs 2002.* New York: W. W. Norton & Company, 2002.

iNDEX

Free Magazine

Read unique articles by Llewellyn authors, recommendations by experts, and information on new releases. To receive a **free** copy of Llewellyn's consumer magazine, *New Worlds of Mind & Spirit,* simply call 1-877-NEW-WRLD or visit our website at www.llewellyn.com and click on *New Worlds.*

LLEWELLYN ORDERING INFORMATION

Order Online:
Visit our website at www.llewellyn.com, select your books, and order them on our secure server.

Order by Phone:
- Call toll-free within the U.S. at 1-877-NEW-WRLD (1-877-639-9753). Call toll-free within Canada at 1-866-NEW-WRLD (1-866-639-9753)
- We accept VISA, MasterCard, and American Express

Order by Mail:
Send the full price of your order (MN residents add 6.5% sales tax) in U.S. funds, plus postage & handling to:

Llewellyn Worldwide
2143 Wooddale Drive, Dept. 0-7387-0742-2
Woodbury, MN 55125-2989, U.S.A.

Postage & Handling:
Standard (U.S., Mexico, & Canada). If your order is:
    $24.99 and under, add $3.00
    $25.00 and over, FREE STANDARD SHIPPING

AK, HI, PR: $15.00 for one book plus $1.00 for each additional book.

International Orders (airmail only):
    $16.00 for one book plus $3.00 for each additional book

Orders are processed within 2 business days.
Please allow for normal shipping time. Postage and handling rates subject to change.